TIMOTHY GARTON ASH
History of the Present

Timothy Garton Ash is the author of *The File, In Europe's Name,* and three other volumes of "history of the present": *The Polish Revolution,* which won the Somerset Maugham Award; *The Uses of Adversity,* which won the Prix Européen de l'Essai; and *The Magic Lantern,* his personal account of the Central European revolutions of 1989, which has been published in fifteen languages. Garton Ash is a regular contributor to *The New York Review of Books,* among other journals. He was named Commentator of the Year in 1989 and has been honored with the David Watt Memorial Prize, the Premio Napoli, and both the Polish and German Order of Merit. A Fellow of St. Antony's College, Oxford, and the Hoover Institution at Stanford University, he lives in Oxford with his wife and two sons.

HISTORY OF
THE PRESENT

HISTORY OF THE PRESENT

Essays, Sketches, and
Dispatches from Europe
in the 1990s

TIMOTHY
GARTON ASH

VINTAGE BOOKS

A DIVISION OF RANDOM HOUSE, INC.

NEW YORK

FIRST VINTAGE BOOKS EDITION, SEPTEMBER 2001

Copyright © 1999 by Timothy Garton Ash

All rights reserved under International and Pan-American Copyright
Conventions. Published in the United States by Vintage Books, a division of
Random House, Inc., New York, and simultaneously in Canada by Random
House of Canada Limited, Toronto. Originally published in the United
Kingdom by Penguin Books, London, in 2000, and in hardcover in the United
States by Random House, Inc., New York, in 2000.

Vintage and colophon are registered trademarks of Random House, Inc.

Owing to limitations of space, the permission acknowledgments
can be found on pages 455–456.

The Library of Congress has cataloged the Random House edition as follows:
Garton Ash, Timothy.
History of the present : essays, sketches, and dispatches from Europe in the
1990s / Timothy Garton Ash.
p. cm.
Originally published: New York : Random House, c1999.
ISBN 0-375-72762-0 (trade paper)
1. Europe—Politics and government—1989– 2. Europe, Eastern—Politics
and government—1989– 3. Europe, Eastern—Ethnic relations. 4. Europe—
Foreign relations—1989– I. Title.
D2009 .G37 2000
940.55'9—dc21
2001026037
CIP

Author photograph © Caroline Forbes

www.vintagebooks.com

Printed in the United States of America
10 9 8 7 6 5 4 3 2 1

TO ROBERT SILVERS

CONTENTS

INTRODUCTION

Even at one minute past midnight on 1 January 1990, we already knew that this would be a formative decade in Europe. A forty-year-old European order had just collapsed with the Berlin Wall. Everything seemed possible. Everyone was hailing a "new Europe." But no one knew what it would look like.

Now we know: in Western Europe, in Germany, in Central Europe, and in the Balkans. Of course, in all these parts, the future will be full of surprises. It always is. But at the end of the decade we can see the broad outline of the new European order that we have already ceased to call new. Only in the vast, ethnically checkered territory of the former Soviet Union is even the basic direction of states such as Russia and Ukraine still hidden in the fog. And perhaps also, at Europe's other end, is that of the decreasingly United Kingdom.

This book does not pretend to be a comprehensive account of the 1990s in Europe. It is a collection of what are rightly called pieces—in other words, fragments—that reflect my own interests, expertise, and travels. However, a chronology running through the book not only supplies missing links between the pieces but also records significant European developments not covered in any of them. Into this time line I have inserted some short, diarylike sketches, drawn mainly from my own notebooks and recollections. There are also several longer sketches in the main text. The largest part of the book consists of analytical reportages, mostly published in *The New York*

Review of Books, after the skilled attentions of the editor to whom this book is dedicated. Finally, there are a few essays in which I attempt an interim synthesis on a larger subject, such as the development of the European Union, Britain's troubled relationship with Europe, or the way countries deal with the legacy of a dictatorship.

As befits "history of the present," everything in the main text was written at or shortly after the time it describes. The pieces have been edited lightly, mainly to eliminate repetition, but nothing of substance has been added or changed. I compiled the chronology and short sketches more recently. Occasionally, I have also added a comment at the end of a piece.

HERE I WANT to reflect on writing "history of the present." The phrase is not mine. It was, so far as I know, coined by the veteran American diplomat and historian George Kennan in a review of my book about Central Europe in the 1980s, *The Uses of Adversity.* It is, for me, the best possible description of what I have been trying to write for twenty years, combining the crafts of historian and journalist.

Yet it immediately invites dissent. History of the present? Surely that's a contradiction in terms. Surely history is by definition about the past. History is books on Caesar, the Thirty Years War, or the Russian Revolution. It is discoveries and new interpretations based on years of studying documents in the archives.

Let's put aside straightaway the objection that "the present" is but a line, scarcely a millisecond wide, between past and future. We know what we mean here by "the present," even if the chronological boundaries are always disputed. Call it "the very recent past" or "current affairs" if you would rather. The important point is this: Not just professional historians but most arbiters of our intellectual life feel that a certain minimum period of time needs to have passed and that certain canonical kinds of archival source should be available before anything written about this immediate past qualifies as history.

It was not ever thus. As the formidably learned German intellectual historian Reinhart Koselleck has observed, from the time of Thucydides until well into the eighteenth century, to have been an eyewitness to the events described or, even better, to have been a participant in them was considered a major advantage for a writer of history.[1] Contemporary history was thought to be the best history. It is only since the emergence of the idea of progress, the growth of critical philology, and the work of Leopold von Ranke that historians have come to believe that you understand events better if you are farther away from them. If you stop to think about it, this is actually a very odd idea: that the person who wasn't there knows better than the person who was.

Even the most ascetic neo-Rankean depends upon the witnesses who make the first record of the past. If they do not make a record, there is no history. If they do it badly or in pursuit of a quite different agenda (religious, say, or astrological or scatological), the historian will not find answers to the questions he wants to ask. It's therefore best to have a witness who is himself interested in finding answers to the historian's questions about sources and causes, structure and process, the individual and the mass. Hence, for example, Alexis de Tocqueville's personal account of the 1848 revolution in France is worth twenty other memoirs of that time.

This need for the historically minded witness has become more acute in recent times for a simple reason. In Ranke's day, politics was put on paper. Diplomacy was conducted or noted immediately in correspondence. Politicians, generals, and diplomats wrote extensive diaries, letters, and memorandums. Even then, of course, much that was vital was not written down—murmured private understandings in the corridors of the Congress of Vienna, the pillow talk of queens. Then, as now, most of human experience was never recorded at all. But most of politics was.

Today, however, high politics is more and more pursued in personal meetings (thanks to the jet airplane) or by telephone (increasingly by mobile phone) or by other forms of electronic communication. Certainly, minutes of meetings are made afterward and, at the highest levels, so are transcripts of phone conversations. But the proportion of important business actually put on paper has diminished. And who writes narrative letters or detailed diaries any more? A dwindling minority.

To be sure, researchers can watch television footage. Sometimes, they can listen to the telephone tapes—or taps—of those conversations. Perhaps in future they will also read the e-mails. The point is not that there are fewer sources than there were. Quite the reverse. Where the ancient historian has to reconstruct a whole epoch from a single papyrus, the contemporary historian has a roomful of sources for a single day. It is the ratio of quantity to quality that has changed for the worse.

On the other hand, politicians, diplomats, soldiers, and business-people have never been so eager to give their own version of what has just happened. Iraqi crises famously unfold in "real time" on CNN. European ministers tumble out of EU meetings to brief journalists from their own countries. Naturally, each gives his own twist and spin. But if you put the different versions together, you have a pretty good instant picture of what occurred.

In short, what you can know soon after the event has increased, and what you can know long after the event has diminished. This is particularly the case with extraordinary events. During some of the dramatic debates between the leaders of Czechoslovakia's "velvet revolution," in the Magic Lantern theater in Prague in November 1989, I was the only person present taking notes. I remember thinking, "If I don't write this down, nobody will. It will be gone forever, like bathwater down the drain." So much recent history has disappeared like that, never to be recovered, for want of a recorder.

Two objections remain strong. First, since those things governments and individuals try to keep secret are often the most important things, the eventual release of new sources will change the picture substantially. This is not a conclusive argument for waiting—in the meantime, other equally important things, well understood at the moment, may be forgotten—but it is a major hazard of the genre. In the preface to my first "history of the present," an account of the Solidarity revolution in Poland, I observed that I would not have attempted to write the book had it seemed likely that the official papers of the Soviet and Polish communist regimes would become available in the foreseeable future. That, I continued blithely, seemed "as probable as the restoration of the monarchy in Warsaw or Moscow." Eight years later, the Soviet bloc had collapsed and many of those papers were available. Fortunately, I also quoted Walter Raleigh's warning, in the preface to his *History of the World,* that "who-so-euer in writing a modern Historie shall follow truth too neare the heeles, it may happily strike out his teeth."

The second strong objection is that we don't know the consequences of current developments, so our understanding of their historical significance is much more speculative and liable to revision. Again, this is patently true. Every high-school senior studying ancient history knows that the Roman empire declined and fell. Writing about the Soviet empire in the 1980s, none of us knew the end of the story. In 1988, I published an essay entitled "The Empire in Decay," but I still thought the empire's fall was a long way off. In January 1989, I wrote an article pooh-poohing suggestions that the Berlin Wall might soon be breached.

Yet there is also an advantage here. You record what people did not know at the time—for instance, that the Wall was about to come down. You dwell on developments that seemed terribly important then but would otherwise be quite forgotten now, because they led nowhere. You thus avoid perhaps the most powerful of all the optical illusions of historical writing.

One of the real pleasures of immersing yourself in the archives of a closed period is that you gradually, over months and years, see a pattern slowly emerging through the vast piles of paper, like a message written in invisible ink. But then you start wondering, Is this pattern really in the past itself? Or is it just in your own head? Or perhaps it is a pattern from the fabric of your own times. Each generation has its own Cromwell, its own French Revolution, its own Napoleon. Where contemporaries saw only a darkling plain, you discern a tidy park, a well-lit square, or most often a road leading to the next historical milestone. The French philosopher Henri Bergson talks of the "illusions of retrospective determinism."

American journalists writing books of recent history sometimes modestly refer to them as "the first draft of history." This implies that the scholar's second or third draft will always be an improvement. Well, in some ways it may be, having more sources and a longer perspective. But in others it may not be, because the scholar will not know, and therefore will find it more difficult to re-create, what it was really like at the time; how places looked and smelled, how people felt, what they didn't know. Writers work in different ways, but I can sum up my own experience in a doggerel line: There is nothing to compare with being there.

KENNAN OBSERVED THAT history of the present lies "in that small and rarely visited field of literary effort where journalism, history and literature . . . come together." Again, this seems to me exactly right. The corner of Europe where Germany, France, and Switzerland meet is known in German as the *Dreiländereck,* or Three Country

Corner. "History of the present" lies in a Three Country Corner between journalism, history, and literature. Such frontier areas are always interesting but often tense. Sometimes working in this one feels like walking in a no-man's-land.

The shortest and best-marked frontier is that between history and journalism on the one side and literature on the other. Both good journalism and good history have some of the qualities of good fiction: imaginative sympathy with the characters involved, literary powers of selection, description, and evocation. Reportage or historical narrative is always an individual writer's story, shaped by his or her unique perception and arrangement of words on the page. It requires an effort not just of research but of imagination to get inside the experience of the people you are writing about. To this extent, the historian or journalist does work like a novelist. We acknowledge this implicitly when we talk of "Michelet's Napoleon" as opposed to "Taine's Napoleon" or "Carlyle's Napoleon."

Yet there is a sharp and fundamental difference, which concerns the kind of truth being sought. The novelist Jerzy Kosinski, who played fast and loose with all facts, including those about his own life, defended himself aggressively. "I'm interested in truth not facts," he said, "and I'm old enough to know the difference." In a sense, every novelist can say that. No journalist or historian should. In this, we also differ from the father of contemporary history. Thucydides felt free to put words into Pericles' mouth, as a novelist would. We do not. Our "characters" are real people, and the larger truths we seek have to be made from the bricks and mortar of facts. What did the prime minister say *exactly*? Was it before or after the explosion in the Sarajevo marketplace, and whose mortar actually fired the fatal shell?

Some postmodernists disagree. They suggest that the work of historians should be judged like that of fiction writers, for its rhetorical power and capacity of imaginative conviction, not for some illusory factual truth. Eric Hobsbawm has given a finely measured response: "It is essential," he writes, "for historians to defend the foundation of their discipline: the supremacy of evidence. If their texts are fictions, as in some sense they are, being literary compositions, the raw material of those fictions is verifiable fact."[2]

That applies equally to journalism. We all know about fabrications at the bottom end of journalism, in the gutter press. Unfortunately, the frontier with fiction is also violated at the top end of journalism, especially in reportage that aspires to be literature. Any reportage worth reading involves rearranging material, highlighting, and, to some extent, turning real people into characters in a drama. But the line is crossed when quotations are invented or the order of events is changed. There is one genre of modern journalism, the "drama-documentary" or "faction," which does this avowedly. Faction is, so to speak, honestly dishonest. But more often this is done behind a mask of spare authenticity.

The precedents are distinguished. John Reed's account of the Russian Revolution, *Ten Days That Shook the World*, is probably one of the most influential pieces of reportage ever written. Yet he spoke virtually no Russian, regularly made up dialogue, offered secondhand accounts as firsthand, mixed up dates, and added imaginative detail. As Neal Ascherson observes, in a fine essay on his work, Reed "gives a thrilling account of Lenin's appearance at a closed Bolshevik meeting in Smolny on 3 November, allegedly communicated to him outside the door by Volodarsky as the meeting went on. No such meeting took place."[3]

To save us from Reed's disease—and to spoil our best stories—great American journals such as *The New Yorker* employ factcheckers. As they drag their fine combs through your text, it is horrible to find how many small errors of fact have slipped into your notebook or intruded on the path from notebook to text. But sooner or later you come to the passages, often the most important ones, that they annotate in the margin, "On author." This means you are the only source for the fact (if fact it be) that, for example, a church door in the Krajina was stained with blood, or a Kosovo rebel leader said what your notebook records that he said. Then you are alone with your notebook and your conscience. Did he really say that?

Ideally, I suppose, one should be permanently wired for sound, like a superspy. Or, even better, have a miniature video camera implanted in one's skull. And certainly some of the very best contemporary history has been done on television. I think of documentary series such as *The Death of Yugoslavia*. Although the television camera can also be made to lie by tendentious selection and manipulative editing, at best it brings you closer than any other medium to how things really were.

For the writer, however, the conventional, handheld, visible tape recorder and television camera have major disadvantages. They are cumbersome, even in their latest, slimmed-down, high-tech versions. Try using one at the same time as taking notes during a fast-moving demonstration. It is, in practice, very difficult to see simultaneously with both the camera's and the writer's eye. You're always liable to miss the telling detail that is vital to good reportage because you're fiddling with a tape or lens. And then you keep worrying about whether and what they are recording. Tape recorders and cameras put people off. Politicians and so-called ordinary people speak less naturally and freely as soon as the machines come out. Worse still, cameras and microphones also turn people on. Demonstrators or soldiers strike heroic poses and make portentous statements they would not otherwise make. So these apparently neutral, mindless recorders of reality actually change it by their mere presence. Yet even the visible notebook does that.

I occasionally use a tape recorder for an important conversation, but my inseparable companion is a pocket notebook. The notebook is often open when the person is speaking, but sometimes, when I think they will talk more freely or simply when walking or eating or whatever, it is not. Then I write the conversation down as soon as possible afterward. I am obsessed with accuracy and, after twenty years, rather well practiced in this kind of remembering. But as I look back through my notebooks there is always this nagging concern: Did he really say that?

Take the opening passage of my reportage from Serbia in March 1997 (see p. 226): the student named Momčilo exclaiming "I just want to live in a normal country," and so on. Now Momčilo said this, in his imperfect English, as we hurried through the streets of Belgrade toward a students' meeting. I wrote it down as soon as we got there. If I had a tape recording of what he actually told me, it would probably be slightly different—a bit more awkward and less sharp. But I don't have a tape recording. The verifiable historical truth of that fragment of the past is gone for good. You just have to trust me. A little later, I relate excited exchanges at the student meeting. These I scribbled down as they happened. But I don't speak Serbian, so what you read is my interpreter's version—and we both have to trust her.

Altogether, the business of language is crucial. Most of what is quoted in this book was said or written in languages I understand. But some, especially from Albanian and the southern Slav languages now called Serbian, Croatian, Bosnian, and Macedonian, was translated for me by an interpreter, with the inevitable loss of accuracy and nuance. The first thing to ask of anyone writing about anywhere is, Does he or she know the language?

Finally, it seems to me, the key to trust is not the technical apparatus of audiovisual recording and sourcing and fact-checking, invaluable though that is. It is a quality that may best be described as veracity. No one will ever be completely accurate. There is a margin of unavoidable error and, so to speak, necessary license if cacophonous, Babel-like reality is to be turned into readable prose. But the reader must be convinced that an author has a habit of accuracy, that he is genuinely trying to get at all the relevant facts, and that he will not play fast and loose with them for literary effect. The reader should feel that while the author may not actually have a video recording of what he is describing, he would always like to.

George Orwell's *Homage to Catalonia* is a model of this kind of veracity. The book is a piece of literature. It is inaccurate in many details, not least because Orwell's notebooks were stolen by the communist goons who came to arrest him as a Trotskyist.[4] Yet you don't doubt for a single moment that he is striving for the greatest possible accuracy, for the fact-based truth that must always set apart the plains of history and journalism from the magic mountains of fiction.

THE FRONTIER BETWEEN journalism and history is the longest in our Three Country Corner. It is also the least well marked and therefore the most tense and disputed. I can testify to this, having lived on both sides and in between. In journalism, to describe a piece as "rather academic"—meaning jargon heavy, boring, unreadable—is the surest path to the spike. In academe, it's a put-down to say that somebody's work is "journalistic," meaning superficial, racy, and generally not serious. "Contemporary history?" sniffed an elderly don when I returned to my Oxford college from a job in journalism at the end of the 1980s. "You mean journalism with footnotes?"[5]

I think it's important to understand that the reasons why so much is made of the differences between journalism and academic or professional history have at least as much to do with the practical exigencies, self-images, and neuroses of the two professions as they have with the real intellectual substance of the two crafts. Granted, the qualities of bad journalism and bad history are very different: sensationalist, intrusive, populist tosh with millions of readers on the one side; overspecialized, badly argued, ill-written doctorates with no readers on the other. But the virtues of good journalism and good history are very similar: exhaustive, scrupulous research; a sophisticated, critical approach to the sources; a strong sense of time and place; imaginative sympathy with all sides; logical argument; clear and vivid prose. Was Macaulay, in his essays for the *Edinburgh Review*, a historian or a journalist? Both, of course.

Yet, in modern Western societies, profession is a defining feature of personal identity, and the professions that are closest together take most pains to distinguish themselves. I say modern *Western* societies, incidentally, because this was not so true in the communist world, where the most important social identification was with a broad class: intelligentsia, workers, or peasants. One of the interesting experiences of the last decade in formerly communist parts of Europe has been to see friends rapidly becoming differentiated by profession, Western style. Where once they were all fellow members of the intelligentsia, now they are academics, lawyers, publishers, journalists, doctors, and bankers, with diverging ways of life, styles of dress, homes, incomes, and attitudes.

Now, because of the ways in which the professions of journalism and history have developed and because of the edginess between them, the writing of "history of the present" has tended to fall between the two. That no-man's-land is perhaps wider and more tense than it was when Lewis Namier put aside eighteenth-century English politics to chart the European diplomatic history of his own times and Hugh Trevor-Roper turned from Archbishop Laud to write *The Last Days of Hitler.*

Every profession has its characteristic fault. If I had to summarize in a word, I would say that the characteristic fault of journalistic writing is superficiality and that of academic writing is unreality. Journalists have to write so much, and they are so pressed for time. Sometimes they are "parachuted" into countries or situations about which they know nothing and expected to report on them within hours. Hence the famous, horrible line "Anyone here been raped and speak English?" Then their copy is cut and rewritten by editors and subeditors who are working to even tighter deadlines. And, anyway, tomorrow is another day, another piece.

Academics, by contrast, can take years to finish a single article. They can (and sometimes do) take infinite pains to check facts, names, quotations, texts, and contexts, to consider and reconsider the validity of an interpretation. But they can also spend a life describing war without ever seeing a shot fired in anger. Witnessing real life is not what they are supposed—or funded—to do. Methodology, footnotes, and positioning in some ongoing academic debate can seem as important as working out what really happened and why. Participants in the worlds they describe sometimes throw up their hands in laughter and despair at the unreality of what comes out.

Of course, I could equally dwell on the characteristic virtue of each side, which is the opposite of the other's characteristic fault: depth in scholarship, realism in journalism. The interesting question is, Has it gotten worse or better? Well, some things have improved. If you read what passed for contemporary history in Britain in the 1920s, you find a bluff amateurism unthinkable today. In journalism, the growth of world television-news services such as CNN, Reuters, and BBC World Television and that of documentation on the Internet offers wonderfully rich new sources for present history. But, on the whole, I think it has gotten worse.

There is still a handful of great international newspapers of record. Top of my personal short list would be *The New York Times, The Washington Post,* and *The International Herald Tribune, The Financial Times, Le Monde* in France, the *Neue Zürcher Zeitung* and the *Frankfurter Allgemeine Zeitung* in the German-speaking world. You can generally believe what you read in these papers. Yet even with this select group, it is astonishing how many discrepancies you find if you buy them all and compare their accounts of the same event. By and large, they do still separate fact and opinion, although there are exceptions. For example, the coverage of the wars of the Yugoslav succession in the *Frankfurter Allgemeine Zeitung* was for years distorted by the pro-Croat views of one of that paper's publishers.

In my view, the foreign reporting in the leading American newspapers is the best in the world. Senior, highly educated American journalists are proud to describe themselves as "reporters," whereas in Britain every twenty-three-year-old fresh out of college wants to be a "columnist" or "commentator." Standards of editorial accuracy and fact-checking are second to none, and corrections are published when errors are made. Moreover, extensive space is given to foreign coverage. You have a definite sense that what happens almost anywhere in the world matters, because the country in which the paper appears is a world power. What was true of the *The Times* of London a hundred years ago is true of *The New York Times* today. For an Englishman, the contrast in quality of foreign coverage between the New York and the London *Times* is now painful to observe.

Outside this small group, the value as historical record of most other newspapers in most other countries is slight, and diminishing. This is particularly true in Britain, where the fierce commercial competition for readers—above all between the groups headed by the Australian-American owner of *The Times,* Rupert Murdoch, and the Canadian proprietor of the *Daily Telegraph,* Conrad Black—has resulted in a further erosion of the journalism of record. I'm talking not just about the quite astonishing levels of routine inaccuracy and distortion, for reasons of both sensationalism and ideology—although in Britain this is especially apparent in anything to do with the European Union. As important are two other traits: featurism and futurism.

A large part of most newspapers is now taken up not, as their name would suggest, with news, but with features: lifestyle, beauty, fashion, medicine, food, holidays, etc. This is what readers are said to want. Meanwhile, in what remains of the news pages, there is the more subtle disease of futurism. More and more space is devoted to speculating about what may happen tomorrow rather than describing what happened yesterday—the original mission of journalism. When read any time after today, this stuff is useless, except as an illustration of what people did not know at the time. Reading my own pieces for this book, I am again reminded that nothing ages more quickly than prophecy—even when it was prescient.

For all these reasons, the history of the present gets written less in its first natural home, the newspapers. But there are also problems on the academic side of the frontier. Some professional historians do tackle subjects in recent history. Even the Oxford history faculty, long accounted conservative (with a small *c*), now has a history syllabus that is open-ended toward the present. Nonetheless, in my experience, most academic historians are still reluctant to venture much closer to the present than the canonical thirty years after which official papers are released in most democracies. They still incline to leave this territory to colleagues who have made it their own in subjects such as International Relations, Political Science, Security Studies, European Studies, or Refugee Studies.

Yet these relatively new specialisms often feel the need to establish their academic credentials, their claim to the high name of Science (in the German sense of *Wissenschaft*), by a heavy dose of theory, jargon, abstraction, or quantification. Otherwise—horror of horrors—their products might be confused with journalism. Even when those involved have been trained to write history, the results often suffer from overspecialization, unreadable prose, and that characteristic fault: unreality. At the same time, the pressures of American-style "publish or perish" mean that a huge amount of academic work in progress is hastily thrown into book form. Here, too, the ratio of quantity to quality has surely changed for the worse.

So I MAINTAIN THAT, for all its pitfalls, the literary enterprise of writing "history of the present" has always been worth attempting. It is even more so now because of the way history is made and recorded in our time. Sadly, it has suffered from developments in the professions of journalism and academic history.

Yet you can soon have enough of such methodological self-examination. Altogether, the habit of compulsive labeling, pigeon-holing, and compartmentalizing seems to me a disease of modern intellectual life. Let the work speak for itself. In the end, only one thing matters: Is the result true, important, interesting, or moving? If it is, never mind the label. If it isn't, then it's not worth reading anyway.

T.G.A., Oxford–Stanford, March 2000

HISTORY OF THE PRESENT

CHRONOLOGY

1990

1 JANUARY.   *Introduction of economic "shock therapy" to make the transition to a free market in Poland. This is called the "Balcerowicz Plan," after the finance minister Leszek Balcerowicz.*

11 JANUARY.   *Soviet president Mikhail Gorbachev visits Lithuania, attempting to stop the movement for independence.*

12–13 JANUARY.   Oxford. At a Franco-German-British conference to discuss what the West should do about the great changes in the former East, senior politicians, officials, and diplomats express blank horror at the suggestion that Poland, Hungary, and Czechoslovakia should join NATO.

20–22 JANUARY.   *The Fourteenth Special Congress of the League of Communists of Yugoslavia ends with the virtual dissolution of the party that held Yugoslavia together.*

27–30 JANUARY.   *The Polish communist party is succeeded by two "social democratic" parties. Youthful former Central Committee member Aleksander Kwaśniewski is elected leader of one of them.*

JANUARY–FEBRUARY.   *Albanians in Kosovo protest against their province being stripped of its autonomy by Serbian leader Slobodan Milošević.*

1 FEBRUARY.   *East German prime minister Hans Modrow announces a plan for "Germany, United Fatherland."*

6–7 FEBRUARY.   *The Central Committee of the Communist Party of the Soviet Union accepts Mikhail Gorbachev's proposal to abandon the "leading role" of the Communist Party and move toward political pluralism.*

10–11 FEBRUARY.   *West German chancellor Helmut Kohl and Foreign Minister Hans-Dietrich Genscher visit Moscow. President Gorbachev gives the green light for unification of Germany.*

12–14 FEBRUARY.   *A formula for negotiations on the external aspects of German unification is agreed at an Ottawa "open skies" meeting between NATO and the Warsaw Pact, with the participation of the two German states and the four postwar occupation powers: the United States, Britain, France, and the Soviet Union. The occupying powers call this formula "4 + 2"; the Germans call it "2 + 4."*

17–21 FEBRUARY.   Berlin. "You can't come through here," says the East German frontier officer at the Brandenburg Gate. Why not? "Haven't you heard of the four-power status?" And then, rather wittily, "It's your government which prevents you crossing here!" When an East German frontier officer starts appealing to the four-power status of Berlin, I think the end of the East German state is in sight. When he finally lets me through—saying, with a shrug of his shoulders, "Anyway, it's the British sector"—I know the end is near. Further on, an East German guard stands on top of the Wall, while under his very feet people chip away pieces to sell as souvenirs. High up on the Brandenburg Gate itself, I spy a large, white graffito. It says, *"Vive l'Anarchie."*

I visit Egon Krenz, the last communist leader of East Germany, in the pleasant East Berlin villa to which he has moved from the politburo compound at Wandlitz. In real life, his white teeth are every bit as distractingly large as on the photographs. ("Granny, what large teeth you have!" said the posters at last autumn's demonstrations.) He has time on his hands and tells me his life story. The illegitimate son of a Pomeranian peasant woman, he knew poverty in his childhood. What did socialism mean to him as a young man? "A better life!" Then he hastily adds, "I mean—also for other people." Krenz is working on his memoirs and has published advanced tidbits in the *Bild-Zeitung*. So, just weeks after being deposed as communist leader, he has sold himself to a right-wing West German tabloid that stands for everything he has denounced for forty years.

One thing he wants to tell me. He much admires Margaret Thatcher's stalwart and farsighted opposition to German unification. A great woman, that Mrs. Thatcher.

24 FEBRUARY.   *Lithuanian elections are won by the independence movement Sajudis.*

26 FEBRUARY.   *Social Democrat Ingvar Carlsson is reappointed prime minister of Sweden.*

26–27 FEBRUARY. *The Soviet Union agrees to withdraw its troops from Czechoslovakia by July 1991.*

23–27 FEBRUARY. Prague. I find Václav Havel installed in the magnificent Castle, traditional home of rulers of the Czech lands. The presidential office still contains some of the old communist furniture: square brown armchairs of superhuman size, set yards apart, silently eloquent of endless fraternal nonconversations between totalitarian rulers. The ghastly pictures have mostly been removed from the walls, to be replaced by large nudes and a prayer rug from the Dalai Lama. Unlike Egon Krenz, Havel now has no spare time at all. But, dashing along the long back corridors to a press conference, he pauses for a moment to show me a room with a huge, ancient metal door. This is the starvation chamber traditional in Central European castles. "We shall use it for talks."

Walking down Wenceslas Square, I bump into an old friend, the Hungarian writer Árpád Göncz. We go for a coffee in the marvelous Jugendstil café of the Hotel Evropa. "It seems we have reached a compromise on the matter of the new president of Hungary," he tells me. Oh yes, and who will it be? "It seems it will be me."

4 MARCH. *Democratic elections to republican parliaments and local councils in the Soviet Union.*

10 MARCH. *The Soviet Union agrees to withdraw its troops from Hungary by July 1991.*

11 MARCH. *The Lithuanian parliament votes to "reestablish" the independence of Lithuania.*

15 MARCH. *Gorbachev is given the powers of an executive president in the Soviet Union.*

17 MARCH. *Warsaw Pact foreign ministers, meeting in Prague, agree that both the Warsaw Pact and NATO should continue to exist.*

18 MARCH. *Free elections to the "People's Chamber" in East Germany.*

THE SOLUTION

THE SOLUTION
After the rising of the 17th June
The secretary of the Writers' Union
Had leaflets distributed on the Stalinallee
In which one could read that the people
Had forfeited the confidence of the government
And could only recover it through
Redoubled work. Would it not then
Be simpler, if the government
Dissolved the people and
Elected another?

THUS BERTOLT BRECHT—BUT ONLY PRIVATELY—AFTER THE EAST German workers' rising in the summer of 1953.

In the summer of 1989, on 31 August to be precise, Erich Mielke, the eighty-one-year-old minister for state security of the German Democratic Republic, held a conference with his regional commanders to discuss growing discontent in the state. Extracts from the transcript of that meeting are among the first documents from the now dissolved Ministry for State Security to have been published, in a remarkable book commissioned by the East German "Round Table" of government and opposition groups.[1] At one point in this meeting, Mielke interrupts the report of Comrade Colonel Dangriess from Gera to ask, "Is [the situation] such that tomorrow the 17th June will break out?"

All along one had guessed that the old men at the top were haunted by that memory. But it is still extraordinary to find the fear so plainly expressed, black on white. "That is [sic] not tomorrow," replies the Comrade Colonel, "that will not happen, that's why we exist." A little later it is the turn of the Comrade Lieutenant General from Leipzig. "The atmosphere is wretched," he says. But, "so far as the question of power is concerned, Comrade Minister, we have things firmly in hand."

How wrong they were, how the protests grew, how Leipzig in particular became the center of enormous but peaceful popular protests—these events I have described elsewhere.[2] The documents reinforce the impression that the GDR came close to bloodshed. Here, for example, is the text of Erich Honecker's telex message to regional party secretaries on 8 October, the day after the GDR's fortieth anniversary, ordering that further disturbances are "to be prevented from the outset." And here is the matching order from the minister for state security, including the following: "Members [of the State Security Service] who are regular weapon-carriers should carry their service weapons with them, appropriately to the given challenges." In a long conversation, Egon Krenz, Erich Honecker's successor as party leader for just forty-four days, told me that in his view the country did come to the verge of bloodshed, for in such a tense situation one spark—one shot fired in panic—could have set the country alight.

The turning point was probably 9 October, when a large peaceful demonstration in Leipzig was not dispersed by force. While local initiatives, rather than Krenz, were responsible for averting violence at that critical moment, these documents give some credence to Krenz's claim to have maintained the line of nonviolence. Thus, his otherwise combative message to regional and local party secretaries on 24 October contains the crucial phrase, "We assume that all problems will be solved by political means."

By 4 November, the day of a huge opposition demonstration in Berlin, Mielke is sending a pathos-laden telex to his deputies and regional leaders. He offers thanks to all his "dear Comradesses and Comrades" for their "staunch behavior and responsible fulfillment of their duty." "I know," he writes, "how difficult it is [not to be provoked or unsettled] especially in this tension-loaded atmosphere, how much self-restraint, staunchness, and courage that requires." The crimes of the Stasi are truly not comparable with those of the SS, yet the language of this message recalls nothing so much as Himmler's infamous Posen speech of 1943.

The last document in the collection is a report from Erich Mielke to Krenz and other party leaders, dated 7 November. It records how church and opposition groups such as the New Forum have begun to defend State Security buildings against angry demonstrators. A few days later, this terrible, pathetic old man stood before the "People's Chamber," East Germany's previously rubber-stamp parliament, and said, in words that provide the title for this first documentation and will surely become immortal, *"Ich liebe doch alle"*: "But I love everyone."[3]

That was the revolution, phase one: a peaceful popular uprising that grew slowly through the summer and early autumn and flowered from 9 October. A new "17 June." Phase two of the revolution began a month later, on 9 November, with the opening of the Berlin Wall. Within a very few weeks, the tidal wave of popular demands turned decisively in the direction of unification. Instead of *"Wir sind das Volk"* ("We are the people") the crowd chanted, *"Wir sind EIN Volk"* ("We are ONE nation").

Meanwhile, thousands voted for unification with their feet, moving to West Germany and taking up their automatic rights of citizenship. First the power of the party and the Stasi, then the authority of the government collapsed. Even after taking opposition leaders into his cabinet, in a so-called Government of National Responsibility, Prime Minister Hans Modrow could not slow the internal collapse or the external hemorrage. So the promised free election was hastily brought forward, from 6 May to 18 March.

By this time, West German politicians from all the major parties were already stumping the country, and it was clear that the main contestants in the election would be the East German partners or protégés of the main West German parties. The East German Social Democrats, who had originally called themselves the SDP (Sozialdemokratische Partei) precisely to distinguish themselves from the West German SPD (Sozialdemokratische Partei Deutschlands), changed their name to SPD. Although their leading candidate was called Ibrahim Böhme, their chief crowd-puller was the legendary former West German chancellor Willy Brandt. The West German Free Democrats helped put together a Federation of Free Democrats, whose chief crowd-puller was the West German foreign minister, Hans-Dietrich Genscher. The West German Christian Democrats were instrumental in forging a so-called Alliance for Germany out of the formerly puppet CDU (East), under its new leader, Lothar de Maizière; the newly founded German Social Union (DSU), under the Leipzig pastor Hans-Wilhelm Eberling; and the smaller opposition group, Democratic Awakening (DA), which chose as its leading candidate a lawyer, Wolfgang Schnur, who had been active for several years in church-based opposition circles. But here, too, there was no doubt that Helmut Kohl was the key man. During the campaign, he spoke at six mass meetings across the land.

In the case of these three parties or party groupings, the West German influence was overwhelming. It was not just that prominent West German politicians of the appropriate party came over to support them. It was not just the financial support, important though that was. Their very posters looked the same: those of the SPD (East) in the distinctive colors and orthography of the SPD (West). So, too, for the CDU and the Free Democrats, while the DSU, based in Saxony and Thuringia, took its symbolic cue from its Bavarian neighbor, the Christian Social Union (CSU). Their language was increasingly the same: so many little Genschers, Kohls, and Brandts springing fully armed out of the television screen. Indeed, most of them had learned the language of democratic politics while watching West German television. Moreover, the actual content of their campaigns was inseparable from the impression and promises made by their West German patrons.

The only major contestant with substantial resources of its own was the former ruling communist party (SED), now renamed the Party of Democratic Socialism (PDS) and fiercely insisting that it was a completely different outfit. "We are the new," said one of its posters, showing Hans Modrow ogling a baby in a studiedly informal group of mostly young and casually dressed people on a Berlin street. Besides the two former puppet, or "block," parties, the Democratic Farmers' Party and the National Democratic Party, the other parties or party groupings on the ballot paper—twenty-four in all—included such exotic flowers as the Spartacist Workers' Party, the Carnations, and the German Beer-Drinkers Union. Seriously notable was the Alliance '90, a coalition of three opposition groups—New Forum, Democracy Now, and the Initiative for Peace and Human Rights—which, as the Stasi documents amply confirm, had been instrumental in preparing and leading the country's "October revolution."

The election campaign, fought at mass meetings, on posters and fly sheets, and on both East and West German radio and television, was quite bitter, with two basic themes. The first theme was the past. Charges of collaboration with the former communist dictatorship flew to and fro like custard pies in a bad comedy. Thus, for example, the western CDU, desperately conscious that the eastern CDU was compromised by having been a puppet party, whereas the eastern SPD was a wholly new organization, tried to make up for it by reminding voters of the awful way in which the western SPD had previously chummed up with the ruling communists in the east. One poster showed the western SPD's candidate for chancellor, Oskar Lafontaine, waving brightly next to the former East German leader Erich Honecker, a fellow Saarlander. Underneath it said, "Now what belongs together is growing together"—the already famous words with which Willy Brandt greeted the opening of the Berlin Wall. (Yet the Social Democrats would have had little difficulty finding photographs of leading Christian Democrats grinning broadly while shaking hands with Honecker, starting with Franz Josef Strauss.) When accusations about the lawyer Wolfgang Schnur's past collaboration with the Stasi began to be made, leading Christian Democrat politicians dismissed them as outrageous electoral mudslinging—until, just a few days before the election, they turned out to be true.

Yet the results suggest that the issue of the past was not decisive. If it had been, the group with much the strongest claim to be uncompromised, the Alliance '90, would have gotten more votes than it did. What decided the issue were the contrasting proposals for the immediate future, which boiled down to one essential question: How far, how fast, and by what means should East Germany be united with West Germany? The differences between the SPD and Kohl's Alliance for Germany on this issue were not fundamental. Both said unity should come, and both said they would protect the people of East Germany against the economic and social costs. But there was a significant difference of emphasis. The Alliance for Germany and, above all, Chancellor Kohl himself, made a clear, simple case for the fastest possible integration into the existing structures of the Federal Republic. There should be a rapid currency union. "We," the Alliance said in effect, "will give you the deutsche mark." Then, following intergovernmental negotiations and the reconstitution of the historic states (*Länder*) in East Germany, they should join the West under Article 23 of the Federal Republic's constitution, which is called the Basic Law. This, after listing the *Länder* of West Germany in which the Basic Law applies, says simply, "In other parts of Germany it [i.e., the Basic Law] is to come into force after their entry." *Basta!*

The SPD, by contrast, argued for a somewhat slower and more considered process in which East Germany would bring more of its own "identity" into the new Germany. Although it did not absolutely preclude unification by Article 23, the SPD inclined more to the path envisaged in the final article of the Basic Law, Article 146, which says, "This Basic Law loses its validity on the day on which a constitution comes into force which has been resolved upon by the German people in a free decision." In other words, there would be some sort of constituent assembly that would write a new constitution, perhaps formally incorporating some of the different property rights or so-called social rights established in the GDR. Altogether, the SPD offered more ifs and buts about the process of unification.

The renewed communist party, the PDS, put the ifs and buts before the "yes" to unification, although the practical difference between the "confederation" or "treaty community" for which it originally argued and de facto unification became increasingly thin. One of its two leading candidates, Hans Modrow, had, after all, as prime minister, himself put forward at the beginning of February a plan for what he called, echoing a slogan from the streets, which in turn took up a line from East Germany's national anthem, "Germany, United Fatherland." The other leading candidate of the PDS, a clever lawyer named Gregor Gysi, said, "We want a new Germany, better than the GDR but also better than the Federal Republic."

Curiously enough, the party closest to the postcommunists in its reservations about what was described as an *Anschluss* by the Federal Republic was the grouping of those whom the communist party had previously considered its worst enemies, the Alliance '90. When a telephone number is unavailable in Germany, you hear a message saying, "No *Anschluss* [i.e., connection] on this number." The Alliance '90 had an election poster saying, "Article 23—no *Anschluss* on this number!"

Yet the opinion polls soon showed that the Alliance '90 had no chance of winning with this slogan. The SPD initially had an overwhelming lead in the polls, but as the campaign progressed the Alliance for Germany, which people increasingly referred to just as the CDU, gained on it rapidly. The choice was clearly going to be between the medium track and the fast track to unification. As this became apparent, one had the curious spectacle of the communists and the dissidents joining together at the Round Table talks, and in the Government of National Responsibility, to try to save what they thought deserved to be saved from the ruins of the GDR. Sitting in his Spartan government office, one of the most determined and longest-serving dissidents, Gerd Poppe, now a minister without portfolio, explained to me how the government had hastily put together a "social charter" and laws on different ownership, so that there would be at least some formal, codified starting point for the discussion of what "good" from the GDR could be preserved in a larger Germany. The feelings of the former dissidents during this period were profoundly mixed, for whereas in the rest of East Central Europe the Round Tables and the provisional governments were clearly laying foundations for the (re-)building of democracy, here their work was more like throwing up temporary huts, which would be bulldozed away as soon as the real builders moved in.

1

Sunday, 18 March, was a beautiful spring day—almost a summer's day, in fact. The sun shone without ceasing. People voted early, then took off into the countryside. There seemed to be universal good humor. An old lady in Pankow asked how many times she should fold the ballot paper. "You can fold it as many times as you like," said the volunteer official—"it's a free election!" By the time I got to the polling station in the small village of Seeberg at midday, nearly 80 percent of the electors had voted. When I say "polling station," I mean the back room of the local pub. And when I say "80 percent," I mean about fifty people, for there were only sixty-five electors in this village—and eight of them were on the supervisory electoral commission.

These electoral commissions, containing, where possible, representatives of the main parties, took their tasks very seriously indeed, scrupulously checking off names and insisting that people use the polling booths. Previously, to use the polling booth was a sign that you were not toeing the line: Good conformists openly marked and folded their paper and put it straight into the box. A friend once described the few paces to the polling booth as "the longest walk of my life." Another recalled how, at the local government elections only last May, her hand was shaking so much that she could not get her deliberately spoiled ballot paper into the slot. Today, these sounded like tales from a distant epoch.

In Buckow, where Brecht, in his charming lakeside house, probably wrote his poem about the 17 June rising, there was the same quiet excitement, especially among younger voters. However, when I asked one old woman how it felt to take part in her first free election, she grunted and said, "Well, it was rather complicated." The agonies of choice! Actually, compared with the system in Poland or Hungary, the election procedure was simplicity itself. All you had to do was put one cross or other clear mark next to the party or party grouping of your choice. According to the election law, no party propaganda was allowed within "some 100 meters" of the polling station. So instead of the canvassers there were the journalists. Interviewers from West Germany's television asked thousands of voters to repeat their votes on simulated ballot papers.

Within a few minutes of the polling station closing at 6 P.M., television was able to announce the shock result: a triumph for the CDU. As the evening wore on, the simulated results were replaced by real ones, slightly reducing the scale of the triumph so that the Alliance for Germany narrowly missed an absolute majority. But the message was plain. In the huge metal and glass Palace of the Republic in the center of East Berlin, where three competing German television channels (two West, one East) had their studios on the *belle étage*, a desperate scrum of reporters mobbed the winners and collared anyone who seemed interesting, while yesterday's men, such as Mieczysław F. Rakowski, former leader of the former Polish communist party, peered longingly at the limelight. In one corner I spotted Daniel Cohn-Bendit, the hero of '68 in Frankfurt and Paris, known as Danny the Red. As I approached, he was saying to an interviewer, "You know, I was never a communist."

The balladeer Wolf Biermann wandered like a friendly bear through this frantic scene. "Today," he said, "here in this glass palace, is the funeral of the GDR." In another corner, the writer Stefan Heym observed, "There will be no more GDR. It will be nothing but a footnote in world history." The Republic had voted to end the Republic.

I say "the Republic" advisedly, for in East German popular usage "the Republic" is counterposed to Berlin. And Berlin voted differently: nearly 35 percent for the SPD, only 18 percent for the CDU, and nearly 30 percent for the PDS, the renamed communist party. This last rather astonishing figure may be explained partly by the heavy concentration of former party functionaries and state employees of all sorts in the capital. Yet it seems that the PDS also managed to attract both old and young voters by its skillfully propagated warnings against the cost of "capitalist" unification: unemployment, higher rents, and so forth.

But Berlin was outvoted by the rest of the country—"the Republic"—and above all by the lands of the south: Thuringia, Saxony, and Sachsen-Anhalt. Before the war, these were strongholds of social democracy. (It is sometimes claimed—although this is hotly disputed—that in the 1950s the West German chancellor Konrad Adenauer pressed less hard for reunification than he might otherwise have done because he feared these constituencies would have swung the electoral balance against him.) But now the electoral regions of Dresden, Erfurt, Gera, Suhl, and Karl-Marx-Stadt—that is, as Chancellor Kohl repeatedly insisted, Chemnitz—all turned in votes for the Alliance for Germany of around 60 percent, with less than 20 percent for the SPD and less than 15 percent for the PDS. According to a survey, some 58 percent of workers throughout the country voted for Kohl's Alliance.

To label this a "swing to the right" would be, at best, a half-truth. It is true that, as elsewhere in the former Eastern Europe, the more straightforwardly anticommunist the party, the better its chance. Here, as elsewhere, forty years of communism calling itself social-ism has made *socialism* a dirty word. But it would be wrong to sug-gest that people went from one extreme to the other. The neo-Nazi far-right groups that made such a terrible impression on interna-tional television with their rowdy behavior and chants of "Foreigners out!" at the later Leipzig demonstrations remained marginal. Even the markedly conservative DSU got no more than 15 percent of the vote in its original southern heartlands, and just 6.3 percent overall. What people chose—in spite of its past as a puppet party—was the moderate, liberal conservative CDU, which alone got almost twice the SPD vote (40.9 percent to 21.8 percent). This was, first and last, a vote for Chancellor Kohl and the fast track to unity. *Anschluss?* Yes, please!

Bärbel Bohley, the artist who was one of the founders of the New Forum, commented bitterly that "people really have no more trust in their own strength. They are swapping the tutelage of the old SED for that of the CDU and hope that not the red but the black state will do everything for them." Again, this seems to me at best a half-truth, seen from the rather special and atypical viewpoint of East Berlin. An old friend in Dresden drew my attention to an article in the West German weekly *Der Spiegel* by an East Berlin intellectual that said, in effect, "We don't need unification now that the Wall is open." If I want to get a Western book, observed the author of this article, I just take the train to Bahnhof Zoo (in West Berlin) and pop down to the Heinrich Heine Bookshop there. But, said my friend, that's precisely what you *can't* do from distant Dresden. If you want to have easy ac-cess to books—or building materials or clothes or cars—from the West, then you need unification. And, anyway, only the privileged in-tellectual would have the hard currency to slip over so casually to pick up a book—hard currency earned, for example, by writing an article against unification in the West German weekly *Der Spiegel*.

Moreover, for the people of Dresden, this is not a loss but a gain in identity. For what they identify with is not the GDR but the old *Land* and former kingdom of Saxony. (The grand duke, I understand, proposes to move back to Schloss Moritzburg.) Here, on the dusty housefronts and outside the neglected, antiquated factories, you see everywhere two flags: black, red, and gold for Germany; green and white for Saxony. And it is as the reconstituted *Land* of Saxony, not as the former GDR, that the Saxons wish to join the Federal Republic.

In the country at large, it seems to me, the real motto of the campaign—though no one, to my knowledge, actually used it—was Adenauer's slogan from the 1950s: "No Experiments!" They had experienced enough experiments to last several lifetimes: Hitler's experiments, Stalin's experiments, Ulbricht's and Honecker's. They'd had quite enough of being guinea pigs. There were certainly aspects of West German life and attitudes about which they had reservations. But so far as the economic, political, and legal system was concerned, West Germany's was the best one going. Arguably, it was the best system Germany had ever had. Now they wanted to have it as fast as possible: first the deutsche mark of course, but not just the deutsche mark, also the free press, the rule of law, local self-government, and federal democracy. In many ways, their priorities also recalled those of the 1950s in West Germany—starting with the passionate drive to rebuild for private happiness from the ruins. Understandably, the enthusiasm was greatest among the young, while the middle-aged were more worried about their abilities to adapt, and the old were concerned about the conversion rate and the values of their pensions. Indeed, the old might remark wearily, like the grandmother in Edgar Reitz's film *Heimat*, "Yet another new era!"

There are plainly immense problems of learning democracy for people who have lived even longer than Czechs or Poles under successive dictatorships, although the Czechs and Poles, unlike most East Germans, were not able to watch democracy in practice every night on their television screens. But it is deeply condescending to suggest that this vote was simply a sellout or a cop-out and little short of revolting for intellectuals in the West to suggest that the East Germans should try—as it were, on our behalf—yet another experiment. (Why the hell should they? If you want to make another experiment, kindly perform it on yourself.)

To be sure, in comparison with Poland, Hungary, or Czechoslovakia, there *is* a certain special melancholy about East Germany's transition to democracy. For it is only of the first phase of the revolution—from the great Leipzig demonstration of 9 October 1989 to the opening of the Wall on 9 November—that people can say, with justified pride and unqualified truth, "We stood up for ourselves! We did it our way!" The first peaceful revolution, the first *self*-liberation in German history, did not remain a self-liberation. East Germany did not first build its own democracy and then join hands with West Germany. From 9 November, the liberation, though still the work of Germans, was led as much by West as by East Germans. But it remains a liberation. And, with all due caveats, the prospects for a swift, successful transition to a flourishing market economy, a stable parliamentary democracy, and the rule of law are now brighter in this central patch of old Europe than east of the Oder or southeast of the Erzgebirge.

2

The reunification of Germany began on 9 November 1989. It happened from below. Wherever I went in East Germany, I found evidence of new ties: from person to person, family to family, enterprise to enterprise, town to town, *Land* to *Land*. I talked to a floor tiler in Buckow. His cooperative had established links with a West German firm. They just came knocking on the door. I gave a cheerful agricultural worker a lift home from the pub/polling station in Seeberg. Yes, he said, a baron from West Germany was going to invest in their poultry farm. The Reclam publishing house (East) has come to an arrangement with the Reclam publishing house (West). And so on.

Yet this election was a turning point. It closed the second phase of the revolution and opened the period of formal negotiation about the terms of unification between the democratically elected governments and parliaments of the two postwar German states.

The process of unification is of such complexity, with so many interacting unknowns, that merely to indicate the main issues would require another essay. Whereas the Bundesbank president initially observed that the currency union should come at the end of the transformation to a market economy, it will now come at the beginning: probably by early July, according to the Bonn government. "Engagement in spring, marriage in the summer, and then off on holiday," said the West German economics minister blithely. But who knows what will come after the honeymoon? Inflation for the West? Mass unemployment for the East? How will a swift currency union be reconciled with East Germany's Soviet and East European trade? And how will the new government resolve the ghastly tangle of claims on expropriated, nationalized, collectivized, or socialized property in the GDR?

The critical argument for a hasty currency union was to stem the hemorrhage of emigration from East Germany, and the Bonn government announced that the special treatment for migrants from East Germany will end simultaneously with the introduction of the deutsche mark. But what guarantee is there that this will halt the flood? The *Länder* of East Germany will still be much poorer than those of West Germany, with lower wages for the same work and a condition of profound social and economic dislocation. How will the social and economic strains of unification affect popular attitudes in East and West? Could they boost the vote for the far-right Republicans? East German society has scant experience of living peacefully with either political conflicts or foreigners. One of the more worrying side effects already observable in both East and West is a street-level tendency to see an answer to the problem of accommodating more Germans (including those from elsewhere in Eastern Europe) in the accommodation of fewer foreigners (Turks in the West, Vietnamese in the East, and Poles all over). Then there is the terrible problem of so-called *Vergangenheitsbewältigung*—"overcoming" the past—in East Germany: Witness the Schnur case and the beginning of a verification procedure to check that the people elected on 18 March had not formerly worked for or collaborated with the Stasi. There are no completely reliable figures, but if one takes the estimates made by the commission dissolving the State Security Service, then it would appear that at least one in every hundred GDR citizens was an official or unofficial collaborator.

And these are only a few of the internal aspects of unification. I have not begun to list the problems that most exercise the outside world: the so-called external aspects of unification, the stuff of the "2 + 4" talks, the ending of Allied rights over Berlin and "Germany as a whole," the Polish frontier treaty, the difficult substantive issues of integration into the European Community and, most intractable of all, the whole complex of political-military security arrangements, the future of NATO and the Warsaw Pact.

For years, German politicians have never tired of repeating that the key to German unity lies in Moscow. Recently Chancellor Kohl's main foreign-policy adviser, Horst Teltschik, was reported as saying that the key to German unity now lies in Bonn. Even if he actually formulated it a little more cautiously, the basic point is right. Moscow has, of course, still a great deal to say, above all on security issues. But even on security issues the first question at the moment is, What do the Germans want? Yet they disagree among themselves about what they want, as the SPD leader Oskar Lafontaine has recently demonstrated once again in advocating what would amount to German withdrawal from NATO.

ON THE EVENING of 18 March, Chancellor Kohl was so full of himself that I was afraid he might burst. Exuding sentimental assurance, he obviously felt that the CDU had won not only the East German elections but also the West German elections in December and that he would therefore go down in history as the chancellor of German unity. The SPD, by contrast, had hoped to sail into the federal elections with the wind from an East German triumph behind it and was shocked by the defeat. I would not be quite so confident as the chancellor. As the East German elections themselves showed, the firmest predictions can be overthrown. We are in unchartered waters: The chancellor has raised great expectations, and there are any number of things that can go wrong in the process of unification. Nobody knows exactly what has begun. All that is certain is what has ended. This has a name. It is called the German Democratic Republic.

Late that night, I found myself wondering how Brecht would have reacted. Had he offered himself, like Heym and Biermann, to the television interviewers in the frantic melee of the Palace of the Republic, he would probably have said something clever and dishonest. But, in the tranquil privacy of Buckow, I think his lyric spirit—honest in spite of the man—might perhaps have written:

> THE SOLUTION
> *In the election of 18th March*
> *The people*
> *Dissolved the republic and*
> *Chose another.*

CHRONOLOGY

1990

24 MARCH. Margaret Thatcher summons a group of historians and specialists on Germany to a private meeting at Chequers to discuss German unification. See below, p. 50.

8 APRIL. *The second round of Hungarian parliamentary elections produces a government majority for the nationalist Hungarian Democratic Forum.*

9 APRIL. *Leaders of Czechoslovakia, Hungary, and Poland meet in Bratislava to discuss Central European cooperation. They will subsequently become the "Visegrád group."*

18 APRIL. *French president François Mitterrand and German chancellor Helmut Kohl send a joint message to the current president of the European Council of the EC, proposing an intergovernmental conference on "political union" of the existing EC, as well as that already planned on economic and monetary union (EMU).*

3 MAY. *Árpád Göncz—writer, translator, and former political prisoner— becomes acting president of Hungary.*

4 MAY. *The Latvian parliament proclaims the country's independence from the Soviet Union.*

6 MAY. *The nationalist Croatian Democratic Union wins parliamentary elections. Its leader, Franjo Tudjman, becomes president of Croatia.*

8 MAY. *Estonia declares independence.*

11 MAY. *Lech Wałęsa declares a "war at the top," which will divide Solidarity in Poland.*

16 MAY. *Nationalist conservative József Antall forms a right-wing coalition government in Hungary.*

20 MAY. *The National Salvation Front, led by the former communist Ion Iliescu, wins elections in Romania. Iliescu becomes president.*

29 MAY. *Creation of the European Bank for Reconstruction and Development (EBRD) to finance reconstruction of postcommunist countries.*

30 MAY. *Boris Yeltsin is elected president of the Russian Republic.*

MAY–JUNE. *Continental European countries impose ban on imports of British beef, for fear of bovine spongiform encephalopathy or "mad cow disease."*

7 JUNE. *A Moscow summit of the Warsaw Pact seeks to transform it into a "political-military" rather than a "military-political" body.*

10 JUNE. *In the first free elections in Czechoslovakia since 1946, victory for the movements that led the "velvet revolution": the Civic Forum in the Czech lands, the Public Against Violence in Slovakia.*

10 AND 17 JUNE. *In Bulgaria, former communists—now called Socialists—win parliamentary elections, followed closely by the Union of Democratic Forces, an opposition coalition.*

14–15 JUNE. *Romanian miners are bused in from the provinces to attack protesting students, "intellectuals," and opposition parties in Bucharest.*

20 JUNE. *In Yugoslavia, the Croatian Republic removes "Socialist" from its name and adopts the checkerboard flag of the wartime fascist Croat state. Serbs in the Croatian province of Krajina start forming their own de facto authority.*

25–26 JUNE. *As urged by President François Mitterrand and Chancellor Helmut Kohl, European Community leaders, meeting in Dublin, decide that an intergovernmental conference on political union should be held parallel to that already planned on economic and monetary union.*

26 JUNE. *The Hungarian parliament votes for the country to negotiate its withdrawal from the Warsaw Pact.*

28 JUNE. Vienna. I hear Lech Wałęsa speak at a conference on "Central Europe on the Way to Democracy," together with several former Solidarity leaders against whom he has declared his "war at the top." Wałęsa is given a tour of the Habsburg capital. His guide points out a statue of the empress Maria Theresa. A little later, Wałęsa muses, "Hm, interesting that Mother Teresa already has a monument."

1 JULY. *German "Monetary, Economic and Social Union." The deutsche mark comes to East Germany.*

1–13 JULY. *The Twenty-eighth Congress of the Communist Party of the Soviet Union.*

2 JULY. *The Slovenian parliament issues a declaration of sovereignty, giv-*

ing republican laws priority over federal ones. The Kosovo assembly declares the province to be an "independent republic" in the Yugoslav federation.

5 JULY. *Václav Havel is reelected president of Czechoslovakia.*

5–6 JULY. *A NATO summit in London concludes with a declaration marking the end of the cold war.*

14–16 JULY. *Helmut Kohl and Hans-Dietrich Genscher visit Moscow and the Caucasus. Crucial German-Soviet agreements on the external aspects of German unification, with Gorbachev accepting that united Germany will be in NATO.*

14 JULY. *British trade and industry minister Nicholas Ridley resigns after telling* The Spectator *that the proposed European monetary union is a "German racket designed to take over the whole of Europe."*

16 JULY. *Slobodan Milošević is elected leader of the postcommunist Socialist Party of Serbia.*

Après le Déluge, Nous

I telephoned Jacek Kuroń, the veteran oppositionist, now Poland's minister for labor and social affairs. A woman answered the phone.

"Could I speak to Minister Kuroń, please?"

"But this is the censors' office!" the woman replied politely. (The telephone numbers differ by only one digit.)

"I thought censorship had been abolished?"

"Yes it has, but our contracts run until the end of July, so we're still here."

"Well, I wish you pleasant inactivity."

"Thank you, and all the very best to you."

She sounded charming.

Former censors, former border guards, former apparatchiks, former secret policemen: What is to be done with them? Or, rather, what is to be done with Them—*Oni*—as the communist power holders, great and small, were universally known. There is the question of justice. Should the men at the top be brought to trial for the evil they did or that was done under them? If so, on what charges and by what laws? At a lower level, it becomes almost a question of social justice. Is it fair, people ask, that those who had comfortable office jobs under the communists should still have them today, when ordinary people are having to tighten their belts yet more? Is it fair that members of the *nomenklatura* (those nominated to leading positions by the ruling communist party) are exploiting the unclear legal conditions of privatization to take over as capitalists the enterprises they have previously commanded as communists?

Yet the requirements of justice can clash with those of efficiency. If the choice is between a compromised, incompetent person and an uncompromised, competent one, then the decision is easy. But what if the choice is between a compromised but relatively professional person and an uncompromised but wholly amateur one? I dine with the new ambassador of an East Central European country, a charming person, Catholic, brave, honest, unbowed. The number-two man at the embassy, by contrast, is plainly from the old guard, at best an unprincipled careerist, complete with regulation dandruff and greasy smile. He starts telling me how this year he hoped they would lay a wreath at the monument to the American rather than the Soviet liberators. A perfect turncoat. Yet at least he has some rudimentary professionalism in foreign affairs, whereas the ambassador tells me that "our foreign minister has introduced a new element into international relations—it's called trust." Oh dear.

There is the problem of Them, but there is also the problem of Us. "We are not like Them," chanted the crowds in Prague during the revolution of 1989. Six months later, some of those same people can be heard muttering about how the new power holders resemble the old. In Poland, the disgruntled now speak of a "new *nomenklatura*." The Citizens' Committees, they claim, are beginning to work like the Party Committees of yore. As in the old days, they say, a telephone call from the Committee decides the issue.

Many things contribute to this inchoate discontent. Partly it is that, having known no other power holders than the communists, people do not distinguish between what is common to all power holders and what was peculiar to communist ones. Partly it is that, in the first postrevolutionary phase, these countries' new would-be democratic leaders are almost bound to resort to the method of placing "one of Us" instead of "one of Them" on the commanding heights, whether of the secret police or of the media, by nomination rather than election or free competition. This has been true of Czechoslovakia—one writer called it Havel's "anti-February," referring to the communists' February 1948 coup—and of Poland under its post-Solidarity prime minister Tadeusz Mazowiecki, although the nominations are often the outcome of complex negotiations and in no case imposed by force or the threat of force.

One may have some sympathy with those at the top, for they are damned if they do and damned if they don't. If they leave old communist appointees in place, people say it's not fair and nothing has really changed. It's like the Polish police cars: same vehicles, same colors, same people inside, but where before it said *Milicja* it now says *Policja*. If, however, they replace the communist appointees with their own, then people cry, "Foul!" and "New *nomenklatura!*" On the one hand they are required to make changes fast and effectively, on the other hand democratically and constitutionally. As one speaker remarked at a stormy session of Lech Wałęsa's Citizens' Committee, the trouble is that there are no generally accepted "rules of the game." This leads into temptation.

Visiting old friends catapulted from jail to cabinet, from stoker to parliamentarian, from being a victim of the secret police to being the head of it, I was interested to see how the acquisition of power had changed them. Could they prove exceptions to Lord Acton's rule that power tends to corrupt?

Everyone, but everyone, is changed. It's not just the externals, although these are important. Offices with secretaries—most of them ladies of a certain age, inherited from the ancien régime. Chauffeur-driven cars—avoiding, if at all possible, the old black Tatras in favor of Volvos, Mercedes, or, as in Havel's new presidential motorcade, supersexed BMWs. Suits and ties instead of the regulation dissident sweaters (with the exception of the former dissident Adam Michnik—still defiantly wearing jeans—and the Hungarian Young Democrats, who, even in the sumptuous, gilded Budapest parliament, have a quite distinctive line in casual summer wear; "yes, they discuss it in their caucuses," an MP told me). The unaccustomed press of business, exacerbated by deep tiredness, poor institutional backup, and the endless flow of Western visitors. Changes in bearing, manner, and manners. When Havel became president, he adopted a ramrod-straight posture and a rather gruesome imperial stare that I had never noticed before. One sees it often now, on television, far away. Just playing the part?

Many others exhibit the same features to a lesser degree. "I feel as if I'm two different people," says one. "My old, private, writer self and a new public self." There is irony here. Against what did they set out to do battle? Why, against the double life, against the split between public and private selves, the daily toll of public conformity and mendacity which, as Havel demonstrated better than anyone in his essays, played a vital role in sustaining the previous system. Yet now they are themselves condemned to live sorts of double lives. Not that the new public language is comparable to the old. The Havel-speak now used by Czechoslovak television commentators is quite depressing, but it is still a world away from Newspeak. Nonetheless there is—in Poland and Hungary as well as in Czechoslovakia—a certain incipient divergence between the public and private language of the new leaders.

Corruption by power? The germs of it, in some cases, yes: a little too much enjoyment of the new privileges; perhaps a few too many trips abroad—"for the good of the country," of course. (Oh, the hard life of luxury!) The arrogance of power, subtly reinforced by the feeling that you have deserved it after so many long years of struggle. "Where were you in November?" Havel recently retorted to a crowd of Slovak hecklers. "Where were you in August?" "Where were you in '68?" "Where were you in '56?" Explicitly or implicitly, these are also the challenges made in Polish and Hungarian politics. But this line of argument is as dangerous as it is understandable. When the writer Wiktor Woroszylski attacked the Polish parliamentarian Ryszard Bender for having been a member of parliament under the Jaruzelski "normalization" regime, Bender retorted by recalling Woroszylski's own communist past. Where do you stop with the reckoning? Where do you draw the line?

Everyone finds it difficult to come to terms with the loss of the common enemy. Of course, there were endless personal conflicts inside the opposition movements, as well as deeper differences of tradition and ideology. But, sooner or later, people pulled together against the common oppressor. This was true, at a rather basic level, of all the East Central European societies under communism. In your circle of friends you could always find common ground in grumbling about Them. A young Dresdener described to me his shock at discovering, during the election campaign, that his friends could actually think differently. Unheard of! What was true of the majority of the population in a mild way was true of the politically engaged minority in a much stronger way. For all the tensions and conflicts, the emotional experience of Solidarity in Poland was, indeed, that of solidarity. The heyday of the Civic Forum in the Czech lands was a shorter but no less intense experience of triumphant social unity. Yet, to put it in Hegelian terms, the triumph of unity was also the beginning of its negation.

The one great conflict is succeeded by many small conflicts. However much you may rationally appreciate that there is no pluralism without conflict, the mere fact of these conflicts is somehow felt to be abnormal and disturbing. Often they involve the severing of old friendships, with sadness and bitterness. There is a lack not only of the forms and procedures in which to regulate these conflicts but of the language in which to express them. In Poland and Czechoslovakia, the civic movements came to power with a rhetoric derived from the antipolitical language of the democratic oppositions—a language of philosophic and moral absolutes, of right against wrong, love against hate, truth against falsehood. To communism as a monopoly system of organized lying they counterposed the antipolitical program of "living in truth."

Now we expect many things of politicians in a well-functioning parliamentary democracy, but "living in truth" is not one of them. In fact, the essence of democratic politics might rather be described as "working in half-truth." Parliamentary democracy is, at its very heart, a system of limited adversarial mendacity in which each party attempts to present a part of the truth as if it were the whole. When Václav Havel was asked at a public discussion in London whether he thought it would prove possible for the new politicians to continue to "live in truth," he replied, "Either yes or no. If it proves not, I certainly won't go on being one." Now it may just be possible for the president, as moral father-figure, to go on "living in truth"— although some might think that campaigning for the Civic Forum in the election while protesting that you are not campaigning at all comes pretty close to the line. But it is certainly not possible for any lesser mortals who actually have to compete for power.

Partly for tactical or strategic reasons—"unity is strength," as the crowds chanted in Prague—but also for intellectual and emotional ones, there is a reluctance to move from antipolitical to explicitly political language. Instead, there is a tendency on all sides toward Manichean overstatement. Having lost the communist devil, says Adam Michnik, we find the devil in each other.

1

New political divisions are clearly emerging. But how to describe them? Western observers grasp for simple, comprehensible dichotomies: the functional equivalents of the categories of "reformists versus hard-liners" or "regime versus opposition," which served understanding (and misunderstanding) in the past. Polish, Hungarian, Czech, and Slovak participants and analysts are only too happy to offer new, clear dichotomies—partly in an attempt to understand the situation, partly to mold it. Unfortunately, they offer not just one or two but ten or twenty new dichotomies.

The real issue is pluralism versus the "new monopoly" of his former advisers, says Lech Wałęsa. No, it is parliamentary constitutionalism versus extraparliamentary populism, says Solidarity's parliamentary floor leader Bronisław Geremek. It is Europeans against nationalists, says Adam Michnik. No, say others, the real conflict is between underrepresented workers and overrepresented intelligentsia. Or between country and city. Or simply between those who now have power and those who want it: the Ins and the Outs. Then someone else comes along and says, to the relief of many baffled Westerners, that, after all, the fundamental argument is still between left and right. But no, says another; the crucial difference is rather between liberals of right or left and illiberals of right or left.

In the U-shaped Hungarian parliament you have, starting from the speaker's left, a few independent members, then Socialists (i.e., former communists), Young Democrats, Free Democrats, Smallholders, the Democratic Forum, and the Christian Democrats. That looks clear enough: left to right. But, wait a minute: the economic policy of the Free Democrats is far more radically free market—or "Thatcherite"—than that of the Democratic Forum, while at the far right of the Democratic Forum sit members of what is described as the Protestant, populist *left:* communitarian and anticapitalist.

Let's try again. The basic divide is between two Hungaries: the cosmopolitan, urbanist, Western-oriented Hungary represented archetypally by the multilingual Jewish intellectuals of the Free Democrats; and a nationalist, populist, sometimes anti-Semitic, Transylvania-oriented Hungary, represented by the monolingual intellectuals of the Democratic Forum. But then the Forum's foreign minister, Géza Jeszenszky, a diplomatic historian, spends twenty minutes explaining to you with eloquence and passion, in fluent English, why this is a caricature. And the populist "left" (or is it "right"?) rather prove the point by their furious attacks on their own prime minister, József Antall, and his cozy cabinet of Christian Democrat or Gladstonian-liberal gentlemen. But, then again, it is Antall, a devout Catholic, rather than the Protestant populists who has pressed one of the policy proposals most offensive to Free Democrats and Young Democrats: that there should be religious instruction—initially it was even implied that this might be compulsory Catholic instruction—in schools. So is that all clear?

In Poland, things are no less complicated. Take, for example, two prominent exponents of opposing points of view: Adam Michnik, chief editor of the Solidarity daily, *Gazeta Wyborcza,* and Jarosław Kaczyński, chief editor of the Solidarity weekly, *Tygodnik Solidarność,* and a leading light of the so-called Center Agreement, a pro-Wałęsa party. Michnik essentially argues that the basic divide in Polish politics today is still that which can be found, in one form or another, in the histories of all East and Central European countries—between Slavophiles and Westernizers, populists and urbanists, *Kultur* and *Zivilisation.*

One problem with his position is that it does not really allow for the possibility of a modern, liberal, European Christian Democracy in East Central Europe. Early in July, Prime Minister Tadeusz Mazowiecki attended a meeting of, precisely, European Christian Democrats hosted in Budapest by József Antall and starring the German chancellor, Helmut Kohl. Some politicians close to Mazowiecki founded a Forum of the Democratic Right, which clearly aimed to be just that. But in Michnik's judgment the dynamics of Polish politics would almost certainly sweep a would-be liberal, tolerant, European Christian Democracy into the flood waters of an intolerant, nationalistic, chauvinist National Democracy.

Kaczyński offers a quite different dichotomy. Michnik and Geremek, he says, represent "the left." He, by contrast, claims to represent the "center-right." What, I asked him, distinguished this "left"? Without hesitation, he spelled out four points. First, he said, there was the attitude toward property. He and his colleagues were unambiguously in favor of private property, "the left" much more ambiguously so. Second, there was Michnik and Geremek's attitude toward communists. For a year since last June's election they had been far too ready to make compromises with the communists. As late as the autumn, Michnik had argued that the most important thing was to forge an alliance with reformist (ex-)communists. According to Kaczyński, this also reflected ideological preferences: a red–pink continuum. Third, there was the attitude toward the church. To be sure, Michnik often referred to Christian values and professed admiration for the historic antitotalitarian role of the church, but there was still an underlying suspicion, an anticlericalism, which they, the "center-right," did not share. Fourth, Michnik and Geremek had a basic, underlying mistrust of ordinary Polish people; they, the "center-right," by contrast, believed in the common sense of the common people.

Kaczyński is a clever man, and there is something in at least the last three of these points. Yet the truth of the whole is less than that of any one of its parts. For the whole picture he paints is that of a conspiracy: a conspiracy to dupe the common people, organized in what *Tygodnik Solidarność* writers refer to as the "Warsaw–Kraków salon" and led by the satanic pair, "Michnik and Geremek," whose names are repeated over and over again.

To suggest this is covert anti-Semitism (both Michnik and Geremek are of Jewish origin) would be as crude as it would be to suggest that Polish-Jewish history has nothing to do with the argument. The best way to describe it is, I think, in terms of residual images. In what Jarosław Kaczyński says, and even more in what some of the more explicitly right-wing groups say, there is the residual image of a Jewish conspiracy. In what Adam Michnik says, there is the residual image of a pogrom. (Of course, these residual images are not histor-ically symmetrical, for there never was a Jewish conspiracy, whereas there were pogroms. Indeed, it must not be forgotten that Poland saw a communist-led anti-Semitic campaign as recently as 1968.) Yet the emphasis in both cases should be on the word *residual*. To suggest that this is somehow the "real" difference, the bottom line, would be as wrong as it would be to reduce the present arguments to any other single dichotomy: left-right, European-nationalist, mo-nopoly-pluralism, workers-intelligentsia, Ins-Outs.

Perhaps the beginning of wisdom is to recognize that what the communists have left behind is an extraordinary mishmash, a pro-found fragmentation and cacophony of interests, attitudes, views, ideals, traditions: what in Polish is called a *miazga*. The system of late communism may not have qualified for the label "totalitarian-ism," but it was certainly posttotalitarian. Many elements of civil society—elementary property rights, legal structures, intermediate institutions that still existed under the dictatorships in Spain, Greece, or Latin America—were destroyed in Eastern Europe and even more thoroughly in the Soviet Union. In this sense, the totali-tarian-authoritarian distinction may yet be found to have some va-lidity.

A Russian joke about the transition from communism makes the point better than any learned disquisition: "We know that you can turn an aquarium into fish soup; the question is, Can you turn fish soup back into an aquarium?" In East Central Europe, things are not quite so hopeless. Here one has something more like a goulash than a fish soup. (After goulash communism comes the postcommunist goulash.) There are large lumps of civil society swimming around like meat in the goulash: private farmers, churches, universities, small-scale entrepreneurs. But it is still a very long way from the reg-ular meat and two vegetables of developed Western societies, with relatively coherent blocs of interests, aspirations, and traditions finding their political expression through a small number of rela-tively durable political parties.

In East Central Europe today there are a few elements of political differentiation based on socioeconomic positions. For example, ever since the formulation of the Mazowiecki government, private farmers have been the most clearly defined and determined interest group in Polish politics. But it is still very difficult to imagine a class-based politics. Wałęsa and his political allies may still sometimes speak in the name of "the workers," but in reality the working class is almost as divided as the intelligentsia is between those who stand to gain from this or that measure or marketization and those who stand to lose by it. In Poland, there is still no significant property-owning middle class. In Hungary, the sociologist Elemér Hankiss argues that one can already identify a small *grande bourgeoisie* (the "red barons" of the cities and the "green barons" of the agricultural cooperatives) and a larger *petite bourgeoisie,* numbering perhaps as many as two million. But he cannot yet offer any significant correlation between these new-old classes and particular parties.

Indeed, in both Poland and Hungary the more important divide may be between those who believe that parliamentary politics can change something in their everyday lives and those who do not. In these countries' first free elections in more than forty years, the rate of abstention was staggeringly high: nearly 40 percent in Poland's parliamentary elections in 1989, nearly 60 percent in the local elections in May 1990; 35 percent in the first round of Hungary's parliamentary elections, 55 percent in the second.

It would be wrong to say that there are no ideological divides. Of course there are. They emerge, for example, in one of the most important debates in all contemporary East Central European politics: how to proceed with privatization. Should the present management of state enterprises be allowed to turn them into joint-stock companies? Or should ownership be given to the workers? Or should shares be distributed to the whole population, perhaps through a system of holding companies or investment funds? And what, if any, should be the limitations on foreign ownership? But, again, these differences are not sufficiently clear and simple to form the basis of different political parties. The arguments are precisely about how to proceed with privatization, not about whether to.

If the basis of postcommunist politics is neither class nor ideology, then what is it? At the moment, the answers would seem to be history and the West. Western models play a major role, both in the design of the new political institutions of East Central Europe and in the formation of parties. Everywhere, teams of Western experts have been called in to give their advice. In domestic debates about the new constitution, the "French model," the "Italian model," and the "German model" are basic terms of reference. The last mentioned is particularly noteworthy.

Germany has offered many things to East Central Europe over the centuries, but democracy has rarely been among them. Now, however, the German model of democracy is arguably the most relevant of all, because it is a model built on the rubble of a totalitarian dictatorship and very deliberately designed to prevent the return of such a dictatorship. It is, one might say, a Western system built on Central European experience. Constitutional elements such as the rule that parties must win more than 5 percent of the popular vote to gain any seats in parliament or the parliamentary institution of the "constructive vote of no confidence"—that is, a vote of no confidence that simultaneously appoints a new prime minister—have been copied directly in Czechoslovakia and Hungary respectively. The West German parties, together with their wealthy and active party foundations, also play important roles. At the moment, the CDU seems to be most successful, while the SPD has the problem that all over East Central Europe ex-communists are now calling themselves Social Democrats.

On the other hand, there is history. I have referred already to some residual images that shape and color Polish and Hungarian politics. In Czechoslovakia, the only relatively clear divides at this moment are historical-national ones, with separate Czech and Slovak versions of the revolutionary civic movement dominating the Czech and Slovak governments, while both are challenged by Slovak nationalists, by Hungarian nationalists in Slovakia, and by Moravian and Silesian autonomists. But these echoes of the interwar period are only one part of the story. Both the more recent and the more distant past also play roles.

To understand present conflicts, you really need a collective biography of the last forty years. Members of the Hungarian Democratic Forum, for example, often charge the Free Democrats with being former Marxists, while claiming they themselves had no illusions about communism. Similar charges are heard in Poland. Yet many of those who never had any illusions about communism were also never particularly active against it. Gáspár Miklós Tamás, the Transylvanian philosopher and Free Democrat MP, memorably calls them "the sleepers." In present-day politics, you have the class of '48, the class of '56, the class of '68, the class of '80, and—largest of all—the class of '89. Both between the classes and within each class there is a complex personal history of friendships and rivalries. You cannot begin to understand the personal alignments of today unless you know *who did what to whom* over the last forty years.

Sometimes, however, one can dig too deep. For example, there were, to be sure, obvious differences of tone and style between Tadeusz Mazowiecki and Lech Wałęsa over the last ten years: Mazowiecki always diplomatic, cautious to a fault, a cabinet politician; Wałęsa direct, instinctive, a tribune of the people. Yet the origins of the conflict between them essentially lie in developments over just the last year (1989–1990), when Mazowiecki was sitting in the prime minister's office in Warsaw while Wałęsa was sitting in Gdańsk.

"How you see things depends on where you sit," as Wałęsa himself put it. Last autumn, the civic movements in Poland and Czechoslovakia believed that they were embarking on a sort of "march through the institutions," to recall the German student slogan of '68. But what we have seen was almost the opposite: a march of the institutions through people. It is remarkable how quickly and fully people identify with that particular part of the political system in which, initially almost by chance, they have come to serve: with government as opposed to parliament, with parliament as opposed to the extraparliamentary movement, with the presidency (in Prague Castle) as opposed to the government, and so on.

At the same time, one cannot ignore the elements of history, tradition, and political culture stretching back not months but centuries. Obviously, these are more difficult to analyze and assess. But they are certainly there. Watching a meeting of Lech Wałęsa's Citizens' Committee in the main lecture hall of Warsaw University, with people making theatrical entrances and exits, passionate speeches, and furious interjections from the floor, and then plotting in the corridors, I wrote at the top of my notes one word: *sejmik* (literally "little parliament"—that is, the gentry parliaments of prepartition Poland). Then the film director Andrzej Wajda slipped into the chair beside me and said, "You see, all they need is sabers and they'd be fighting each other outside."

Amid this baffling cacophony of intelligentsia politics—baffling to a large part of the population as well as to the outsider—with its strange admixtures of Piłsudski and Olof Palme, Horthy and Thatcher, Masaryk and Weizsäcker, Bundestag and *sejmik*, the only serious path to real understanding is a detailed historical and, in the case of the leading actors, biographical narrative. But, short of that, there are still a few generalizations that might be risked.

2

A friend of mine has a thick file labeled simply "TD." It contains invitations to conferences on the subject of the "Transition to Democracy" in Eastern Europe. "TC" might be a more accurate label. What one can certainly observe in the whole of Eastern Europe, and in much of the Soviet Union, is the Transition from Communism. But the only case in which one can be almost 100 percent certain that the transition will indeed be *to democracy* is that of the former German Democratic Republic, which will cease to be called democratic but actually become so. It is, however, no disrespect to the people of East Germany to say that this will be as much an imported as a homegrown democracy.

Inside the Soviet Union, the aspirations of such European peoples as the Lithuanians, Estonians, and Latvians, and of European Russians are clearly in the same basic direction—toward liberal democracy, the market economy, and the rule of law—but the problems they face are both of a different kind (being part of a multinational internal empire) and of a different degree (fish soup rather than merely goulash). In the Balkans, too, there is a rather different pattern, with what seems at the moment to be a transition from a (notionally) communist dictatorship to a non- (or ex-?) communist dictatorship in Romania, and Yugoslavia facing ethnic-national problems more comparable with those of the Soviet Union than with those of East Central Europe.

The heartlands of East Central Europe—Poland, Hungary, and Czechoslovakia—are therefore, at the moment, something of a special case. One might also say a test case, for the success or failure of their attempts will influence future developments in the countries of the Balkans and the Soviet Disunion. Poland, Hungary, and Czechoslovakia are the three ex-communist countries that are at the moment clearly attempting to build their own democracies on the ruins of dictatorship. Hungary and Czechoslovakia have had wholly free parliamentary elections, which all observers accept to have been fair. Poland has had partly free but wholly fair parliamentary elections and wholly free local elections. These elections were not contested by a "normal" party spectrum, as in Western Europe, but nonetheless they produced real parliaments. New constitutions are being written. There is already legally guaranteed freedom of speech, assembly, and worship. There are a free press and free media, although the practice of independent journalism still leaves much to be desired—especially in the all-important medium of television. People can travel freely, limited only by shortage of hard currency. The increasing convertibility of their own currencies is itself a vital element of freedom and dignity. Everyday life is less abnormal.

So these countries are traveling hopefully, but will they arrive? It is a commonplace to say that the chances for the political transition from dictatorship to democracy depend to a very large degree on the economic transition from a planned to a market economy. However, it is also true that the chances for the economic transition depend on the politics of transition. It is, I think, slightly misleading to describe the problem as that of a possible "failure" of the economic transition, for even "success" will be agonizing in the early stages. This transition is, as Ralf Dahrendorf has written, unavoidably a valley of tears. The valley may be shallow or deep, short or long, but a valley there will certainly be. Even the Germans, with far better starting conditions in 1948, got poorer before they got richer. (There is also a problem of unrealistic popular expectations in East Central Europe, based on a mental elision of the idea of the 1950s *Wirtschaftswunder* with the visible reality of West German prosperity in the 1990s. Perhaps the Goethe Institute should organize a traveling exhibition showing everyday life in Germany in the early 1950s.) In

Czechoslovakia, there is talk of achieving a soft landing. But the real question is whether they can achieve a soft takeoff. Even East Germany is not going to have that.

The immediate question, therefore, is, What variant of democratic politics can, on the one hand, provide sufficiently strong, stable, consistent government to sustain the necessary rigors of fiscal, monetary, and economic policy over a period of several years, while, on the other hand, being sufficiently flexible and responsive to absorb the larger part of the inevitable popular discontents through parliamentary or, at least, legal channels, thus preventing the resort to extraparliamentary, illegal, and ultimately antidemocratic means? This challenge has already been posed in a quite direct way in Poland, with peasant farmers physically occupying the agriculture ministry and blocking highways across the country.

For some in Poland and Czechoslovakia, the requirements implicit in this question seem to point to the need for a strong presidency. In an opinion poll conducted in Poland in mid-July 1990, 52 percent of those asked said the highest power in the state should be the president, against 43 percent for parliament. In Hungary, by contrast, the argument seems already to have been decided in favor of parliament, with a presidency having little real power although lots of real influence. The American political scientist Alfred Stepan has argued forcefully that the South European and Latin American experiences of attempted transitions from dictatorship to democracy suggest that an unambiguously parliamentary system has a better chance of striking the necessary balance than a presidential one. Executive presidents are less able to create consensus behind painful (e.g., anti-inflationary) policies than parliamentary coalitions are. The executive president therefore becomes either a weak president, because he bows to the majority, or a strong but antidemocratic one, because he does not. It is, of course, questionable how far such experience is applicable to a regime with a very different history and with the unprecedented task of transforming not just an authoritarian but a posttotalitarian polity, not just a controlled but a central-command economy.

Nonetheless, what I have seen on the ground in East Central Europe would support the general argument. Given the fragmentation and confusion of interests, aspirations, and traditions that I have sketched above, it is very difficult to see how any president, however popular or charismatic, could sustain a voluntary consensus over a sufficient period for those painful policies of economic transition to have a chance to work, unless it was by mobilizing nationalistic fervor against a real or alleged common enemy: a new devil—Russian? German? Jewish? Romanian?—to take the place of the communist one. But such an undemocratic, nationalist mobilization would itself undermine the proposed economic transition, which depends crucially on the continued goodwill and active engagement of Western democracies.

No, the political key to creating such a consensus must be the creation of strong, freely elected coalition governments. At the time of writing (July 1990) each of the East Central European countries has fulfilled two of these conditions, but none has fulfilled all three. Hungary has a freely elected coalition government. But thus far it seems to be a weak coalition government, one in which junior coalition partners (e.g., the Smallholders) behave as if they hardly belong to the coalition, while the main partner, the Democratic Forum, is itself a coalition with a coalition. Nor has the Antall government found an architect of economic transformation to compare with Leszek Balcerowicz in Poland or Václav Klaus in Czechoslovakia.

Czechoslovakia has a freely elected government—in fact, it has three freely elected governments: federal, Czech, and Slovak. If President Havel were to put his authority firmly behind the policies proposed by the finance minister, Václav Klaus, who knows that there is no such thing as a soft takeoff, then the federal government might also be a strong government. But it is not a coalition, in the sense of a government constructed as a negotiated deal between distinct parliamentary parties. For here there is at present really only one party, or rather movement. Since the 5 percent rule (taken over from West Germany) led to the elimination at the polls of virtually all the minor parties contesting the election, the Civic Forum in the Czech lands and, to a lesser extent, the Public Against Violence in Slovakia are left as overwhelming blocs, with a parliamentary opposition composed only of communists and nationalists (plus some Christian Democrats in Slovakia).

The competing parties will therefore have to form out of the body of the Civic Forum. There are already nascent political groupings within the Forum, and one proclaimed protoparty, the neoliberal (or is it neoconservative?) Civic Democratic Alliance. These parties will have to separate out in time to compete in the next election, scheduled for 1992. The tendency must therefore be for the Civic Forum to pull apart, rather than to pull together. How this necessary pluralization can be combined with the unity required to sustain the hard policies of economic transition over the two-year period nobody in Prague could tell me.

As for Poland, from the formation of the Mazowiecki government in September 1989 until the spring of 1990, it had something that it has not often had in its history: a strong coalition government. This was a broad coalition, dominated by ministers from the Solidarity side but containing communists in key positions (defense, interior ministry) as well as representatives from the formerly puppet Democratic and Peasant parties. It was a strong coalition, which managed to sustain, in its first six months, a remarkable degree of national consensus through the most radical and painful economic shock therapy that had yet been seen anywhere in the ex-communist world: the so-called Balcerowicz Plan.

The trouble is that it was not a freely elected coalition government. And when free parliamentary elections had been held everywhere else in Eastern Europe, when Czechoslovakia and Hungary had their playwright presidents (Václav Havel and Árpád Göncz), then it began to seem anachronistic and shameful that Poland—the pioneer throughout the 1980s—should still have a rigged parliament and, heaven help us, General Jaruzelski as president. A seemingly transformed General Jaruzelski to be sure, as mild and discreet and civil and cooperative as any West European constitutional monarch, but nonetheless—Jaruzelski.

In the event, Polish politics were transformed by Lech Wałęsa's challenge from Gdańsk. But even if Wałęsa had behaved like—well, like Jaruzelski—the problem would still have become acute. It seems to me quite unlikely that, in these external circumstances, the Mazowiecki government and, so to speak, the Geremek parliament could have stuck to the timetable of first holding completely free parliamentary elections in 1991 and only then electing a new president. Even if they had, there would still almost certainly have been a crystallization of competing parties from within the broad Solidarity movement and its Citizens' Committees.

These Citizens' Committees are strange creatures. The central one started life as a group of intellectual advisers to Lech Wałęsa. In the first half of 1990, it was expanded to include representatives of very different political groupings, at Wałęsa's behest but against the wishes of many of its founding members. The regional Citizens' Committees were set up on the initiative of the Solidarity leadership (Wałęsa, Geremek, and Mazowiecki, then working in close harmony) to win the historic June 1989 election. They had no clear structure or membership. Anyone "who felt good there" could come, as one member explained. This sort of spontaneous, quasi-revolutionary grassroots democracy has, of course, led to countless tensions and conflicts ever since that glorious fourth of June.

In fact the dilemma of the Citizens' Committees in Poland is comparable to that of the Civic Forum in the Czech lands. Once the electorate had shown that its confidence still lay with the heirs of the revolution (and the Citizens' Committee lists secured over 41 percent of the vote in the May 1990 local elections), then it was clear that the process of democratic pluralization must occur inside the movement as well as outside it.

This is one of the things that Lech Wałęsa said most forcefully. But it is not the only thing that he said. In fact, in a series of pyrotechnic interviews and speeches, he said many different and contradictory things—some very acute, some very stupid, some funny, and some less so. There are two ways of viewing the "war at the top" that Wałęsa launched in spring 1990. One is that Wałęsa, being in touch with ordinary people, saw that all was not going well with the government he had done so much to create. His former intellectual advisers and comrades were growing too comfortable in their undemocratic, rigged Warsaw coalition: their "new monopoly." Meanwhile, both political and economic changes were going too slowly. Privatization, insofar as it was happening at all, was benefiting the old *nomenklatura* rather than ordinary people. As prices and unemployment rose, so did popular discontent: Witness the railwaymen's and other strikes, which only Wałęsa, with his authority and charisma, managed to pacify.

What was needed, therefore, was an "acceleration"—acceleration of privatization and marketization, to be sure, but above all political acceleration, meaning free parliamentary elections, Wałęsa for president, and the faster removal of communists at all levels. Wałęsa sometimes adopted the argument, made by Jarosław Kaczyński and others, that, since people could not be offered economic goods, in the short term they should be offered symbolic political goods instead—that is, communist heads on a silver platter. Not salami tactics but Salome tactics.

The other way of describing Wałęsa's campaign is more simple. Having contributed more than any other single human being, with the exceptions of the pope and Mikhail Gorbachev, to the end of communism in Eastern Europe; having won the elections; having formed the Mazowiecki government; he suddenly found himself marginalized, up there in Gdańsk, while all the action was in Warsaw. Then he found that his popularity was slipping in the opinion polls prominently published by *Gazeta Wyborcza*—the paper whose editor, Adam Michnik, he, Wałęsa, had chosen personally. According to one of these polls, he even scored lower than Jaruzelski as a suitable candidate for the presidency. His former advisers made it plain that they, too, did not see him as president. Then news leaked out from the Belweder, the presidential palace, that Jaruzelski, resenting the attacks upon him and realizing that his time was past, was ready to resign. So, if Wałęsa wanted to be president, it was now or never.

There is truth in both versions. The discontents and problems to which Wałęsa pointed were real, but so was his personal sense of destiny. Like a commander in chief, he replaced the chairman of the Citizens' Committee with his own appointee, Zdzisław Najder. Then he sacked—by public letter—the secretary of the Citizens' Committee, Henryk Wujec, for many years one of his closest comrades. When Wujec politely objected that, since he had been elected by the Citizens' Committee, only the committee could dismiss him, Wałęsa wrote back, no longer to "Henryk" but to "Representative Henryk Wujec," the now famous line, "feel yourself dismissed." Then he attempted to sack Adam Michnik from *Gazeta Wyborcza*. Then he peremptorily summoned the prime minister to a meeting in front of the workers in the former Lenin Shipyard, now once again called simply the Gdańsk Shipyard. "Let us meet at the source," he wrote, as if "the source" of the prime minister's power was somehow still the workers' muscle that gave birth to Solidarity in August 1980, rather than the election of June 1989 that gave birth to the Mazowiecki government. (But then, and here's the catch, it wasn't a wholly free election, and people were voting for the "candidates of Lech Wałęsa.")

In a newspaper interview in mid-June, he said:

For today, when we are changing the system, we need a president with an ax: decisive, tough, straightforward, doesn't mess around, doesn't get in the way of democracy, but immediately fills the holes. If he sees that the people are profiting from the change of system, stealing, he issues a decree, valid until the parliament passes a law. I would save half of Poland if I had such powers.

3

Is this merely a specific, Polish problem, with one very special history and one very special person, or is it a more general one? Bronisław Geremek has spoken dramatically of the "totalitarian temptation" in postcommunist countries. As an analytical (as opposed to a rhetorical) proposition, this goes too far. One cannot see in any East Central European country today the combination of specific features that the French philosopher Jean-François Revel characterized as the totalitarian temptation. But one can see the seeds of an authoritarian temptation.

This is least apparent in Czechoslovakia, the country with the strongest twentieth-century democratic tradition. To be sure, one can hear criticism of Havel's high-handed, arbitrary style, and, as you would expect, much more outspoken criticism of his "court." But, in his speech to the newly elected Federal Assembly, Havel himself came out in favor of somewhat reducing the powers of the presidency from those he currently enjoys. If the government(s) can remain coherent and strong, even while the Civic Forum breaks into different protoparties—a very big if—then there is a chance that Havel could withdraw slightly farther from the everyday political arena, in the best case becoming to the Czechoslovak transition what King Juan Carlos was to the Spanish one.

In Hungary, the temptation is perhaps slightly greater. As one Hungarian writer put it to me a short time ago, "The Czechs are so lucky. When they look under the carpet they find Masaryk, whereas we find Horthy." Fortunately, Hungary's new president is no Horthy but instead is that same Hungarian writer: the liberal, genial, and charming Árpád Göncz. In the present design of Hungary's new political system, if there were to be a new "strongman," it would probably be in the position of prime minister rather than president. His rule would be reinforced, it is suggested, by an alliance with an extra-parliamentary "movement," a *Bewegung,* and buttressed by weak, government-dominated media. But the Democratic Forum really does not yet qualify as a *Bewegung.* Although the press may not be as fiercely independent as it should be—ironically enough, the former party paper *Népszabadság* is now said to be one of the best dailies—it is still very far from being a transmission belt for government policy.

Even in Poland, where the authoritarian temptation actually has a name and a mustache, the immediate danger is certainly not that of a Balkan-style transition from communist to noncommunist dictatorship. In fact, one might say that the immediate danger here is of too much democracy, not of too little. The immediate effect of Wałęsa's extraordinary campaign was to accelerate—to use his own buzzword—the process of pluralization and political fragmentation.

If Hungary needs the element of strength, and Czechoslovakia the genuine coalition, Poland needs the free election. But will the freely elected government then be a strong coalition, as the half freely elected Mazowiecki government was for its first six months? Or will it rather be a weak coalition, with members from numerous smaller parties or factions, subject to endless conflicts and frequent reshuffles? This is, after all, what happened last time Poland regained its independence and attempted to build a parliamentary democracy, in the years from 1918 to 1926. Then, as the historian Norman Davies observes jocularly, "the proliferating profusion of possible political permutations . . . palpably prevented the propagation of permanent pacts between potential partners."

At a meeting of Lech Wałęsa's central Citizens' Committee in late March, at the very beginning of the "war at the top," Tadeusz Mazowiecki expressed his fear that the fledgling Polish democracy could turn into "a Polish hell. A Polish hell of squabbles, intrigues, and conflicts." At the dramatic thirteenth meeting of that committee, in June, Wałęsa said, "Maybe we have to go through the Polish hell." And that is rather how it looks at this writing. One could, perhaps, afford such fissiparous politics—the Italians seem to manage—if one already had a flourishing free-market economy, with only a small state sector, and a developed civil society. But here, in the immediate postcommunist period, too much still depends on the state. It is the state that has to organize the withdrawal of the state from the economy, the state that has to create the conditions for "building" civil society. One might, therefore, offer an alternative definition of the Polish hell: Italian politics without the Italian economy.

Altogether, if there is a threat to democracy in East Central Europe, it will probably come through a period of, so to speak, excessive democracy. In Czechoslovakia and Hungary, as well as in Poland, one can see three major elements that give cause for concern. First, there is popular disgruntlement, not only about the costs of economic transition, such as price rises, reduction of subsidies, and unemployment, not only about new injustices and the slowness of visible change but also about the processes of parliamentary democracy, which are themselves held to be responsible for the slowness of change. It is difficult to adapt psychologically from the dramatic fast-forward of last year's revolutions to the slow motion of this year's parliamentary democracy. Seeming indifference to the new politics (reflected in the very high abstention rates in Poland and Hungary) and revolutionary impatience are, in fact, two sides of the same coin.

Second, the processes of the fledgling democracy are, indeed, often slow, ramshackle, and flawed. If there is abnormally low popular tolerance or understanding of political conflict ("Why can't we still be united?"), there is also an abnormally high level of political conflict inside the new political elites: because there are no clear dividing lines, no proper parties, and few "rules of the game"; because the new leaders, too, are unused to living with routinized, multilateral conflict and have difficulty moving from antipolitical to ordinary political language; and, yes, because power is a dangerous drug. Finally, the inevitable dislocation and distress associated with the conversion to a market economy could increase both the fissiparousness of the elite and the disillusionment of the populace. One could then all too easily imagine these three elements—elite dissension, popular disillusionment, economic distress—combining in a vicious circle, each exacerbating the other.

After 1918 came 1926 and Piłsudski's coup. Yet although in so many ways the past seems to be returning with a vengeance, there are at least two powerful reasons for believing that history will not simply repeat itself. The first is the popular experience of dictatorships (of right and left) over the last half century. When the expatriate Nobel Prize–winning Polish poet Czesław Miłosz was asked, on a recent trip to Poland, what he thought people might have learned from the years under communism he replied, "Resistance to stupidities." An optimistic interpretation, you may say, but there are some grounds for believing that fifty years of bitter experience have given the people of East Central Europe a resistance to certain kinds of stupidity. The kinds of stupidity associated with dictatorships, for example.

As we have seen, people are unfamiliar with, and therefore sometimes distrustful of, the forms and habits of democracy. But the habits of dictatorship? With these they are all too familiar. "Though I may not be able to define freedom," wrote another Polish poet, "I know exactly what unfreedom is." Suppose a would-be strongman comes along and, using populist demagogy, attempts to overturn the parliamentary government. How, then, would he rule? By an extraparliamentary mass movement? By police terror? By censorship? By martial law? The repertory of dictatorship is relatively small and, in this region, quite comprehensively discredited.

Against this argument you may cite Romania, where an authoritarian regime has succeeded the Ceauşescu dictatorship. Without insisting too much on differences of tradition and political culture between East Central Europe and the Balkans, I would point to a second, powerful, reason for believing that these countries can after all resist the authoritarian temptation. This is the international context. If more or less authoritarian regimes flourished in East Central Europe between the wars, this was partly because there were examples of authoritarianism elsewhere in Europe that could somehow be associated with the dream of modernity. Today there are no such examples, and modernity is unambiguously associated with democracy.

It would be nice to think that Poland, Hungary, and Czechoslovakia could coordinate their "return to Europe," supporting each other's fledgling democracies. But, despite the goodwill of the new leaders, symbolized by the Bratislava summit in April, the present reality is as much one of competition as it is of cooperation. In almost every field, at almost every international gathering, one finds the Polish, the Hungarian, and the Czechoslovak representatives quietly pushing their own particular claims for the special attention of the West. This competition is not unhealthy, but it underlines the new-old dependency of these countries—on the West.

Part of the attraction for Czechoslovakia and Hungary of the so-called Pentagonale cooperation between them, Yugoslavia (especially Slovenia and Croatia), Austria, and Italy may be the sentimental revival of old Habsburg ties. But there is also the more vulgar charm of being closely involved with two highly developed Western countries—one a leading member of the EC, the other trying hard to get in. In their different ways, the Czechoslovak, Polish, and Hungarian foreign ministers have all observed that if these three countries are to achieve a new democratic partnership, it will be only in the context of belonging to a larger European community—and by that they mean, above all, a larger European Community.

The responsibility of the West in general, and Western Europe in particular, is therefore immense. A cartoon on the front page of the leading Czech independent daily, *Lidové Noviny*, expressed a sentiment about the West that can be encountered in Budapest and Warsaw as well as in Prague. It showed a rather gloomy man saying, "The European Home is shut. If we want to get in, we have first to solve all our key problems." At times, the attitude of some Western leaders does still recall Dr. Johnson's famous definition of a patron: "Is not a

Patron, my Lord, one who looks with unconcern on a man struggling for life in the water, and, when he has reached ground, encumbers him with help." Of course, Western investors have no moral obligation at all to invest unless the conditions are right. But Western democracies do have a moral obligation and, what is more, a hard political interest in helping the man while he is struggling in the water—provided, of course, he is really trying to swim and not just shouting about swimming.

Perhaps the greatest risk of the kind of superdemocratization that I have suggested is possible—with more shouting but less swimming—is that it will diminish the overall Western interest in the transitions in East Central Europe, an interest which may yet prove to be as shallow as it is currently broad. "Why should we help them if they cannot help themselves?" will be the cry.

There are two sides to this coin too. The West, if it is to help, has a right to ask for certain rigorous, consistent economic policies—let us call them, in shorthand, a Balcerowicz or Klaus plan—and for the kind of governments that will be able to sustain such policies. The political desideratum may, I have suggested, be summarized as strong, freely elected coalitions. But, if the countries of East Central Europe produce such governments, then they must be confident that the help will really be there. For without it, such policies are simply unsustainable.

West Germany is currently reckoning to pay something in the order of three hundred billion marks over the next three years for the transition in East Germany. As with all building plans, the final bill will almost certainly be higher. And that is for a ready-made transition—a turnkey democracy, so to speak—for just sixteen million people in the most prosperous country of the former Eastern Europe. How much larger then would be the bill for homemade, trial-and-error democracies for sixty-three million people in three rather poorer countries?

There is, to be sure, a general consensus among Western governments and political elites that "we should help" the transition to democracy in East Central Europe. But how many politicians are prepared even to contemplate action on a scale comparable to that which West Germany, after a very sober examination, considers to be necessary for East Germany? Above all, how many politicians are prepared seriously to make the case to their own electors for such help? If presented with such a prospective bill, most West European electors would, I fear, say, "Sorry, no!" Ironically, the kind of West European consumer democracy to which East Central Europeans so passionately aspire may be the kind least likely to help them. If West German taxpayer electors are so reluctant to pay even for their fellow Germans, who would seriously expect them to cough up for Poles?

Nonetheless, the challenge of democratic leadership would be precisely to make this unpopular case as eloquently and convincingly as possible, stating plainly that this is a moment when short-term personal and material interests should be sacrificed to long-term national and European ones. What we are witnessing is therefore not just a testing time for the fledgling democracies of East Central Europe but also a testing time for the established democracies of Western Europe.

Finally, my exclusive emphasis on just three countries of East Central Europe may raise an objection. What about all those other Europeans to the east and to the southeast who are also crying out for democracy? My answer is a purely pragmatic one. Poland, Hungary, and Czechoslovakia are the countries where the fate of democracy hangs in the balance today and where the weight of the West can make the difference between success and failure. You cannot do everything at once. With German unification, the eastern frontier of democratic Europe has already moved from the Elbe to the Oder. I sincerely hope (against hope) that in ten or fifteen years the frontier of democratic Europe may be at the Urals and the Black Sea. But the question for today is, Will democratic Europe end on the Oder or on the Bug?

THE CHEQUERS AFFAIR

IN JULY 1990, IN THE MIDST OF FAR, FAR MORE IMPORTANT DEVEL-
opments, such as NATO's London Declaration, the Twenty-eighth
Congress of the Communist Party of the Soviet Union, and the
Stavropol accord giving Soviet approval to the full sovereignty of a
united Germany, Anglo-German relations suffered a little shake.
The first part of this little shake was an interview given to *The Spec-
tator* by Britain's then secretary of state for trade and industry,
Nicholas Ridley, in which, after lunch, but only one glass of wine,
Mr. Ridley talked about the proposed European monetary union as
"a German racket designed to take over the whole of Europe," and
declared that, if you were prepared to give up sovereignty to the
Commission of the European Communities, "you might just as well
give it to Adolf Hitler, frankly." Saltily written up by the new editor of
The Spectator, Dominic Lawson, son of former chancellor of the exchequer Nigel Lawson, and adorned with a characteristically vivid
cartoon by Nicholas Garland showing a schoolboylike Mr. Ridley
daubing a poster of Chancellor Kohl with a Hitler mustache, this
"outbreak of the Euro-hooligan Ridley," as the normally restrained
Frankfurter Allgemeine Zeitung described it, caused a political storm
and the resignation of the trade and industry secretary.

The second part of this little shake was the publication in *The Independent on Sunday* and *Der Spiegel* of a leaked, highly confiden-
tial memorandum of a meeting between Mrs. Thatcher and a small
group of historians held at Chequers, the prime minister's country

residence, on 24 March to discuss Germany. The memorandum, which I had not seen until its publication, although I participated in the Chequers meeting, was written by Mrs. Thatcher's private secretary for foreign affairs, Charles Powell. "Ver-bloody-batim" was how one British minister reportedly described this singular document. But ver-bloody-batim is precisely what it was not. Rather it was a report, with no views attributed specifically to anyone but some by implication to all. And, like all good Whitehall rapporteurs, Mr. Powell managed to flavor this rich cream soup with a little of his own particular spice.

One sentence was particularly rich: "Some even less flattering attributes were also mentioned [at the meeting] as an abiding part of the German character: in alphabetical order, angst, aggressiveness, assertiveness, bullying, egotism, inferiority complex, sentimentality." Well, perhaps in the course of a long discussion those attributes were mentioned by some participants, along with many more positive ones. But plainly they were never listed like that by anyone; nor, indeed, was there anything like a collective view of "the German character"—if such a thing exists. Still, as one might expect, this was the sentence that made the headlines, whether in London, Paris, or Frankfurt.

What really happened was this. Mrs. Thatcher invited six independent experts on Germany to give their views at a private meeting in which the foreign secretary, Douglas Hurd, also participated. Besides two leading American historians of Germany, Fritz Stern of Columbia University and Gordon Craig of Stanford, there were four British historians and commentators: Lord Dacre (Hugh Trevor-Roper), Norman Stone, George Urban, and myself. This was no ideological cabal. The guests had different views on Germany and different views on Europe. Thus, for example, Norman Stone is a member of the Bruges Group, named after Mrs. Thatcher's Bruges speech, which opposes further steps of federal integration in the European Community, while I have repeatedly criticized Mrs. Thatcher for not going farther in that direction. Fritz Stern is not only an outstanding authority on German history but also an outspoken defender of the "*l* word" (liberalism). All spoke their own minds. Fritz Stern said nothing that he has not said already in his published work; I said nothing that I have not said in mine.

Yet the most remarkable feature of this quite diverse group was the degree of unanimity that emerged in answering the central questions of whether and how Germany has changed and what we might expect from the new, united Germany. As the main body of Mr. Powell's memorandum fairly indicated, the weight of the argument was overwhelmingly positive. We explained why 1945 was a great caesura in German history. We described how, self-consciously but increasingly self-confidently, the democratic West Germany differed from its predecessors; and how the unification of Germany in one democratic state, bordering on East Central European states that were also choosing their own governments, was a development heartily to be welcomed. And we argued that it should be, precisely, welcomed.

Of course, concerns were also expressed about this new Germany. Historians will always find continuities as well as discontinuities. But almost every doubt or question that was raised by the guests around the Chequers table could also have been heard in Bonn from distinguished German historians, commentators, and, indeed, leading politicians. For, as several participants pointed out, one of the signal strengths of West Germany has been its capacity for constant, relentless, sometimes almost masochistic self-examination and self-criticism, based soundly on a strong, free press and an exemplary historiography. Neither Japan nor Italy, nor indeed Austria, could match this. Thus, I think it is fair to say that if Chancellor Kohl himself had sat in on that meeting he would have agreed with, or, at the very least, accepted as fair comment, 90 percent of what was said around the Chequers table.

For a private, no-holds-barred brainstorming session, that is not a bad percentage. After all, everyone but everyone speaks slightly differently *about* his neighbors than he does *to* them. Auden says somewhere that if men knew what women said about them in private, the human race would cease to exist. The same might almost be said about the nations of Europe and the European Community. (Men as much as women, of course.) If we had a completely frank account of, say, President Mitterrand's discussions with some French intellectuals on this issue, would the score even be as high? Or, for that matter, in a comparably frank discussion between Chancellor Kohl and some German specialists about Britain?

The remaining 10 percent was as much a matter of style as of content, of tone rather than analysis. This was, of course, the problem a fortiori with Nicholas Ridley's remarks, as presented in *The Spectator*. As it happens, Mr. Ridley's analysis was wrong. (If there is a danger, it is not Germany's commitment to further West European integration but rather a weakening of that commitment as a result of the new possibilities opening to the east.) But, even if he were right, he would have been wrong for the way he said it. I have thought a good deal about this particular British tone and style in discussing Germany and Europe—a tone and style reflected outrageously in Mr. Ridley's remarks, somewhat also in *The Spectator*'s representation of them, but also, to a much more limited degree, and in a more defensible way, in the personal spice of Mr. Powell's memorandum.

I am told this is a matter of age and personal experience, and no doubt it is easier for someone of my generation, born after the war, to come to like and admire present-day Germany and to make friendships unburdened by the past. Yet the generation gap does not quite account for this peculiar British tone—a unique mixture of resentment and frivolity. It may, I think, be explained partly by geography and history. America is far enough away and still big and powerful enough to be relaxed about the reemergence of Germany as a great power in Central Europe. France is too close, too small, and relatively too weak to be anything but deadly serious about it. But Britain is somewhere in between: close enough to be worried and weak enough to be resentful ("Who won the war anyway?"), yet also far enough away, and still self-confident enough, to be outspoken and outrageous.

This slightly resentful insouciance is, like so many national weaknesses, the flip side of a strength. With a few notable exceptions, most German political speeches and commentaries are still so earnest, learned, scrupulous, and responsible that they are better than any sleeping pill. British political speeches and commentaries, by contrast, are still often amusing, original, and uninhibited—to a fault. But the fault in this case was a serious one.

It is not just that it is profoundly offensive to the leaders and people of a democratic Germany to paint Hitler on the wall (or on the remnants of the Wall). It is also consummately counterproductive. Such sauce does not make the meat of substantive criticism more interesting. It means that the whole dish is pushed away. It does not mean that Britain's voice is listened to more attentively in the councils of Europe. It means that it is listened to even less.

In a sense, the July crisis was just another chapter in a much longer story: the story of how numerous responsible British policy makers, including successive foreign secretaries, have worked extraordinarily hard to produce a positive yet still distinctive British contribution to the development of Europe, and how this work has again and again been frustrated. There are many reasons for this frustration—in the EC itself, in the legacy of past mistakes, in the Labour Party as well as in the Conservative Party—but some of the responsibility must plainly lie with Mrs. Thatcher. The buck stops there. A large part of this most persistent problem lies in that 10 percent region of tone and style: in the failure to find a distinctive language of British Europeanism—a language in which criticisms do not automatically become accusations and praise does not sound like blame.

The very fact that Mrs. Thatcher invited six independent experts for a day's seminar, and listened, shows a genuine wish to come to a serious, informed judgment on these extraordinary developments in the center of Europe and hence to find an appropriate response to them. There are those, including some in Bonn, who say that her interventions on these issues were more obviously measured, informed, and helpful in the second quarter of 1990 than perhaps they were in the first. Yet the effect of the leaked Powell memo, coming on top of the Ridley affair, was to set things back once again.

Chancellor Kohl took it all very sportingly, saying that Mr. Ridley was not the only person to have made tactless remarks, recalling his own gaffe a few years ago when he compared Gorbachev to Goebbels. In Britain, an investigation was ordered into the source of the leak. Few thought the culprit would ever be found. Questions were asked in the House of Commons. The prime minister defended Mr. Powell. The foreign secretary invited his counterpart, Hans-Dietrich Genscher, to the Glyndebourne Opera. Then the Germans went on uniting and the British went on holiday.

However, the "Chequers seminar" has entered the mythology of Anglo-German relations. For several years after 1990, I was tackled by people in Germany who started by telling me that of course they hadn't taken the incident at all seriously, and then talked about it very seriously for hours. In 1996, George Urban published a very extensive account of the meeting, drawn from his diaries. He records Mrs. Thatcher saying at the end of the meeting, "Very well, very well . . . I promise you that I shall be sweet to the Germans." Now I vividly remember her sitting up like a schoolgirl and saying, "All right, I shall be very nice to the Germans." I wonder how many of the other participants (including Douglas Hurd, well-known as a diarist) have recorded slightly differing versions of the same event.

CHRONOLOGY

1990

1 AUGUST.   Noncommunist philosopher Zhelyu Zhelev becomes president of Bulgaria.

2 AUGUST.   Iraq invades Kuwait.

3 AUGUST.   Árpád Göncz is elected president of Hungary.

17 AUGUST.   Beginning of a Serb insurrection in the Croatian province of Krajina.

23 AUGUST.   The East German "People's Chamber" votes for East Germany to join the Federal Republic under Article 23 of the West German constitution.

31 AUGUST.   Signature of the Unification Treaty between the Federal Republic and East Germany.

7 SEPTEMBER.   Ethnic Albanian delegates of the recently dissolved Kosovo assembly meet secretly in Kaçanik and adopt a constitution for their "independent republic."

11–12 SEPTEMBER.   The concluding "2 + 4" meeting and signature in Moscow of the "Final Treaty with Respect to Germany"—informally known as the "2 + 4 treaty."

17 SEPTEMBER.   Lech Wałęsa declares that he will stand for the presidency of Poland. The European Community agrees on arrangements for the former East Germany to join the EC.

1 OCTOBER.   Britain joins the Exchange Rate Mechanism of the European Monetary System at a central rate against the deutsche mark of DM 2.95 to £1.

3 OCTOBER.   East Germany joins the Federal Republic. The "Day of German Unity."

GERMANY UNBOUND

———

HE WISHED TO BE THE CHANCELLOR OF A LIBERATED, NOT A DE-
feated Germany, said Willy Brandt on the evening of his election victory in 1969. Yet only on 3 October 1990 did Germany liberate itself.
Not all alone, of course. Every German politician pays tribute to
Gorbachev, to the pioneers of emancipation in Eastern Europe, to
the Americans, French, and British, without whom, as authors say in
their acknowledgments, this book could never have been written.
But it was the Germans who wrote the book.

For all the discontinuities of West German policy since 1949, one
can but admire the grand continuity in which all chancellors from
Adenauer to Kohl, all foreign ministers, all federal governments over
forty years, now this way, now that, now in the West, now in the East,
pursued the cause of German liberation.

Historians will argue whether Adenauer's integration into the
West or Brandt's Ostpolitik contributed more to the success of the
past year. There is much to be said for the claim that the East Central European year of wonders, 1989, was a late triumph of Adenauer's "magnet theory"—the idea that the attraction of a free and
prosperous West Germany embedded in a free and prosperous Western Europe would sooner or later draw the unfree and impoverished
East Germany irresistibly toward it. But could the magnet have exerted its full attractive force if the blocking Iron Curtain had not first
been drawn back by the Ostpolitik, which Willy Brandt launched in
the late 1960s? And it was not Bonn's Western but rather its Eastern

ties—above all, those to Moscow—that directly permitted the transformation of an East German movement for freedom into an all-German state of unity.

Yet this East German rising for freedom was not contemplated in Bonn's policy toward East Germany. Those in the GDR who contributed most to Germany's peaceful October revolution—the tiny minority of human- and civil-rights campaigners—had benefited least from the Federal Republic's governmental policy toward the GDR. Bonn politicians now ritually celebrate the "peaceful revolution." Two years ago, most of those same politicians would have described it as "dangerous destabilization." Yes, it was a "dangerous destabilization" that made German unification possible. Without the brave minority that faced down armed police on the streets of Leipzig, Dresden, and Berlin, the ultimate goal of Bonn's policy would never have been achieved—Gorbachev or no Gorbachev. (The real greatness of this year's Nobel Peace Prize winner consists in the ability to accept often undesired and unintended faits accomplis—or what Mr. Gorbachev likes to call "life itself.")

The pioneers of social emancipation and democratization in the GDR were then overtaken rapidly by those who wanted to have done with the GDR altogether. By this time, the two parallel sets of negotiations for unification—the "internal" ones, between the two German states ("1+1"), and the "external" ones, between the two German states and the four post-1945 occupying powers ("2+4")—were already under way.

Chancellor Kohl, after giving initial consideration to alternative models, such as that of a "treaty community" or confederation, had decided by the end of January to go full steam ahead for one federal republic. The votes of the East German population gave him the domestic political strength to do this. It was his political decision, against the advice of most experts, to introduce monetary union on 1 July and to do so with a large degree of one-to-one parity (deutsche mark to GDR mark). This had a traumatic impact on the East German economy—according to West German statistics, industrial output in August 1990 was down 51 percent from that of August 1989—which in turn imparted a desperate urgency to the last months of negotiation.

To describe these seven hectic months of intricate negotiation would require not an essay but a compendium. The 31 August treaty on unification between the two German states is a book in itself— 243 pages of small print in the official government bulletin. Formally, they were "1+1" and "2+4" negotiations. In practice, they were "1+¼" and "1+1+1" negotiations. The first and last freely elected East Berlin government was not an equal partner in the German-German talks. The Bonn government basically set the terms of the internal unification, its officials drafting treaties that bore a remarkable resemblance to the finished product. Many East German politicians and intellectuals in both halves of Germany were understandably miffed by this procedure. "*Anschluss,*" said some. Yet was it not for this that the majority of the people had voted in March? And, despite widespread economic distress, the majority expressed its basic satisfaction with the result, on 14 October, in the first elections for the five reconstituted *Länder* of the former GDR. Chancellor Kohl's CDU was the overall winner everywhere except in Brandenburg (where the Social Democrats' leader is a prominent Protestant churchman) and secured more than 45 percent of the vote in Saxony and Thuringia.

The external negotiation was basically between the Federal Republic, the Soviet Union, and the United States, in that order. The Bonn government makes no secret of the fact that it was the United States, rather than France or Britain, that was its crucial Western supporter in the whole process. Washington was not just self-evidently more important in talks with Moscow but also more unreservedly supportive than London or Paris—a fact that has done some damage to the Franco-German "axis." Yet the central negotiation was that between Bonn and Moscow. In Moscow in February, Chancellor Kohl secured Gorbachev's assent to unification in one state. In Stavropol in July, he secured Gorbachev's assent to the full sovereignty of the united state, including its membership in NATO—although a NATO redefined by the "London Declaration" a few days before. Soviet troops would leave Germany by 1994.

In return, the united Germany would have no atomic, biological, or chemical ("ABC") weapons and no more than 370,000 men and women under arms; it would make a hefty financial contribution to the repatriation costs of Soviet troops; and it would become, even more than it was already, Gorbachev's leading partner in his desperate attempt to modernize the Soviet Union and bring it "to Europe." That was the essential German-Soviet deal, which opened the door to unification on Adenauer's terms. To celebrate this remarkable deal, Kohl and Gorbachev appeared in V-necked cardigans and open shirts. Surrounded by men in suits, they peered into a Caucasian river and mused upon the meaning of life itself.

In Europe these days, "sovereignty" is a controversial word—and not just for Mrs. Thatcher or Jacques Delors. When German conservatives celebrate Germany's recapture of full sovereignty, German liberals (and liberal conservatives) hasten to say, "But of course this is no longer sovereignty in the classical sense," and "After all, we share sovereignty in the European Community." So let us put it more precisely. Until 3 October 1990, the Federal Republic had somewhat less freedom of action than the United Kingdom or the French Republic, both de jure and de facto. After 3 October 1990, it has almost precisely as much de jure, and de facto slightly more. Britain and France have no comparable international treaty restrictions on their armed forces. But their relative economic weaknesses and their geographical positions give them less room for maneuver than Germany, which is once again the great power in the center of Europe.

The liberation from the bonds of the Western Allies' residual rights over Berlin and "Germany as a whole" is but a marginal advantage by comparison with the liberation from the half-nelson grip of Soviet control over East Germany. At a meeting in Moscow just a few days after unification, I heard a very senior German official say simply, "Now we are no longer open to blackmail." "Are the Russians our brothers or our friends?" asked an old East German joke. Answer: "Our brothers—you can choose your friends." By 1994, at the latest, the brothers will be gone—and Germany can choose her friends.

3 October will now officially replace 17 June, the anniversary of the East German rising of 1953, as "the day of German unity." A better description might be "the day of German liberty." Externally, the new German state is free—and can use its freedom of action for

good or ill. Internally, more than sixteen million men and women are free who until a year ago were not. Of course, they have hard times ahead. Of course, their new freedom is relative. But one of the messages of the East Central European 1989 is precisely to warn against the confused and exaggerated relativization of values in which all too many German intellectuals indulged so wordily throughout the 1980s.

A few weeks before the great day, we had to stay with us in Oxford a young man, Joachim. As the son of a very remarkable Protestant priest in East Berlin, he had been prevented from completing an ordinary secondary schooling. When I visited him in the early summer of 1989, at the rectory behind the Wall, he described to me how small demonstrations to protest against the falsification of the local-election results in May, as well as the East German leadership's endorsement of the repression on Tiananmen Square in early June, had been brutally dispersed. Here, in this very garden, the marchers had assembled. There, on that street, they had been "pulled away," the police dragging them along the cobblestones by their long hair. He was pale, nervous, angry.

In the early autumn of 1989 he wrote to me from West Berlin. He had fled across the frontier from Hungary to Austria. (On the first attempt, the Hungarian border guards had caught him and turned him back.) Life in the West seemed to him in some ways poorer than in the East, he wrote—"inwardly poorer." But he was still glad to be here—"and I hope to remain so." Yet the separation from his family, just a few miles away in East Berlin, was very bitter. His little brother and sister had insisted that their mother take them to a point near the Wall where, clambering on some stones, they could at least see their big brother, a distant figure waving from a platform on the other side.

Now, in the early autumn of 1990, he was a different man: bronzed, confident, relaxed. He had just been to America for the first time. "That's great!" he kept exclaiming colloquially. He was just off to Dublin to improve his English. But he would probably go back to join his family in Berlin for Christmas. Suddenly he was the citizen of a free, prosperous, and—dare one say?—normal country. The word *liberation* has long been tainted in Central Europe, and most especially since the Soviet "liberation" of 1945. But there comes a time when even the most polluted words must be reclaimed. This, in a single life, was liberation.

So when, around half past two on the morning of 3 October, as we wandered through the streets of Frankfurt, none of our party being perhaps entirely sober, Adam Michnik turned to me and said, "Now tell me, Tim, what do you really feel about German unification?" my immediate response was, "You know, I really *am* pleased." And when, seven hours later and not perhaps entirely rested, I set out from the Hotel Unter den Linden in the former East Berlin to walk westward through the Brandenburg Gate (look for the new asphalt, it's all that's left of the Wall) and across a corner of the Tiergarten to the official ceremony for German unity in the Berlin Philharmonic concert hall, my step was light.

At first glance, I thought the governing mayor had acquired a wig. But when he began to speak, I, together with the rest of the gala audience in the Philharmonic, soon realized that this was an uninvited guest. He had walked through all the security controls and right up to the microphone. Before him, in the first row, sat President Richard von Weizsäcker, Chancellor Helmut Kohl, Foreign Minister Hans-Dietrich Genscher, and grand old Willy Brandt, and behind them the country's most important political leaders. If the uninvited guest had been a terrorist with a gun, he could have decapitated the German body politic on the day of unification.

Fortunately, he was just a nutcase with a cardboard folder, containing a long speech. "Allow me fifteen minutes," he said, and began a complicated tale of some outstanding grievance against the justice ministry. After several seconds of silent bewilderment, the audience began loudly to applaud him, hoping to clap him away. He would not stop. The master of ceremonies, in white tie and tails, politely asked him to leave the stage. On he went, describing in detail the excellent wine he had drunk in the course of his extensive litigation. The interior minister, Wolfgang Schäuble, could be seen rising from his seat. After whispered consultations and a good minute more of barmy speech plus ironic applause, two plainclothes policemen very gently led this Herr Walter Mitty away. (According to subsequent press reports, they simply took him out to the entrance and released him into the holiday crowds.) Then, at last, we looked down on the familiar bald pate of the governing mayor of Berlin, the next speaker on the official program.

Far more than any of the official speeches, the proclamation of peace and goodwill to all men, the painfully responsible press commentaries, more even than the grave and beautiful cadences of Richard von Weizsäcker, this little incident exemplified everything that was good about the forty-one-year-old Federal Republic of Germany: civil, civilian, civilized. The small deed matched the big words—and the music, which was splendid.

With hindsight, since Wolfgang Schäuble was actually shot and badly wounded by another disturbed man at a rally less than a fortnight later, the episode looks less amusing. And of course, the German police are not always so civil. That same afternoon, there was what seemed a quite excessive police turnout in the center of Berlin to control a demonstration against unification by squatters, anarchists, and the far left. Riot-squad vans roared through the former Checkpoint Charlie (now a flea market) into the former East Berlin, and police helicopters clattered overhead, as if to say, "We are the masters now." Yet the way in which Herr Mitty was treated was nonetheless representative of celebrations that were peaceful and merry without being triumphalist.

In fact, it all seemed almost too good to be true. Like the East Central European revolutions of 1989, the German wonder of 1990 was so swift, peaceful, and civil that it is still hard to believe it has really happened. If the first unification of Germany was made with blood and iron, the second took only words and money. Among the countless intellectuals asked by newspapers for their response to unification, the (once East) German writer Reiner Kunze stood out. "I expect of Germany," he replied, "that after 3 October 1990 it will prepare itself for this day."

There is still a vast gulf between the new *pays légal* and the *pays réel*, between the legal fact of unity and the social fact of continued division. On the backstreets, in the factories, and in many, many heads, the GDR still exists. Something like one out of every ten from the former GDR workforce is unemployed. Pensioners have been terribly hard hit by the upward leap in prices. Tenants fear for their security—not to mention their low rents—as old private landlords return or new ones arrive. And the psychological adaptation after forty years of socialism is perhaps even more difficult than the material ups and downs.

How long will it take before Germany is prepared for 3 October 1990? One reads widely varying estimates of the number of years it will take before the five *Länder* of the former GDR are pulled up to a level comparable with that of even the poorest *Land* of the old Federal Republic. Undeterred by their failure to reveal the full disastrous state of the East German economy in the past, the economists and research institutes are making confident predictions about its future. As diverse are the estimates of the financial cost of reconstructing East German industry. The round figure of a trillion deutsche marks over ten years is tossed about. Chancellor Kohl has bravely promised an official guess at the costs, even before the federal election on 2 December. The finance minister, Theo Waigel, does not quite say, "Read my lips," but reckons the government should be able to get by without major tax increases. In the former GDR, as elsewhere in the former Eastern Europe, the costs and problems of economic transformation are far bigger and more fundamental than in Western Europe after 1945. But if anyone in Europe can master the task of postcommunist economic reconstruction, it is the Germans.

The real question is less the economic cost than the political implications of the economic cost. These will be seen first on the streets rather than in parliament. The enthusiasm with which ordinary West Germans greeted their liberated compatriots a year ago has largely evaporated, as the newcomers take scarce housing and jobs from poorer West Germans and jam the checkout lines at the cheaper supermarkets. But the swelling resentment against the so-called *Ossis* is sweetness and light compared with street attitudes toward Poles, Romanians, and Turks. In a West Berlin supermarket, a sign says, "Polish citizens may only purchase one carton."

At present, the new Germany is home to some five million foreigners, out of a total population of seventy-eight million. With the social tensions that will arise from the reconstruction of the East, the tolerance even of those foreigners who have lived in Germany for a long time is likely to diminish. Already one hears of second-generation Turkish-German citizens losing their jobs to East Germans. It is here, on the streets, that the political culture of the Federal Republic will be put to the test.

At the same time, with the combination of political liberation and economic disintegration in the former Eastern Europe and Soviet Disunion, the press of would-be immigrants or *Gastarbeiter* ("guest workers") will increase, adding to the existing pressure from across the Mediterranean. A new specter is haunting Western Europe: the specter of a huge postcommunist movement of peoples, something like the great *Völkerwanderung* of the early Middle Ages. This is a formidable challenge for the whole European Community but for Germany above all.

How will it cope? By building a new wall along Germany's new eastern frontier, the Oder-Neisse line? Or by opening to the East while supporting, with more billions of deutsche marks, the transformation to a market economy from Poznań to Vladivostok, thus encouraging people to stop wandering westward? The answer given by Germany's political leaders is, not surprisingly, a qualified version of the latter possibility rather than the former. "We lift our voice for a constructive and common Ostpolitik," said President Weizsäcker in his 3 October speech. "All the frontiers of Germany should become bridges to our neighbors." But, even as he spoke on the day of unity, a visa requirement was introduced for all Poles, many of whom had previously been able to travel without visas to East Germany and West Berlin. So, if the German-Polish frontier is a bridge, it is a half-closed one. Reality did not quite match up to rhetoric. However, the Bonn government has now declared its readiness in principle to lift the visa requirement for Poles as it has already done for Hungarians, Czechs, and Slovaks.

Altogether, the problem with the foreign policy of the new Germany would seem to be not that it has any bad intentions but that it has too many good ones. Hans-Dietrich Genscher says, "We Germans want nothing else than to live in freedom, democracy, and peace with all the peoples of Europe and the world." A modest aspiration: Germany as Europe's "honest broker." But, as Richard von Weizsäcker's unification speech reached its climax with an appeal to Germans to set about "preserving the creation" (i.e., the natural world), I could not help recalling the description of Germany's possible role that Bismarck rejected in his "honest broker" speech. Germany, said the chancellor of the first unification, should not aspire to be the schoolmaster of Europe.

The schoolmaster of Europe—that seems to me perhaps the best phrase to summarize the aspirations of Germany's present political leadership. The schoolmaster has passed his own exams over the last year with flying colors. There is a great deal of sense in what he has to say. But one does wonder how much of the schoolbook can ever be translated into practice, even by the Germans themselves—let alone by more recalcitrant pupils (J. Delors, smirking in the front row; F. Mitterrand, looking grandly out the window; M. Thatcher, giving her own lesson in the corridor). Are they not perhaps aiming a little too high? As Robert Browning has it in "A Grammarian's Funeral":

> That low man goes on adding one to one,
>   His hundred's soon hit:
> This high man, aiming at a million,
>   Misses an unit.

In the immediate future, German foreign policy will face some hard choices. American readers may think first of the decision about how far and in what form Germany should take greater responsibility outside Europe. Within Europe, I see two major choices, which in a deeper sense are one. The first concerns the former Eastern Europe and the Soviet Union, the second the (West) European Community.

Since 1955, when Adenauer opened diplomatic relations with the Soviet Union (but with no other Soviet-bloc state), then very clearly since the Moscow Treaty of 1970, the relationship with the Soviet Union has taken top priority in Bonn's Ostpolitik. On a sober analysis of national interests, this has been wholly understandable. As many observed, "The key to German unity lay in Moscow"—from 8 May 1945, one might say, until 3 October 1990. Plainly, this priority remained throughout the negotiations on German unity. Chancellor Kohl emphasized that he would have liked to have signed a comprehensive friendship treaty with Poland at the same time as he signed the treaty with the Soviet Union. As it turned out, in 1990 as in 1970, the Moscow treaty preceded the Warsaw one, which is still to be negotiated. And what a treaty this Moscow one is!

Francis Fukuyama has proclaimed the end of history, but the German-Soviet friendship treaty, initiated in Moscow on 13 September, goes one step further. "The Federal Republic of Germany and the Union of Soviet Socialist Republics," says its preamble, "wishing finally to put an end to the past." To put an end to the past! "Determined to follow on from the good traditions of their [i.e., Germany and the Soviet Union's] centuries-old history," the two sides produce another catalogue of good intentions, mainly gluing together prefabricated phrases from German-Soviet documents of the last twenty years but also declaring that "they will never and under no circumstances be the first to use armed force against each other or against other states. They call upon all other states to join in this commitment to nonaggression." If we take this literally, it means that Germany is joining the Soviet Union in calling upon, say, the United States not to use armed force against, say, Iraq.

"But," your German colleague will respond privately, "you mustn't take it literally!" Then why write it if you don't mean it? Well, to get Russian agreement to unification, of course! Fair enough: Machiavelli dressed as Luther. The question then becomes, Is this really the last page of an old chapter—the forty-five-year-long story of German liberation—or the first page of a new one? (GERMANY AND THE SOVIET UNION AT A NEW BEGINNING, a headline in the *Frankfurter Allgemeine Zeitung* memorably announced at the time of the Stavropol agreement in July.) Time will tell—meaning the Germans will decide. Or perhaps will not decide. For my impression is that German policy makers do not at the moment have a private set of priorities in foreign policy that is much clearer than the public rhetoric.

The consciousness of promises made, gratitude, habit, the faint hope of a great market to open, above all a deep fear of disorder and chaos—the dreaded "instability"—all these will incline Bonn to make quite substantial efforts to help the Soviet leadership (and the *Soviet* leadership rather than, say, the Russian, Ukrainian, or Baltic leaderships) to proceed along the path of economic transformation. Yet the Soviet Union is collapsing at such a rate that these efforts are probably doomed to failure, at least in this well-ordered form (Germany–Soviet Union). Moreover, so long as the Soviet-American relationship remains highly cooperative, German-Soviet cooperation need not adversely affect German-American relations. In the short term, then, the "Big Three" of post–cold war Europe—America, Germany, and Russia—can probably remain more or less in sync.

The immediate problem lies closer to home. At the same time as they promise extensive help to the Soviet Union—to be set out in a second comprehensive treaty on economic, scientific, and technological cooperation—German policy makers say they want especially to help their neighbors in "Central, Eastern, and Southeastern" Europe. But, as the Germans have themselves discovered in the GDR, the problems and costs of the transition from a planned to a market economy are vast. If this is true of the small and relatively prosperous GDR, how much more is it true of Czechoslovakia, Hungary, and Poland, let alone of Romania and Bulgaria—not to mention the East European republics of the Soviet Union? If German, European, and Western help is spread more or less indiscriminately across this whole vast region, then the three mutually dependent transitions—to market economy, to parliamentary democracy, and to the rule of law—will not succeed even in the nearest east of Europe, in East Central Europe. And then that region could indeed become Europe's Near East: not the Central Europe of the intellectual antipoliticians' dreams, but the *Zwischeneuropa* of a nightmare—an area of weak, undemocratic states, riven by social and national conflicts. This would obviously be bad for all of Europe, but it would be especially bad for Germany, since the resulting chaos would be just thirty miles east of the capital, Berlin. The pressure of immigrants would grow, not decline, and they would be knocking first at Germany's doors.

"The western frontier of the Soviet Union must not become the eastern frontier of Europe," says President Weizsäcker. A noble sentiment but open to question in two respects. First, the Soviet Union is ceasing to exist, and Lithuanians, Estonians, Latvians, and Ukrainians no longer wish to recognize "the western frontier of the

Soviet Union" as "the eastern frontier of Europe." (The Ukrainian republic recently signed a separate treaty with Poland, including mutual recognition of frontiers.) Second, if we understand by "Europe" a community of more or less liberal democratic states with social-market economies, then the real question for the next five to ten years is not "Will Europe end on the present western frontier of the Soviet Union?" but rather "Will Europe reach even that far?" Unless a clear and very high priority is given by Germany and the whole European Community to East Central Europe, where the transition still has a sporting chance, Europe—in the constitutional and economic sense—will not end on the river Bug. It will end on the Oder and Neisse.

This relates intimately to the second hard choice that faces German policy: that about the (West) European Community. As national unification reached its climax, so German policy makers and commentators redoubled their insistence that the EC must move forward in both domestic and external policy. Where Bismarck said, "Let us put Germany in the saddle," the Nestor of German liberal journalism, Theo Sommer, says, "Now we must put Europe in the saddle." Poor girl: up into the saddle, whether she wants it or not! And, of course, she herself is, as always, of several minds. A significant part of Germany's present political elite still has a genuine commitment to moving forward to closer integration at the EC intergovernmental conferences on political and on economic and monetary union (although there are also substantial reservations, for example on the part of the Bundesbank, which fears a softening of the deutsche mark). This commitment is shared, in different ways and varying degrees, by significant parts of the political elite in most of the other Continental members of the EC. But there is one quite fundamental and immediate problem.

Germany's present political leadership says it wants to deepen the community but also in the foreseeable future to widen it to include East Central Europe and some countries from the European Free Trade Association (EFTA). But many people at the highest levels of the EC consider deepening and widening to be not complementary but contradictory goals. Jacques Delors argues that if you are to deepen, for example by adopting a common currency and a central bank, then you cannot afford to widen. Mrs. Thatcher advocates a rapid widening, partly out of genuine concern for the fledgling democracies of East Central Europe but also to foil Brother Jacques's designs of rapid deepening.

One can quite plausibly argue that the EC is on the horns of a dilemma. If it moves forward soon in the general direction of a United States of Europe, then East Central Europe will join it only late or never. If East Central Europe joins soon, then the EC will move forward in the direction of a USE only late or never. In the former case, the position of the former Eastern Europe will differ from that of the former Soviet Union in degree but not in kind. "Europe" will, in some very significant senses, end on the Oder-Neisse line. In the latter case, however, in a looser *"Europe des Patries,"* Germany would willy-nilly come back somewhat more to the old post-Bismarckian dilemmas of the nation-state in the middle. So German policy makers quite rightly see that they must try to both deepen and widen the community. But how?

There are a few people in Germany seriously seeking answers. (Perhaps it is always only a few.) Whether they find any, and, if so, what those answers will be, we will probably begin to learn only after the federal election on 2 December. The starting point must surely be, as it was for Adenauer and Brandt, the definition of national interests. For the last forty years (some would say for the last two hundred), the question of German national *identity* has provoked some of the longest, deepest, most contorted answers ever given to any question by any branch of humankind. The question of national *interest,* however, has been much easier to answer. For the last forty years, the answer was, in a nutshell, "recovery of sovereignty and overcoming the division of Germany."

Now, in one united, western Germany, the question of national identity should be easier to answer—although to judge by the hypochondriac effusions in recent weeks of many German writers lamenting unification (such as Günter Grass) or discovering a late love for the cozy old Federal Republic (such as Patrick Süskind), there is no guarantee that their answers will actually become any simpler. The question of national interest, by contrast, necessarily becomes more complicated. On my analysis, besides the consolidation of the constitution of liberty and an open society inside Germany, the first strategic answer would be: "to combine in one design the enterprise of sustaining the democratic transition in East Central Europe and that of further, primarily political, integration of the EC."

If, however, such a design is not spelled out clearly, if the hard choices are ducked, then national (and therefore European) interests will be defined on the hoof—dictated by dramatic external developments, such as the further collapse of the Soviet Union, or by domestic pressures, such as swelling resentment against immigrants, or by a combination of both.

The second part of my answer to Adam Michnik, on the streets of Frankfurt, at two-thirty on the morning of German unification, was: "If I have a fear for the next few years, it is not that Germany will turn outward in any sort of bid for domination as an economic great power. It's rather that it will turn inward, become obsessed with the problems flowing from unification, a little self-pitying, self-protective. And build a new wall on its eastern frontier, which its other West European partners will only help to reinforce."

In short, the German eagle is unbound. The broken chains lie on the hillside. He has raised his wings a little and given a few friendly cries. Will he now spread his wings and rise up, this time to help, not to attack? Or will he rather, like the eagle donated to Washington Zoo by Chancellor Helmut Schmidt, sit sulkily on his perch, gobbling his ample food and disconsolately scratching his breast feathers with that great beak?

CHRONOLOGY

1990

12 OCTOBER. *Signature of a German-Soviet treaty on the arrangements for remaining Soviet troops in Germany and their planned withdrawal by December 1994.*

15 OCTOBER. *Mikhail Gorbachev is awarded the Nobel Peace Prize.*

25 OCTOBER. *The Slovak parliament votes to make Slovak the official language of Slovakia.*

28 OCTOBER. *At the Rome summit of the EC, eleven leaders agree to proceed to a "second stage" of monetary union on 1 January 1994 and to achieve full monetary union by 2000. British prime minister Margaret Thatcher refuses to join them, denouncing this as the "back door to a federal Europe."*

1 NOVEMBER. *British deputy prime minister Geoffrey Howe resigns in protest at Mrs. Thatcher's attitude to Europe.*

6 NOVEMBER. *Hungary joins the Council of Europe—the first postcommunist country to do so.*

7 NOVEMBER. *Mary Robinson is elected president of the Republic of Ireland.*

9 NOVEMBER. *Chancellor Kohl and President Gorbachev sign a German-Soviet friendship treaty on the first anniversary of the opening of the Berlin Wall.*

14 NOVEMBER. *Signature of a German-Polish frontier treaty.*

19–21 NOVEMBER. *Paris summit of the Conference on Security and Cooperation in Europe. Launch of the Paris Charter for a New Europe. Member states of Warsaw Pact and NATO sign the Treaty on Conventional Armed Forces in Europe.*

28 NOVEMBER. *Margaret Thatcher resigns as prime minister of Britain and leader of the Conservative Party. She is succeeded by John Major.*

2 DECEMBER. *The first all-German elections to the Bundestag result in a clear victory for the existing center-right coalition government led by Helmut Kohl.*

9 DECEMBER. *Lech Wałęsa is elected president of Poland, promising an "acceleration" of decommunization. Slobodan Milošević is elected president of Serbia on a nationalist platform.*

14–15 DECEMBER. *The European Council in Rome launches twin intergovernmental conferences on economic and monetary union and on political union.*

20 DECEMBER. *Soviet foreign minister Eduard Shevardnadze resigns, warning of the risk of a renewed dictatorship in the Soviet Union.*

22 DECEMBER. *In its "Christmas constitution," the Croatian parliament proclaims Croatia "the national state of the Croatian people."*

1991

4 JANUARY. *Liberal Jan Krzysztof Bielecki becomes prime minister of Poland.*

11–12 JANUARY. Paris. At a grand dinner in the Hôtel de Ville, Henry Kissinger twits Jacques Chirac, the Gaullist mayor of Paris, about his earlier admiration for the Iraqi leader Saddam Hussein. Chirac replies, "Oh, he's changed you know." Politician's wisdom.

13 JANUARY. *"Bloody Sunday" in Vilnius. Some fifteen Lithuanians are killed following action by Soviet forces.*

17 JANUARY–8 FEBRUARY. *Gulf War to liberate Kuwait from Iraq under Saddam Hussein.*

JANUARY–FEBRUARY. *A wave of emigration by Albanian "boat people" attempting to enter Italy.*

27 JANUARY. *Former communist leader Kiro Gligorov becomes president of the Yugoslav republic of Macedonia.*

6 FEBRUARY. Stockholm. A memorable conversation with Carl Bildt, leader of the Swedish conservatives. The social-democratic "Swedish model" or "third way" has failed, he says. For too long, Sweden has stood apart, considering itself somehow closer to Africa than to Germany. And he talks, almost like a Polish or Czech politician, about the need for his country to "return to Europe."

9 FEBRUARY. *Overwhelming vote for independence in a Lithuanian referendum.*

15 FEBRUARY. *The "Visegrád Declaration" constitutes the so-called Visegrád group for Central European cooperation, comprising Hungary, Czechoslovakia, and Poland.*

23–25 FEBRUARY. *A congress of the Solidarity movement in Poland elects Marian Krzaklewski to succeed Lech Wałęsa as its leader.*

25 FEBRUARY. *The Warsaw Pact agrees to dissolve its military structures by 1 April. The trial of former Bulgarian communist leader Todor Zhivkov begins.*

3 MARCH. *Referendums produce clear majorities for independence in Estonia and Latvia.*

4 MARCH. *The Supreme Soviet ratifies the "2+4 treaty" together with the accompanying German-Soviet treaties.*

11 MARCH. *John Major declares that Britain is "at the very heart of Europe." In Greece, former prime minister Andreas Papandreou goes on trial, charged with bribery and embezzlement.*

11 AND 14 MARCH. *Rallies for Slovak independence in Bratislava.*

14–16 MARCH. Dresden. For forty years, the British-German Königswinter Conference has met either in Königswinter on the Rhine or in Cambridge. Now, for the first time, it breaks this tradition to meet in Dresden, the beautiful city—"Florence on the Elbe"—destroyed by British and American bombs in February 1945. This is a moving event in many ways, but it is striking that, in the first Königswinter meeting after the liberation and unification of Germany, we come to the place in Germany where Britain has most to apologize for. It's almost as if, after forty years of apologizing for Hitler, the Germans are saying, "Now it's your turn." The balance of apologies shifts with the balance of power?

LATE MARCH. *First outbreaks of interethnic fighting between Serbs and Croats, in Serb-populated Krajina and eastern Slavonia regions of Croatia.*

MARCH–APRIL. *The Civic Forum in the Czech lands splits into three successor parties.*

1 APRIL. *Formal dissolution of the military structures of the Warsaw Pact.*

16 MAY. *Serbs in the Croatian province of Krajina call for the union of their territory with Serbia.*

19 MAY. *Croatians vote for independence in a referendum boycotted by Serbs living in Croatia.*

29 MAY. *Basque terrorists (ETA) bomb a Civil Guard barracks, killing nine people.*

12 JUNE. *Boris Yeltsin is elected president of the Russian Federation.*

12–14 JUNE. *In Prague, François Mitterrand attempts to launch his European Confederation.*

12–14 JUNE. Prague. I am among those invited to found the European Confederation. Even before we arrive, it is clear that this is essentially a French scheme for a grand, velvet-wallpapered waiting room in which the former communist countries can wait a long, long time before joining the EC. The EC, meanwhile, would remain a right, tight little West European affair with—and here's the real point—France at its political center, as it had been throughout the history of the European Community in the cold war. At the political center of an enlarged EC, by contrast, would be Germany.

Fortunately, in the first day of discussions, it soon emerges that many other delegates see and object to this, too. Although Václav Havel had agreed to host the meeting, the Czechs also understand that it is not really in their interest to make it work. Soon, the French participants are fighting a magnificent rearguard action, with all the formidable intellectual brilliance and diplomatic trickiness at their command. The French justice minister, Robert Badinter, who serves as President Mitterrand's field commander, pleads eloquently for a *"structure très légère, très légère."* The Germans, Britons, Dutch, and others present are not having even that.

In the concluding session, Mitterrand gives one of the finer rhetorical performances that I have witnessed, disguising what is, in fact, a quadruple backward somersault as a great, balletic leap forward. But the European Confederation will remain a joke.

17 JUNE. *Signature of a German-Polish treaty on good neighborliness and friendly cooperation.*

20 JUNE. *The Bundestag votes to move the federal capital from Bonn to Berlin.*

25 JUNE. *Croatia and Slovenia declare their independences.*

25 JUNE. A newspaper photograph shows men having their beards shaved off in Prague. They began to grow these beards on 21 August 1968, when Soviet troops invaded, and swore they would shave them off only when the last Soviet soldier had left their land. Now he has.

27 JUNE. *Additional units of the Serb-dominated Yugoslav federal army enter Slovenia but subsequently withdraw after Slovene armed resistance and Western diplomatic protests. The "ten-day war."*

27 JUNE–1 JULY. *EC dispatches the current "troika" of foreign ministers—Jacques Poos of Luxembourg, Gianni de Michaelis of Italy, and Hans van den Broek of the Netherlands—to bring peace to Yugoslavia. Poos declares, "The hour of Europe has dawned."*

28 JUNE. *Comecon, the economic organization of the former Soviet bloc, is formally dissolved.*

1 JULY. *The Warsaw Pact is formally dissolved.*

26 JULY. *The Central Committee of the Communist Party of the Soviet Union approves Gorbachev's party program leading to a free market and multiparty democracy.*

30 JULY. *Russian president Boris Yeltsin signs a treaty recognizing Lithuania's independence.*

JULY–AUGUST. *Fighting between the Serb-dominated Yugoslav federal army and Croatian troops in eastern Slavonia.*

29 JULY–1 AUGUST. *A Bush-Gorbachev summit in Moscow. Signature of the Strategic Arms Reduction Treaty (START).*

19–21 AUGUST. *A coup is attempted against Mikhail Gorbachev, intended to reverse changes in the Soviet Union. Yeltsin leads resistance in Moscow.*

23 AUGUST. *The Communist Party is suspended in Russia.*

27 AUGUST. *EC countries agree to establish diplomatic relations with the Baltic states.*

29 AUGUST. *Soviet legislators vote to suspend all activities of the Communist Party of the Soviet Union. Formation of the "Weimar Triangle" of foreign-policy cooperation between France, Germany, and Poland.*

7 SEPTEMBER. *An EC peace conference on Yugoslavia opens in The Hague under the chairmanship of Lord Carrington.*

17 SEPTEMBER. *Estonia, Latvia, and Lithuania are admitted to the UN.*

26–28 SEPTEMBER. Kraków, Poland. At a conference to mark the end of the Fondation pour une Entraide Intellectuelle Européenne, a foundation dedicated to helping opposition intellectuals in Eastern Europe during the cold war, Adam Michnik warns in dramatic terms of the danger of a new clerical, nationalist authoritarianism in Poland. I think he overdramatizes the danger, partly in a quest for the kind of clear, Manichaean dichotomy between good and evil in which dissidents lived under communism. We argue all the way to passport control at Warsaw Airport.

26–30 SEPTEMBER. *Kosovar Albanians hold an unofficial referendum on independence.*

3 OCTOBER. *Carl Bildt heads a new center-right coalition government in Sweden.*

4 OCTOBER. *The Czechoslovak federal parliament passes a "lustration" law, providing for the vetting and banning from public service of people who collaborated with the communist secret police or held certain positions in the communist state.*

8 OCTOBER. *The Soviet Union agrees to withdraw its troops from Poland by November 1992.*

13 OCTOBER. *The opposition Union of Democratic Forces wins Bulgarian parliamentary elections.*

15 OCTOBER. *Bosniak (or "Muslim") and Bosnian Croat members of the parliament of Bosnia-Herzegovina vote for independence. Bosnian Serbs leave in protest.*

27 OCTOBER. *The first free parliamentary elections in Poland produce a fragmented parliament.*

OCTOBER–NOVEMBER. *The Serb-dominated Yugoslav federal army destroys the Croatian city of Vukovar and attacks Dubrovnik.*

14 NOVEMBER. *The German Bundestag passes a law giving people access to their Stasi files from January 1992.*

21 NOVEMBER. *Following a referendum, the Macedonian parliament proclaims the sovereign, independent Republic of Macedonia. The head of state is the former communist leader Kiro Gligorov.*

1 DECEMBER. *In a referendum in Ukraine, a clear majority votes for independence. Former communist Leonid Kravchuk is elected president.*

8 DECEMBER. *Leaders of Russia, Ukraine, and Belarus agree to establish the Commonwealth of Independent States (CIS).*

9–11 DECEMBER. *The EC's Maastricht summit agrees terms of the Treaty on European Union. Monetary union is to happen by 1 January 1999 at the latest, providing that "Maastricht criteria" are met. EC and other "pillars" of institutionalized cooperation between its member states will be combined in a "European Union."*

14–16 DECEMBER. Oxford. At the suggestion of the Czech prime minister Petr Pithart, a conference brings together, in Magdalen College, a

Czech delegation led by him and a Slovak delegation led by their prime minister Ján Čarnogursky. Pithart, who spent some time in Oxford after the Soviet invasion in 1968, touchingly hopes that they will all see reason in these civilized, dignified, and neutral surroundings. Czechoslovakia will be saved in Oxford.

At the meeting, the Czechs talk grandly about the "civic principle." The Slovaks talk bitterly about the way they have been exploited in the shared state. A Slovak literary historian reels off fantastical statistics about Czech economic discrimination against Slovakia. Then they all slip away together to do their Christmas shopping at Marks and Spencer department store.

15 DECEMBER. *The UN Security Council resolves to send peacekeeping forces to former Yugoslavia. These will become known as the United Nations Protection Force: UNPROFOR.*

16 DECEMBER. *The signature of so-called Europe Agreements between the EC and Poland, Hungary, and Czechoslovakia. Under pressure from Germany, EC foreign ministers agree to diplomatic recognition of former Yugoslav republics on 15 January, if certain conditions are met.*

19 DECEMBER. *The Bonn government announces that it is going ahead with the recognition of Slovenia and Croatia before Christmas, as it had previously, unilaterally promised. Serbs in Croatia proclaim the "Serb Republic of Krajina," with its capital in Knin.*

21 DECEMBER. *At Alma Ata, eleven republics of the former Soviet Union sign agreements creating the Commonwealth of Independent States.*

23 DECEMBER. *The conservative anticommunist Jan Olszewski forms a government in Poland.*

25 DECEMBER. *Gorbachev resigns as Soviet president, marking the effective end of the Soviet Union.*

1 9 9 2

15 JANUARY. *The EC's "Badinter Commission" says only Slovenia and Macedonia among former Yugoslav republics qualify for diplomatic recognition. Most EC states nonetheless proceed to recognize Croatia as well as Slovenia but not Macedonia, because of opposition from Greece.*

19 JANUARY. *Zhelyu Zhelev is confirmed as president of Bulgaria in direct elections.*

3–10 FEBRUARY. Moscow. I meet General Sergei Kondrachev, once head of KGB operations in Western Europe but now rapidly retooling as "historian" and "archival specialist." He argues that the spies in East and West saved us from a third world war, since through their efforts both sides knew so much about each other's defenses that the danger of either risking a nuclear attack was diminished. On the moral chessboard of the post–cold war world, I call this the Kondrachev Defense.

Kondrachev was stationed in London during the 1950s. In perfectly modulated, slightly old-fashioned English, he tells me, "I have the fondest memories of my trips to Cambridge."

7 FEBRUARY. *Signature of the Maastricht Treaty on European Union.*

28 FEBRUARY. *Slovak prime minister Ján Čarnogursky says he would like Slovakia to enjoy international recognition.*

FEBRUARY. *Beginning of arrests in a growing Italian political-corruption scandal. The first focus of investigation is the Italian Socialist Party of Bettino Craxi.*

3 MARCH. *President Alija Izetbegović declares Bosnian independence, after a referendum boycotted by Bosnian Serbs.*

5 MARCH. *German foreign minister Hans-Dietrich Genscher presses for international recognition of Bosnia-Herzegovina.*

6 MARCH. *Formation of a Council of Baltic Sea States, including Denmark, Estonia, Finland, Germany, Latvia, Lithuania, Norway, Poland, Russia, and Sweden.*

11 MARCH. *After a year of failed attempts to negotiate a new Czecho-Slovak federation, the heads of the Czech and Slovak parliaments suspend talks until after June elections.*

27 MARCH. *Bosnian Serbs, led by Radovan Karadžić, declare a "Serb Republic" in Bosnia-Herzegovina.*

LATE MARCH/EARLY APRIL. *Outbreak of war in Bosnia.*

2 APRIL. *President Mitterrand appoints socialist Pierre Bérégovoy prime minister of France.*

5 APRIL. *The siege of Sarajevo begins.*

6 APRIL. *Sali Berisha, a cardiologist from the northern part of the country, is elected president of Albania.*

7 APRIL. *The USA recognizes Bosnia-Herzegovina, Slovenia, and Croatia.*

9 APRIL. *A general election in Britain returns to office a Conservative government under Prime Minister John Major.*

27 APRIL. *Declaration of a new Federal Republic of Yugoslavia (FRY), consisting of Serbia (including Kosovo and Vojvodina) and Montenegro. Not recognized by the West.*

29 APRIL. *A list of suspected agents of the communist secret police is published in Prague.*

18 MAY. *Hans-Dietrich Genscher resigns after eighteen years as German foreign minister. He is succeeded by Klaus Kinkel.*

22 MAY. *Slovenia, Croatia, and Bosnia-Herzegovina are admitted to the UN.*

24 MAY. *Kosovar Albanians hold clandestine elections. Ibrahim Rugova is elected "president of the republic." In Austria, Thomas Klestil is elected president, replacing disgraced Kurt Waldheim.*

25 MAY. *Oscar Luigi Scalfaro becomes president of Italy.*

27 MAY. *Massacre of civilians in Sarajevo.*

30 MAY. *The UN agrees on sanctions against the Federal Republic of Yugoslavia.*

2 JUNE. *In a referendum, Danish voters reject ratification of the Maastricht Treaty by a narrow majority.*

5 JUNE. *The Olszewski government falls in Poland after identifying leading politicians as former collaborators with the communist secret police: the "night of the files."*

5–6 JUNE. *Parliamentary elections in Czechoslovakia. The Civic Democratic Party of Václav Klaus wins in the Czech lands, and the Movement for a Democratic Slovakia of Vladimír Mečiar wins in Slovakia.*

15 JUNE. *Serbian writer Dobrica Ćosić becomes president of the Federal Republic of Yugoslavia.*

17 JUNE. *The Slovak parliament votes a declaration of "sovereignty."*

18 JUNE. *Giuliano Amato becomes prime minister of Italy.*

JUNE. *Serious escalation of the war in Bosnia and the siege of Sarajevo. Student protests against Milošević in Belgrade.*

JUNE–AUGUST. *Czech prime minister Václav Klaus and Slovak prime minister Vladimír Mečiar agree to dissolve the Czecho-Slovak federation by the end of the year.*

3 JULY. *Bosnian Croats declare their own statelet in western Bosnia-Herzegovina.*

10 JULY. *A summit meeting of the Conference on Security and Cooperation in Europe, which now has fifty-one member states.*

12 JULY. *Hanna Suchocka, from a liberal-conservative post-Solidarity party, forms a coalition government of seven parties in Poland.*

14 JULY. *Milan Panić, a Serb-American businessman, becomes prime minister of the Federal Republic of Yugoslavia.*

17 JULY. *Following Slovakia's "declaration of sovereignty," Václav Havel announces his resignation as president of Czechoslovakia, as of 20 July.*

2 AUGUST. *Croatian nationalists (HDZ) led by Franjo Tudjman win Croatian parliamentary elections. Tudjman is reelected president of Croatia.*

26–28 AUGUST. *At the London Conference on the former Yugoslavia, it is agreed that borders should not be altered by force and that ethnic cleansing should cease. War and ethnic cleansing continue.*

30 AUGUST. *Sarajevans standing in a breadline are killed and wounded.*

3 SEPTEMBER. *Lord (David) Owen and Cyrus Vance become joint chairmen of a new EC-UN conference on former Yugoslavia.*

4 SEPTEMBER. *Former Bulgarian communist leader Todor Zhivkov is found guilty of embezzlement.*

16 SEPTEMBER. *Massive speculation against the pound forces Britain to "suspend" its membership in the Exchange Rate Mechanism of the European Monetary System: "Black Wednesday."*

17 SEPTEMBER. *The Italian lira is also forced out of the Exchange Rate Mechanism.*

20 SEPTEMBER. *In a referendum called by President Mitterrand following the Danish referendum, 51 percent of French voters approve ratification of the Maastricht Treaty. In Estonia, parliamentary elections are won by parties of the center-right. Only Estonian citizens are enfranchised, so most of the nearly 40 percent non-Estonian population is not able to vote.*

27 SEPTEMBER. *Ion Iliescu is confirmed in office as president of Romania. His authoritarian National Salvation Front wins most seats in parliament.*

5 OCTOBER. *Nationalist intellectual Lennart Meri becomes president of Estonia.*

11 OCTOBER. *Former Soviet foreign minister Eduard Shevardnadze becomes head of state in Georgia. He faces a Russian-supported revolt in Abkhazia.*

13 OCTOBER. *The veteran socialist Andreas Papandreou again becomes prime minister of Greece, replacing the right-wing government of Constantine Mitsotakis.*

25 OCTOBER. *Lithuanian parliamentary elections produce a landslide victory for former communists under Algirdas Brazauskas.*

26 OCTOBER. *Czech prime minister Václav Klaus and Slovak prime minister Vladimír Mečiar agree on a customs union after Czechoslovakia will be divided on 1 January 1993. Erich Mielke, former head of the East German State Security Service (Stasi), is convicted for his part in the murder of a policeman in 1931.*

3 NOVEMBER. *Bill Clinton wins the U.S. presidential elections.*

THE VISIT

"ARE YOU BRINGING ANY LAUNDRY?" ASKS THE PORTER AT THE fortified entrance to Moabit prison.

When I laugh, he says defensively, "I was only asking," and grimly stamps my permit to visit remand prisoner Honecker, Erich.

Into a waiting room full of chain-smoking wives and lowlifes in black leather jackets. Wait for your number to be called from a loud-speaker. Through an automatic barrier. Empty your pockets and put everything in a locker. Body search. Another automatic barrier. Un-smiling guards, barked orders. *"Moment! Kommen Sie mit!"* Then you've come to the wrong place. Collect all your belongings again. Pack up. Walk around the redbrick fortress to another gate. Unpack. Sign this, take that. Another huge metal door. The clash of bolts. A courtyard, then the corridor to the prison hospital, bare but clean.

Somehow this all seems increasingly familiar. I have been here be-fore. But where and when? Then I remember. It's like crossing through the Friedrichstrasse underground frontier station into East Berlin, in the bad old days. West Germany has given Honecker back his Berlin Wall.

Inside, it is warm and safe. There is food to eat—plain fare, to be sure, but regular and ample. There is basic, free medical care for all. Good books are to be had from the library, and there is guaranteed employment for men and women alike. And life is, of course, very se-cure. Just like East Germany.

THE FIRST TIME I saw, at close quarters, the chairman of the Council of State of the German Democratic Republic and general secretary of the Socialist Unity Party of Germany was at the Leipzig trade fair in 1980. A horde of plainclothes Stasi men heralded the arrival of the leader. Eastern functionaries, West German businessmen, British diplomats all flapped and fluttered, bowed and scraped, as if at the Sublime Porte of Suleiman the Great. His every move, every tiny gesture, was studied and minutely interpreted, with all the arcane science of Sovietology. Significantly, graciously, the chairman and general secretary stopped at the Afghan stand, which displayed rugs and nuts. "And these are peanuts, and those are salted peanuts," came the breathless commentary of the rattled Afghan salesman. Graciously, significantly, the chairman and general secretary clapped him on the shoulder and said, "We regard your revolution as a decisive contribution to détente. All the best for your struggle!" Ah, happy days, the old style.

Now, the door opens, and there he stands in a tiny corner room, sandwiched between the doctor's washbasin and a table. He is very small, his face pallid and sweaty, but he still stands bolt upright. "Bodily contact is not permitted," says my permit. But he extends his hand—graciously, significantly—and I shake it. He is clad in khaki prison pajamas, which remind me of a Mao suit. But on his feet he still wears, incongruously, those fine, black leather slip-on shoes in which he used to tread all the red carpets, not just in Moscow and Prague but in Madrid, in Paris, and in Bonn. "Fraternal greetings, Comrade Leonid Ilyich" and a smacking kiss on each cheek. "How do you do, Mr. President." *"Guten Tag, Herr Bundeskanzler."*

We sit down, our knees almost touching in the cramped room, and the accompanying warder wedges himself into a corner. All my notes and papers have been impounded at the gate, but fortunately the doctor has left some spare sheets of lined paper and a pencil. Fixing me with his tiny, intense eyes—always his most striking feature—Honecker concentrates on answering my questions. He talks at length about his relations with Moscow, his friendship with Brezhnev, his arguments with Chernenko and then Gorbachev. Even under Gorbachev, he says, the Soviet Union never ceased to intervene in East Germany. The Soviet embassy's consular officials behaved, he says, like provincial governors. So much for the sovereignty of the GDR that he himself had so long trumpeted! At one point, he shows staggering (and I think genuine) economic naïveté, arguing that East Germany's hard-currency debt, in deutsche marks, has to be set against its surplus in transferable rubles.

His language is a little stiff, polit-bureaucratic, but very far from being just ideological gobbledygook. Through it come glimpses of a real political intelligence, a man who knows about power. Was it his conscious decision to allow many more ordinary East Germans to travel to the West in the second half of the 1980s? Yes, definitely, a conscious decision. He thought it would make people more satisfied. But did it? "*Nee*," he says, "*offensichtlich nicht.*" "Nope, obviously not."

With the tiny pupils of his eyes boring into mine, he speaks with what seems like real, almost fanatical, conviction—or at least with a real will to convince. This is somehow more, not less, impressive because of the humiliating prison surroundings and because of the obvious physical effort it costs him. (He has cancer of the liver. The doctors give him only months to live.) Once he has to excuse himself to go to the lavatory, accompanied by the warder. "You noticed I was getting a little restless," he says apologetically on his return.

Then he resumes his defiant refrain. East Germany, he insists, was "to the end the only socialist country in which you could always go into a shop and buy bread, butter, sausage etc." Yet people wanted more? Yes, but now they regret it. Look at the unemployment in the former GDR! Look how few apartments are being built! He gets hundreds of letters from people in the east. They say they lived more *quietly* in the old days: "*Sie haben ruhiger gelebt.*"

And look what's happening on the streets now: the racist attacks, the fascists. It reminds him of 1933. Really? 1933? Well, he concedes, perhaps 1923. Hitler's first attempt was also a flop. But look what happened then. He's warning us. We've been here before. At least, he's been here before—which, indeed, he has: held as a political prisoner in this very prison in the years 1935–1937, after being caught working for the communist resistance.

And now he is here again. West Germany's leaders denounce him as a criminal. Yet only yesterday the same politicians were competing for the privilege of being received in audience by him. Oh, the tales he could tell! His talks with West German Social Democrats were, he says, "comradely." Some other West German politicians were more reserved. He had great respect for Franz Josef Strauss. Helmut Schmidt was the most reliable and punctilious partner. But he also got on well with Helmut Kohl. He had often talked on the telephone to Chancellor Schmidt and to Chancellor Kohl. Why, he had even dialed the number himself.

Then the former chairman of the Council of State of the former German Democratic Republic and former general secretary of the former Socialist Unity Party of Germany pulls out of the pocket of his prison pajamas a slightly dog-eared card on which his former secretary had typed the direct telephone number to the chancellor in Bonn. He places it before me, urges me to copy the number down. 0649 (West Germany) 228 (Bonn) 562001. (I try it later. It takes you straight through to the chancellor's office in Bonn.)

A quarter century of divided Germany's tragic, complex history is, it seems to me, concentrated in this one pathetic moment: the defiant, mortally sick old man in his prison pajamas, the dog-eared card with the direct number to Chancellor Kohl.

The warder clears his throat and looks at his watch. Our time is up. Honecker rises, again standing almost to attention. A formal farewell. Then the bare corridors, the clashing gates, the unsmiling guards, the belongings from the locker, the fortified entrance. But now I *am* carrying laundry. Scribbled in pencil on a doctor's notepad: the dirty linen of history.

CHRONOLOGY

1992

6 DECEMBER. *In a referendum, Swiss voters reject membership in a European Economic Area, seen as a stepping-stone to membership in the EU. Milan Kučan is elected president of Slovenia.*

9 DECEMBER. *John Major announces that the prince and princess of Wales are to separate.*

11 DECEMBER. *EC summit in Edinburgh.*

20 DECEMBER. *Slobodan Milošević is reelected president of the republic of Serbia.*

1993

1 JANUARY. *The Single European Market comes into effect in the EC, now renamed the EU. Czechoslovakia splits into the Czech Republic and Slovakia: the "velvet divorce."*

2 JANUARY. *Presentation in Geneva of the "Vance-Owen plan" for Bosnia as a federal republic with ten ethnically based cantons enjoying substantial autonomy.*

3 JANUARY. *US president George Bush and Russian president Boris Yeltsin sign the START II treaty, eliminating all multiple-warhead intercontinental ballistic missiles and reducing their stocks of strategic nuclear weapons by two thirds.*

20 JANUARY. *Bill Clinton takes office as U.S. president.*

26 JANUARY. *Václav Havel is elected the first president of the Czech Republic.*

JANUARY–DECEMBER. *Italy is engulfed in a massive political-corruption scandal, which effectively destroys the political system that had survived throughout the cold war. In the so-called Mani Pulite ("Clean hands") investigation, numerous senior politicians, including four former prime ministers, and many business leaders are arrested or interrogated on charges of corruption.*

1 FEBRUARY. *Sweden, Norway, Finland, and Austria—all members of the European Free Trade Association (EFTA)—begin negotiations to join the EU.*

14 FEBRUARY. *Former communist Algirdas Brazauskas is elected president of Lithuania.*

22 FEBRUARY. *UN agrees that there should be criminal prosecution of those responsible for war crimes in former Yugoslavia.*

5 MARCH. *Michal Kováč, an independent-minded former associate of Prime Minister Vladimír Mečiar, becomes president of Slovakia.*

MARCH. *UN convoys reach the besieged Bosnian town of Srebrenica.*

MARCH–APRIL. *The center-right Swedish government of Carl Bildt pushes through major cuts in public expenditure, especially on welfare programs.*

20 MARCH. *Russian president Boris Yeltsin attempts to impose "special rule," effectively suspending parliament until fresh elections.*

29 MARCH. *A new government of the center-right in France, under Prime Minister Édouard Balladur. "Cohabitation" with socialist president François Mitterrand.*

7 APRIL. *Macedonia is admitted to the UN as "The Former Yugoslav Republic of Macedonia" (FYROM), despite Greek opposition.*

12 APRIL. *NATO begins enforcement of a no-fly zone over Bosnia.*

24 APRIL. *The Dutch government under Christian Democrat Ruud Lubbers agrees on a program of radical reductions of the Netherlands' generous welfare spending.*

APRIL. *A referendum on political reforms in Italy. President Scalfaro asks nonparty Carlo Azeglio Ciampi, governor of the Bank of Italy, to form a government, following the resignation of Giulio Amato. Veteran Christian Democrat politician Giulio Andreotti, seven times prime minister, is accused of complicity with the Mafia.*

1–2 MAY. *Representatives of the main combatants in Bosnia sign the "Vance-Owen plan." Thorvald Stoltenberg replaces Cyrus Vance as UN cochairman of the London Conference on the former Yugoslavia.*

5–6 MAY.   *The Bosnian Serb assembly in Pale rejects the "Vance-Owen plan."*

6 MAY.   *UN Security Council Resolution 824 declares Sarajevo, Tuzla, Žepa, Bihać, Goražde, and Srebrenica to be "safe zones." These are often called "safe areas" or "safe havens."*

18 MAY.   *In a second referendum, Danish voters approve ratification of the Maastricht Treaty, after their government has negotiated a number of "opt-outs."*

31 MAY.   *Serbian writer Dobrica Ćosić is compelled to resign as president of the Federal Republic of Yugoslavia.*

6 JUNE.   *Spanish elections return the Socialists under Prime Minister Felipe González to power, though dependent on Catalan and Basque votes for a majority.*

21 JUNE.   *The Copenhagen summit of the EU sets out basic criteria for postcommunist countries to become members of the European Union.*

14 JULY.   *The Belgian parliament votes to complete federalization of the country, with far-reaching devolution to largely Flemish-speaking Flanders, French-speaking Wallonia, and the mixed city of Brussels.*

1 AUGUST.   *After intensive speculation against the French franc, remaining currencies in the Exchange Rate Mechanism are allowed to fluctuate within margins of 15 percent above or below the central rate. Only the deutsche mark and the Dutch guilder remain within a narrower band.*

2 AUGUST.   *Britain ratifies the Maastricht Treaty.*

LATE SEPTEMBER–EARLY OCTOBER.   *President Yeltsin suspends the intransigent parliament and calls for fresh elections. Following resistance by parliament and some armed forces, forces loyal to President Yeltsin bombard and storm the parliament building, Russia's "White House."*

3–15 OCTOBER.   Germany. I spend the evening of the third anniversary of German unification in the beer tents of the Oktoberfest in Munich. The editor of a women's magazine tells me how they live on images of Princess Diana. Every time they put her on the front cover, sales go up by at least 20 percent. On television, I see Chancellor Kohl toasting German unity in Saarbrücken. "Here's to Gorbi," says someone from the crowd. "Yes, here's to Gorbi," says Kohl. Forgotten or abhorred in Russia, Gorbachev is still a hero here. But Kohl has a new friend: Boris Yeltsin.

In Bonn, the Social Democrat leader Rudolf Scharping hastens to tell me about his early contacts with dissidents in Poland. I ask him what he replies to German voters who ask, "Why do we need Europe now?" "I have only fragments of an answer," he says. An associate of Helmut Kohl tells me that the chancellor is adamant that other EU states must agree to the European Monetary Institute, and hence the European Central Bank, being located in Frankfurt—"Otherwise," Kohl apparently said, "I'll enter the election campaign in short trousers."

In an east German city, I share a platform with a new dean at the local university, a west German. He's an example of the kind of second-rater who would never have got such a senior position in the west but now lords it over the east Germans like a British district commissioner in nineteenth-century India. He hardly lets the east Germans in our audience get a word in edgeways. Germany has another political first: colonialism in one country.

12 OCTOBER. *The German Constitutional Court rules that Germany can ratify the Maastricht Treaty.*

26 OCTOBER. *Following a decisive victory in Polish elections held in September under a new electoral law, a coalition government of postcommunists and the Polish Peasant Party is formed under Prime Minister Waldemar Pawlak.*

29 OCTOBER. *EU leaders agree that the European Central Bank will be in Frankfurt and that monetary union should happen at the latest by 1999.*

1 NOVEMBER. *The Maastricht Treaty comes into force in all member states of the EU.*

1–4 NOVEMBER. Amsterdam and Antwerp. A tour for the Dutch edition of my book about German Ostpolitik. For these purposes, Flanders is treated as a part of Holland. It's as if Belgium does not exist.

The Dutch, in both Holland and Belgium, are better informed about Germany than the Germans themselves are. But they are also astonishingly suspicious and fearful of Germany and the Germans. Several times, I am told the story of the banner, held up to greet German visitors at some large public event, saying, "Give us back our bicycles!" (During the wartime occupation, bicycles were confiscated.) And when young German tourists ask the good people of Rotterdam, "Excuse me, where's the old town?" they receive the acid reply, "Ask your grandfather." (The old town of Rotterdam was destroyed by the Germans during the war.)

This suspicion and fear is mitigated but also strengthened by the present relationship with their mighty neighbor. For the Dutch accept, almost fatalistically, that their economy, and therefore their fate, is inextricably bound up with that of Germany; that their interest rates automatically follow the Bundesbank's; that the Dutch guilder will merge with the deutsche mark in monetary union. One Dutch journalist confides, "You know, in the end, we're left saying, 'We hope they'll be nice to us!' " The national purpose is to preserve nothing so grand as sovereignty—just their language and a distinctive way of life. From "Give us back our bicycles!" to "Please let us keep our bicycles."

9 NOVEMBER. *The old bridge in Mostar is destroyed in fighting between Bosniaks and Bosnian Croats.*

11 NOVEMBER. *The UN Tribunal on War Crimes in former Yugoslavia is inaugurated in The Hague.*

12 DECEMBER. *The first free multiparty parliamentary elections in Russia since 1917. Strong vote for communists under Gennady Zhuganov and for the far-right nationalist "Liberal Democratic Party" of Vladimir Zhirinovsky. A new constitution is approved, giving more powers to the president.*

15 DECEMBER. *British prime minister John Major and Irish prime minister Albert Reynolds issue the "Downing Street Declaration" on the way forward in Northern Ireland.*

19 DECEMBER. *Milošević's Socialist Party wins parliamentary elections in Serbia.*

21 DECEMBER. *Former interior minister and moderate nationalist Peter Boross becomes Hungarian prime minister following the death of József Antall.*

1994

1 JANUARY. *The "second stage" of economic and monetary union comes into effect with the establishment of a European Monetary Institute as a precursor to a European Central Bank.*

10–11 JANUARY. *At a Brussels summit, NATO leaders launch the Partnership for Peace with former members of the Warsaw Pact.*

14 JANUARY. *The U.S., Russian, and Ukrainian presidents sign an accord detailing arrangements for the transfer of Ukrainian nuclear warheads to Russia.*

5 FEBRUARY. *A mortar attack on the marketplace in Sarajevo, with heavy loss of life. UN secretary-general Boutros Boutros-Ghali asks NATO to prepare for possible air strikes against Serb artillery positions around Sarajevo.*

16 FEBRUARY. *Greece imposes a trade embargo on Macedonia. The EU declares this to be in violation of European law.*

23 FEBRUARY. *The Russian parliament votes an amnesty for those involved in the October 1993 revolt by the Russian parliament.*

9–10 MARCH. *The EU's Committee of the Regions, established under the Maastricht Treaty, holds its first session.*

14 MARCH. *Vladimir Mečiar resigns as prime minister of Slovakia after losing a confidence vote.*

18 MARCH. *The Washington Agreement creates the Federation of Bosniaks and Bosnian Croats.*

26–27 MARCH. *The new "Forza Italia" party of business magnate Silvio Berlusconi wins Italian parliamentary elections as part of a "Freedom Alliance."*

27 MARCH. *A referendum called by the pro-Russian president of the Ukrainian republic of Crimea results in a vote for greater autonomy for the Crimea.*

SEVEN CITIES

Vienna

Driving into town from the airport, I pass a café called the Espresso Ilidza. On the radio, a reporter discusses the arrangements in Austrian schools for teaching in Croatian. Then comes the weather forecast: for Austria, Hungary, Slovenia, Croatia, and northern Italy. I read the diminutive *Neue Kronen Zeitung,* clipped to its *Zeitungshalter* (newspaper stick) like a little flag. In a fighting interview, Frau Klestil, the jilted wife of Kurt Waldheim's successor as president, tells us she is determined to remain Austria's first lady. The operetta continues. I am back in Central Europe.

Later, at the editorial meeting of a more elevated journal, a German feminist exclaims, "Eastern men are such pashas." Yes, a colleague agrees, they could do with some "reeducation." I glimpse a new Central Europe, where Polish men are to be "reeducated" by German feminists.

Then to the fellows' meeting of the Institute for Human Sciences, a meeting place to rival even the Café Landtmann. Bronisław Geremek lectures on "The Collapse of Communism and European Security." He makes a politician's speech, mustering every argument for Poland to be admitted to NATO. Eloquent, as always, but some in the audience are disconcerted. Somehow, they had expected him to speak as an intellectual to intellectuals. But times and roles have changed, and Geremek, unlike many from the anticommunist oppositions of the 1970s and 1980s, has made a clear choice: While he is a politician, he will be a politician. I'm sure he's right. All we've seen in Central European politics since 1989 confirms an old truth. You may, in the course of your life, be both intellectual and politician. Try to be both at once, and you'll be neither.

Bratislava

Before the wars—Second World and cold—you went by tram from Vienna for an evening at the theater in the Slovakian capital of Bratislava, or vice versa. Now you could do so again, if the authorities would only relay a few miles of track. Meanwhile, it is just over an hour by train, and you slide across the border as if the Iron Curtain had never been. Amid the seemingly endless, dusty allotments—small plots of land on which people grow vegetables—I spy garages flying the flags of Volkswagen and Audi, like crusader castles. Giggly Slovak schoolgirls scream pop songs out of the train windows, startling the people digging in their gardens below. But the nice girl sitting next to me demurely studies a German textbook on management economics. She hopes to work in the hotel trade.

As I arrive, the government falls. The populist prime minister, Vladimír Mečiar, has been ousted by a parliamentary vote, following outspoken criticism of him by the president, Michal Kováč.

On the evening television news, the chubby, avuncular president is shown sitting beside a carefully polished tile oven, with a large bunch of flowers in a vase on the table before him. At one side of the screen you see a large microphone, held motionless by a female hand with brightly painted fingernails. The president talks about democracy, constitutionalism, civic engagement, on and on, but the more he talks, the less he convinces me—because of that painted hand. After about five minutes, we briefly catch sight of the woman interviewer. Her feeble "question" gives the cue for another five-minute sermon, delivered to the long-suffering painted hand. President Clinton, President Mitterrand, or, for that matter, President Klestil can only dream of such a complaisant medium; but then they work in fully fledged democracies.

My acquaintances are divided over whether Mečiar's fall is a good thing. All sigh with relief that the vulgar, nationalist rabble-rouser has got the boot. But some fear this ouster gives him the perfect chance to bounce back—as self-styled victim—in the elections that are due to be held in September. After all, he did it once before, in 1992, after being ousted by the parliament in 1991. Well, we shall see.

Meanwhile, I am in search of old Bratislava—that is, the German-Hungarian-Jewish-Slovak city of Pressburg, and before that the Hungarian royal capital of Pozsony. As I walk the dilapidated streets of the old town in the company of a local journalist, we meet an elderly gentleman in a black felt hat and formal gray coat, with a semiprecious stone on a ribbon around the collar of his slightly grubby white shirt. "Ah, here is the oldest Pressburger!" says my acquaintance and makes the introduction. This is Jan, Hans, or "Hansi" Albrecht, a retired musicologist and son of a celebrated local composer.

Later, over coffee and cognac in the inspissated gloom of his cluttered apartment, Albrecht tells tales of old Pressburg, while kids smash out the window glass from a derelict house across the road. ("Yes, that house belonged to the Esterházys," he says; *crash* goes another window.) He shows me a program for one of his father's concerts: printed in German, Hungarian, and Slovak. The Pressburg of his youth really was trilingual, he says. Someone would address you in Hungarian, you might reply in German, another would interrupt in Slovak.

Even after the first wave of Slovakization, which began with the establishment of Czechoslovakia in 1918, the statistics still show a population of some 15,000 Jewish, 20,000 Hungarian, and 30,000 German citizens of Pressburg, as well as 60,000 Slovaks. It was only the next two waves of Slovakization that effectively purged the city of all but a very few survivors of the other nationalities. First came the proclamation of Slovak independence under Hitler's protection in March 1939. (Outside the Slovak Philharmonic's concert hall, a pathetic gaggle of old men in shabby suits and cheap ties can be seen gathering to celebrate the anniversary.) The fascist puppet state of Father Jozef Tiso got rid of the Jews, and made the Hungarians unwelcome too.

After 1945, the new Czechoslovak government got rid of the Germans. Finally, to celebrate the enhanced status that Slovak Bratislava received after the Soviet invasion of Czechoslovakia in 1968, the communist authorities drove a huge suspension bridge, the "Bridge of the Slovak National Uprising," across the Danube and through the heart of the old town, destroying the synagogue and much of the old Jewish quarter. On a high wall they inscribed in large letters, "Bratislava, City of Peace."

Alas, poor Pressburg! Hansi Albrecht, the musicologist, argues that there has also been some cultural gain—the effete, decadent bourgeois culture of the late Habsburg empire has been reinvigorated by an injection of raw Slavonic folk spirit—but one feels an overwhelming sense of loss. Alma Münzová, another charming survivor of old Pressburg, well-read, multilingual, soignée, gives me the text of a talk she recently delivered (in German) on the history of the city. In it, she quotes a wry old joke: "When will things finally get better?" "What do you mean? They already were!" In many ways, to propose multiculturalism in Central Europe really is to suggest going forward to the past.

However, one must beware the siren song of nostalgia. The balance was never even. Before the Austro-Hungarian *Ausgleich,* or compromise, of 1867, the Austro-German element dominated Pressburg life. After the *Ausgleich,* the Hungarians there launched a program of systematic Magyarization. At the end of the century, this would arouse the sympathy of visitors such as the historian R. W. Seton-Watson, who described it under the pseudonym "Scotus Viator" in *The Spectator.* So at the end of the First World War he was among those who advocated that Slovakia—"Northern Hungary" as it then was—should be taken away from Hungary and joined with the Czech lands, in the newly independent state of Czechoslovakia.

All this is not just history. It has immediate political relevance. For, as a result of the post-1918 territorial settlement, reaffirmed after 1945, and again in the Helsinki Final Act of 1975, some half million Hungarians now live just inside the Slovak frontier, on the north bank of the Danube. In Czechoslovakia, they were a small minority: about one in thirty of the population. In Slovakia, they are a much larger minority: about one in ten.

The Slovak government, under Mečiar, has been a model of na-

tionalist stubbornness in resisting even the most reasonable demands for bilingual road signs, the restoration of the Hungarian
forms of personal names, and so on, despite pressure from, among
others, the Council of Europe. On the other hand, it was the now
deceased Hungarian prime minister József Antall who famously declared that he wished to be the prime minister of 15 million Hungarians—that is, roughly 10 million inside Hungary's frontiers and 5
million beyond them. When Czecho- and Slovakia were splitting up,
radical Hungarian nationalists even argued that what was laid down
by the Allies in 1920, in the Treaty of Trianon, was the new frontier
of Czechoslovakia, not of Slovakia—which would therefore have to
be negotiated anew. Incredibly, though Slovakia and Hungary are
both members of the Visegrád group, together with the Czech Republic and Poland, Slovakia currently has no ambassador in Budapest.

Slovakia's Hungarians are represented in the Slovak parliament
by their own Hungarian parties. Except on a few tactical votes (and
to some extent, interestingly, in the ex-communist party), they do
not mix with the Slovak parties. Regrettably, the Hungarian and Slovak sides seem to be getting not closer together but farther apart. I
am told that, in a recent poll, 35 percent of those asked thought the
Hungarian parties should not be in the Slovak parliament.

It is a worrying state of affairs.

Budapest

I cross the Slovak-Hungarian border on the so-called Balkan–Orient
Express. Its Romanian carriages provide a very credible setting for a
murder. The old peasant woman sitting opposite me puts the Hun-
garian-Slovak conflict in its proper place. To the Slovak passport officer she says, in Slovak, "I'm Slovak." To the Hungarian passport
officer she says, in Hungarian, "I'm Hungarian." To neither does she
show a passport. Maybe there's hope for Central Europe yet.

I tell a Hungarian friend that I'm staying at the Hotel Gellért, that
splendid art-nouveau blancmange on the right bank of the Danube,
with its majolica-walled thermal baths and granite-faced masseurs.
"Oh," she says, looking disapproving, "it's a Forum hotel." Thinking

of the rather good Forum Hotel on the Pest side of the river, I'm about to exclaim, "So has the Forum taken over the Gellért?" Then I realize that she means the Hungarian Democratic Forum, the conservative nationalist party which has been in power since 1990 and now faces an election in which the former communists are favored to win. How out of touch can you get?

She's right, too. I had forgotten how the tone, the decor, the very smell of the Gellért exude that particular aesthetic of populist Hungarianness. Even the "Do Not Disturb" signs to hang out on your doorknob are done in the national colors of red, white, and green. Meanwhile, the modern Forum Hotel is bursting with Western consultants, most of them wasting large sums of our (that is, Western taxpayers') money which is meant to be going to the struggling new democracies of postcommunist Europe. In German, one talks of *Spesenritter*: expense-account knights. O brave new world, that has such people in't.

This evening, however, something of the old world—almost a flashback—can be witnessed just along the embankment. A large crowd gathers at the invitation of the Democratic Charter, a liberal civic initiative, or anti-Forum forum, to protest against the recent sacking of 129 state radio employees. This was the latest act in the so-called media war, and a quite blatant attempt by the government to skew the radio still further to its side during the election. As dusk falls, the crowd, in which I meet several old friends, moves picturesquely down the left bank of the Danube, flaming torches held aloft, to reassemble at the statue of the poet Sándor Petőfi.

It was 146 years ago tomorrow, on 15 March 1848, that Petőfi led a Budapest crowd in what is generally taken to be the beginning of the country's "lawful revolution"—Hungary's 14 July. And tomorrow it will be celebrated as a national holiday, with all the fetid pathos of which the Forum is capable. But this evening, the liberals have stolen a march on them. At the feet of the poet, fine speeches are delivered by flaming torchlight: for democracy! for civil rights! for freedom! O brave old world, that had such demos in't.

As we watch the march, a publisher friend explains to me his worry that Hungary is once again being polarized into two nations, locked in a *Kulturkampf*. If someone talks of "structural problems," of "this country" or "this agricultural country," you know at once that they come from the camp known before the war as "urbanist." If someone talks of "fate issues," of "my land," or "our homeland," they belong to the camp known before the war as "populist." He fears history is repeating itself.

Another friend puts his personal dissatisfaction, frustration, and melancholy in a different way. "I grew up," he says, "in what I knew was an 'abnormal' state. I thought that, if the communists and the Soviet Union went, Hungary would be a 'normal'—that is, a Western—country. Now they've gone, and it isn't. We're governed by the Forum, and I have to accept that Hungary is in some ways an Eastern country."

He gropes for an image and finds it. "There was a statue, covered by a heavy sheet. We believed it was beautiful. One day, miraculously, after forty long years, it was uncovered. Our hearts rose, great were our hopes. But then we found that the statue was chipped and dirty and not so handsome after all."

Prague

The sleeping beauty of Central Europe has not merely been awakened by a prince's velvet kiss. She has put on black tights and gone off to the disco. (That is, after all, what contemporary princesses do, whether in Monaco or Mayfair.) While Budapest developed gradually into a modern consumer city, starting in the 1970s, Prague has emerged from its time warp suddenly and explosively. Instead of the magical museum, lovely but decaying, there is color, noise, action: street performers, traffic jams, building works, thousands of young Americans—would-be Hemingways or Scott Fitzgeralds—millions of German tourists, betting shops, reserved parking places for France Telecom and Mitsubishi Corporation, beggars, junkies, *Spesenritter* of all countries, car alarms, trendy bars, gangsters, whores galore, *Bierstüben*, litter, graffiti, video shops, and Franz Kafka T-shirts.

I have mixed feelings about this transformation scene. But I am quite won over by walking the streets with my friend Jáchym Topol, a young poet, novelist, and editor of the formerly samizdat journal *Revolver Revue*. Jáchym—longhaired, chain-smoking, deeply Bohemian in both senses of the word—stalks along simply fizzing with enthusiasm for the way Prague has come alive. "Look at it—it's great!" he exclaims, as we are nearly run down by a speeding car. The rock groups now write their lyrics in English, he says. Street kids use the Albanian word for prison, because there is now a strong Albanian "mafia," beside the Russian and local ones. And there's a new kind of savory bread roll. It's called a *crazy chleba,* a grammatically eccentric name translatable roughly as a "bread crazy."

Jáchym's new novel, out of Döblin and Joyce by way of Hrabal, is to be published next month, and he's dashing around trying to arrange publicity for it. But he has to do almost everything himself. The publicity department, so important a part of most Western publishers, is still almost unknown here.

The cliché is that the Czechs are the Prussians of the Slavs. Certainly the orderly, Western qualities of Bohemia, its prewar industrial record, the economic credibility of premier Václav Klaus, and, above all, its cheap skilled labor have combined to attract foreign, and especially German, investment. (An hour's skilled labor costs the employer about DM 35 in Germany compared to just DM 4 in Bohemia.) Yet even here there is the characteristic postcommunist mixture of enterprise and corruption: large kickbacks paid in the course of privatization, mysterious enhancement of party funds, the dubious involvement of ex-*nomenklatura,* criminal, semicriminal, and corrupt official elements, all combining to give many ordinary people a slightly jaundiced view of both capitalism and the politicians who preach it.

The frequently encountered and loosely used term *mafia* points to the ubiquitous element of organized crime. The Russian word *prikhvatizatsiya*—that is, roughly, pritheftization (*khvatat* = seize, grab)—catches another aspect of the postcommunist scene; as does the phrase "the privatization of the *nomenklatura.*" Alfred Stepan, the American political scientist and new rector of George Soros's Central European University, reminds me of the term *kleptocracy,* already used in Latin America and Africa. The former foreign minister Jiří Dienstbier talks of an "Italian-type political system." And, finally, there is the special part played by the consultants and the *Spesenritter.* German businessmen, I am told, are particularly free with the bribes. What we need, however, is a term that encompasses the whole distinctive postcommunist combination of all of these.

A friend who works for the Helsinki Committee for Refugees adds another colorful tessera to the postcommunist mosaic. She tells me the story of a former Afghan police chief who had fled with his family to Moscow. There, he was told that he could get to Germany, at a cost of $12,000 per head. He paid up for himself, his wife, and their two youngest children, leaving two older children behind. (How an Afghan police chief had collected $48,000 one can perhaps imagine.) They were given false passports, traveled for many hours by train, by bus, by train again, until they finally arrived. "Well," said the Russian who escorted them, "here you are, in Germany." Setting them down in the station buffet, he asked for their false papers back and then went, as he said, to get some cash. Of course he never returned. So there they were, without papers, money, or a single acquaintance, in what they thought was Germany. That is, in Prague.

Walking along Národní Street, I suddenly notice a black metal plaque inscribed simply with the date 17 November 1989. It marks the student demonstration that began the "velvet revolution." But you feel that event is already almost as remote as the resistance to Nazi occupation commemorated by other plaques around the city. Here more than anywhere else the last forty years seem just to have evaporated, almost as if they had never been. Certainly no one, except a very few historians, is interested in the communist past. Inasmuch as anyone is interested in the past at all, it is that of Tomáš Garrigue Masaryk's first republic, before 1939.

NEXT DAY, I am driven out to Masaryk's country house at Lány, to see President Havel. Recovering from the flu, he sits with a small group of friends and counselors in a rather formal salon, while the rain buckets down on the park outside. Watched by the ghost of Masaryk, we talk about the idea and the reality of Central Europe. Masaryk's definition of Central Europe, or *Střední Evropa*, elaborated in London during the First World War in R. W. Seton-Watson's journal *The New Europe*, included "Laplanders, Swedes, Norwegians and Danes, Finns, Estonians, Letts, Lithuanians, Poles, Lusatians, Czechs and Slovaks, Magyars, Serbo-Croats and Slovenes, Romanians, Bulgars, Albanians, Turks and Greeks"—but no Germans or Austrians. The German liberal politician Friedrich Naumann articulated a very different vision of Central Europe at the same time. His *Mitteleuropa* was all about the Germans and Austrians, with the others included only insofar as they were subjects of the German and Austro-Hungarian empires.

One of the great questions of the new "New Europe" is whether this old tension between *Mitteleuropa* and *Střední Evropa* can finally be laid to rest. Very much with this in mind, Havel has invited seven presidents to an "informal" meeting in Litomyšl, the birthplace of the composer Smetana. Besides the presidents of the "Visegrád four" (Poland, Hungary, the Czech Republic, and Slovakia) and the president of Slovenia, a country with which the Czech Republic has developed its own miniature special relationship (some make jokes about "Czecho-Slovenia"), the "L7"—as Havel's foreign-affairs adviser Pavel Seifter wryly christens it—will include Austria's President Klestil and Havel's good friend, the outgoing German president, Richard von Weizsäcker, whose birthday will also be marked by the occasion.

The inclusion of Germany in the group may raise a few eyebrows, not least in France or Italy, but I think it is vital. Even if Germany only stands in Central Europe "with one leg," as Havel himself observes, it is the biggest leg in town. There is a lively debate about Germany inside East Central Europe, and there is a lively debate inside Germany about East Central Europe: It is vital that the two debates should intertwine.

At one point, I ask Havel when he is going to write his fundamental essay about the intellectual and the politician. "Only when I stop being president," comes the instant reply.

Back in Prague, I visit another old friend, Petr Pithart, a highly respected opposition intellectual who in 1990 became prime minister of the Czech Republic but is now—with relief—an intellectual again. After working hard to keep Czechoslovakia together, he now finds himself being invited to Belgium and Quebec, to tell them how you make a velvet divorce.

ON SUNDAY, I drive myself out, along bad roads, through poor, dusty villages—no Prague transformation scenes here—to the castle of Častolovice, in northeastern Bohemia. Diana Phipps—née Sternberg—has had the castle returned to her, under the so-called resti-tution law. Not so many great families of the Bohemian aristocracy have in fact been eligible for this restitution, because the condition sine qua non is that they were still there at the time of the February 1948 communist coup. Many, seeing the writing on the wall, had al-ready left. Of those eligible, by no means all have reclaimed their property, which often requires a large investment for a very doubtful return. Diana has, with enormous difficulty, gotten back more than seven thousand acres of the estate that originally sustained the cas-tle, mainly forest, with herds of white deer and gruntles of wild boar. But, as for all but a very few country houses or castles in the world today, Častolovice's future will depend on people coming to see it. Častolovice will be well worth seeing. There is the breathtaking Re-naissance Knight's Hall, the dining room adorned with portraits of all the kings of Bohemia, the library left virtually untouched for forty years, like Miss Havisham's boudoir in *Great Expectations,* the rusty old weapons, the furniture (much of it "restituted" from other loca-tions), the ancestral portraits—Diana's great-grandfather in the full splendor of a general in the service of Emperor Franz Joseph, her fa-ther as a dashing dragoon galloping through some Ruthenian hamlet in the First World War; then the "English" park and the boar-filled woods; and all this restored with Diana Phipps's rare taste and imag-ination. If you stand with eyes half closed, you can almost see Count Leopold Sternberg's hunting party lined up in the great courtyard, waiting impatiently for the American ambassador to join them, as described in Cecilia Sternberg's memorable autobiography, *The Journey.*

Here as elsewhere in the Czech lands, the local people do not seem to be overwhelmingly enthusiastic about the return of the aris-tocrats. (There is perhaps a contrast to the traditional gentry nations of Poland and Hungary.) I personally find it not just fabulous, in the original sense of the word, but also moving. Like, at the other social extreme, Jáchym Topol's street kids tossing off Albanian slang be-tween bites of *crazy chleba,* this is all part of the larger return to di-versity, to history and to freedom—with all the tensions and conflicts that necessarily brings.

In the anteroom to the "museum" part of the castle, we con-template a display, left over from the communist period, listing the successive owners with their coats of arms. The Sternberg arms show a star with the motto "*Nescit occasum*"—"It will not set." Underneath, the communist curators have written, "Sternberk family (1694–1948)"—as if the star had set. We discuss how this entry should be amended. Perhaps the simplest and most eloquent thing would be just to add, "(1992–)."

Warsaw

In the evening, I fly, with a planeload of screaming French teenagers and wearily networking American, German, and British consultants, to Poland, where it is the ex-communists' star that has risen again. For me, this is really just a stopover on the way to Lithuania, but there is time to see a few old friends.

Konstanty Gerbert, who still sometimes uses his underground pen name of Dawid Warszawski, takes me out to lunch in an unexpectedly good Chinese restaurant (culinary worlds apart from the old, state-owned Shanghai). He talks, vividly as ever, about Bosnia, where he now spends much of his time. "But," I ask, "what about Poland?"

"*Sluchaj, nudnie!*" he says. Boring! "Poland has become an ordinary, provincial country with ordinary, provincial problems." We both agree that this is a very great achievement indeed. After all, until 1989, boring, provincial normality was beyond all but the most far-fetched dreams. And the fact that this can more or less continue to be the case under a government dominated by the ex-communists (or ex-ex-communists) levered out only five years ago is a twist that nobody imagined.

EVERYWHERE JACKETS AND TIES, suits and ties—scarcely a trace of the old underground sweaters and jeans. I feel almost underdressed.

GRZEGORZ BOGUTA, once the tyro of the underground publisher Nowa and now the smartly suited head of Polish Scientific Publishers (PWN), gives me the 1992 supplement to their dictionary of the

Polish language. It contains words that have entered the language since the dictionary was first published in 1978 and those that had been excluded for political reasons (including reasons of communist prudery). This is a fascinating semantic register of fifteen years in which so much has changed: from *aborcja* (abortion, one of the most controversial issues in Polish politics over the last few years) to *żydokomuna* (a hateful new-old term for communists of—or allegedly of—Jewish origin). The entries under *B* include *beton* ("concrete," referring to communist party hard-liners), *bingo, bioenergoterapia, bogoojczyźniany* (one of my favorites, meaning literally "god-fatherlandized," and used to refer to excessively pious patriotic persons), *bolszewik, briefing,* and *broker. V,* a letter not generally used in Polish, has just three entries: *video* (explained as "wideo"), *video-* (as prefix), and *votum separatum.*

Vilnius

Puttering along in yet another twin-propeller plane, across snow-covered fields, enchanting lakes, and enchanted woods, I arrive in Vilnius. Like Bratislava, this is a capital city that lies in one corner of its country and is in many ways quite untypical of it. Where Bratislava (Pressburg, Pozsony) was once German, Hungarian, and Jewish as well as Slovak, Vilnius (Wilno, Vilna) was once Polish and Jewish as well as Lithuanian. Memorably evoked in recent times by two of its native sons, the Polish poet Czesław Miłosz and the Lithuanian poet Tomas Venclova, Vilnius is a wonderful irregular composition of baroque churches, small palaces, and town houses, courtyard leading into courtyard—"a city of clouds resembling baroque architecture and of baroque architecture like coagulated clouds," as Miłosz puts it in his *Native Realm.*

However, Vilnius is Central Europe only from the knees up: The pavements and roads are full of Soviet-style potholes and slush. Near the university, I see a car with its rear wheel completely jammed in a three-foot-deep pothole. An acquaintance tells me you can actually get some modest compensation for the damage from the local authorities, but only if you land in a registered pothole.

A Lithuanian poet shows me around the Jewish museum, which

goes by the curious name of the Jewish State Museum of Lithuania. The exhibition is striking because, even when you have found it, which is not altogether easy, there is almost nothing there. A few Torah scrolls and Hanukkah lamps, some prints ("Portrait of Sir Moses Montefiore, Lithograph, Warsaw"); that's about it. Fragments of fragments from a lost world. "We rely on the visitors to tell us what we have," says the poet. In the visitors' book, a young German thanks the museum for this reminder of "our very, very bad history."

NOT FAR AWAY, on Gedimino Boulevard, there is another exhibition. In the basement of what until just three years ago was still the KGB headquarters, you can visit the cells. I am shown around by a former inmate, Stasys Katauskas. Speaking Polish with the rolled Lithuanian *l*, he tells me how he was caught in 1946 after passing a radio set to the anti-Soviet partisans. Then he takes me through the cells as if I myself were being admitted—first the strip search; then locked up in a tiny, windowless cupboard; then the registration, photographing, and fingerprinting (the original equipment is still there); finally, into the cells. These were repainted by the KGB before they left, but the association of former inmates has paid a picture restorer to strip off the paint, layer by layer. On a small, two-foot-square patch, you have twenty carefully numbered layers: So many despairing messages, so much filth, so much blood have these walls seen. Down the corridor there is the freezing solitary-confinement cell and, most horrible of all, a cell heavily padded with stuffed canvas, still bloodstained. The torture room.

To sophisticated Western ears, Lithuanian nationalism often sounds strident and crude. But if you walk through these cellars, contemplate the catalog of occupation that this one building has seen over the last century—tsarist Russian courts, Polish courts, NKVD, Nazi *Sicherheitsdienst*, KGB—and look at the grainy photographs of the partisans on the walls, then you may have a little more understanding of the traumatic experience from which that raw, naive nationalism comes.

However, I am told that, after the first great wave of recollection and mourning and celebration in the independence struggle, most young Lithuanians, perhaps most Lithuanians altogether, no longer want to look back, whether in sorrow, pride, or anger. They have elected former communists to the government after the anticommunist patriots led by Vytautas Landsbergis turned out to be inept. They are more concerned with today's chances and today's problems, such as the omnipresent mafia, with their car-theft and protection rackets; the *biznes*-men who buy politicians and a favorable press; the politicians enriching themselves from the public purse and the proceeds of privatization. (Once again, I feel the lack of a term to embrace this entire complex phenomenon.)

I VISIT SOME of the politicians in the parliament building which the people of Vilnius defended against Soviet forces in 1991. A section of the concrete and barbed-wire barricade has been left as a memorial, looking strangely like a remnant of the Berlin Wall. Inside, an adviser to the government of ex-communists outlines Lithuania's foreign-policy options: to take the "northern" route to Europe, via Sweden and Denmark, or the "western" route, by way of Poland and Germany. Interestingly, many Lithuanians favor the northern route mainly because it does not involve going by way of Poland, which is still seen here as a historic oppressor.

Romualdas Ozolas, a small, wiry, bristling opposition MP, has a sticker on his office wall in the blue and yellow colors of the European Union. It proclaims, "My Country Europe." Is that his sentiment? *"Ja,"* he says, in his somewhat broken German, *"genau!"* And what is Europe? Strutting up and down, he barks a short and definite answer: *"Europa ist . . . nicht-Russland!"* "Europe is not Russia." Well, that is one definition—and far from just a Lithuanian one. (It's just that the Lithuanians are naive enough to say so.)

Our wide-ranging geopolitical discussion is interrupted by a sharp knock at the door. A young journalist from the sensationalist newspaper *Respublika* comes in and, without so much as an "Excuse me," thrusts a tape recorder under Mr. Ozolas's nose. Mr. Ozolas delivers a few well-chosen words, and the journalist exits as abruptly as he entered.

Playing on the popular theme of political corruption, *Respublika* has offered a large reward to any politician who can prove—against the best efforts of their investigative journalist—that he (or she) is not corrupt. Since politicians have not exactly been rushing to apply, the newspaper has started nominating candidates, allegedly on the basis of a poll of its readers. Mr. Ozolas has been thus nominated. He has just told that probing young Lithuanian Woodward 'n' Bernstein that he would not be accepting the kind offer. *"Ich sage,"* he explains, *"ich nicht nehme, weil ich habe Auto gekauft!"* After further inquiries, I finally establish that, along with other MPs, he had voted himself a car at what was, in effect, a subsidized price.

Saint Petersburg

After a long, cold wait, the Lithuanian Airlines twin-prop just starts up and goes—no safety drill; no "This is your steward speaking." The emergency exit next to me rattles like a loose mudguard.

At Saint Petersburg Airport, however, I am met by a Volvo stretch limo and swept into the Grand Hotel Europe—a Swedish-Russian joint venture and luxurious even by Western standards. "No detail has been overlooked," says the room card, "in creating an authentic Russian environment with all the comforts and services of today." Authentic Russian environment, my foot!

The contrast with the city just beyond the hotel doors is extreme. There, poorly dressed crowds trudge grimly along the muddy pavements—although some stop to indulge in that curious Russian pastime of eating ice cream in the snow. The facades look grubbier than when I was last in (then still) Leningrad, but perhaps it is just the season. What is certainly new is the proliferation of street traders, hawkers, con men, and beggars.

I am here for what turns out to be a fascinating conference, organized by the Hamburg-based Bergedorfer Gesprächskreis with the participation of the German defense minister and the Russian deputy defense minister. Two things strike me particularly. One is that, whereas in Central Europe the central historical reference point is the period before 1939, here it is clearly the period before 1917. This extends even to details of dress and manner. The smart aide-de-camp to the Russian minister looks like an oil painting of a First World War officer. The German military men, by contrast, look like managers in uniform.

The other, more serious, thing is just how difficult even those whom I know to be very liberal Russians find it, emotionally as much as intellectually, to accept the loss of empire. Although the West in general, and the Clinton administration in particular, has done everything to avoid a Versailles-type humiliation, they still feel humiliated. In this, as in other respects, it really is "Weimar Russia."

The crucial psychological test case is not the Baltic states—although Russia's relationship with them is difficult enough, especially because of the position of the Russian minorities there and the Russian military exclave of Kaliningrad. The test is Ukraine. With the best will in the world, most Russians I talk to find it difficult to accept the idea that Ukraine can really be an independent state.

One evening we are treated by Mayor Sobchak to a splendid reception in the extraordinary Yusupov Palace, with its rooms of onyx, marble, and tooled leather, its white-and-gold ballroom, and its own small theater, complete with plush stalls, circle, and the family box. After the usual banquet of *zakuski,* vodka, and speeches, we are shown down to the room in which Prince Feliks Yusupov and his fellow conspirators attempted to poison Rasputin. A wax model of the lubricious monk sits at a table laid with his favorite sweet wine and cakes, while the clean-shaven young prince looks on. A smartly dressed lady guide, exuding perfume and national pride, tells us every last detail of that gruesome night: how the poison was not sufficient to fell the immensely strong Rasputin, how he staggered out into the courtyard, how the conspirators finished him off, how they disposed (or failed to dispose) of the body. His ghost, you feel, has still not quite been laid to rest.

CHRONOLOGY

1 9 9 4

1 APRIL. *Hungary becomes the first postcommunist state to apply for membership in the EU.*

26 APRIL. *The United States, Britain, France, Germany, and Russia form the Contact Group for coordinating policy toward former Yugoslavia. Polish president Lech Wałęsa visits Lithuania and signs a treaty of friendship and cooperation.*

APRIL. *Bosnian Serbs attack the UN "safe haven" of Goražde. The first NATO air strikes on Bosnian Serb forces are abandoned after Bosnian Serbs threaten UN troops.*

6 MAY. *Queen Elizabeth II and President François Mitterrand open the Channel Tunnel between Britain and France.*

11 MAY. *Silvio Berlusconi becomes prime minister of Italy.*

17–19 MAY. Milan: so rich; so beautiful its women; so stylish its men; so glorious its food. I am here at the invitation of my publisher, Mondadori, which is owned by Berlusconi, although the politics of the editors I meet are very different from his. They give me a few glimpses of the crisis that has engulfed the whole Italian political system. One tells me, "You know, we in Milan knew there were politicians in Rome, just as we knew that there are wild boar in the forests of Tuscany." They were strange, remote creatures, southern lawyers and Roman wheeler-dealers. "But now, suddenly, they are real people—even people we actually know."

Berlusconi, I am told, started his eruption into Italian politics by conducting extensive and sophisticated opinion polls. Having found out what people wanted, he then offered it to them, wrapped in glittering paper and sold with the latest advertising techniques on the television channels that he owns. It's almost a parable—or is it a parody?—of contemporary television democracy.

I am taken to a television chat show that addresses the question of whether there is any connection between the success of the Milan football club, owned by Berlusconi, and his recent triumph in politics. Is politics like football? The presenter, himself of the left, suggests one parallel. Berlusconi's success in football, he observes, comes from buying players.

20 MAY. *The Crimean assembly approves an effective declaration of sovereignty.*

20–23 MAY. Sintra, Portugal. Byron's "Eden." A moorish castle, fantastic villas, and exotic trees, their tops disappearing into the hillside mists. What does this small country, at the westernmost end of Europe, helped on its journey from dictatorship to democracy by the prospect and then the reality of joining the European Community, think of doing the same for the small, fragile new democracies in the eastern mists? The answer, roughly, is "We'd really like to support them, as we ourselves were supported, just so long as it doesn't take any of the money that we get from the EU." The money that has, for example, paid for the motorway we drove down on our way from Lisbon.

Talking of money, the Portuguese are determined to be a founding member of the European monetary union. But won't the participation of currencies such as theirs mean that the new single currency will be softer than the deutsche mark? "Yes, exactly," says a former finance minister. "That's just what we want."

23 MAY. *Roman Herzog is elected president of Germany, succeeding Richard von Weizsäcker.*

26–27 MAY. *The inaugural conference for a Pact on Stability in Europe is held in Paris.*

27 MAY. *Alexander Solzhenitsyn returns to Russia.*

29 MAY. *The former East German leader Erich Honecker dies in Chile. Former communists, now called socialists, win parliamentary elections in Hungary.*

30 MAY. *A new currency, the* kuna, *is introduced in Croatia and in Croatian-controlled parts of Bosnia.*

1 JUNE. *Partial legalization of euthanasia in the Netherlands.*

6 JUNE. *Politicians and veterans commemorate the fiftieth anniversary of the D-Day landings in Normandy. Germans are not invited to participate.*

FATHERS AND SONS

LIKE MANY BRITISH CHILDREN OF MY GENERATION, I GREW UP AMID tales of D-Day and the memories of war. When I was six or seven, my mother showed me the citation for my father's Military Cross: "He landed on 6th June 1944 with the first assault wave of 6th Battalion The Green Howards and in the bitter and continuous fighting in the Normandy bridgehead his coolness and disregard of danger were quickly apparent. . . . His conduct, bravery and devotion to duty throughout the whole campaign are deserving of the highest praise." With all their formulaic stiffness, the words move me as deeply now as they did then.

When my children were about the same age, I sat them on a tank outside the D-Day museum in Bayeux and told them how their grandfather had fought to liberate Europe from Nazism. There are few satisfactions to compare with that of passing on history with pride. "This story shall the good man teach his son . . ." It is a satisfaction that many Polish friends of my generation can share, but only a very few German ones. For, while their fathers often fought with extraordinary courage, resourcefulness, and, yes, devotion to duty, they did so in an abominable cause. The brave men and women of the resistance whom Germany will commemorate on 20 July, the fiftieth anniversary of Count Stauffenberg's attempt to assassinate Hitler, are the exceptions.

Yet the subsequent fifty years offer Germany some other causes for quiet pride. Last weekend, I took my eldest son, Thomas, now ten, to visit his godfather in Berlin. Thomas's godfather, Werner Krätschell, is an East German priest with a remarkable story. When East Germany was cut off from the West by the building of the Berlin Wall, in August 1961, Werner was on holiday in the West. He made an extraordinary decision. While thousands of East Germans were still desperately trying to get out, he decided to go back. "People will need me there," he said. And they certainly did. For twenty-eight long years, Werner did what a churchman could do to alleviate the suffering caused by the communist dictatorship, with quiet courage and devotion to duty. And this story, too, shall the good man teach his son . . .

Thomas can be proud both of his grandfather and of his godfather. That is a fine beginning. But if one takes the argument from the individual to the collective, from single people to the nations to which they belong, things are not so easy. So much of our national pride still derives from our part in the defeat of Nazism, and this is remembered not just as a defeat of Hitler but also as a defeat of Germany. Now Thomas's history teacher at the Dragon School in Oxford will remind him of the complicating truth that the Wehrmacht's back was broken by the Red Army, fighting in the service of another tyrant. But in the British memory it is "the longest day." And before that "the finest hour."

Yet, read again today, Churchill's famous remark about the Battle of Britain—"if the British Empire and its Commonwealth last for a thousand years, men will still say, 'This was their finest hour' "—seems to contain the hint of a dark premonition: There might not be many more fine hours to follow. It is, I think, really a little worrying that a British schoolboy in the 1990s is still expected to derive so much of his national pride from the achievements of fifty years ago, as if nothing really important had been done since. But of course he asks questions. What *has* happened since? Is Britain or Germany now the richer and more powerful country? Which has the stronger currency? And it is not easy to avoid, in the substance if not in the phrasing, the hoary old cliché that "Britain won the war but Germany won the peace."

Germany has a different problem—or, rather, the other side of the same one. It was well illustrated by the little rumpus last year

about Chancellor Kohl's possible participation in this year's ceremonies to mark the fiftieth anniversary of D-Day. Denying that
Chancellor Kohl had ever sought to be included, his spokesman remarked at a press conference, "Do you seriously think that the chancellor would wish to take part in a ceremony [marking an event] in
which German soldiers suffered a defeat?" While the spokesman
subsequently elaborated his off-the-cuff remark—the chancellor, he
added, would not want to celebrate the German victories of 1870 either—it in fact perfectly encapsulates a deep ambivalence about a
liberation that was also a defeat.

My father, who as I write these lines is once again embarked for
Normandy, felt the Germans should not be invited to the veterans'
commemoration. It seems to me that the veterans have an absolute
right to say this. They risked their lives so that others—including the
Germans—could be free. They must decide. But, insofar as the
commemoration is also an act of contemporary states, this was, I
think, a missed opportunity.

A missed opportunity, above all, for Germany. Had the German
president, Richard von Weizsäcker, been invited to participate in
some form—and, as head of the state, he would have been the appropriate person to invite—he would have had the opportunity to
deliver one more great speech, comparable to that which he delivered on the fortieth anniversary of V-E Day in May 1985.

This speech would have explained how the defeat of the German
armies meant liberation even for the soldiers who were defeated.
How everything that has been achieved in Germany over the past
fifty years—security, prosperity, democracy, and, finally, unity—
began with and was founded upon that total defeat and uncondi-
tional surrender that precluded any but the civilian path to recovery.
How, in short, the defeat of Germany was a victory for Germany. (He
might have added, but would have been too diplomatic to do so, that
Russia today faces a rather similar question—was the end of the
cold war a defeat for Russia or just for Soviet communism?—but in
a situation more like that of Germany in 1918 than that of Germany
in 1945. For Russia, even more than for Weimar Germany, the military option still remains very much available.)

The German president's great speech would have concluded by

explaining why this memory is still important for a united, fully sovereign Germany, the richest and most powerful country in Europe. For if the danger for Britain is that we dwell too much on the past, often in romanticized, Merchant-Ivory colors, the danger for Germany is now rather the opposite.

The public memory of the old, preunification Federal Republic dwelled almost obsessively on the Nazi past. Everything the Bonn republic did was interpreted in the light of "the past"—meaning the twelve years of Hitler. But, even then, the private memory was rather different. James Fenton captured this wonderfully in a poem called "A German Requiem," which he wrote when living in Berlin in the late 1970s: "How comforting it is, once or twice a year,/To get together and forget the old times." And again: "But come. Grief must have its term? Guilt too, then."

With unification has come a strong inclination to say, "Enough is enough." Germany has done its penance through forty years of division, with the East Germans, such as Werner Krätschell, bearing a disproportionate part of the burden. You cannot walk forever in sackcloth and ashes. What matters now is for the new republic, the Berlin republic, to concentrate on building Europe's future. Anyway, the German past is more than just those twelve years. There are other aspects of German history, before 1933, after 1945, even a very few between those dates, about which Germans can be proud—patriotic, even.

This reaction is not only understandable but right and proper—up to a point. The task, the extraordinarily delicate task, for Germany's political, intellectual, and spiritual leaders is to determine: up to what point?

Now, one of the passages of history that I think is already slipping down the memory hole is the specifically British contribution not just to the liberation of Germany from Nazism but also to the reconstruction of what was to become West Germany after 1945, the defense of West Berlin, and the secure position in the West from which the Federal Republic could develop its own relations with the East. I am struck by the extent to which, in the German public debate, the three Western Allies have really become two: France and the United States. (German politicians and officials will of course deny this—unconvincingly.)

This has happened partly because France and the United States have known how to combine the proper memory of war with effective signs of reconciliation—like the "Eurocorps," in whose ranks German troops will march through Paris on 14 July. But it is even more because France and the United States both seem to have some vision of a new partnership with Germany in Europe, while Britain does not. At which it will be the turn of British politicians and officials to protest—unconvincingly.

In 1944, Britain had a policy for Europe: to liberate as much of it as possible and then to help reconstruct it. Fifty years on, Britain has neither a policy for Europe nor any coherent vision of our own place in Europe. If we carry on like this, I fear to think what my sons will have left to teach their children.

CHRONOLOGY

1994

9 AND 12 JUNE. *Direct elections to the European Parliament.*

12 JUNE. *In a referendum, 66.4 percent of Austrian voters support their country joining the EU.*

22 JUNE. *Russia signs a Partnership for Peace agreement with NATO.*

24 JUNE. *The UN endorses deployment of Russian "peacekeeping" forces in Abkhazia, which has effectively seceded from Georgia.*

24–25 JUNE. *An EU summit in Corfu. Signature of accession treaties for Austria, Finland, Sweden, and Norway. A partnership and cooperation agreement is signed with Russia.*

2 JULY. *Former Albanian president Ramiz Alia is condemned to nine years in prison for abuse of power.*

6 JULY. *The Contact Group unveils its proposal for division of Bosnia, giving 51 percent of the territory to the Bosniak-Croat federation and 49 percent to the Bosnian Serbs.*

10 JULY. *Leonid Kuchma, a former director of a missile factory, is elected president of Ukraine. Alexander Lukashenka is elected president of Belarus on a pro-Russian and anticorruption platform.*

12 JULY. *The German Constitutional Court decides that it is constitutional for German forces to participate in operations outside the NATO area.*

15 JULY. *Jacques Santer is appointed president of the European Commission as of 1 January 1995. A new Hungarian government is formed, with postdissident Free Democrats serving under postcommunist prime minister Gyula Horn. Horn promises a "historic reconciliation" with Romania.*

23 JULY. *Tony Blair becomes leader of the British Labour Party.*

29 JULY. *Former Italian prime minister Bettino Craxi is sentenced to*

eight and a half years' imprisonment for fraudulent bankruptcy but remains in Tunisia, enjoying "ill health."

5 AUGUST. *The Federal Republic of Yugoslavia imposes an economic blockade on Bosnian Serbs.*

29 AUGUST. *The Basque terrorist organisation ETA calls on six hundred imprisoned members to go on hunger strike.*

29–30 AUGUST. *The last Russian forces leave Estonia and Latvia.*

31 AUGUST. *The IRA declares a cease-fire in Northern Ireland.*

1 SEPTEMBER. *The last Russian troops leave Berlin, completing their withdrawal from Germany.*

6 SEPTEMBER. *Irish prime minister Albert Reynolds meets Sinn Fein leader Gerry Adams and SDLP leader John Hume to talk about peaceful solutions in Northern Ireland.*

8 SEPTEMBER. *The United States, Britain, and France withdraw their remaining troops from Berlin. The last Soviet forces leave Poland.*

SEPTEMBER–NOVEMBER. *NATO member Turkey threatens war against NATO member Greece if the latter extends its territorial waters in the Aegean.*

1 OCTOBER. *Vladimír Mečiar's Movement for a Democratic Slovakia wins the Slovak parliamentary elections.*

7 OCTOBER. *Swedish social democrats return to power, with Ingvar Carlsson as prime minister. Ex-king Michael of Romania is refused entry at Bucharest airport.*

16 OCTOBER. *In a referendum, Finns vote to join the EU. Bundestag elections in Germany.*

INTELLECTUALS AND POLITICIANS

IMAGINE A THEATER CRITIC WHO IS SUDDENLY HAULED UP FROM THE stalls to act in the play he meant to review. What should he do then? Write the review without mentioning his own part? Appraise his own performance? This is the strange dilemma in which I find myself as I sit down to write this essay. Yet it is a dilemma curiously appropriate to the subject—as will, I trust, emerge. Let me explain.

Earlier this year, I received a letter informing me that I had been elected an honorary member of Czech PEN. I was touched by the gesture. The letter also invited me to attend the Sixty-first World Congress of International PEN, which would be held in Prague in November.

Now there is a great deal to be said against attending any international congress of writers, anywhere, any time. But Prague is a city where writers and intellectuals, especially the numerous banned writers and intellectuals, published only in samizdat or in the West, had a singular importance up to 1989. This occasion was to take place five years to the month after the "revolution of the Magic Lantern" that had catapulted many of them quite unexpectedly into positions of power, which some retain but others have in the meantime left or lost.[1] Those characteristic postcommunist mutations, dilemmas, and ironies are concentrated—almost as in an archetype—in the person of the writer-president Václav Havel. All this, I thought, might make this particular writers' congress more than usually interesting.

It did.

1

On the plane out, I looked back through my notebooks from the heady days of November 1989 in the Magic Lantern theater, and recalled the leading actors in the play then directed by and starring Václav Havel. Among my visiting cards I found one given me in the Magic Lantern by someone who, at the time, had only a minor part—as an economist prized for his professional expertise by the writers, philosophers, journalists, and historians then leading the Civic Forum. I have the card before me as I write. Actually nothing more than a typewritten slip of paper, it reads, "Dr. Václav Klaus, Head of Department for Macroeconomic Analysis, Institute for Forecasting, Czechoslovak Academy of Sciences."

In Prague, I soon found that the position of intellectuals was very much a live subject and one that, like so many others in the Czech lands today, had come to be politicized around the, so to speak, magnetic polarity between the two Václavs, now better known as President Havel and Prime Minister Klaus. Havel was understood to be calling for the voices of independent intellectuals to be heard more clearly, enriching the country's political debate. Klaus, the intellectual anti-intellectual, was heard to be skeptical of this notion, both on general grounds and because Havel was for it.

I talked briefly to the prime minister in the days before the PEN congress opened. Dr. Klaus received me in his tastefully appointed office, its walls decorated with framed honorary doctorates, prizes, and photographs of himself with very important persons. In the course of an interesting conversation, mainly about Europe, he thrust into my hands a selection of his lectures and speeches from the last three years, which he had gotten his office to type up, photocopy, and bind. This collector's item of, as it were, prime-ministerial samizdat—entitled *Dismantling Socialism: An Interim Report*—documents well his characteristic mixture of sharp economic analysis and bold political salesmanship. Helpfully, he pointed out the best pieces.

The PEN congress itself was opened by President Havel. Welcoming his fellow writers from around the world "first and foremost as a colleague and only secondarily as a representative of the Czech

Republic," he went on to express the hope that our presence would "introduce important spiritual and intellectual stimuli into this sometimes too materialistic and somewhat provincial setting." Intellectuals, he argued, have a responsibility to engage in "politics in the broadest sense of the word." And not just in the broadest sense:

> I once asked a friend of mine, a wonderful man and a wonderful writer, to fill a certain political post. He refused, arguing that someone had to remain independent. I replied that if you all said that, it could happen that in the end no one will be independent, because there won't be anyone around to make that independence possible and stand behind it.

However, "I am not suggesting, dear colleagues, that you all become presidents in your own countries, or that each of you go out and start a political party." But we should, he suggested,

> gradually begin to create something like a worldwide lobby, a special brotherhood or, if I may use the word, a somewhat conspiratorial mafia, whose aim is not just to write marvelous books or occasional manifestos but to have an impact on politics and its human perceptions in a spirit of solidarity and in a coordinated, deliberate way.

He continued:

> Politicians—at least the wiser ones—will not reject such activity but, on the contrary, will welcome it. I, for instance, would welcome hearing, in this country, a really strong and eloquent voice coming from my colleagues, one that could not be ignored no matter how critical it might be, a voice that did more than merely grumble or engage in esoteric reflection but became a clear public and political fact.

He then concluded with an eloquent appeal for us all to stand up for Salman Rushdie, for Wole Soyinka, and for Bosnian intellectuals. Emboldened by this speech, the assembled PEN delegates could begin their usual round of reports, resolutions, and the all-important business of supporting persecuted and imprisoned writers—work in which Czech writers who had themselves long been persecuted or imprisoned could now join. But you could see at once (though I'm not sure how many of the international PEN delegates did see at once) that Havel's speech was addressed to the domestic audience as much as to us. And it was a blow—a pen thrust—at Klaus, whom Czech readers, radio listeners, or television viewers would immediately understand not to be among those "wiser" politicians who would welcome independent intellectual criticism.

Indeed, that very day, Czech readers could find in the newspaper *Lidové Noviny* a column by Václav Klaus rejecting, in the name of liberalism, the demand recently made by a group of intellectuals that the showing of violence on television be regulated by the state. President Havel had come out in support of the intellectuals' petition.

In the evening, the prime minister, who as a regular newspaper columnist and essayist is himself a member of Czech PEN, gave a reception for the PEN delegates. His speech of welcome was also in part an answer to Havel's welcome speech in the morning, thus producing further symptoms of slight bafflement among those delegates who thought they were just attending a writers' congress. As we left the reception, officials distributed free copies of two books (in Czech) by Klaus, almost as if to say, "Look, *he* writes books too!" One of the books is called *Why Am I a Conservative?* and begins with a glowing tribute to Margaret Thatcher, entitled "Inspiration."[2]

The next day there was a panel discussion on the very general theme of "Intellectuals, Government Policy, and Tolerance" in a large hall at the foreign ministry. The most prominent panelist was none other than the writer-premier Václav Klaus. He was joined on the platform by the Hungarian essayist György Konrád (himself a former president of International PEN and someone who has written extensively on the role of intellectuals), the Czech novelist Ivan Klíma, writers from Germany, Sweden, and Turkey, and myself. Extracts from the discussion were to be broadcast on Czech television. Good press coverage for the prime minister among these intellectuals would no doubt enhance his public image, which might be useful in the imminent local-government elections. In fact, the prime minister was going straight from this discussion to campaign for his party in the provinces.

Before the discussion, we were handed copies of an essay on tolerance, nicely printed in five languages. And whom was the essay by? Comenius? John Locke? Voltaire? No, by Václav Klaus. That philosopher of tolerance then opened the discussion with a remarkable short statement in which he announced that in a free country, such as the Czech Republic had now become, the distinction between "dependent" and "independent" intellectuals no longer had any real importance. Some intellectuals were in politics, others not. Expert advice was always welcome. But it made no sense to speak any more about a special role for "independent" intellectuals.

Now the critic was hauled onstage. For this sally could not go unanswered. I began my reply by saying that it was both appropriate and moving to discuss the subject of "Intellectuals, Government Policy, and Tolerance" in Prague, where, for twenty-one long years, from the Soviet invasion of 1968 until the "velvet revolution," some individual Czechs—and Slovaks—had given us a shining example of what intellectuals can do in opposition to a repressive state. The names of Jan Patočka and Václav Havel must stand for many, many more whom I would have liked to name.

Five years on, however, we happily found ourselves in very different times in Central Europe. What was the role of intellectuals now? I argued, against Klaus, that independence is a crucial attribute of what it should mean to be an intellectual. Not just in a dictatorship but precisely in a liberal, democratic state, independent intellectuals have a crucial role to play.

There should be, I suggested, a necessarily adversarial (but not necessarily hostile) relationship between the independent intellectual and the professional politician. The intellectual's job is to seek the truth and then to present it as fully and clearly and interestingly as possible. The politician's job is to work in half-truth. The very word *party* implies partial, one-sided. The Czech word for party, *strana,* meaning literally *side,* says it even more clearly. Of course, the opposition parties then present the other side, the other half of the truth. But this is one of those strange cases where two halves don't make a whole.

The position of a nonexecutive president or constitutional monarch may, I noted, be a partial exception to this rule. Such a person, standing above party politics, may contribute to setting certain higher intellectual or moral standards in public life. But as a rule, there is a necessary and healthy division of labor in a liberal state between independent intellectuals and professional politicians. Arguably, this is as important as the formal separation of powers between executive, legislature, and judiciary. It is part of the larger and all-important creative tension between the state and civil society.

Having made my main point about "intellectuals," I commented briefly on the other words in the theme that PEN had asked us to discuss: "government policy and tolerance." The liberal state—but mainly the legislature and the judiciary rather than the executive branch of government—may sometimes have to limit the freedom of the enemies of freedom. If, say, a private television channel were to mix popular light entertainment with consistent advocacy of the extermination of Gypsies, a liberal state should stop it being used for that purpose. If a writer is threatened from abroad with assassination, like Salman Rushdie, the government has a duty to protect him.

Beyond this, however, the contribution of politicians in power to "tolerance" lies less in specific acts or policies than in a certain attitude and style of political conduct. No politician likes being criticized. Mrs. Thatcher often complained about "the media." Her successors blame "the chattering classes," which, I noted, is the current English phrase for intellectuals. Yet the closer the politicians can stick to the attitude summed up in the famous phrase "I do not agree with what you say, but I will defend to the death your right to say it," the more secure freedom will be. This, I suggested, is where the business of PEN and the business of prime ministers meet.

Now if these thoughts were expressed around a seminar table at Harvard or Oxford they might be questioned for their simplicity or banality, but they would hardly be thought provocative.[3] Here, with the Czech television cameras rolling and the famously arrogant prime minister locked in this strange intellectual-political wrestling match with his own president, they were accounted so.

Dr. Klaus was not amused by my comments. He wanted to reply immediately. He sat fuming while our strong-minded American chairwoman let all the other panelists have their turn. Then he let rip. In his essay on tolerance, he had written, "The responsibility of a tolerant person is to listen attentively to others and to attempt to understand what they are saying." This was not my experience of Dr. Klaus. Instead, I found him a sharp political debater, happy to twist an argument in order to score a point. But then, what else would you expect of a politician sitting in front of TV cameras at the beginning of an election campaign?

Yet by behaving in this way, he actually made my point far more effectively than I could myself. If he had listened attentively and then calmly made a reasoned argument in response to mine, he would have brilliantly illustrated his own proposition that there is no fundamental difference or clear dividing line between the roles of independent intellectual and professional politician. There he would have been: a professional politician, yet arguing as an intellectual among intellectuals.

But, instead, he began by exclaiming, in his peculiarly effective tone of aggressive exasperation, that he found what I had said "incredible." He knew me as an intellectual, an essayist, he said, but I had just delivered a "political speech." But there again he was, in a backhanded way, making my point. For the criticism has meaning only if there is, indeed, a fundamental difference between an intellectual speech and a political speech, between the way intellectuals use words and the way politicians do.

He went on to say that there is nothing worse than an intellectual delivering a political speech. Politicians may not like to be criticized, he observed, but do intellectuals? And he also found "incredible" my observation that politicians "live in half-truth." This was a rather revealing misquotation, since one of the most famous leitmotifs in the whole Central European debate about intellectuals and politics is Václav Havel's pre-1989 formula "living in truth." But what I said was that politicians *work* in half-truth.[4] The phrase characterizes the professional party politician's job, not his life.

No politician worthy of the name will seriously maintain in private that what he has said in a public, party-political speech is the whole truth on a particular issue. It may possibly have been the truth; it might even have been nothing but the truth; but it is most unlikely to have been the whole truth—or he will not be a very effective party politician. Every time a politician says to a journalist, "Off the record," he is recognizing this elementary fact about his profession. Off the record, Václav Klaus would doubtless acknowledge this.

Here I need to explicate two issues that were not clarified in the subsequent discussion—partly, I would have to add as a critic, through my own fault. Both were raised by Ivan Klíma, in interventions that effectively supported his prime minister. First, Klíma objected to what he saw as the implication that intellectuals are morally superior to politicians or somehow possessed of "Truth" with a capital *T*. We have heard too much of these claims, especially in Central Europe, suggested Klíma, in a discussion which we had begun earlier and subsequently continued in private.

Look what a mess intellectuals in power have made of things! Look at the damage done by their utopias! And look what monsters they have been in their private lives! In which connection he quoted Paul Johnson's book *Intellectuals*. The charge about private lives is probably the least pertinent, but there is much in the rest of the indictment. Intellectuals obviously do bear a heavy load of responsibility as architects or accomplices of some of the greatest political crimes of the twentieth century. As George Orwell caustically observed of fellow-traveling intellectuals, "No ordinary man could be such a fool."

Yet I am not making any such high moral, let alone ideological or metaphysical, claim for intellectuals. Many politicians are no doubt better people than many intellectuals. They may also be more intelligent, better read, more cultured. My argument is only that they have, and should have, a different role, which is reflected, crucially, in a different use of language. If a politician gives a partial, one-sided, indeed self-censored account of a particular issue, he is simply doing his job. And if he manages to "sell" the part as the whole, then he is doing his job effectively.

If an intellectual does that, he is not doing his job: He has failed in it. The intellectual is not the guardian or high priest of some metaphysical, ideological, or pseudoscientific Truth with a capital *T*. Nor is he simply the voice of the "ethics of conviction" (*Gesin-*

nungsethik) against the politician's "ethics of responsibility" (*Verantwortungsethik*), to use Max Weber's famous distinction. But he does have a qualitatively different responsibility for the validity, intellectual coherence, and truth of what he says and writes.

I therefore have an answer to the question that Ivan Klíma injected into the discussion: "What do you mean by an intellectual?" What I mean is a person playing a particular role. It is the role of the thinker or writer who engages in public discussion of issues of public policy, in politics in the broadest sense, while deliberately not engaging in the pursuit of political power.

I certainly don't mean all members of the "intelligentsia," in the broad sociological definition of *intelligentsia* officially adopted in communist Eastern Europe; that is, everyone with higher education. Nor do I mean the "intellectuals on the road to class power" of György Konrád and Ivan Szelényi's book of 1974.[5] Or the pre-1989 Václav Klaus, an employee of the Czechoslovak Academy of Sciences under President Husák. These were all intellectuals, but in a different sense.

My description of the intellectual's role, which is both a Weberian ideal type and simply an ideal, certainly has more in common with the self-understanding of the opposition intellectuals in Central and Eastern Europe before 1989; of the pre-1989 Václav Havel (who barely qualified as an "intellectual" in communist sociology, since he had scant formal higher education and for a time did manual labor); of the patriotic Polish, Czech, or Hungarian "intelligentsia," in their idealistic, pre- and anticommunist interpretation of their own role. Yet it differs also fundamentally from this. In the "abnormal" conditions that have actually been normality for much of Central Europe over much of the last two centuries, intellectuals have been called upon, or have felt themselves called upon, to take roles that they did not take in the West. The conscience of the nation. The voice of the oppressed. The writer as priest, prophet, resistance fighter, and substitute politician.

Since the liberation of 1989, all these extra roles have fallen away with stunning rapidity. This is healthy and long overdue. As Brecht's Galileo exclaims, "Unhappy the land that has need of heroes." The role of the intellectual as critic of a democratically elected government cannot be equated with that of the intellectual as leader of the opposition against an alien, totalitarian power. But I am deeply convinced that Hans Morgenthau expressed a universal and not a particular truth when he observed: Truth threatens power, and power threatens truth. That applies not just to totalitarian or authoritarian power, as described in Václav Havel's great essay "The Power of the Powerless," but also, albeit to a lesser degree, to democratically elected and constitutionally limited power.

Now, obviously, this ideal of the intellectual has never fully been achieved. Indeed, as the twentieth century closes, the catalog of the *trahison des clercs* is a thick volume; the list of those who preserved real independence is a thin one. In our own free societies, we see examples of journalists who have been corrupted by their proximity to power. American academics will perhaps know, in their own universities, scholars who have politically trimmed their analyses, or at least their conclusions, in the hope of following Kissinger or Brzezinski to a job in Washington. But to say that an ideal has never fully been achieved is merely to say that it is an ideal.

We have Orwell. We have Raymond Aron. We have other writers, academics, and journalists who have maintained a high standard of intellectual independence while engaging in political debate. Even in a free society, there is still an important part to be played by the *spectateur engagé*. By the critic on stage.

2

And by the playwright on stage? Václav Havel was, of course, the invisible panelist in our discussion. Klaus certainly interpreted much of what I said in the light of his running argument with Havel. Doubtless many Czech listeners did. And from what I have written so far you might also think that I was, so to speak, taking Havel's part—breaking a lance for Václav I against Václav II. That would be a misunderstanding.

It is wholly true that I feel strong ties of admiration for and friendship with Václav Havel. It will also be clear that I think he is right to argue that independent intellectuals should take an active part in the public life of a democracy. Yet I also have a serious disagreement with him about the role that intellectuals can play in politics, in the narrow sense of competing for power and holding office. The sharp distinction I drew on that panel between the roles of the intellectual and of the politician is one that ever since Havel became president of Czechoslovakia at the end of 1989 he has consistently refused to accept. As it happened, I went straight from the panel discussion in the foreign ministry to a lively private discussion with the president on precisely this issue, in the more congenial surroundings of a riverside pub. (György Konrád also came from the panel to the pub and joined cannily in the debate.)

Now on this particular issue, a discussion with Havel is obviously far more important than any argument with Klaus. Klaus will be judged on his record as a politician and on his very considerable achievements in the rapid transformation of the Czech economy. Despite his at times almost comical desire to be taken seriously as a writer, his views on intellectuals are, so to speak, an optional extra. By contrast, the subject is central to Havel's whole life and work. His essays, lectures, and prison letters from the last quarter century are, taken altogether, among the most vivid, sustained, and searching explorations of the moral and political responsibility of the intellectual produced anywhere in Europe. Indeed, it is difficult to think of any figure in the contemporary world who has more cumulative authority to speak on this issue than Václav Havel.

If you said "the intellectual and politics" in the 1960s, the immediate free association might be Sartre or perhaps Bertrand Russell. Say it now, whether in Paris, New York, Berlin, or Rome, and one of the first associations will be Havel. If he is right, what he says will be important not just for the Czech lands; if he is wrong, it matters for the rest of us too.

Fortunately, I don't just have to rely on a pub conversation for this judgment. Three volumes of Havel's speeches have now appeared in Czech, and a Prague publisher has just issued a selection in English, entitled *Toward a Civil Society.*[6] Although the English selection is biased heavily toward his major foreign appearances and to that extent gives a slightly misleading impression of what he has been doing for the last five years, it does contain the most important and systematic statements of his views since he became president. Havel told me that he regards his presidential speeches as the intellectual continuation of the essays, lectures, and prison letters of the dissident years. "Then I wrote essays, now I write speeches," he said, suggesting that only the form of what he does with words has changed, not the essential content of the intellectual activity.

Certainly as presidential speeches go, these are extraordinary. Extraordinary in the range of subjects they address, from Maastricht to the Anthropic Cosmological Principle, from European security to the legacy of the Czechoslovak security police, from Kafka to the need for a higher something that Havel cannot quite bring himself to call God. Extraordinary in their literary quality. Extraordinary in their frank and vivid insights based, like his earlier work, on a kind of wry agonizing about his own existential dilemmas. Since his present dilemma—or, at least, one of them—is that of the intellectual in politics, there is much on that in his speeches. And sometimes in unlikely places.

Nearly two years ago, a mutual friend brought me, with the president's greetings, the typescript of a speech delivered in the Asahi Hall in Tokyo in April 1992 and now reproduced in this volume. The speech is devoted to the place of the intellectual in politics. Having described the peculiar postcommunist situation in which "poets, philosophers, singers became members of Parliament, government ministers or even presidents," he proceeds to take issue with "a British friend of mine" who "has said that one of the biggest problems of the postcommunist states lies in the inability of their leaders to make up their minds about who they are. Are they independent intellectuals or practising politicians?"

Having explained that he understands only too well what I have in mind, he goes on to ask if this may actually be "not a dilemma, but a historic challenge? What if in fact it challenged them to introduce a new tone, a new element, a new dimension into politics?" Based on their specific experience under totalitarianism, might they not inject "a new wind, [a] new spirit, a new spirituality . . . into the established stereotypes of present-day politics?" Faced with the huge challenges of overpopulation, poverty, pollution, ethnic and social unrest, what is needed is a change "in the sphere of the spirit, of human consciousness and self-knowledge."

Politics is increasingly becoming the domain of specialists, but it should be the domain of people

with a heightened sense of responsibility and heightened understanding for the mysterious complexity of Being. If intellectuals claim to be such people, they would virtually be denying the truth of that claim if they refused to take upon themselves the burden of public offices on the grounds that it would mean dirtying their hands. Those who say that politics is disreputable in fact help make it so.

He does not know, he says in conclusion, who will be proved right, but he regards it as "a challenge to take a great risk and launch a great adventure. It is up to those of us whom fate has put in this position to demonstrate whether my British friend has shown foresight, or has simply been too influenced by the banal idea that everyone should stick to his own trade."

Heaven only knows what the Japanese audience made of the president from Prague conducting a long-range discussion with someone in Oxford from a platform in Tokyo. But the result is certainly one of the clearest and fullest statements of his position. Elsewhere, he restates and elaborates on various parts of it. Right at the outset, in his 1990 New Year's address, he expresses the hope that the new Czechoslovakia can "permanently radiate love, understanding, the power of the spirit and of ideas," with a new version of the founding president Tomáš Garrigue Masaryk's concept of politics based on morality. ("Jesus, not Caesar," as Masaryk famously wrote.)

"If the hope of the world lies in human consciousness," Havel tells a joint session of the U.S. Congress in February 1990, "then it is obvious that intellectuals cannot go on forever avoiding their share of responsibility for the world and hiding their distaste for politics under an alleged need to be independent." And he says there what he repeated in opening the PEN congress nearly five years later: that if everyone remained independent then in the end nobody would be independent.

Perhaps his most remarkable treatment of the subject, however, is a speech he delivered in Copenhagen in May 1991. Here he confronts head-on what he calls the "diabolical" temptations of power. He now finds himself, he writes,

> in the world of privileges, exceptions, perks, in the world of VIPs who gradually lose track of how much a streetcar ticket or butter costs, how to make a cup of coffee, how to drive a car, and how to place a telephone call. In other words, I find myself on the threshold of the very world of the communist fat cats whom I have criticized all my life. And worst of all, everything has its own unassailable logic.

"Someone who forgets how to drive a car, do the shopping, make himself coffee, and place a telephone call is not the same person who had known how to do those things all his life." The politician becomes "a captive of his position, his perks, his office. That which apparently confirms his identity and thus his existence in fact subtly takes that identity and existence away from him." This is vintage Havel, probing through a combination of ironical observation and agonized introspection to a larger truth, as he did in "The Power of the Powerless." It hints at a great essay to come: on the powerlessness of the powerful.

Yet the conclusion of this speech is surprising. It does not follow, he says, "that it is not proper to devote oneself to politics because politics is in principle immoral." What follows is that politics requires people of higher responsibility, taste, tact, and moral sensitivity. "Those who claim that politics is a dirty business are lying to us. Politics is work of a kind that requires especially pure people, because it is especially easy to become morally tainted."[7]

He returns to the theme in a speech at New York University in October 1991, comparing himself to a literary critic well known for his sharp judgments who is suddenly called upon to write a novel. First he quotes his own refutation of the charge that politics is "an essentially disreputable business":

> Of course, in politics, as anywhere else in life, it is impossible and pointless to say everything, all at once, to just anyone. But that does not mean having to lie. All you need is tact, the

proper instincts, and good taste. One surprising experience from "high politics" is this: I have discovered that good taste is more useful here than a degree in political science.

(This may be less surprising to anyone who has studied political science.)

Then he notes that in the few weeks since he wrote those words, "fate played a joke on me. It punished me for my self-assurance by exposing me to an immensely difficult dilemma. A democratically elected parliament passed a bill I considered to be morally flawed, yet which our constitution required me to sign." This was the so-called lustration bill, which, as Havel explains, banned from public service whole categories of people who had been implicated in the communist regime, with inadequate rights of individual appeal. He describes his decision: to sign the bill and then propose an amendment to parliament.

He does not know, he concludes, whether his decision was the right one, whether this part of the "novel" he is writing would meet the standards he set earlier as a critic. "History can probably be the only judge of that." He still does not think that politics requires one to behave immorally. "My latest experience, however, makes me want to underline five times a sentence that, until a few weeks ago, I thought unnecessary to underline even once: that the way of a truly moral politics is neither simple nor easy."

Six months later comes the Tokyo long-range argument with me, which is, so far as I can judge, his last major stab at this issue before his resignation as the president of a now clearly dissolving Czechoslovakia in July 1992. (The English edition rather glosses over this discontinuity, but what is described as his "abdication speech" can be found in the relevant Czech volume.)[8] Since he came back to the Castle as president of the Czech Republic in January 1993, courtesy of the votes of Václav Klaus's party and with much reduced powers, he has returned to the theme on various occasions, most recently in his welcome speech to the PEN congress, but without, so far as I can see, adding significant new elements to his argument.

I have quoted what Havel has to say on this subject at some length because his reflections are always interesting but also because only through extensive quotation does a problem become apparent. The problem is that what he has to say is often vague and confused, and this analytical confusion reflects a deeper confusion about his own role.

In his PEN speech, for example, he confuses the intellectual's engagement in politics in the broader sense (that is, without being directly involved in the pursuit of power or office) and in the narrower sense (the anecdote about urging his writer friend to take office). But, as I argued against Klaus, the distinction is very important.

The argument in the Copenhagen speech is also confused. Is he saying that politics is or is not a dirty business? If it isn't a dirty business, then why should it require exceptionally "pure" people to get involved without being corrupted? Anyway, why should we imagine that intellectuals are any better equipped to resist the temptations of power, to remain decent, upright, and uncorrupted, than ordinary mortals? One might well argue, with Ivan Klíma, quite the contrary: the record of intellectuals in power in the twentieth century suggests that they are among the least likely to resist the insidious poison, precisely because they are most able to rationalize, intellectualize, or philosophically justify their own submission or corruption by referring to higher goals or values. Orwell's faith in "ordinary men" may also be misplaced, but the history of Europe in the twentieth century gives us no grounds for believing that intellectuals will do any better.

The argument about the irresponsibility of not taking political responsibility is also a highly questionable projection from the very particular situation of postcommunist Central Europe, and specifically of V. Havel, to the general one. Of course, in the unique situation of 1989, in countries where the only alternative to the *nomenklatura* was a new political elite drawn largely from the ranks of more or less independent intellectuals, it would have been shirking responsibility not to take office. "Someone had to" is, for 1990, an entirely valid observation. But even then it could be the polite and, as it were, p.c. (or, rather, m.c.—morally correct) guise for personal ambition. Lech Wałęsa's *"Nie chcę, ale muszę"* ("I don't want to, but I must") has become proverbial in Poland. In any case, this is the particular problem of a particular historical moment. As a new class of professional politicians emerges, there is no reason at all why those intellectuals who do not feel comfortable in professional politics—with its different rules of play, its different way with words—should not return to their desks, laboratories, or studios.

Then there is Havel's powerful argument about the need to change consciousness. But why need intellectuals be in politics in order to change the consciousness of their own societies or a wider world? To be sure, it is good to have politicians with larger visions. In conversation, Havel mentions the examples of de Gaulle, Adenauer, and Churchill. But, if the point is to change consciousness, then the classics of the samizdat reading list—Orwell, Hayek, Popper, and, of course, Havel—have done as much or more. You don't have to be a president or a prime minister to change consciousness. In fact, you may stand a rather better chance if you're not.

There remains the general claim about introducing a new moral, intellectual, and spiritual dimension into our routinized, specialized, unimaginative party politics—a "new wind," to recall Havel's own metaphor. At this point, at the latest, one has to turn from the writing to the man. For Havel now differs fundamentally from most writers or philosophers, in that the test case of the truth of the propositions he is advancing is himself. As he constantly points out, the test of what Václav Havel argues in these speeches is what Václav Havel does as president—which is, of course, now mainly to give speeches.

3

So how far has Havel achieved the very high goal that he set himself five years ago? Particularly in his first two years as president of Czechoslovakia, the achievement was immense. Through his words and deeds, he both preached and practiced a resolute and morally sensitive moderation, civility, tolerance, and decency that contributed a huge amount to the peaceful, civilized nature of the transition from communism in Czechoslovakia. There was nothing inevitable about this. Were it not for him, it could have been much messier, dirtier, even bloody. Beyond that, he has been an extraordinary and much-needed voice in Europe and beyond. While the response of West European leaders to what happened five years ago was woefully inadequate, while they fiddled as Yugoslavia began to burn, he has constantly and eloquently reminded us of the larger historical dimensions of what has happened in Europe, and—if one can say this without too much pathos—of our duty.

Of course he did not become Plato's philosopher-king, or even, to take the obvious comparison, a second Masaryk. At times, he does seem to hold the peculiar Masarykian belief which Ernest Gellner ironically sums up as "No State Formation without Philosophic Justification." But he is not a systematic philosopher, and 1989 was not 1918. Yet measured by any but the vertiginous standards he has set himself, the first two years of the playwright-king would be accounted a remarkable success.

Since then, however, and especially since his abdication in 1992 and his return as Czech president in 1993, it has been, to say the least, a more mixed picture. There are many reasons for this, but the one most relevant here is his refusal to choose between the roles of intellectual and politician.

If, when the Civic Forum broke up on the initiative of Václav Klaus in 1991, Havel had allowed himself to be identified clearly with the remaining movement or some new political movement or even—perish the thought—a political party, he would certainly have stretched the terms of his office, but he might also have had a real political power base as well as his own charisma and popularity. As it was, he refused to engage in those normal, partisan (and often dirty) politics. His power slipped away. Up came Václav II, on whose reluctant sufferance he was, in a quite humiliating way, elected Czech president in 1993, with very limited powers. Havel himself recalls with anger how members of the Czech parliament openly ignored him, reading newspapers or chatting while he addressed them. Wryly, but with more than a touch of bitterness, he mutters, in English, the word *clown*.

Yet at the same time, his image and voice as an intellectual have become blurred. It's not just the suits and ties (in which he says he still feels uncomfortable), the ceremonial duties, and the compromises, such as that on the "lustration" law. It's not just the privileged isolation from ordinary life—the life in a velvet cage that he describes so vividly in his Copenhagen speech but that has nonetheless alienated many former close associates and friends. All that apart, there is simply the plain fact that a president's speeches are not a writer's essays. Text and context interact in a different and much less favorable way. Life contradicts art.

Even the outward form of *Toward a Civil Society* somehow speaks to us of the blurring of the voice that comes from the confusion of roles. The copyright page tells us this book is published with financial assistance from the Czech foreign ministry. Does a book by Havel really need a subsidy to be published? It comes with jacket endorsements from Zbigniew Brzezinski, Eduard Shevardnadze, and one Thomas Klestil, who, readers may like to know, is the president of Austria. Does Havel really need to be puffed by a Klestil? The cover photograph shows a man in a pinstriped suit and tie speaking in front of the yellow-stars-on-blue-background of the Council of Europe and the EU. In other words, this book looks just like a professional politician's piece of government-subsidized vanity publishing—which, of course, it definitely is not. But it looks like it.

"The strongest poison ever known / Came from Caesar's laurel crown," wrote William Blake. I do not believe that Václav Havel has been poisoned by power in any normal sense. If mildly infected at all, it is in the rather unusual form of being, so to speak, aesthetically enamored of the theater of high politics—which, as he is the first to point out, is even more the theater of the absurd than the most absurdist of his own plays.

Earlier this year, I heard him give a brilliantly funny description of the stage management of President Clinton's visit to Prague and, in particular, of his visit with Clinton to a typical Prague pub with a typical gathering of typical locals—all carefully identified by the American embassy beforehand. (The typical locals included the writer Bohumil Hrabal.) It was a wonderful foretaste of the book he might write when he ceases to be president. But I must admit that for a moment I did find myself uneasily wondering what the dissident writer Václav Havel would have made of such a stage-managed scene, what subtle lessons he would have drawn about the alienation of the powerful.

Probably the shortest and best retort ever made to Plato's vision

of the philosopher-king is Kant's remark that for philosophers to become kings is neither desirable nor possible, because "the posses-
sion of power unavoidably spoils the free use of reason." Havel's case
is an interesting variation on this eternal truth, because it seems to
me that the greater threat to his free use of reason may actually be
the relative *loss* of power he has experienced since 1992—a loss that
Václav Klaus misses no occasion to rub in. Havel is now fighting to
regain some of the lost power, staking out his own political agenda in
a series of speeches stressing the importance of education, local government, civic engagement, and so on. He now even seems prepared, at least on some issues, to be a focus for opposition to
Klaus—an opposition that is to be found not least within the prime
minister's own governing coalition. But to use his "spoken essays" in
this instrumental way would seem to be a departure from the standards he has set himself—and simply a sad comedown from his position five years ago.

Anyway, this is not a French-style *cohabitation,* in which an executive president with great powers can, as it were, win the political battle. Havel's present constitutional position as nonexecutive president
is more comparable to that of the president of the Federal Republic of
Germany, an office held until recently by a man whom he much admires, Richard von Weizsäcker. In his *Summer Meditations,* Havel
wrote that, in his dream vision of (as he then still hoped) Czechoslovakia, "At the head of the state will be a grey-haired Professor with
the charm of a Richard von Weizsäcker." And as I read Havel's
speeches, especially the more recent ones, I notice some similari-
ties—not least in a small but revealing feature of the prose. The most
characteristic feature of President Weizsäcker's style was the rhetorical question. "Of course my office only permits me to ask questions,"
he would say, before launching a series of rhetorical questions that
added up to an extremely clear statement of his own views. Am I
imagining things, or is Havel increasingly using the same device?

One can take this particular comparison a stage further. It is an
open secret that there was considerable tension between the patri-
cian, Protestant, intellectual President Weizsäcker and the provincial, Catholic, and less ostensibly intellectual Chancellor Kohl. In
private, they could be quite rude about each other. In public, some

of President Weizsäcker's elegant rhetorical questions could be understood as digs at the chancellor; some of the chancellor's remarks could be interpreted as barbs in the other direction. But they certainly never descended to anything like the public Punch and Judy show that the Klaus-Havel duel has at times become, with everyone knowing who is the unnamed object of each elliptical speech; every occasion being interpreted in that light; and ordinary Czechs sometimes having the impression that if Havel came out in favor of eating spinach then Klaus would be sure to come out the next day against eating spinach—on impeccable neoliberal grounds, of course.

Instead, both Kohl and Weizsäcker scrupulously observed the constitutional proprieties and, at best, tried to turn their differences into complementarity rather than discord. The result was one of the most effective double acts to lead any European state in recent history. It contributed very substantially to the peaceful achievement of German unity. If the Czech president and prime minister were to achieve such a division of labor, it would doubtless be a great service to the Czech Republic—at home, in Europe, and in the wider world.

To be sure, this, so to speak, Weizsäcker role would be some miles down from that new spiritual dimension that Havel dreamed, and perhaps still dreams, of introducing. Indeed, as the German example illustrates, in the wider European context it would not even be new. There is also a real question whether the ex-president of Czechoslovakia might not actually have a greater influence in Europe and the world today were he again able to speak with his own unique voice as an independent intellectual. But the die is cast. For another few years, at least, he will go on in the Castle, suffering up there for us; a living exemplar of the dilemmas of the intellectual in politics; condemned, like the central character in one of his own plays, to play out a role that he feels is not truly his own; and haunted and taunted by a slightly threatening character who even bears the same name. Such absurdist tricks the divine playwright plays.

4

With that somewhat Havelesque reflection, my Prague tale of intellectuals and politics is told, five years, almost to the day, after I told the story of the revolution of the Magic Lantern. Now, as then, I have tried to tell the story as honestly as I can, at the risk of indiscretion and of causing offense. Are there any conclusions to be drawn, any lessons even? There are, I think, possible implications for the Czech Republic, for the position of intellectuals in postcommunist Europe, and, most tentatively, for the place of intellectuals in Europe altogether.

For the Czech Republic the immediate question is, Can the premier and the president possibly achieve the kind of moderately harmonious public relationship which Kohl and Weizsäcker achieved? Almost certainly not. Since this is a new democracy, the constitutional roles are not defined as clearly by law or by precedent. The two have very different political views of the way the new Czech state should be built. Klaus, the Thatcherite, gives absolute priority to economic transformation, even at the cost of corruption and illegality on the way. "Speed," he says, "is more important than accuracy." At times he seems inclined to Mrs. Thatcher's view that "society" does not exist. Havel, whose politics, inasmuch as they can be defined in ordinary terms, are those of an ecologically minded social democrat, stresses the importance of culture, local government, civic participation, and civil society.

Above all, though, it is a clash of personalities and biographies. The Tale of Two Václavs is not simply that of the intellectual Havel versus the politician Klaus. To be sure, Havel is a more important intellectual and Klaus a more effective politician. But what makes it so difficult is precisely that both are intellectuals in politics, as the PEN episode vividly illustrated.

This is what makes the story at once unique and representative, for all over postcommunist Central Europe intellectuals are wrestling with similar dilemmas. Many who have gone into and remain in politics will find the dichotomy I present too sharp. The former dissident and former foreign minister Jiří Dienstbier, now the leader of a small opposition party, commented in a newspaper interview after our PEN discussion that, while he agreed with my basic argument, he did not feel that as a minister he had been working in half-truth. Those, now quite numerous, who after 1989 went into but are now again out of politics will find it easier to accept such a clear dichotomy. Those who never ventured into politics will find it easier still. But they have their own problems.

The intelligentsia—one of the characteristic phenomena of modern Central and East European history—is now everywhere engulfed in sweeping change. This world of "circles of friends," of *milieux,* where artists, philosophers, writers, economists, journalists all felt themselves to belong to the same group and to be committed to a certain common ethos (albeit often honored in the breach), was something anachronistic in late-twentieth-century Europe—but also something rich and fine. Its extraordinary character was summed up for me in a phrase that Ivan Klíma used in describing how he and his fellow writers had set out to revive the dormant Czech PEN club in 1989. "I was," he said, "authorized by my circle of friends." The peculiar world of the intelligentsia under communism was one in which you sought authorization from your circle of friends.[9]

Freedom has changed all that. With remarkable speed, the intelligentsia has fragmented into separate professions, as in the West: journalists, publishers, academics, actors, not to mention those who have become officials, lawyers, diplomats. The *milieux* have faded, the "circles of friends" have dispersed or lost their special significance. Those who have remained in purely "intellectual" professions—above all, academics—have found themselves impoverished. Moreover, it is the businessmen and entrepreneurs who are the tone-setting heroes of this time. Thus, from having an abnormal importance before 1989, independent intellectuals have plummeted to abnormal unimportance.

Yet to say that is to assume that we know what their "normal" importance would be. But do we? Is there any wider European normality in this respect, toward which postcommunist Central Europe might be either moving or contributing? In Britain the term *intellectual* is used rarely, being regarded as something Continental and slightly pretentious. Yet, as Byron said of the word *longueurs,* though we have not the word, we have the thing in some profusion. And the things exist on both left and right—although here, as elsewhere, the right tends to identify the very idea of "intellectuals" with the left.

In Germany, the days of the great public role of writers such as

Heinrich Böll and Günter Grass seem to be over. However, some of the country's most interesting political debates are actually conducted by intellectuals, on the *Feuilleton* pages of the *Frankfurter Allgemeine Zeitung* and in smaller journals. Yet here, too, you have the phenomenon of right-wing intellectuals denouncing "the intellectuals," meaning left-wing intellectuals: in this case, for their failure to welcome the unification of Germany.

In France, there have been writers and thinkers identified and identifying themselves as "intellectuals" at least since the time of the Dreyfus affair and the *Manifeste des Intellectuels*. Yet I doubt that anyone would today venture to write a *Plaidoyer pour les intellectuels*, as Sartre did in 1972. Partly, no doubt, out of an awareness of the awful misjudgments and moral failures of intellectuals in the twentieth century—and not least French intellectuals, including, notably, Sartre. Partly because there are no obvious new utopias to be embraced—except utopian liberalism, which is a contradiction in terms. Partly, perhaps, because they are too busy appearing on television and generally competing in a crowded entertainment market.

Yet at the same time, there is, in all the major West European countries, a real crisis of popular confidence in the professional politicians, seen to be out-of-touch, self-interested careerists, tainted by corruption. The Italian debacle haunts us all.

In this sense, Havel's call for a new spiritual and moral dimension to be introduced into politics might seem to be relevant, after all, for Western Europe. That was what many in Western Europe felt and hoped at the moment of the Magic Lantern five years ago. But the lesson is surely not that this is a time for intellectuals to enter politics, in the narrow sense of trying to become prime ministers or presidents. No, this is a time for intellectuals to be both resolutely independent and politically engaged—which means, among other things, criticizing prime ministers and presidents. Politely, of course. Constructively, wherever possible. But above all, clearly.

Four years later, in November 1998, Havel returned to this subject when receiving an honorary doctorate at Oxford. Referring in his acceptance speech to our earlier exchanges, he acknowledged that intellectuals have borne a heavy responsibility for some of the worst regimes in history. But he argued that, at a time when politicians tend to follow opinion polls and the media rather than to lead their citizens, there is a crying need for men and women of larger vision to enter politics. Intellectuals, he said, can participate in politics either by holding office or by holding up a mirror to those in power. You can be an office-holder or a mirror-holder. But I would continue to insist that a healthy democracy requires a very clear separation of roles between the two, and that the primary, even the defining, role of the intellectual in politics should be that of mirror-holder.

MARTA AND HELENA

────────

IT'S NOVEMBER 1994, AND WE'RE AT THE LUCERNA PALACE IN Prague, built by a millionaire developer in the early years of this century, expropriated by the communists, but now returned to his sons, Ivan and Václav Havel. Tonight's guest stars are the Golden Kids, a sixties pop group whose members haven't performed together for nearly twenty-five years, since they were banned by the communist authorities after the Soviet invasion. They are Marta Kubišová, now aged fifty-three; Václav Neckář, fifty-two; and Helena Vondračková, forty-seven. They wear black. They jive. They sing "Hey Jude" and "Massachusetts" and "The Times They Are a-Changin'" and "The Mighty Quinn" and even, God save us, "Congratulations."

The audience, like the Golden Kids, is middle-aged: men in shiny suits, white shirts, and ties, women in blouses, as if for the opera. They sweat amid the faded *Jugendstil* gilding and candelabra. Sometimes they clap along. But when the Golden Kids sing "Suzanne," there's just total silence:

> *Suzanne takes you down*
> *To her place near the river.*
> *You can hear the boats go by:*
> *You can spend the night beside her.*

Tense and heavy with regret: the silence of the middle-aged remembering sex.

There's another story being played out on stage this evening: the story of Marta and Helena. Marta Kubišová was a Czech heroine of the Prague Spring in 1968. A song called "Hymn for Marta" became a rallying song of the time. After the Soviet invasion, she was banned. For twenty long years, until 1989, she did odd jobs, worked as a clerk, had close friends among the dissidents. In the middle of the "velvet revolution" she made her first comeback—a moment I will never forget, at once rapturous and terribly sad. Barely able to sing, due to the engulfing emotion, she whispered into the microphone, *"Časy se měni."* "The Times They Are a-Changin'."

Helena Vondráčková took a quite different path after 1969. She continued performing and was seen often on state television. She collaborated.

Now their paths have met again. Will virtue have its reward? Or does none of that matter anymore? Helena—tall, blonde, and still very much in practice—seems to dominate at first. She's younger, more professional, and the audience knows her from television. Perhaps they even feel a little easier with her, for most of them collaborated, too, or at least made little compromises to keep their jobs. Marta—older, shorter, black haired—is a shade slower, and you feel the nervousness in her voice.

But, somewhere in the middle of the evening, the emotion begins flowing toward her. People bring bouquets of flowers up onstage after every number (opera habits), and the flower count is going Marta's way. Then the whole concert stops, and the stage is full of embarrassed men in suits. They represent Supraphon, Fiat, Interbanka, Seagram—the commercial sponsors of the evening. Awkwardly, they hand out platinum discs and bottles of champagne. And there's a raffle; first prize, a Fiat Punto. The prize-winners come up onstage, say a few words into the mike, and kiss the stars.

One, a comfortable-looking man in jeans, shambles up and says he'd like to thank all the performers, every one, "but above all, above all, Mrs. Kubišová." And we all applaud loud and long, and we know what he's thanking her for, and it's not for her singing this evening—it's for her twenty years of silence.

But now everyone is sweating, and everything is mixed up together, the Marta of then and the "Mrs. Kubišová" of now, the pop heroes of the 1960s and the business heroes of the 1990s, the memories of sex and the memories of national protest, and today's hope of a Fiat Punto.

Yet there's an ever bigger circle closing here: a European circle. For these are also our songs: This is our past. Sixty-eight was one of those very rare moments when the experiences of people in Western and Eastern Europe really did meet. For all the differences between Prague and Paris, Liverpool and Leipzig, people under thirty here and there moved to the same rhythm, sang the same lyrics, shared something of the same protest, the same emancipation. Then the Russian tanks rolled in, and the paths of experience diverged, as did those of Marta and Helena, and the years slipped away.

Now, a quarter century on, East and West have come together again, like Marta and Helena, here in the Havels' Lucerna Palace, in this postmodern stew of middle-aged longing and regret, under the sign of Seagram, and the shared meaning of history is:

> *Yeh yeh yeh yeh yeh yeh yeh da da da da*
> *Hey Jude.*

Chronology

1994

25 October. *British prime minister John Major announces an inquiry into standards in public life, headed by a senior judge, Lord Nolan. The "Nolan committee."*

11 November. *The United States announces that its troops will no longer enforce the arms embargo against Bosnia.*

13 November. *In a referendum, 52.2 percent of Swedish voters approve of their country joining the EU on the terms already negotiated.*

15 November. *The EU's Court of Auditors highlights the problem of fraud in the Common Agricultural Policy and the so-called structural funds.*

27–28 November. *In a referendum, 52.4 percent of Norwegian voters oppose their country joining the EU on the terms already negotiated.*

9–10 December. *An EU summit in Essen outlines the "pre-accession strategy" for enlargement of the EU to include some former communist countries. It also discusses terms of the EU's relationship with states across the Mediterranean. Other major summit themes are improving competitiveness and creating jobs.*

11 December. *Russian forces invade the breakaway republic of Chechnya.*

13 December. *Italian prime minister Silvio Berlusconi is questioned by magistrates investigating corruption in three subsidiaries of his Fininvest business empire. Vladimír Mečiar becomes Slovak prime minister for the third time, leading a "red-brown" coalition of right- and left-wing parties.*

22 December. *Berlusconi resigns as Italian prime minister after the Northern League withdraws its support from his coalition.*

1 9 9 5

1 JANUARY. *Austria, Finland, and Sweden join the EU. Establishment of the World Trade Organization. A four-month cease-fire in Bosnia, negotiated by former U.S. president Jimmy Carter, comes into effect but is ignored in Bihać, one of the UN's "safe areas."*

9 JANUARY. *Seven former members of the East German politburo, including former party leader Egon Krenz (see above, p. 4), are charged in connection with shootings at the Berlin Wall.*

13 JANUARY. *In Italy, former treasury minister Lamberto Dini forms a government, after the collapse of the Berlusconi government.*

27–30 JANUARY. Davos, Switzerland. The World Economic Forum, an extraordinary annual gathering of business and political leaders, with a scattering of intellectuals thrown in for stimulation and entertainment. A giant ego-feast on Thomas Mann's "magic mountain." (His great novel *Der Zauberberg*, "The Magic Mountain," was set here.) I have a memorable dinner with the financier and philanthropist George Soros, whom I know from his pioneering charitable work for open societies in Central and Eastern Europe. He is one of a very small group of people who have been good both at making money and at spending it.

We meet at a restaurant that is called, promisingly, Der Zauberberg, but turns out to be Chinese. Soros says he has always thought of himself as first and foremost a philosopher, not a moneyman. When he was still a poor exile, he took several years of his life to write a philosophical work called *The Burden of Consciousness*. But nobody really wanted to know. Then he went off and made his billions. Now everyone is eager to hear his lectures on philosophy; great universities and institutions vie to offer him a platform. Yet he can never quite be sure whether it is his philosophy that they are interested in or his money. In a way, his personal experience is an illustration of his own central philosophical principle, which he calls "reflexivity."

With its human and philosophical ironies, this seems to me a tale worthy of Mann's magic mountain.

LATE JANUARY. *Russia claims victory in Chechnya.*

7 FEBRUARY. *Polish prime minister Waldemar Pawlak resigns. He is succeeded by the postcommunist Józef Oleksy, heading the same coalition of the postcommunist Democratic Left Alliance and the Polish Peasant Party.*

21 FEBRUARY. *Belarus president Alexander Lukashenka signs comprehensive cooperation treaties with President Yeltsin. Substantial reintegration of Belarus with Russia.*

22 FEBRUARY. *Irish prime minister John Bruton and British prime minister John Major present a framework document for all-party constitutional talks on Northern Ireland, including proposals for a cross-border body.*

12 MARCH. *The Hungarian government proposes drastic new austerity measures.*

20–21 MARCH. *A pan-European "Stability Pact" is signed in Paris.*

26 MARCH. *The Schengen agreement comes into effect, abolishing border controls between France, Germany, Belgium, Luxembourg, the Netherlands, Spain, and Portugal. "Schengenland" is born.*

7 APRIL. *In Poland, General Wojciech Jaruzelski is charged with involvement in the shooting of protesting workers in 1970.*

29 APRIL. *The British Labour Party votes to replace clause four of the party's constitution, which had advocated "common ownership of the means of production, distribution, and exchange."*

1 MAY. *Heavy fighting erupts in Grozny, capital of Chechnya, after Chechen forces return to the city.*

1–2 MAY. *Croat forces recapture the Serb-controlled enclave in eastern Slavonia.*

7 MAY. *Jacques Chirac wins the runoff election for the presidency of France. Alain Juppé is named prime minister, heading a center-right coalition government. In Bosnia, another attack on a marketplace in Sarajevo.*

CATCHING THE
WRONG BUS?

Five years ago, in the euphoria at the end of the cold war, it looked as if we could discern the shape of the twentieth century in Europe. That shape seemed to be a V. The line descended from the first and second Balkan wars before 1914, through what Churchill called Europe's second Thirty Years War, to the depths of Auschwitz and the Gulag, but then gradually rose again from mid-century, through the reconstruction of Western Europe to the liberation of Eastern Europe in 1989. For Poland, V-E Day came only in the summer of 1989—just forty-four years late. And for Germany, that autumn. "Only today is the war really over," said an improvised poster in East Berlin as the Berlin Wall came down. So in 1989 the shape of the century looked like a V for Victory. But since then, the upward line has faltered, perhaps even turned downward, as we once again witness a Balkan war.

Fifty years on, we remember Britain's unique contribution to the Victory in Europe with wholly justified pride. But we had to fight that war partly because of an earlier British policy based on the mistaken belief that Britain could, by a diplomacy of detachment, insulate itself from those European quarrels in faraway countries of which Chamberlain knew nothing. Wrong then; even more wrong now.

So, fifty years after the end of what we still call *the* war in Europe and five years after the end of the cold war, what has Europe come to, and where, if anywhere, is it going? And is there, could there be, a British way of "thinking Europe"?

Most contemporary British discussion of "Europe" is not about Europe at all. At best, it is about EU-rope—that is, some aspects of the collective political and economic life of the western, northern, and southern European states now organized in something rather misleadingly called the European Union. But mainly it is about Britain. Our so-called European debate is part of a tortured national self-examination, an English, Scottish, Welsh, and Irish agonizing about self. In this debate, "Europe" appears as a threat to the very existence of Britain for (mainly English) "Euro-skeptics" of the right; as a chance to transform the very nature of Britain for (often Scottish or Welsh) "Euro-enthusiasts" of the left; as both opportunity and problem for the large center, but for all sides as something basically external. There is "Europe" over there and "Britain" here, and the argument is about the relationship between them and us.

Penser l'Europe is a French book title, inconceivable as a British one. Thinking Europe is an un-British activity. Those who do it, even as consenting adults in private, risk being stigmatized as "Euro-intellectuals"—a neologism that neatly combines two things the British deeply distrust.

In the circumstances, it is not surprising that most of our Continental partners regard the very notion of "a British idea of Europe" as a contradiction in terms. This is a pity. It is a pity for Britain: We lose influence because we are seen on the Continent to be opposed or at best marginal to the mainstream of European development. But it may also be a pity for Europe, since Europe, and especially EU-rope, could perhaps use a little more British thinking at the moment—with "British" here meant in the deeper sense of our particular intellectual tradition: skeptical, empirical, and pragmatic.

For "Continental" ways of thinking about Europe also have their problems. To use a simple dichotomy of "British versus Continental" would, of course, be to make precisely the British mistake. There is a huge variety of different ways of thinking about Europe across the Continent. Yet certainly there are some common characteristics of the main French and German approaches that have had a formative influence on the development of EU-rope over the past half century.

Where British politicians make an artificial separation of the national and the European, ignoring the degree to which the two are already intertwined, French and German politicians utterly conflate the national and the European, so it is almost impossible to distinguish when they are talking about Europe and when about their own nations. Now the instrumentalization of "Europe" for the pursuit of national ends is an old European habit. Bismarck famously observed that he had always found the word *Europe* in the mouths of those politicians who wanted from other powers something they did not dare demand in their own name. His conclusion was *"Qui parle Europe a tort. Notion géographique."* British Euro-skeptics applaud Bismarck.

Yet in truth things are now a little more complicated. For in the half century since 1945, there has also been a great deal of genuinely idealistic commitment to Europe among French and German politicians and opinion-formers—a commitment born from personal experience of revolution, war, genocide, defeat, and occupation. The trouble is that the conflation of national and European—part instrumental, part idealistic—has become so habitual that they themselves sometimes don't quite know when they are talking about Europe and when about France or Germany.

Idealism in a different though related sense—the tendency to represent things in an ideal form rather than as they are: idealism as opposed to empiricism—is the other salient common characteristic of this French and German Euro-thinking. The "Europe" of which they have spoken for the past half century is an idea and an ideal, a dream, a vision, or a grand design; this is *faire l'Europe, Europa bauen,* Europe as project, process, progress toward some *finalité européenne;* Europe as *telos.* At its most vertiginous, this comes as dialectical idealism. *"Europa der Gegensätze auf dem Wege zu sich selbst,"* proclaims a German publication: "The Europe of contradictions on the way to itself." Which, in English, makes about as much sense as "The London of traffic jams on the way to itself."

The difference between the teleological-idealistic and the empirical-skeptical approaches leads to profound misunderstandings. For the former, the great end justifies the often unsatisfactory means. Eurocratic nonsense from Brussels is a price worth paying for the larger political sense. But the teleologists are in trouble. In the Continental elites' building plans for EU-rope, from Messina to Maastricht, the *telos* was a substitute for the absent *demos*—with the hope of eventually contributing to the creation of a new European *demos* from above, by education and example. But it has not happened. There is still no European people, or *demos*. And, after the signature of the Maastricht Treaty, the peoples of the very heartlands of EU-rope turned to question what was being dished up in their name. "For we are the peoples of Europe, that never have spoken yet," as Chesterton might have written.

In this sense, EU-rope is perhaps now ready for a more (intellec-tually) "British" approach. But is any constructive "British" ap-proach on offer? An approach, that is, which cares about Europe as Europe and not just as a threat or opportunity for a greater or lesser Britain. What follows is an attempt to "think Europe" in English: to see Europe plain and to see it whole.

FOR A START, does Europe exist? This most ill-defined of continents has, after all, been open for long stretches of its history not just on one but on three sides: to the south across the Mediterranean, throughout most of what we call "ancient history" and in some ways again today; to the east, where Europe does not end but merely fades away, into Asia; and to the west, across the Atlantic, especially in our post-1945 "West." The "globalization" caused by the technological developments of the past half century further calls into question the coherence or validity of the unit "Europe" as compared with smaller entities (state, region, firm) or larger ones (Eur-atlantic, OECD, world).

And what of its internal makeup? What are Europe's essential constituent parts? Its hundreds of millions of individual people who more or less—mainly less—identify themselves as "Europeans"? Its regions? Classes? Societies? Nations and states? But to say "nation-states," as most British politicians do, obscures the huge diversity of European combinations of nation and state, from the national state, with citizenship rights conditional on membership of one dominant ethnic *Volk,* or the classic east European variant of ethnic nations distributed between several states, through the French civic *état-nation,* to Britain itself: a nation-state containing several nations.

Nonetheless, in most of western, southern, and now also northern Europe, these individuals, regions, societies, nations, but above all states are now organized in something new—EU-rope—that differs qualitatively both from any previous arrangement of states and from any current arrangement of states on any other continent. The nature of this arrangement is, however, very hard to define. The German Constitutional Court has described it as a *Staatenverbund*. In English, we might call it a thing. This thing is less than a federal superstate but more than an alliance: an unprecedented, unique, and horribly complex combination of the supranational and the intergovernmental, of economic integration and political cooperation.

This thing evolved in the cold war, like NATO and with NATO, as the western half of a European order that we called in shorthand "Yalta." Its development was directly and indirectly influenced, to a degree many devoted advocates of European integration find hard to acknowledge, by that of the cold war—and of détente, the Siamese twin of cold war. But, five years ago, this "Yalta" order ended in a way quite different from that in which previous European orders, whether of "Versailles," "Vienna," or "Westphalia," had ended. Essentially, its eastern half just fell away, with the largely peaceful death of communism in Eastern Europe and the rather less peaceful dissolution of the Soviet Union. The western half remained intact— or at least apparently so.

So today this now slightly expanded western part, this EU-rope, with its fifteen states and some 370 million people, faces the other Europe from which it was so long insulated by the Iron Curtain. (For we lived, as the Hungarian writer György Konrád put it, with our backs to the Berlin Wall.) This other Europe may itself be subdivided very crudely into a second and a third Europe. The second Europe has in all some twenty states, of which fifteen have only recently been liberated from communism, and some 140 million people. The states of this second Europe, among which I do not include Turkey, are mainly small. Except for Poland and Romania, none has more inhabitants than Greater London, and most have far fewer. Most of them, or at least most of their political elites, more or less clearly want to join the Europe of the EU and NATO; to "return to Europe," in the slogan of 1989. More important, their theoretical claim to belong, sooner or later, is more or less accepted by the political leaders of the EU—although with the emphasis in practice often on the less and later.

Clearly, this is to paint with a very broad brush. Having spent much of the past fifteen years trying to explain to Western readers that Prague, Budapest, and Warsaw belong to Central and not to Eastern Europe, I am the last person to need reminding of the immense differences between Poland and Albania. But to suggest that there is some absolutely clear historical dividing line between the Central European democracies in the so-called Visegrád group and, say, the Baltic states or Slovenia would be to service a new myth.

The third Europe comprises two much larger states, Russia and Ukraine, together with Belarus, and perhaps also Serbia. They have a very large combined population of more than 210 million—or 220 million if one includes Serbia. These states are themselves, especially in the case of Russia, somewhat more ambivalent than the second Europe about their own historical belonging to Europe and their current desire to join the first Europe of EU and NATO. But, more important, the political leaders of the EU and NATO do not agree even on the long-term principle of these states' claim to membership.

Again, the division between the second and third Europes is crude, probably unfair to Ukraine, and may understate the long-term possibility of a democratic Serbia reoriented toward Europe. But, wherever the exact lines fall at any given moment, for the foreseeable future this other Europe will certainly be subdivided between states that are recognizably set on a course toward EU-rope and those that are not—with, no doubt, a number straggling in between.

The central political question about the composition of Europe today is therefore whether and how EU-rope can gradually include an ever larger part of the second Europe, while itself continuing to "work" in the unique, complex, unsatisfactory, but nonetheless real way it does; and how this process will both affect and be affected by relations with the third Europe, above all with Russia.

At issue right across the other Europe is the choice not just between democracy and dictatorship but also between war and peace.

Banishing the specter of war between European states and peoples was, of course, the first great purpose of EU-rope's founding fathers. Economic integration was the indirect means chosen to achieve that end, especially after a more direct approach—the European Defense Community—was voted down in the French National Assembly. Now it is a fair question how far it really was the (then still) EEC/EC that kept the peace in Europe, inasmuch as it was kept, up to 1990, and how far NATO and the East–West nuclear standoff in the cold war. But certainly the habits and institutions of peaceful conflict-resolution and permanent cooperation in the EC made a contribution.

Yet, while our leaders still mouth the platitude that "war has become unthinkable" in Europe, war not only has again become thinkable across much of postcommunist Europe but is, even as they speak, actually being waged, bloodily and brutally and—with almost too crude an irony—in a place called Sarajevo.

One lesson of the short twentieth century is that political ends are not separable from the means used to attain them. Today, EU-rope's means are threatening its ends. The process of "making Europe" proceeds *pars pro toto*. The elites negotiate for the people and ask them only afterward, if at all, whether they agree. In this sense, as process, what is happening now is already "a second Maastricht." EU-rope also decides for Europe, and future members have to accept the given shape. The Poles send up their old cry, *"Nic o nas bez nas"*—"Nothing about us without us!"—but, as usual, the West hardly listens.

Within the EU, a number of states—and crucially France and Germany—are contemplating "going ahead": *pars pro toto* again. Following German unification, France's political leaders feel it to be more urgent than ever to bind Germany into Europe and—curious but true!—Germany's political leaders want their own country to be bound in, so they are not left alone to face the temptations of the past in the center of Europe. True to the functionalist tradition of proceeding through economic means to political ends, the chosen path is monetary union. This, with its desired political consequences, is to make the process of integration "irreversible." The Franco-German avant-garde will form a "magnetic core" of a uniting

Europe, with monetary union as the hard core of the hard core. But where they lead, other states, including Britain, are to follow, as they have done throughout the previous history of the EEC/EC/EU. EU-rope after Maastricht (1 and 2) will be "multispeed" but still moving in one direction.

Here, stripped to essentials, is the bold—even breathtaking—Franco-German project for EU-rope in the closing years of the century and the immediate European challenge for Britain. The trouble is that this project is very likely to fail. Monetary union itself might fail, obviously, at the first or second fences, because even the core economies are not close enough to stand the strains, or because either French or German political opinion turns against it. Monetary union might also fail after the event. Nothing except death is irreversible, and European history offers several examples of failed monetary unions.

Yet it may also fail by succeeding. That is, succeed in the narrow, technical, sense but fail in the broader purpose. A single market is perhaps difficult to sustain without a single currency, but it may be even more difficult to sustain with a clear, formalized division between monetary core and periphery. And how would this work in the councils of EU-rope? Would representatives of the core states have separate meetings on those fundamental issues of fiscal and macro-economic policy on which they would now need a common stance? (The idea of EMU as gold standard, with each state bound to keep its own budgetary house in order or go broke, is theoretically attractive but not practical European politics.) Or would the core group be a permanent caucus, coming to each Council with an agreed position? One of the great strengths of the EU is its flexibility: You have changing national alliances on different issues. Set one alliance in concrete, and you risk breaking the whole structure.

The great gamble of this Continental project is that the Franco-German core will indeed be magnetic, that where Bonn and Paris lead others will sooner or later follow. And the reason why people in Bonn and Paris (and quite a few older "pro-Europeans" in London) think this will happen is that that is roughly what did happen for about thirty-five years, from 1955 to 1990. But a process that worked, almost with the regularity of a physics demonstration, in the air-cooled laboratory of "Western Europe" in the cold war will not necessarily work in the same way in the much larger, messier, post-Wall Europe of today.

Anyone who has played with magnets as a child knows that they can have two effects: one way around they attract, the other way they repel. There is now a serious danger of the would-be magnetic core exerting magnetic repulsion. The best can be the enemy of the good. The rationalist, functionalist, perfectionist attempt to "make Europe" or "complete Europe" through a hard core built around a rapid monetary union could well end up achieving the opposite of the desired effect. A procedure aimed at finally overcoming the bad old European ways of competing nation-states and alliances risks hastening a return to precisely those bad old ways. Press the fast-forward button, and you go backward.

Yet even if it succeeds, both economically and politically, even if Britain and others in the EU once again follow where France and Germany have led, this in itself offers nothing to the rest of Europe knocking at our door. Indeed, the current Inter-Governmental Conference threatens to be "Maastricht 2" in another sense—with the leaders of EU-rope so totally preoccupied with the EU's own internal reforms that they simply don't have enough time, energy, and attention left for the parts of Europe where our actions might actually make the difference between democracy and dictatorship, war and peace.

Yet it is not enough to point out—empirically, skeptically, and pragmatically—the flaws and dangers in a Franco-German project that is, characteristically, at once teleological, idealistic, and instrumental. For the French and Germans will quite rightly retort, Do you have a better one? For anyone who cares about Europe, the task is therefore to come up with a better one. Or, at the very least, to ensure that there is something else under way so that the whole "European enterprise" at the end of the twentieth century is not seen to stand or fall with this hair-raising adventure, this *Europe as Will and Idea*, of unification through money.

That "something" should, I believe, be a detailed project both for the enlargement of the present EU to include, over the next twenty years, the recently liberated second Europe, and, simultaneously, for a more closely coordinated and in some respects "common" foreign, security, and defense policy, to meet the challenges and dangers both within Europe itself and from the dangerous world around. This project would therefore approach the political goal directly, by political means, not by the functionalist diversion through economics. Unlike EMU, it would not be one simple big thing but a whole jigsaw of complex, piecemeal things, since it would necessarily involve many other, overlapping European institutions, and, above all, EU-rope's second true pillar: NATO. But, however precisely it were done, it would require more sharing of power and sovereignty—both in the form of Qualified Majority Voting, without which an EU of twenty and more member states would simply not work, and in the rather different procedures for what one might call Qualified Minority Acting (by varying groups of states, but usually involving France, Germany, and Britain), which are what is needed in foreign, security, and defense policy.

But if you don't care about Europe as Europe, just about Britain as Britain, why bother and why pay the price? For two reasons: because if we don't we'll be left out, and because if we don't we'll be dragged in. Left out, in the short term, from the next stage of Franco-German EU-ro-building, with (at the very least) high risks for Britain; but then dragged in by the probable failure of that design and by the disorder of the rest of Europe, which that design does so little to address.

There is a surreal, even a grotesque, discrepancy between the contorted, rapidly sleep-inducing, acronym-ridden, polit-bureaucratic detail of the current debate about reforming EU-rope and the huge, fateful, almost melodramatic challenges facing us across the rest of Europe after the end of the cold war. And yet our answer to the latter must start from the former—for where else should we start except where we are?

And going where? All divisions of time are artificial, and perhaps the last five years of the twentieth century and the second millennium A.D. should be considered no differently from any other five years. But the millennial deadline does concentrate the mind. In these next five years, we probably have a larger chance but also a greater danger than at any time in the past fifty. The chance is that in

2000 more of Europe will be more peaceful, prosperous, democratic, and free than ever before in its history. The danger can also be
described simply. If we get things wrong now, some time in the early
part of the next century we will stop talking about 8 May 1945 as the
end of the war in Europe—because there'll be another.

*I develop this argument further in "The Case for Liberal Order,"
p. 279.*

CHRONOLOGY

1 9 9 5

16 MAY. *Milan prosecutors propose that 160 politicians and business people should be tried for bribery and corruption. They also request the indictment of Silvio Berlusconi, Italian prime minister until December 1994.*

25–26 MAY. *NATO bombs Bosnian Serb targets. In revenge, Bosnian Serbs take UN peacekeepers hostage and shell "safe areas."*

31 MAY. *Prince Charles becomes the first member of the British royal family to visit Ireland since it gained independence in 1922.*

3 JUNE. *Creation of a NATO "rapid-reaction force" to support UNPROFOR in Bosnia.*

9 JUNE. *Russian president Yeltsin and Ukrainian president Kuchma sign an agreement on the future of the Black Sea fleet.*

11 AND 18 JUNE. *In French local elections, the far-right National Front makes major gains.*

19 JUNE. *Árpád Göncz is reelected president of Hungary.*

26–27 JUNE. *An EU summit in Cannes. Agreement on an "irreversible" move to economic and monetary union by 1999.*

3 JULY. *Serious rioting in Northern Ireland follows the early release of Private Lee Clegg, a British soldier serving a life sentence for shooting dead a Catholic driving a stolen car.*

4 JULY. *British prime minister John Major wins the election for leadership of the Conservative Party, defeating John Redwood, who receives votes from Major's "Euro-skeptic" critics.*

11 JULY. *Bosnian Serb forces take the UN "safe area" of Srebrenica. Dutch UN peacekeepers offer no resistance. Local Bosniak men of military age are subsequently massacred by Bosnian Serbs; older men, women, and*

children are forced to flee. In Russia, President Yeltsin suffers a heart attack, starting a long period of impaired health.

25 JULY. *Bosnian Serb forces take the UN "safe area" of Zepa. The UN War Crimes Tribunal in The Hague indicts Bosnian Serb president Radovan Karadžić and military commander Radko Mladić on charges of genocide and crimes against humanity.*

30 JULY. *A Chechnya peace agreement provides for withdrawal of Russian troops. The issue of formal independence is left unresolved.*

4 AUGUST. *The Italian parliament approves a pension-reform plan, cutting public expenditure.*

5–9 AUGUST. *Croatian forces retake Serb-held Krajina in "Operation Storm." More than 150,000 local Serbs flee.*

AUGUST. Holidays in a part of western Poland that was Germany until 1945. The architecture is still overwhelmingly, unmistakably German. The redbrick Gothic church is a German Protestant church with a Virgin Mary and twelve stations of the cross slapped around the walls to make it a Polish Catholic one. Many of the place-names are just Polish translations of the original German names. On the murderously busy main road from Poznań to Berlin, a billboard advertises "New Cars—after accidents in Germany." The Germans are not yet coming back in any great numbers, whether as landowners, factory owners, or pleasure seekers. But as Poland comes closer to the West, and the German capital moves to nearby Berlin, they surely will.

28 AUGUST. *Another mortar bombing of a marketplace in Sarajevo.*

AUGUST–SEPTEMBER. *NATO responds by a series of air attacks on Bosnian Serb positions, including their artillery emplacements around Sarajevo.*

31 AUGUST. *The son of Slovak president Michal Kováč is kidnapped and taken to Austria. Operatives of the Slovak intelligence service, answerable to Prime Minister Vladimír Mečiar, are almost certainly involved.*

14 SEPTEMBER. *Bosnian Serbs remove their heavy weaponry from around Sarajevo.*

27 SEPTEMBER. *The European Court of Human Rights condemns the 1988 Gibraltar killing of three unarmed IRA terrorists by British security forces.*

7 OCTOBER. *Representatives of Greek and Turkish political parties in Cyprus express commitment to a negotiated solution for the island.*

12 OCTOBER. *A sixty-day cease-fire in Bosnia, negotiated by U.S. mediator Richard Holbrooke, comes into effect.*

CLEANSED CROATIA

Zagreb

I NEED NO VISA TO ENTER CROATIA. PLANINKA FROM BELGRADE does. She had to wait for weeks and got one only because Slavko Goldstein, her editor here, intervened with the Croat authorities. But others have been refused, in both directions. It's as if I, as an Englishman, were suddenly forbidden to visit Cardiff. "Yugoslavia was a small country," says Slavko, "and now we've made five even smaller ones."

At dinner in one of Zagreb's plush restaurants, we talk about the siege of Sarajevo. "The Serbs" did this, a Croat friend tells us; "the Serbs" do that. Planinka, a lady of a certain age, smartly dressed, and immaculately made up, has an almost permanently fixed smile. But I wonder how she feels. Serb?

"Before the war," says Slavko, and for a moment I think he means, "Before the war . . ." This is Europe's new semantic dividing line. In Britain, France, or Germany, "the war" still means 1939–1945. Here it means 1991–1995. So far, that is, since no one knows whether the war has really ended or merely paused for a year.

To Glina

With Slavko, his son Ivo, and Planinka packed into a puttering Renault 4, we drive south from Zagreb to the Krajina, under Serb rule for nearly four years but now "liberated" by the Croatian army in "Operation Storm." At Karlovac, where Slavko lived as a boy, we visit the marketplace bombed by the besieging Serb forces. Look, here's the mark of the mortar bomb on the pavement; that's where the shoppers died.

On the way out of town, we pick up Mate, an elderly Croat farmer who hid Slavko in his village during the war (the last war, that is), when the Ustasha—the Croat fascists—were rounding up the Jews of Karlovac. Slavko then went off to fight with Tito's communist partisans, but Mate hid in the woods, refusing to fight for any side. The old man has a broad, nut-brown face, a ready smile beneath the cloth cap, and quiet dignity.

Leaving Karlovac, we cross what for the last four years was the Serb front line. Suddenly all the houses are roofless, scorched, plundered, or simply reduced to rubble. It's like the photographs of German cities in 1945, except in color and 3-D. We come upon a man demolishing, brick by red brick, a wall that is still standing. The bricks are then passed down a line, composed mainly of women and children, to a woman who crouches in the ruins. She carefully brushes off each intact brick and places it on a pile, ready for the rebuilding. In Germany in 1945 they called such women *Trümmer-frauen,* the women of the ruins.

We drive eastward along the valley of the river Kupa, which for much of its length was the front line, just twenty miles south of Zagreb as the missile flies. In the Croat villages, almost every house has been plundered and had the roof burned or blown out by the occupying Serbs. Here and there, we see Croats returning to their houses, starting over, with the checkerboard flag of Croatia flying from the balcony. But for the most part the villages are still deserted.

We stop off at the house of Mate's son-in-law, well built, with a still intact solid concrete roof and a good view down the valley. It has survived because the Serbs used it as a command and observation post. Inside, red-painted graffiti in the Serbs' Cyrillic script say, "Welcome to the heroes," "Keep this place clean!" and "If you want to eat, wash up the dishes!" Orderly folk.

On down the valley, and then—*bang! bang!*—two tires on the little Renault have blown as we hit a giant pothole. A passing farmer takes Mate and Slavko off in his trailer to find someone who has the right kind of spare tire. Planinka, still smiling, wanders off into the bushes to have a pee, but Ivo shouts at her: "Stop! The verges are mined!" Half an hour later, Mate and Slavko come back in a lorry with a spare tire and a thickset farmer, grinning from ear to ear. He is a Serb, married to a Croat, and during the Serb occupation he protected the houses of his Croat neighbors. We can see their roofs along the skyline of a nearby hill, miracles of intactness. Now, we are told, he is a hero to the local Croats. But he does seem desperately eager to please. Fear lines his grin.

Mate's village, Kovačevac, has hardly a house intact. He leads us through some long grass to an area of rubble and twisted metal: all that is left of an eighteenth-century wooden church, a fine and rare example of its kind. Planinka picks up a small piece of twisted bronze and turns it around. It is beautiful. I feel that she would love to place it on her studio table. But then she puts it back. After all, she, too, is a Serb.

When Mate came back from hiding in the woods in 1945, he was elected mayor of Kovačevac. He helped rebuild not just his own village, but also the neighboring Serb village of Prško, which had been the victim of an Ustasha atrocity. In 1941, some four hundred women and children had been rounded up by crack troops of the Ustasha leader Ante Pavelić and slaughtered in the forest. So in 1991, when most of the Croats fled before the advancing Serbs, Mate stayed. He'd seen out four regimes, he said, and he'd see out this regime, too. But one night Serb friends came to his house and told him to escape at once. You've seen too much, they said. You know who did the plundering and killing. They're coming to get you. So once again—fifty years on—Mate took to the woods. He stole down to the river Kupa, found a boat, and rowed across to the Croat-controlled side. Next night, Serbs—"Chetniks" says Mate, using the old term for Serb nationalist partisans—came and killed several of the elderly Croats who had stayed in Kovačevac.

Now Mate and his friends are putting their farms together again. They find the barn roof stacked up as spare timber in a farmyard two villages away. They find the tractor abandoned in a field. And, if they don't find their own possessions, they take someone else's. Mate's immediate neighbor came back with a trailer, which Mate recognized as his own. "Give it me back," said Mate. "No," said his neighbor. "I found it. You take another one!"

We leave Mate to attend the first normal funeral in this village for four years. A normal death—a cause for celebration. In Prško, the bust of the local Serb hero—a close comrade of Gavrilo Princip, the man who shot Archduke Franz Ferdinand in Sarajevo in 1914—has been hacked off and thrown into a hedge. Serb houses are still flying white flags. But virtually all the inhabitants have fled, in the exodus of the Serb population of the Krajina, the biggest single exodus of the war. More than 150,000 people filled the roads to Serbia and Serb-controlled Bosnia. A village became a hundred yards of traffic—vans, tractors, and trailers piled high with baggage and pets and wailing children. Again, I think of 1945, and the endless columns of Germans fleeing westward before the Red Army, from East Prussia and Silesia. Here, as there, the war has come full circle. Innocent women and children are punished for the crimes of their compatriots. Nemesis.

In one low wooden house we find an old peasant woman, with a deeply lined face, black woolen headscarf, gnarled hands. She, too, had fled with the village, seven days on the road to Belgrade. "Ay, ay," she sighs, and lifts her hands. But her son went via Hungary to Belgrade and brought her back again. They were lucky to get through. Although paying lip service to the refugees' "right to return," the Croat authorities are making it very difficult for anyone to do so.

We drive through more eerily empty villages, with just the occasional pig wandering along the verge, to the town of Glina, scene of another Ustasha massacre during the Second World War. Here, Serbs from the local area were told they would be spared if they converted to Roman Catholicism. They marched, singing, along the road into Glina. Then they were herded into the Orthodox church and massacred.

Today, this is a ghost town. The Croats fled in 1991; now the Serbs have fled, too, while most of the Croats have yet to return. However, the Croat administration has started the work of reconstruction by converting a memorial pavilion to the victims of the Ustasha massacre into a "Croat House." They have removed the marble tablets bearing the names of the Serb victims, raised the checker-board flag, and held a liberation concert to inaugurate this Croat cultural institute. Western civilization has triumphed.

The Waste Land

Two more days in the "ethnically cleansed" Krajina, this time heading south with my friend Konstanty Gebert, a Polish writer, and Ana Uzelac, his Serbo-Polish colleague from Belgrade. On the roads, there is no traffic except the Croat military police at the roadblocks, a few white-painted UN vehicles, and, incongruously, the occasional smart BMW or Mercedes with German number plates racing past. Presumably Croat *Gastarbeiter* revisiting family homes or just on safari.

For hour after hour, we drive through the most spectacularly beautiful countryside, along the wooded valleys of the Plitvicka National Park, across the karst uplands, and down to the fortress of Knin. For hour after hour we see nothing but devastated, burned, plundered houses. Roofs burned out; windows smashed; clothes, bedclothes, furniture, papers strewn across the floor. Everything of value removed. Orchards, vineyards, fields, all with their crops gone to waste. No cars left, no tractors, no farm equipment, no cattle, no dogs. Only a few cats survive.

And, for mile upon mile upon mile, we see no single human being. Nobody. Ana has brought from Belgrade the addresses of Serb families that fled, but their houses are very difficult to find, because the villages no longer have the landmarks the inhabitants remember. Could this have been a grocer's shop? Was that once a white wall? But there is no one to ask for directions.

Cleansing is in an awful way the right word for what has been done here. The Krajina, an area the size of several English counties, has literally been picked clean. This was not random looting. The plundering and burning has been done quite systematically—for the most part, it seems, by Croats in one uniform or another. The object, apart from booty, is simple: to ensure that the Serbs don't come back. Croatia is to be, so far as possible, Serb-free. *Serbenrein*.

According to the local UN office, some one hundred elderly Serbs who stayed in their homes have been murdered since Croat forces retook the area. At Gračac, we find fresh graves in the cemetery, numbered neatly on the identical wooden crosses. However, here, as elsewhere, the Orthodox church has been left standing, to show that the Croats are western, civilized people, unlike those barbaric Orthodox Serbs, who raze Catholic churches to the ground. But the vicarage has been torn apart. A children's Bible and a church calendar for 1996 lie among the litter on the floor.

At Kistanje, once a pretty, small town, we find three family photo albums laid out on stone tables in the marketplace. The wedding. A son's christening. The ceremony to celebrate his joining the Yugoslav army. As we turn the pages, a white armored personnel carrier of UNPROFOR, the so-called United Nations Protection Force, roars through the deserted town. Ludicrous protectors of nothing. The UN self-protection force.

In places like this, journalists say, "the story writes itself." Wherever we look, journalistic "color" and clichés offer themselves wantonly, like the whores in Amsterdam. Outside a plundered home, a doll is sprawled across the road, one foot torn off. In the ruins of the family home of Milorad Pupovac, leader of a small would-be liberal Serb party in Croatia, I find a book of children's verse, *Robber Katja and Princess Nadja,* published in Sarajevo in 1989. Ana can recite some of the verses from memory. The last poem is entitled "How Our Yugoslavia Grows." In the rubble of another house I see what looks like a white scroll. Unrolling it, I discover a black-and-white photograph of Tito—the kind that once hung in every public place and in many private houses too. It has a bootmark pointing toward the face.

Knin was the capital of the self-styled Serb Republic of Krajina. Now "liberated," its imposing hilltop fortress, with the checkerboard flag flying from the top, forms the background to the main election poster for President Tudjman's nationalist HDZ movement. In the foreground you see Tudjman himself, waving both fists above his head like a victorious football manager. Before the war, some 37,000 people lived in Knin; now even the local government claims only 2,000. Croat soldiers and military police, baseball caps reversed, speed along the deserted streets in their stolen—sorry, "liberated"—

cars: a smart Mercedes, a Renault, a Mitsubishi Jeep with the name of the German dealer still advertised on the back. We climb to the top of the fortress and discover the largest flag I have ever seen in my life. It must be at least thirty feet long. Young girls in black jeans and T-shirts are photographing each other literally wrapped in the flag. The cliché made flesh.

As the sun sets over the mountains like a holiday advertisement, we drive down to the Adriatic, across the invisible line to the part of Croatia the Serbs never occupied, and suddenly there is ordinary life: houses with roofs, electric light, curtains, cars, a young couple canoodling on a scooter. In Šibenik, one of the beautiful resort towns on the Dalmatian coast, we gape at the cheerful, well-dressed crowds, the nice hotels and the Café Europa.

Ah, Europe—but we've been there all the time.

Three years later, British television commentators celebrated the World Cup soccer match in which plucky little Croatia defeated Germany. The cameras showed, draped across one side of the stadium, a huge Croatian flag. The Croatian team played well and sportingly, but I could only think of the cleansed Krajina, and of the huge flag flying over Knin, and of how the same people cheering their soccer players now must have been cheering their soldiers then. Perhaps it was the same flag.

BOSNIAN GLIMPSES

Tuzla

WE ARRIVE IN THE LATE EVENING, AFTER AN EXHAUSTING SIXTEEN-hour bus journey across Bosnia, and enter the dim and cavern-ous Hotel Tuzla, instantly recognizable as the kind of grimly modernist tower-block hotel built all over communist Europe in the 1970s and 1980s. I step into the lift, press the button for the second floor, and at once subside, powerless, into the cellar. The re-ception committee in the bar consists of Christopher Hitchens, Susan Sontag, and David Rieff. When I join them, Sontag is just say-ing to Michael Ignatieff, "I can't believe that this is your first time here."

Next morning, we are bused to a large congress hall, with ush-erettes in red jackets and black miniskirts. Mary Kaldor, chair of the Helsinki Citizens Assembly, welcomes us "after this long journey, so difficult for all of us." But she came by helicopter. Julie Christie reads a poem which goes, according to my notebook, "Sarajevo, glowing white . . . as a translucent china cup."

Then four local politicians, middle-aged men in suits, make their appeals for international support. Sturdy Selim Beslagić, the mayor of Tuzla, tells us that our planet is based on natural laws and har-monies, and asks us to help defend Europe from fascism. The provincial governor, who comes from President Izetbegović's Mus-lim-led Party of Democratic Action (SDA), says Europe must do something to prevent genocide happening one hour's flying time from its capitals. The president of the Bosnian parliament says, according to the simultaneous interpretation, "We are defending the basic principles of the world system," while the head of the Tuzla Citizens' Forum, which cohosts this meeting, talks of "the spirit of progressive mankind" represented by the Helsinki Citizens Assembly and asks, "is Europe dying in Bosnia?" He insists that two things are vital: the right of refugees to return to their homes and the punishment of war criminals.

We have been told that Tuzla is an island of liberal, multiethnic, multicultural coexistence. The reality I discover over the next three days is more complicated. The style of these men, like that of the congress hall and of the hotel, is unmistakably communist. And one reason—perhaps the main reason—why Tuzla is still relatively tolerant of ethnic diversity is precisely that it was such a strongly communist, Yugoslav industrial city. Yet even Tuzla isn't that multiethnic anymore. According to the 1991 census, only 55 percent of the Tuzla region's population identified themselves as Muslim; now the UN estimate is 96 percent. The Serb Orthodox church is beautifully kept, but the old caretaker says they haven't had a priest here since 1992. For three years, the remnants of the congregation have been improvising, intoning half-remembered chants and hymns but with no christenings, marriages, or funerals. And then, when you talk to people from Mayor Beslagić's city council, you find that for them the main enemy seems to be not the Serbs but rather their Bosnian political rivals from President Izetbegović's SDA.

Like the complex landscape of physical destruction on the way out here, these political complexities spoil the simple picture with which many people started the journey of solidarity: immaculate Bosnian victims ("Sarajevo, glowing white . . .") against child-eating Serb villains. But this is one very good reason for coming. It's what I call the *Homage to Catalonia* test. Can you, like Orwell in Spain, maintain solidarity with the victims without compromising the truth about the faults on the victims' side? When the assembly's concluding statement describes Tuzla as a "multiethnic, multireligious paradise," it has, in my book, failed the *Homage to Catalonia* test. But that's the trouble with assemblies, committees, platforms: They always do.

Survivors of Srebrenica

When Serb forces seized the UN "safe area" of Srebrenica, marching Bosnian men off to killing fields while Dutch soldiers stood by, most of the surviving refugees came to the Tuzla area. In a bar in Tuzla, Michael Ignatieff and I meet one of the few soldiers from Srebrenica to have escaped with his life. He limps in on crutches, one foot still heavily bandaged, and tells his story through our interpreter. After being operated on by Dutch surgeons in a UN camp at Potočari, he was told by the Dutch that he would be evacuated to Tuzla. Instead, Serb officers strode in and ordered that an old man should be transported in his place.

Now he was told he would be taken to another hospital, shown on Bosnian Serb TV as proof of how well the captives were being treated, and then evacuated. Instead, he was taken to a Serb prison camp. The camp commander deliberately kicked his wounded leg. The wound, undressed, was crawling with worms. An old man hanged himself after learning of his son's death. Another prisoner died in the freezing cold. After more than three months in detention, he was brought out in an exchange of prisoners organized by the International Committee of the Red Cross. His father and two brothers have still not made it to Tuzla.

The story is harrowing enough. But he's a bad witness. His tale is poorly told, confusing, and he seems to be mixing what happened to others with what happened to him. Notebooks open on the table, Ignatieff and I find ourselves pummeling him with questions to get the bloody story straight. Anyone here been crippled and speak English?

In the nearby town of Živinice, a refugee camp was hit by a Serb mortar bomb just a fortnight ago. Six children were killed, four wounded. The camp turns out to be an incongruous toy town of Scandinavian-built terraced houses, each designed as an idyllic suburban home for a nuclear family of four but now sleeping forty. Old peasant women in headscarves, grubby children with large brown eyes. No work, no money, nothing to do. Empty, numbing hopelessness. Suddenly, there is another visiting party, with Julie Christie in black trousers and gray sweater, camera at the ready. The children immediately form into a group to have their photograph taken. They raise their hands and make the V sign. V for Victory.

Dijana

In a coffee break, I talk to a girl called Dijana, from Sarajevo. She is in her early twenties and beautiful, with high cheekbones and large, liquid, oval eyes; stylishly dressed in black, carefully made up in white. At first, she is unforthcoming, almost hostile, until I mention the name of a good friend who has been coming regularly to Sarajevo in the worst times of the siege. I add, "You must be totally fed up with all these well-intentioned foreigners always asking the same questions." "Yes," she says, and smiles for the first time. "A lot of people come just for themselves, to say they've been here, to show off."

Now she'd like to ask me something. Why did the West do nothing to help Sarajevo? Sarajevo was a very special place before the war. They lived well, better than many in the West. Now their life is utterly destroyed and degraded. Her brother was just starting to study. But he's been four years a soldier, and she doesn't think he can ever return to normal life. And the West has done nothing—nothing—just watched them being killed. She wants to say to UNPRO-FOR, "just clear out and give me a weapon to fight with, and I'll see if I can avoid being raped or whatever." Anger polishes her English.

What is she to do? Perhaps she could emigrate, but she doesn't want to be a dishwasher somewhere. "My children might become Canadian or whatever, but I wouldn't be—I'd always be Sarajevan." At the independent Radio Zid, she and her friends try to pretend they live in a normal country. They do reports on films, play pop music, and give their listeners beauty tips. For example, water after rice has been boiled in it is very good for the skin. She smiles, an angry smile.

Like it or not (and she doesn't), Dijana is a Western television producer's dream victim. Beautiful in black and white, eloquent, bitter. *Victim,* the new fragrance from Calvin Klein.

Sarajevo

Dijana's anger was just a small foretaste of what I find here. I have never met such deep bitterness. Despite all the introductions with which I'm armed—several from good friends of mine to people they regard as close friends here—I think some people would hardly have talked to me were it not for the intercession of my interpreter, Senada Kreso. Knowing some of my work, she decides that it may, after all, be worth the effort of helping me. But it's a very bad moment. The American-brokered cease-fire has just come into force— something I didn't anticipate when I planned my trip. Senada and her Sarajevan friends are just emerging from a particularly terrible period of the now three-and-a-half-year-long siege, the worse because it followed a reprieve in 1994.

For days on end, they sat at home, freezing, in the dark, without electricity, gas, or running water, waiting for a mortar bomb to hit them from the hills. Or they forced themselves to walk to work, although often there was no work to do, risking death by sniper fire at every crossroads. However many descriptions you have read and television reports you've watched, until you see the place for yourself you don't really grasp how its peculiar, unique, and beautiful location lays the whole city out as a kind of super bowl-shaped target for the snipers in the surrounding hills.

They saw friends wounded or killed. They were degraded in a hundred small, everyday ways. They had to wash themselves and their clothes in a couple of buckets of water. They had to scavenge for firewood. They were impoverished by the black-market prices and the lack of normal incomes. They were humiliated by having to receive charity from visiting foreigners: the discreet envelope, the embarrassed smile. And then there was the noise, early at morning, late at night, as death rained gigantically down.

Now they are like deep-sea divers dragged too quickly up to the surface. They have psychological divers' bends. If you, the West, could stop it now—they say—why couldn't you stop it three years ago? And, because they're sure we could have stopped it, they feel that what they've been through has been senseless. Worse still, British and French soldiers have been here all the time, patrolling the ghetto walls while they were frozen, degraded, bombarded, and picked off like insects.

Quite a few of those to whom I have introductions—academics, journalists, artists, filmmakers—have their flats in one large modern housing estate in an area called Ciglane. The estate is built up a steep hillside, with staggered balconies and large windows, like a zig-gurat, thus offering perfect target practice for Serb artillery. When I join Senada in the tiny Café Herc, in the middle of the estate (only yesterday they took the sandbags down from the front window), an unshaved, weary, mildly tipsy man says, "How I hate foreigners!" They are bitter about the indifference of the West, about those who didn't come. But now they are also bitter about those who kept com-ing back—on safari—and then flew out to safety with their Sarajevo tales. "It seemed to us a sort of necrophilia," says Senada.

"Who really helped?" I ask Zdravko Grebo, a law professor and di-rector of Radio Zid, whom every visiting foreigner goes to see. "Everyone and no one," he says. Everyone—even Bianca Jagger, who just stayed for a few hours at the airport—helped a little to draw the world's attention to what was happening in Sarajevo. But nobody, because the siege went on and on and on.

But they are bitter, too, about their own friends and colleagues who have left. Sitting in the cramped editorial office of the weekly *Dani,* an open metal oven burning firewood in the corner, Ozren Kebo talks of "cowardice" and "betrayal." He describes a pop concert in Zagreb where thousands of Sarajevans wept as a well-known Sarajevan pop group sang the refrain of their hit song, "Sarajevo, I'm staying here." But they didn't stay here, says Ozren. He did. With the recent easing of the siege, there's been another wave of emigra-tion.

At times, it seems the only people they can still respect, even re-late to at all, are those who have stayed, like them, and gone through the same experience. They are proud of how they've continued to produce newspapers, literary quarterlies, weeklies, concerts, radio programs. The cultural resistance. The black humor of the siege. The wonderful posters by the "Trio" artists: "Enjoy Sara-Jevo," a per-fect parody of the famous red-and-white "Enjoy Coca-Cola" poster, or "Enjoy the Winter Olympics, Sarajevo 1994/95," with the

Olympic rings done in barbed wire. (The 1984 Winter Olympics were held here.)

Suada Kapić, editor of the *Survival Guide to Sarajevo*, gives me her latest production, a large glossy magazine called *LIFE*—its title printed with the *E* reversed—with profiles of people who stayed. (She tells me Time-Life's lawyers have protested at the infringement of copyright.) Sometimes the pathos of the intellectuals seems a little heavy. And the black humor, too. For example, "What is the difference between Auschwitz and Sarajevo?" "In Sarajevo there's no gas." But I hardly feel in a position to say, "Come on, it wasn't *that* bad."

Yet the worst thing is their bitterness about themselves. Four years ago, they led a life as normal and civilized as that of their contemporaries in Budapest or Athens. They enjoyed the easygoing café lifestyle of their own city, went skiing in the hills around Pale, perhaps vacationed in Italy. Now they are reduced to this humiliating role of victim and international zoo exhibit. Zdravko Grebo, unofficial spokesman number one for Sarajevo, says, "You know, since you're here with Senada, as a friend, I'll tell you what I really want. What I really want is to be left alone, to get back to my books and my music, not to have to travel to conferences and endlessly answer these questions."

In the first two years of the siege—the "romantic period"—they still felt they might save their Sarajevo. Fluid. Tolerant. Multiethnic not as the result of a western ideology of multiculturalism—what they ironically call "multi-multi-multi"—but as a historical reality where people of Serb, Croat, Muslim, and increasingly mixed backgrounds and relationships shared the same lifestyle. Or divided, if they divided, not on ethnic lines. (To be sure, all this happened under the authoritarian roof of Titoism. In many places I find black-and-white photographs of the old man still displayed on the wall: in Radio Zid, in the PEN Club, even above two stern rows of Sarajevo rabbis in the headquarters of the Jewish community.) But now they feel this Sarajevo—their Sarajevo—has gone for good.

Even if the peace holds, they will find themselves in the provincial capital of a rump Bosnian state, with a gently corrupt and mildly authoritarian government. And what there is of cosmopolitan culture will be living off foreign money, as artificial and ultimately as in-authentic and corrupt as the subsidized culture of West Berlin during the cold war.

The defense of the café has failed.

But for what some of the same people were saying three years later, see pp. 337–38.

Karadžić

At first glance, the poet and critic Marko Vešović, with a forehead like a small cliff and wild, swept-back hair, bears an alarming resemblance to the Bosnian Serb leader Radovan Karadžić. In fact, they are both Montenegrins and before the war were friends. With only the slightest prompting, Marko unfolds his tale of Karadžić.

Radovan—"Radko" to his friends—came to Sarajevo on his own at the age of fourteen to study at secondary and then medical school. His family had suffered terribly in Montenegro from wartime reprisals by Tito's communist partisans, and he always hated the communists. He was good-looking, bright, one of the lads. But then, as still a very young man, he made the terrible mistake of impregnating the dreadful Delilija, whom Marko describes as hideous and weighing a hundred kilos. Her father, the manager of the Europa Hotel, forced Radko to marry her and to come and live in their house. But secretly he went on womanizing. That was when his chronic lying began.

Sonja, now propaganda minister of the Bosnian Serbs, was the child of this ghastly coupling. Marko was put down as her godfather at the christening, but Radko told him about it only afterwards—otherwise, in the Montenegrin tradition, the godfather would have had the right to choose her name.

Like Marko and Zdravko Grebo, Karadžić took part in the '68 demonstrations in Sarajevo. But then he got a scholarship to study in America, and they were sure he had agreed to work for the secret police. For years, they shunned him. But eventually they made it up and again attended the hard-drinking "salons," which he loved to give. He was a charming host.

He wanted to be a great psychiatrist, but he was too lazy to do any real work. He owed his job at the clinic to his Bosnian Muslim boss, Ismet Cerić, to whom he was devoted. Never—not even in the most intimate, drunken conversation—had Marko heard Karadžić say a word against Muslims. Once he went away to work in Belgrade. But he came back after a few months and told Cerić he couldn't understand the mentality of the people there. (Those Serbs, you know.)

Then he wanted to be a great poet. But had no voice of his own. His poetry was all bad imitations of Georg Trakl, the Austrian poet of decadence. When he published a book of poems in 1992, Marko and Nikola Koljević (now also a leader of the Bosnian Serbs in the hills) had to rewrite half the verses for him.

Just a few months later, Marko turned on the television and there was Karadžić, up in the hills, looking down at Sarajevo through his binoculars and saying, "I could take it in two days." This from someone who never even served in the army. In this, as in all else, a bragging charlatan. A liar, a trickster, a failure at everything he did.

Yet as Marko rumbles to the close of his picaresque tale, I think that, after all, Radovan Karadžić has succeeded. He may have to live out the rest of his days in hiding as a war criminal. He may even be caught and tried or simply shot. But he's famous at last. His name will live on, in the history books and the stories of future generations.

BOSNIA IN OUR FUTURE

ONE DAY, SOON, I WANT TO HIJACK HELMUT KOHL, JACQUES CHIRAC, Jacques Santer, and all the other leaders of the European Union, on the way to their latest summit, and I want to fly them to a neighborhood of Sarajevo called Ciglane. There I will drive them, past the graveyards, to the Café Herc, or perhaps, because it has more room, to the Café London. Just for an hour—since I know how busy they all are—I will have them listen to a small group of articulate, English-speaking Sarajevans. Have them listen, not, as they might expect, to yet one more plangent appeal for help, but to the sheer bottomless contempt and bitterness of people who don't expect anything from them any more. Nothing except empty words.

After three and a half years, this acid bitterness, so deep and tired that even the black humor of the earlier siege time hardly surfaces any more, extends to almost everyone. To anything in a blue helmet, of course. To all the endless foreign visitors on their Sarajevo safaris. But now even to some of those journalists, intellectuals, and aid workers who came early and really tried to help; even to their own Sarajevan friends who have left; even, worst of all, to themselves, for being forced into this humiliating role of victim. Yet somewhere very near the bottom of the pile is this thing which still calls itself "Europe."

Then, when I have got our European leaders safely back to their comfortable hotels in Brussels or Paris or Barcelona, I should like to see if they can still go on smoothly delivering their soft, prefabricated speeches about our Europe of peace and progress and ever closer union.

1

There are so many defeats and failures involved in Bosnia, so many dimensions and intricacies to the whole larger history of former Yugoslavia, that one hardly knows where to begin. But, at a moment when America is calling all the diplomatic shots over Bosnia, I will, perversely perhaps but not illogically, begin with Europe.

Most people brought up in Western Europe during the cold war have imbibed, consciously or half wittingly, a Whig interpretation of European history. European history since 1945 has been told to them essentially as a story of progress toward more prosperity, more freedom, more democracy, more unity in something now teleologically called the European Union. What is more, in the 1970s and 1980s people in Eastern Europe increasingly came to believe this story. This is one of the reasons why, in 1989, they voted communism away and set out to "return to Europe." Nineteen eighty-nine was thus the greatest triumph of this idea—but also, it now seems, its apogee.

For since then we have, in the southeastern part of Europe, gone almost all the way back. Here there was violent conflict in the province of Kosovo already in 1989, even as the Berlin Wall fell. Within two years, there was outright war between Serbia and Slovenia, Serbia and Croatia, then between Serbians, Croatians, and Bosniaks in Bosnia. With it came a rapid descent to atrocities not seen in Europe for fifty years. These atrocities do not merely reproduce but also, so to speak, elaborate upon the already formidable repertoire of European barbarism from 1939 to 1945.

It is not just war without quarter, massacres of civilians, camps, systematic rapes, mutilation of corpses, but also new refinements of the old European art of ethnic cleansing and the refined psychological torture of the siege of Sarajevo—to name but two innovations. Only the worst horror of them all—the systematic attempt to exterminate a whole people, as in the Holocaust of European Jewry—has so far been lacking, although there have been attempts at systematic extermination of Bosnian elites and men of military age. Now, in the Croatian Krajina, we see a familiar last act: Serbian men, women, and children fleeing on their tractors from villages where their people have lived for hundreds of years, as punishment for the sins of their compatriots—just like the Germans from the Sudetenland and Silesia in 1945. But Bosnia has still not reached its 1945.

Early in the siege of Sarajevo, there appeared on the wall of the half-ruined post office the familiar Serb graffito "This is Serbia!" Someone scrawled underneath, "No, you idiot, it's a post office!" My friend Konstanty Gebert has written a whole book about that line, about the defense of the post office. But I want to add a line of my own: "This is Europe!" For all these things have been done by Europeans to other Europeans in Europe. That in itself should be enough to remind us that the story of recent European history that we have been telling ourselves and our children is little better than a fairy tale. And yet our politicians go on telling it.

The double-think is truly surreal. "War in Europe has become unthinkable," say our leaders. Crash go the shells into Sarajevo and Srebrenica and a thousand other towns and villages.

2

Of course, the war in former Yugoslavia, though entirely comparable in brutality with all but the ultimate horror of the Second World War, is not comparable in scale. But, in two respects, our own relationship to it is worse. In the Second World War, most people in the countries fighting Nazism did not, at the time, know the full extent of the horrors; and, anyway, we were at war with Nazism. But here, sitting in peace and comfort, we have watched it all on our television screens. The Warsaw ghetto in installments, every night at nine. Death brought to us live.

If there was then the question "Why did the heavens not open?" there is even more of a question now. Why did all this coverage, these harrowing accounts by brave reporters, fail to mobilize Western European public opinion? Is it because of the Rambo loop? The young male fighters we see charging across our screens, with black headbands and cross-slung ammunition belts, partly model themselves on Rambo, but they also look to the viewer like Rambo—that is, fiction. Reality, partly modeling itself on virtual reality, is taken for unreal. Or is it the sheer complexity of the story? "Bosnia is our Spain," says the French philosopher Bernard-Henri Levy. But this is so much more complicated, and even Spain, as Orwell reminded us in *Homage to Catalonia,* was complicated enough. Another French intellectual, Alain Finkielkraut, has told us how to be Croats; but Croats, too, have now been ethnic cleansers. And so on.

Worse still, we have not just watched from our ringside seats while people are murdered and Bosnia torn apart. Representing the European Community on a diplomatic mission to Yugoslavia as the war began in the summer of 1991, M. Jacques Poos proclaimed that "The hour of Europe has dawned." America should kindly leave this one to us. As foreign minister of Luxembourg, M. Poos informed the peoples of disintegrating Yugoslavia that small states have no future. Ever since that aptly ridiculous moment, the states supposedly united in the European Union, and especially Britain, France, and Germany, have been directly involved in what has happened. At the very latest since the imposition of the arms embargo on Bosnia, we have directly affected the military balance of this war and become, willy-nilly, a party to the destruction. Not just we Europeans, of course. Plainly, the UN bears its own specific responsibility; and the United States and other non-European states, too.

The point here is not to pick over, once again, the whole tortuous diplomatic and military history of the four years from, as it were, Jacques Poos to Richard Holbrooke, deploying the documentary CD-ROM now available with David Owen's memoirs to demonstrate that the Germans were most to blame here, or the British there. Nor is it to distinguish, as one clearly should, between individual politicians, officials, and UN commanders on the ground. The point is simply to restate a few bald facts about Europe's failure. In the last four years, we have failed to prevent the destruction and partition of a once peaceful and still beautiful part of Europe, with perhaps a quarter of a million people killed and more than two million made homeless. To many a professional soldier's profound frustration and anger, British and French soldiers have had to sit there on the ghetto walls while the people inside were humiliated and shot. Worst of all, there is the supposed UN "safe area" of Srebrenica, where Dutch UN soldiers this summer stood by (if not worse) while Bosnian men were taken off to be killed.

Apart from the valiant but largely vain efforts of Hans Koschnick, the EU administrator of Mostar, the EU as such is represented in Bosnia only by its monitors, known locally as "the ice-cream men" because of their ludicrous uniform of white shirts, white pullovers, white trousers, and white plimsolls. Cricket umpires whom no one obeys. Yet when all is said and done, the ice-cream men seem less caricatures than pretty fair representations of the external policy of that thing called Europe, which looked so bright and hopeful just four years ago.

3

Now for the excuses. First, there is the diplomat's eternal refrain: "What would *you* have done?" "What was the alternative?" Well, of course we never can know "What would have happened if . . ." For example, if we had done nothing—including, that is, not stopping anyone get arms—then it is possible that Bosnia would have been simply obliterated, partitioned between a Greater Serbia and a Greater Croatia, as the postcommunist opportunist Slobodan Milošević (who started it) and the postcommunist nationalist Franjo Tudjman (who has come out on top) discussed at their secret meeting at Tito's villa in Karadjordjevo in March 1991. But it is also possible that the Bosnians would somehow have defended more of their territory, as they somehow defended most of Sarajevo in 1992. We can only make an informed guess.

Many of the "What was the alternative?" arguments, however, actually come back to the question of political will in the West, and specifically in Western Europe. Few soldiers will disagree with the proposition that what we have done militarily to stop the worst of the siege of Sarajevo could have been done militarily three years ago. All along, the professional soldiers were saying that we needed a large force—of the order of sixty thousand men—to stop the fighting in Bosnia. If that is what we are proposing to put in now, why did we not do it then? Ah, because there has been "a process of ripening," one is told; because it needed three years of our masterly diplomacy to detach Milošević from Karadžić. But Karadžić himself says that ten thousand men could have stopped him.[1]

And then we get to the point: that we were simply not ready to do it then. But who is "we" in this sentence? The talk turns to the reluctance of parliaments, to how public opinion would have reacted to our soldiers coming back in body bags. Actually, the British and French publics are probably less sensitive to the famous "body bags" than is American public opinion, so long as they can be persuaded that the end is good and the means patriotic. But nobody even tried to persuade them. Whatever you think of Margaret Thatcher, you can't help wondering what might have happened if she had still been in charge.

In the second line of excuses, there is a whole regiment of arguments from cultural prejudice. Here are the old saws about ancient hatreds and atavistic tribes. "We can't stop people who *want* to kill each other," I recently heard a senior EU official say. Here is the view that, after all, what else can you expect of the Balkans? This view is particularly associated in the United States with Robert Kaplan's book *Balkan Ghosts* but implicit in a great many other analyses and commentaries. Unfortunately, too, the idea of "Central Europe," revived in the 1980s as a political-cultural distinction against the Soviet "East," has now been turned southward against "the Balkans," in effect trying to make it easier for Poles and Czechs to get into the EU by suggesting that Croats, Bosnians, or Bulgarians belong to a different world. Cultural determinism as an instrument of foreign policy. And then there is the view, quite widespread among the Western diplomats and soldiers involved, that all sides are as bad as each other—meaning, in particular, that the Bosnian government side is no better than the Serbs or Croats. So a plague on all their houses.

Now, plainly, it is important not to fall into the opposite mistake: selective idealization rather than collective demonization. To suggest that Bosnia was, as it were, a Switzerland invaded by a Nazi Serbia; that Sarajevo in 1990 was a hotbed of European genius, like Vienna in 1900; that the victims must always be guiltless, because that makes things morally and aesthetically easy for their foreign supporters; and that the current Bosnian state is a model multieth-nic, multicultural, multireligious, multieverything liberal democ-racy. This is the story that some Bosnian politicians will still try to tell you, but it is not the story that Messrs. Kohl, Chirac, and Santer will be told when I have sat them down in that café in Ciglane.

With a self-restraint and honesty that is in the circumstances quite remarkable, the surviving liberal intellectuals of Sarajevo (who are obviously, by definition, not typical, here as everywhere else) tell a much more subtle and therefore more convincing story. They are the first to be ironic about the ideological flag of what they call "multi-multi-multi," which has been hoisted over their city and the remains of their country.

In crude summary, the story goes something like this. For cen-turies, Bosnia was, as everyone knows, a unique meeting place of east, west, and south, Orthodox, Catholic, Bogomil, Muslim, Jew, the Ottoman and Austro-Hungarian empires, and, from the late nineteenth century, self-consciously national Serb and Croat. Coex-istence was often fragile, consisting in a peaceful living side by side rather than mixing, a respecting rather than accepting the other's customs. It was punctuated in the first half of the twentieth century by two horrible periods of war and internecine conflict along both ethnic and political lines. After 1945, however, under Tito's iron roof of "brotherhood and unity," not only was coexistence restored but the mixing advanced. To this mixing, many factors contributed—not least urbanization, secularization, and some assimilation to a Yu-goslav identity.

Naturally, this process went furthest in the city of Sarajevo and furthest of all among the younger generation, who had their own zany version of post-'68 youth culture. An editor of the monthly *Dani* tells me he and his friends are fighting for "freedom, human rights, and urban culture," and when I query the term *urban culture* he shoots back, in English, "Sex, drugs, and rock 'n' roll." It may not have been the world's most creative or exciting place. Many of the best and brightest left, especially for Belgrade. But it had real beauty and charm, a civilized lifestyle, the café raised to an art form.

However—and here's the rub—all of this was still under the po-litical roof of an undemocratic, Titoist Yugoslavia. If you talk to the

Croat Catholic Cardinal Puljić of Sarajevo, or to one of the spiritual leaders of the muslim religious community, they both start by explaining how their communities were oppressed under communism. The contortions of Tito's own nationality policy only made things worse, by identifying the heirs of the Bosniak part of the population as a national group called Muslims with a capital *M* (as opposed to the faith, with a small *m*).[2] So here, as elsewhere in communist Europe, there was simultaneously the assimilation and the exacerbation of ethnic, cultural, and religious differences by communist rule and repression.

The end of communism was therefore bound to be a critical moment, and there was always only a small chance that the repressed grievances and tensions between the different traditions and communities could, even in the most favorable circumstances, have been negotiated peacefully into a stable democratic state. After all, even in the peaceful, prosperous, democratic West, Switzerland is still a great exception. Look at Belgium. Look at Canada. This was true of Yugoslavia as a whole but above all of Bosnia, which had a Bosniak plurality but no majority.

Even the slim chance that still existed was, however, then denied them. Tito's heirs, and specifically the postcommunist politicians of first Serbia and then Croatia, either adopted a manipulative nationalist program in order to gain and retain power (Milošević) or used manipulative postcommunist methods of gaining and retaining power in order to realize a nationalist program (Tudjman). As they pulled Yugoslavia apart, they of course found Bosnian Serb and Bosnian Croat leaders ready to join them in the enterprise. Bosnian politics, especially in the country outside Sarajevo, rapidly divided on these lines. The West, and specifically the EC, then hastened to recognize the independence of the former Yugoslav republics of Slovenia, Croatia, and, yes, Bosnia-Herzegovina, without beginning to think through what it would need to turn this unique and delicately balanced historic entity into a viable independent state.

Of course, Alija Izetbegović and his Bosniak-led SDA were not blameless in this whole process. Of course, there are many nasty, corrupt, manipulative, and authoritarian aspects of the present SDA

regime. Perhaps if you are an UNPROFOR commander or a nego-
tiator on the ground it is the Bosnian government and army representatives who are the most slippery and difficult to deal with, as
British and French soldiers in Sarajevo will hasten to tell you. But to
jump from that current experience to an assertion of moral equiva-
lence between the three sides is to lose sight of the forest for the
trees and to forget how we got to where we are now. In terms of historical responsibility, the position is clear.

There is an important difference in the degree of responsibility
between the Serbian and Croatian regimes, but there is a difference
in kind between the responsibility of the Serbian and Croatian
regimes, on the one hand, and that of the Bosnian regime on the
other. Bosnia was the victim of aggression from first one side, then
the other. Bosnia and the Bosnians have suffered most, lost most,
and are still most likely to lose more.

4

It is important to grasp that the reality on the ground today is a
Bosnia split *three* ways: between areas of Bosnian Serb, Bosnian
Croat, and Bosnian-government control. This reality is best represented on paper by an internal UNPROFOR map entitled, pithily,
Warring Faction Update. It shows that the Bosnian Serbs—with
their "Serb Republic" para-state—control some 48 percent of the
territory of Bosnia-Herzegovina, in an unwieldy shape like two lungs
almost cut off in the middle at the so-called Posevina corridor. The
Bosnian Croats control some 21 percent, with the Herzegovinan
part relatively coherent and conveniently contiguous to the Croatian
fatherland, and then some awkward enclaves in the central Bosnian-
government region. Bosnian-government forces themselves actually
control less than one third of the territory, and theirs is much the
most fragmented part.

Their capital, Sarajevo, is still surrounded by Serbs, with the gun-
men still in the surrounding hills and just a stone's throw across the
river Miljacka, in the suburb of Grbavica. Their main portion of central Bosnia is, at this writing, still separated by Croat-held territory
from the Bihać pocket in the northwest. And then there is the re-

maining enclave of Goražde—Bosnia's Leningrad—separated from Sarajevo by some twenty-five miles of Serb-held land. Following the terms of the cease-fire, I was able to visit Goražde, courtesy of a U.S.-embassy armored Land Rover, but there is still nothing like safe access for ordinary Bosnian civilians. Some call this territory "rump Bosnia," but at least a rump is one piece. Their territory is also landlocked. Some supplies come in by air (including arms purchased with Arab money), but for the most part they have to come by land via Croatia—and the Croatians have been taking a large cut of the incoming money, goods, and, of course, arms.

In theory, the Bosnian-government and Bosnian Croat parts are united in a "Federation of Bosnia and Herzegovina," created in last year's Washington agreements. But the evidence on the ground is all of a continued, almost total, division, with the Croat parts wholly run by the para-state of Herceg-Bosna, having its own insignia, police, armed forces linked closely to the Croatian army, and children taught from Croatian schoolbooks, and even, since Croatia's parliamentary elections in October, their own "diaspora" representatives in the Zagreb parliament. In a wood outside the Bosnian Croat exclave of Kiseljak, you suddenly come upon two dirty caravans and two disheveled frontier policemen: a Bosnian Croat/Bosnian-government frontier post. Hans Koschnick will tell you how all the peaceful pressure that the EU has so far been able (or willing) to exert has not brought the Bosnian Croat authorities in the western half of the divided city of Mostar even to let people pass freely across the river Neretva from the pulverized and miserable Bosnian eastern half. Even though Croat forces supported Bosnian ones in the recent campaign, they reportedly twice went back to fighting each other. And President Tudjman's generous offer in an interview with Le Figaro to help "Europeanize the muslims" hardly makes things any better.

Moreover, if you look at the population figures you find that, through war, murder, flight, and expulsion, the ethnic separation, like the territorial, is already far advanced. The Bosnian government maintains a commitment to a multiethnic state. There are Serb and Croat members of its presidency. There is a Serb general on the Bosnian general staff, always wheeled out to talk to foreign visitors.

The Croat cardinal insists he will stay in Sarajevo, and serve all the Catholics in all of Bosnia-Herzegovina. But the fact is that the Bosnian-government parts are becoming increasingly Bosniak or, to use the misleading term, Muslim. As for "muslim" in the religious sense, I did find some anecdotal evidence of the growth of religious belief—"In times of trouble, man remembers his God"—but nothing remotely resembling "fundamentalism." ("I consider myself a muslim," one historian told me, and, as if on cue, someone came in to refill his large glass of local grape brandy.)

What one does find, however, is elements of something that might be described as nascent Bosnian nationalism: for example, the insistence on calling the language "Bosnian." This is entirely understandable, since one could hardly now expect them to call it "Serbo-Croat," or "Serb," or "Croat," but also rather absurd—for if ever there was an area where the Serb and Croat variants of the common language really were intertwined, together with some regional peculiarities and enrichments, it was Bosnia. In a way, this is a *reductio ad absurdum* of nineteenth-century nation-building through language. But then what on earth are they to do if everyone else around them is separating out into national states, with nationality defined in a neo-Herderian way by that combination of blood, language, religion, and culture that supposedly makes a *Volk*?

Moreover, though still chronically short of heavy weapons, they are defending themselves. (Who was it who said that a language is a dialect with an army?)[3] They try to make up in numbers of soldiers for what they lack in weaponry. In Goražde, we were told that, of some 57,000 people crammed into the enclave, as many as 10,000 were now bearing arms. Before the war, the Bosniaks were not famed as fighters. But nor, before the Second World War, were the European Jews. Some Bosnians say despairingly that they are fated to become Europe's Palestinians. Others are determined, however wildly unlikely it may sound, that they should become Europe's Israelis.

Contemptuously dismissing my suggestion that Europe might still have anything to offer them, a Bosnian editor enumerated the three things that they now need: a strong army, help for economic reconstruction, and American support.

5

And so to Dayton, Ohio, where, once again, for the—what? third? fourth?—time this century, America is trying to resolve a European conflict which Europe has failed to resolve for itself.

I believe Europe should prepare to take over the leading role in providing the international roof under which the different communities in Bosnia might live side by side and then perhaps, gradually, over many years, grow together again. As a European, I shall do what I can to try to ensure that this becomes a priority for European leaders. But, alas, here, too, I simply don't believe that it will happen. On the flight out to Zagreb, I read Helmut Kohl telling the *Süddeutsche Zeitung,* "We will make the process of unifying Europe irreversible in the next two years or so." On the flight back, nearly three weeks later, I find the West European papers full of passionate debate about European monetary union.

There are quite other priorities here: no sense of urgency about what is happening just an hour's flying time away; no sense that there is any contradiction between the claim that Europe is peacefully, irreversibly uniting, and the fact that at the very same time a part of Europe is being brutally and, one fears, really irreversibly torn apart. The long tortuous process of polit-bureaucratic negotiation at the EU's next intergovernmental conference, scheduled to open in 1996, is supposed to produce improvements to the Union's so-called Common Foreign and Security Policy. But I'm afraid we can already guess what that will mean for Bosnia. More ice-cream men.

6

If a Swiss diplomatic observer had gone to sleep after the Congress of Berlin, which assigned Bosnia-Herzegovina to Austria-Hungary in 1878, and awoke now, he would of course find much to surprise him in the institutionalized cooperation of Western European states. Here, he might exclaim, is a permanent Congress of Berlin! So far as the diplomacy goes, he might wonder a little about the blue helmets and white vehicles of the UN, and about Mr. Carl Bildt representing the EU. But a great deal would seem very familiar.

In the so-called Contact Group, he would see representatives of the same powers—France, Britain, Germany, and Russia—pursuing their national interests through their national diplomats and national armies, in what he would probably still call "the Eastern Question." Turning to *The Times*, he would read, in a leading article, of a new Franco-British entente "forged in the Bosnian War." The only difference is that he would have to substitute the United States for Austria-Hungary.

To him, what has been happening on the ground would probably also make sense, although as a Swiss he would not like it. "Ah yes," he would say, "this crazy modern passion for separating out into national states has obviously proceeded apace. I remember when the Serbs started it. . . ."

In other words, it begins to look almost as if the whole twentieth-century European story of postimperial federations and communist multinational states was merely an interruption of a longer, underlying process of separating and molding peoples into nation-states. In Western Europe, we did it earlier, by and large, through conquest and forced assimilation. In Central Europe, the first half of the twentieth century saw the job largely done, by war, the redrawing of frontiers, and ethnic "cleansing" on a massive scale (although the two-nation federation of Czechoslovakia still remained, to be finished off in the 1990s). Now this part of southeastern Europe is following suit—catching up, one might almost say, with modern Europe.

Obviously, this thought can be pushed too far. There are quite specific reasons why former Yugoslavia and Bosnia were pulled apart as they were. Even in former Yugoslavia, Macedonia still fragilely holds on as a multiethnic state. There are parts of the former Soviet Union where ethnic groups still coexist. Nor does it follow that "Bosnia is our future." What we have witnessed on our television screens over the last four years is precisely the simultaneous theater of continued peace, normality, and further (though halting) steps of integration in one part of Europe and bloody disintegration in another.

Before 1989, Europe was like Berlin: divided between east and west by a single wall. Now Europe is like a great American city, with prosperous and relatively peaceful neighborhoods, such as George-town or the Upper East Side of Manhattan, existing just a few blocks away from violent and miserable ghettos. There are no concrete walls across the streets. In theory, you can drive anywhere. But in practice the two are still worlds apart. This should shame us in Europe, just as that should shame America. But somehow we live with it.

Yet this simile, too, is misleading. For the cruelest twist is that the formation of postcommunist nation-states with clear ethnic majorities, through policies that combine the philosophy of Fichte with the methods of Stalin, probably does *not* condemn them to the fate of being Europe's permanent slums. They are not doomed forever to be chronically backward states, with corrupt one-party regimes maintaining their hold by television brainwashing, xenophobia, and force. For example, I would say that Croatia has a reasonable chance of evolving gradually into a reasonably liberal, pluralistic, and democratic nation-state over the next ten to twenty years. It might even, in the still longer term, develop a genuine acceptance of minorities and, who knows, eventually a civic rather than an ethnic definition of nationality.

With the Polish experience in mind, Konstanty Gebert sarcastically puts the lesson thus: "If you want to 'return to Europe,' first do your ethnic cleansing, then wait a generation." One can turn it around another way and put it more mildly. Trying to describe the ethnic and cultural mélange of Sarajevo before the war, the painter Edo Numankadić said to me, "We were Europe before Europe." Hyperbole perhaps, but with an element of truth. The democratization of Yugoslavia, and of Bosnia in particular, would, had it worked, have been a unique example of a part of Europe moving peacefully from a truly multiethnic society under an undemocratic (imperial, then communist) political roof to such a society within a democratic framework. That it failed there does not mean it has to fail everywhere or that we should give up trying—let alone that we should accept ethnic cleansing as a necessary evil. But—alas, alas for Europe!—it does seem to be the case that almost nobody has yet been able to avoid the painful path that has led through the formation of nation-states, to—if one is lucky—the securing of human and civil rights by a democratic nation-state, and thence—if one is very lucky—to the peaceful cooperation and integration of those nation-states.

So this is not just a matter of confronting Europe's failure and Europe's continued responsibility in this part of Europe. Properly understood, Bosnia does, I believe, compel us to reexamine some of our most basic assumptions about the shape and direction of European history.

Of course, the view of Europe you get from Sarajevo is partial as well as bitter. But I trust that my hijacked European leaders will by now have seen the point of their involuntary stopover.

We are now coming in to land at Brussels Airport. Please fasten your safety belts and extinguish all easy speeches.

I return to and develop further this argument in "Cry, the Dismembered Country," below, p. 318.

CHRONOLOGY

1995

18 OCTOBER. *The Czech parliament approves the new "lustration" law, overriding the veto of President Havel.*

29 OCTOBER. *Franjo Tudjman's Croatian Democratic Union (HDZ) wins parliamentary elections in Croatia.*

1 NOVEMBER. *Bosnia peace negotiations begin at a U.S. air-force base in Dayton, Ohio.*

5 NOVEMBER. *Eduard Shevardnadze is reelected president of Georgia.*

16 NOVEMBER. *Populist left-winger Oskar Lafontaine is elected leader of the German Social Democrats.*

19 NOVEMBER. *Presidential elections in Poland.*

NOVEMBER–DECEMBER. *In France, the Juppé government announces cuts in welfare spending, designed to meet the Maastricht criteria for participation in monetary union. Widespread popular protests follow.*

ABNORMAL NORMALITY

THE POLISH PHILOSOPHER LESZEK KOŁAKOSKI HAS A LAW OF THE Infinite Cornucopia. This states that there is never a shortage of arguments to support whatever doctrine you want to believe in for whatever reasons. The historian's version of this law is that causes can invariably be found for any event or phenomenon, however extraordinary or unexpected. Whatever happens will be explained.

The election of the postcommunist Aleksander Kwaśniewski as president of Poland, on 19 November 1995, perfectly illustrates this law. Numerous articles have immediately explained, with clarity, vivid supporting detail, and persuasive arguments, why "Poland chose" a former communist apparatchik in preference to the former Solidarity leader, Nobel Prize winner, and incumbent president, Lech Wałęsa. Never mind that if just 2 percent of the votes had gone the other way we would have read numerous articles explaining, with equal clarity and persuasiveness, why Poland had reelected Wałęsa. Thus is history written.

Yet this was an astonishing result. Six years after the end of communism, the country that had the strongest anticommunist opposition and the weakest communist party in the Soviet bloc has both a postcommunist government and a postcommunist president. If anyone had predicted this in the autumn of 1989, they would have been laughed out of the room. But then so would anyone who had predicted in the autumn of 1983 that within six years Poland would have a Catholic prime minister. Or, for that matter, anyone who had suggested in 1977, when the twenty-five-year-old Aleksander Kwaśniewski joined the ruling communist party, that the party state would soon be engulfed by a ten-million-strong national movement called Solidarity. The kaleidoscope keeps turning. Each turn is a surprise. And each turn changes our view of the past as well as of the present.

1

Now for those explanations. First, there is a regional pattern. Most of postcommunist Europe today has postcommunist rulers. In Central Europe, the Czech Republic is the only clear exception. There are major differences between, for example, countries such as Poland and Hungary, which had intervening periods of transformation under liberal or conservative governments, and those such as Romania, which went straight from the communist frying pan into the postcommunist fire. Polish and Hungarian communists in the 1980s were, in important ways, already less communist than their Czech comrades—let alone their Russian ones.

Nonetheless, there is a pattern. Postcommunist parties inherit nationwide organizations, offices, personnel, and funds, which are usually enhanced, at the end of communism, by appropriating the property of the party state. The "privatization of the *nomenklatura*"—itself one of the reasons why communists gave up political power so relatively quietly—produces a new class of communists-turned-capitalists. Actually, the Yugoslav dissident Milovan Djilas famously described the *nomenklatura* itself as "the new class," so this must be the new new class. They back their old-new party by funding or fixing and through the media they own. Former communists also have the habits and discipline for patient, boring political groundwork, which former dissidents and intellectuals generally do not.

To be sure, the business of democratic politics differs from that of communist politics. But there are people slightly lower down the communist hierarchy who very rapidly adapt to the rather different techniques of acquiring and exercising power in a modern television democracy. You may not be able to teach an old dog new tricks, but the young dogs learn them in no time. After all, they joined the party in the 1970s not because they believed in communism but because they were interested in making a career. And in the real politics of power rather than the intellectual and moral "antipolitics" of dissidence.

In the electorate, they have a hard core of the old faithful. Then they pick up votes from those who have suffered from the transition to a market economy: the unemployed, workers in large state-owned factories, the middle-aged and small-town dwellers who have difficulty adapting to new ways, and impoverished pensioners. When people had the basic, minimal security afforded by a police welfare state, they longed for freedom; now that they have freedom they yearn for the old security as well. Postcommunists promise that the state will provide more housing, employment, and social security, while preserving the gains of freedom and the market.

Kwaśniewski's victory partly fits this broad pattern but also has unique Polish features. His Alliance of the Democratic Left incorporates the so-called Social Democracy of the Republic of Poland—the direct successor to Poland's ruling communist party—whose leader he became in 1990. Although it suffers from internal tensions, the Alliance is much the largest, best-organized, and best-funded party in Poland. Its backers are classic exemplars of the new "new class"— corrupt apparatchiks turned corrupt businessmen. During the campaign, it emerged that Kwaśniewski's own wife had a large shareholding—which he had not declared—in one of these *nomenklatura* capitalist companies. Kwaśniewski gave several implausible explanations of why he had not declared this holding in his parliamentary statement of members' interests, including the suggestion that he and his wife had separated their finances and he didn't know about it.

By contrast with the standard practice in many other postcommunist countries, his candidacy was not promoted outrageously by the news and current-affairs program of state television, which rather favored the incumbent, President Wałęsa. However, he did enjoy the support of papers such as the bestselling satirical weekly *Nie* ("No"), the organ of Jerzy Urban, formerly General Jaruzelski's spokesman during martial law.

Kwaśniewski's campaign was a masterpiece of 1990s designer

electioneering, from his immaculate suits and ties to the perfect delivery of his television sound bites. A friend who commutes between Paris and Warsaw told me it was quite as professional as the presidential campaigns in France. Perhaps this is not surprising, since a leading French public-relations consultant, Jacques Séguéla, was advising him. Séguéla, who has worked previously for François Mitterrand (he claims to have been behind the slogan "*La France Tranquille*") and was recommended to Kwaśniewski by the Austrian chancellor Franz Vranitsky, says he helped to invent Kwaśniewski's two main slogans—"Choose the Future" and "A Common Poland"—and to prepare him for his crucial television debates with Lech Wałęsa. In a telephone conversation, M. Séguéla tells me that he likes to do an election campaign every year or two. It is, he says, his "hobby." Besides Mitterrand and Vranitsky, his advisees have included the Bulgarian president Zhelyu Zhelev and the former Hungarian prime minister József Antall. He finds "Alexander" to be young, clever, courageous, and *médiatique*. He is, says M. Séguéla, something between a Kennedy and a Bill Clinton, whom he describes as "a great president"—although adding cautiously "at least from the point of view of communications."

Kwaśniewski also used more old-fashioned methods. He toured the country assiduously, promising good things such as more housing (a major worry for the young), social security, and pensions—things about which, incidentally, the Polish president has little power to decide, even taking the broadest interpretation of his rather ill-defined constitutional powers.

However, the composition of his vote does not entirely bear out the standard interpretation of postcommunist return. It is true that Wałęsa got slightly more votes in cities and large towns—where the effects of economic growth have been more visible—and Kwaśniewski got slightly more in small towns and the countryside. But his was not simply the vote of losers in an economic game in which his close associates are, after all, among the greatest winners. Voting for him, people also chose a personification of success. And he benefited from a "feel-good factor" in a country that has the fastest economic growth in Europe: 6.5 percent in the first half of 1995. The liberal architects of Poland's "economic miracle," such as

Leszek Balcerowicz, now leader of the opposition Freedom Union party, observe wryly that Kwaśniewski reaps the harvest of the changes they introduced.

Moreover, Kwaśniewski got significantly more votes from the young and Wałęsa more from the old. Here was the great role reversal. The former communist became the man of the future, making Wałęsa look like a man of the past. Just forty-three years old (to Wałęsa's fifty-two), suntanned, trim (he dieted specially for the elections), snappily dressed, better educated (although it now emerges that he lied about having received a master's degree from Gdańsk University), smooth-talking, yuppielike, "Olek" Kwaśniewski sold himself as modern, forward-looking, Western. Perhaps inspired by M. Séguéla, his supporters even called him "the Polish Kennedy." And the whole message was "Choose the Future."

2

Yet how could people so rapidly forget the past? In Hungary, one might understand it more easily: 1956 was a very long time ago, and by the 1980s the party's iron fist was hidden deep inside a thick velvet glove. But not in Poland, where just a few years ago this same Aleksander Kwaśniewski was, as editor of the communist youth newspaper and then as minister for youth, justifying the imposition of martial law, the internment of political opponents, and the banning of Solidarity.

Well, first of all, a lot of people have not forgotten. Many voted for Lech Wałęsa simply in order to stop an ex-communist from becoming their president. Conversely, some of Kwaśniewski's party electorate voted for him precisely because he is an ex-communist. Indeed, for all the slimming and suntanning and smart suits, Kwaśniewski, with his hatchet jaw and slab cheekbones, still has something of the face and posture of the Stalinist worker-hero in Andrzej Wajda's film *Man of Iron*. (People are now speculating about a sequel. *Man of Silicon?*)

For the young, however, communism and Solidarity are already ancient history—something they are forced to learn about from boring textbooks. Here, the post-Solidarity leaders are victims of their own success. So rapid have been the changes, so self-evident has freedom become in just six years, that the young can hardly remember anything else. On election day, I had lunch with a friend who was a samizdat publisher in the 1980s. "Yes," he reminisced, "of course in those days you never used to phone beforehand, just appeared at the door." "But *why* didn't he phone?" asked his fourteen-year-old daughter. Long pause. "Oh, you mean because the phone was bugged?" With some young voters, there was an element of conscious revolt. Just because the parents identify so strongly with the post-Solidarity tradition, the children vote against it.

There remains, nonetheless, a question. In 1989, Solidarity leaders negotiated with Polish communists at the Round Table, and made a power-sharing deal summed up in a famous headline in the Solidarity paper *Gazeta Wyborcza:* "YOUR PRESIDENT, OUR PREMIER." The Warsaw Pact still existed, and this seemed the most the Soviet Union would accept. In a spirit of liberal Catholic forgiveness, and having in mind the model of post-Franco Spain, the Solidarity premier Tadeusz Mazowiecki drew what he called a "thick line" under the past. But did that line have to be quite so thick? And was it still right a year or two later, after the Soviet constraint had largely disappeared, to continue without any systematic purges of former communists or secret-police collaborators from public life (such as happened in Czechoslovakia and East Germany), without Latin American–style truth commissions, tribunals (except one specifically on the responsibility for martial law), or other symbolic steps to remind the public, and particularly the young, of what communists had done to Poland?

This question has divided the post-Solidarity opposition. The right say the revolution should have been completed—not with the guillotine, to be sure, but with purges. Then Kwaśniewski would never have got back. One of their representatives put it graphically on election night. In eighteen postcommunist countries, he said, there has been no decommunization and postcommunists are back in power; in two, the Czech Republic and East Germany, there has been decommunization, and they are not. (The figures don't quite hold up, but one gets the general point.)

At the other extreme is the former dissident and now editor of

Gazeta Wyborcza Adam Michnik, who has counted Kwaśniewski among his friends since 1989, written a preface to General Jaruzelski's memoirs, and in September published a highly controversial article arguing that the time had come for the postcommunist and the post-Solidarity sides to sit down together and try to agree on a common version of the history of Poland under communist rule. The significance of the article was less what it said than the fact that it was signed jointly by Michnik and Włodzimierz Cimoszewicz, a postcommunist member of parliament who soon thereafter became Kwaśniewski's campaign manager.

Michnik argues that somebody had to break through the social ostracism of the postcommunists, which he describes dramatically as "apartheid." (But are the former communists now the blacks or the whites in that metaphor?) He also points out that, in spite of decommunization, the postcommunists got nearly a fifth of the vote in East Germany at the last parliamentary elections (not far short of what they got in Poland) and suggests that we should wait a little longer to see what happens in the Czech Republic.

On balance, it seems to me that this very conciliatory "Spanish" approach to the past probably has facilitated the return of the postcommunists to power in Poland, although, of course, one can never prove that a tougher, more "Czech" or "East German," approach would have prevented it.

3

Absolutely peculiar to Poland was the role of the Catholic Church. The Church threw its immense authority and influence not so much, initially, behind Wałęsa—for in the first round there were other conservative Catholic candidates, such as the exceedingly devout president of the National Bank, Hanna Gronkiewicz-Waltz— but emphatically against the atheist postcommunists. In the late summer, a message from the Episcopate warned against "choosing for the highest positions in the fatherland people who during the period of the totalitarian state were involved in exercising power at the highest party-government level." Now who could they mean? The postcommunists' support for a liberal abortion law and resistance to ratifying the concordat with the Vatican further sharpened the Church's opposition.

Primate Glemp denounced the representatives of what he delightfully called "neopaganism." (In a subsequent interview, he averred that *neopagan* is a purely descriptive term for nonbelievers. Such people could not, he explained carefully, be described as "pagans," since "a pagan has a specific faith." Before the second-round runoff, the Church came very close to telling the faithful to vote for Wałęsa, who famously wears a badge of the Black Madonna of Częstochowa on his lapel. The bishop responsible for the pastoral care of farmers sent a special letter to country and small-town dwellers, headed "Don't abandon the fatherland in need!" At the entrance to St. Stanisław Kostki, the famous Warsaw church of a Solidarity priest murdered by secret police in 1984, I found a Wałęsa election poster displayed beneath the timetable of services. On the very eve of the election, Primate Glemp called on the faithful to pray for "the elections, President Wałęsa, and the fatherland."

And still Wałęsa lost—especially in the countryside and the small towns. In spite of the Church's appeals, or perhaps even because of them. Three quarters of those asked in one pre-election opinion poll said that the Church should not try to influence the election result. After the event, the secretary-general of the Episcopate, Bishop Tadeusz Pieronek, told me that he thinks people may well have resented what he called the Church's "paternalistic" approach and that he is sure many good Catholics voted for Kwaśniewski. As for young Poles, I suspect many of them will have said, "Neopaganism? Mmm, yes please!" It would be a fine irony if it was the Catholic Church that won the election for the neopagan.

Yet part of the responsibility must also lie with the whole post-Solidarity side of Polish politics, divided into many, mainly small parties, with several different presidential candidates and as much occupied with fighting among themselves as with serious nation-wide politics. They have, in fact, done much worse in this respect than their counterparts in Hungary or the Czech Republic, where the liberal and conservative parts of the political spectrum are consolidated into fewer, larger, better organized parties. Why? Partly because such falling-out is what tends to happen after a revolution, and what Solidarity did in Poland over the whole period from 1980 to 1989 was a revolution, albeit of a new kind. Just because before 1989 people had been more united than in Hungary and the Czech lands, they are more disunited now.

Yet watching and listening to these theatrical (and sometimes highly enjoyable) quarrels, I am sure that the disunity also has something to do with older Polish traditions. There is the early modern tradition of the so-called noble democracy, with its endlessly disputatious "little parliaments" and with the gentry, great and small, quarreling on the election fields of the Polish kings, perhaps even coming to blows, then as theatrically making it up over innumerable beakers of hooch. There is also the tradition of the intelligentsia, which the urbanized heirs of the gentry became. This heritage was represented vividly in Warsaw at election time by a fine exhibition of intelligentsia family photographs, spanning five or six generations, from the great-great-grandfather who lost his estates after fighting against the Russians in the January Rising of 1863 to the latest scion graduating from Warsaw University in 1987. Such traditions do not translate easily into the workaday, opportunistic politics of a television mass democracy. Former communist hacks, unburdened by pride or principle, take to it much quicker.

Last, but by no means least, there is Lech Wałęsa himself, who has spent much of the last five years destroying his own monument. Already in 1990, he alienated many former associates and supporters with his "war at the top" of Solidarity and his demagogic campaign for the presidency. As president, he has been erratic and often authoritarian in his style. He once suggested that he would change prime ministers "like car bumpers," and he has, in fact, several times destabilized the parliamentary government. He has surrounded himself with a court of mediocre and even shady advisers, some with dubious ties to the security services and the army. Most notoriously, there was his former chauffeur Mieczysław Wachowski, until recently his senior minister of state. Above all, though, the former electrician and workers' leader has failed to become statesmanlike. Not just the Warsaw intelligentsia, whose condescension he so fiercely resents, but many ordinary Poles I have talked to feel that his often undignified manner and broken, ungrammatical Polish do not fit him to represent a proud nation in the world.

Earlier this year, his standing in the opinion polls fell to as low as 6 percent. Then, having changed his staff—Wachowski and others departing—he tried to adopt a more restrained and presidential style while, at the same time, successfully polarizing the campaign in historical terms: Lech against the Reds. This brought him a remarkable recovery, back up to a third of the vote in the first round, with the alternative candidate of post-Solidarity liberals and social democrats, the veteran dissident Jacek Kuroń, getting less than 10 percent. Then most of the post-Solidarity side rallied around Wałęsa. For someone who remembers Solidarity, it was touching to see him together again with former advisers such as Bronisław Geremek and Tadeusz Mazowiecki.

But Jerzy Urban could quote in *Nie*, his satirical weekly, all the devastatingly critical things Wałęsa's former colleagues had said about him over the last five years, giving this mini-anthology the characteristically sarcastic headline WAŁĘSA'S A MONSTER SO VOTE FOR HIM. And many voted for him only as the "lesser evil," with a heavy heart. "I don't want to, but I must," said one voter interviewed on television, ironically using Wałęsa's own words when he announced that he would stand for president in 1990. "For Wałęsa?" asked the interviewer. "Unfortunately!" A friend of mine told me, "All right, I'll drink half a liter and then go and vote for him." Half a liter of vodka, that is. In the event, we got him there on slightly less.

It was very close. When voting ended at 8 P.M., Polish television's exit polls put Wałęsa ahead at 51.1 percent to Kwaśniewski's 48.9 percent. Jubilation and the old street chant of "Lech Wałęsa! Lech Wałęsa!" from the president's campaign headquarters; defiant chants of "Olek! Olek!" from Kwaśniewski's. Every half hour, television gave a later exit-poll result. At 10:30 P.M. the final, cumulative exit poll, up to the close of voting, still put Wałęsa ahead, but now by just 50.2 percent to 49.8. Then, at nine minutes past eleven, came the first unofficial result from slightly more than a thousand polling stations: 51.3 percent for Kwaśniewski, 48.7 for Wałęsa. The final, official result was 51.7 percent to 48.3, with an impressive turnout of 68 percent.

Opinion polls between the two rounds of voting had shown that Wałęsa lost quite heavily from a rude, unstatesmanlike, and incoherent performance in the first of two television debates between the candidates. It is therefore quite possible that, if he had done better and Kwaśniewski worse in that one television debate, the result might have been the other way around. And then, of course, we would all have knowingly explained Wałęsa's triumph, sagely identifying the deeper forces, structures, and patterns.

4

So there they are, back on top, the men and women who lied to us for so many years, the cynics, opportunists, and careerists, still with their apparatchik's jowls and their lavatory-brush haircuts. Yes, often the very same people. That professor of sociology who went around the world selling martial law while his colleagues were thrown into camps. That "expert" on international relations who traveled abroad to talk about peace and the environment while Professor Geremek had to sleep in the crypt of a church to avoid arrest by the secret police. And lower down, in the provinces and local government, hundreds of much cruder specimens. What's more, many of them have become privately rich as well as again being publicly powerful. Look at the millionaire Jerzy Urban, for heaven's sake!

A memoir written a few years ago by the now outgoing foreign minister, Władysław Bartoszewski—one of three so-called presidential ministers to resign following Wałęsa's defeat—was entitled *It's Worth Being Decent*. This from a man who was a political prisoner both in Auschwitz and in Stalinist jails. But, fifty years on, the message for a young Pole would appear to be, *It's Worth Being an Opportunist*.

Aesthetically and morally, the triumph of the postcommunists in Poland is profoundly distasteful. But is it dangerous? Not, I believe, so far as their aims and policies are concerned. The leader of Russia's communist party, Gennady Zhuganov, congratulated "the Polish working masses" on their victory. But you won't catch Mr. Kwaśniewski talking about "working masses." On the contrary, Poland's postcommunists will do everything in their power to live up to the congratulations Kwaśniewski received from Poland's other big neighbor, Germany, and especially those from the new leader of Germany's Social Democrats, Oskar Lafontaine. Kwaśniewski and his friends want desperately to be seen not as eastern postcommunists but as regular Western social democrats. The president-elect immediately reaffirmed his commitment to Poland seeking membership in the European Union and NATO. Within days, the government was going ahead with the distribution of coupons for the long-delayed mass privatization.

5

It is now commonplace to observe that Poland has become a "normal country." But what does this mean? Certainly, to arrive in Warsaw these days is more like arriving in Lisbon or Naples than it is like arriving in Warsaw before 1989. A smart modern airport. No need for a visa. When the passport officers call Polish passport–holders to a separate gate, you simply can't tell the difference—in dress, accoutrements, hairstyles, and so on—between the two lines, Polish and Western. A relatively clean taxi, and you are actually charged the local-currency price on the taxi meter. Familiar shops, goods, cars. The same TV commercials. Smart offices. Mobile phones. Professional friends who are now overworked and defend themselves with answering machines. More and real money, but also more money worries: "Half our income goes in tax, the other half on school fees!" Great contrasts between rich and poor.

Of course, if you dig just a little deeper you find extraordinary things. The man in the Mercedes is a former politburo member. Your mobile-phone salesman is a former secret policeman. In the countryside, you still see peasant houses out of Brueghel. Priests chunter on about "neopaganism." But Europe—our "normal," "Western," Europe—is also full of extraordinary things. Between observing the Polish elections and writing this essay I had to drop in to Naples for the Premio Napoli awards. The Grand Hotel Vesuvio was even better than the Hotel Bristol in Warsaw, but driving through the city I could see the dreadful slums—far worse than anything in Warsaw—where people still go in fear of the Camorra. Among the Premio

Napoli prizewinners was a Jesuit priest, who was being honored for his fight against usury. ("Why don't you in Britain have a law against usury?" he quizzed me.) The popular postcommunist mayor was asked at the televised prize-giving ceremony what he thought of his rival, the postfascist Signora Alessandra Mussolini (daughter of you-know-who). And, incidentally, was it true that they have been romantically involved? While denying romance, the mayor said that Signora Mussolini had made a very positive contribution to solving some problems in the city. All normal?

So the spectrum of contemporary European "normality" is very wide, and Poland is now definitely within it. But there is another measure of "normality": diachronic rather than synchronic. What has been normal for a country historically over, say, the last two hundred years? By this criterion, Poland today is quite spectacularly abnormal. This country is free, sovereign, prospering? Germany is its best ally in the West? It is not immediately threatened even by Russia? Surely we've got our countries mixed up. I asked the Polish historian Jerzy Jedlicki when before in its history Poland had been so well placed. Scarcely hesitating, he replied, "Probably the second half of the sixteenth century."

Poland's transition from normal abnormality to abnormal normality is already a fantastic achievement. The challenge for the next five years is to secure it, internally and externally—which means in the EU and in NATO. Only then will we, and the Poles themselves, begin to see what the Polish version of European "normality" really looks like. This Polish normality may well not be as interesting as the old abnormality. Indeed, it may at first look like a cheap copy of the West. But, if that is freedom's price, it is surely worth paying. And, anyway, who knows? As the British historian Hugh Trevor-Roper once wryly observed: History is full of surprises, and no one is more surprised by them than historians.

CHRONOLOGY

1995

14 NOVEMBER. *The European Monetary Institute publishes a timetable for monetary union.*

21 NOVEMBER. *Bosnian president Alija Izetbegović, Serbian president Slobodan Milošević, and Croatian president Franjo Tudjman initial the Dayton peace agreement. This provides for the formal maintenance of a unitary state but far-reaching de facto division into the Bosniak-Croat Federation, having 51 percent of the territory, and the Serb Republic, having 49 percent. The Bosniaks get suburbs of Sarajevo and a corridor to Goražde; the Serbs retain Srebrenica and Žepa. A NATO Implementation Force (IFOR) is to police the agreement.*

30 NOVEMBER. *President Clinton visits Northern Ireland, encouraging the "peace process" there.*

6 DECEMBER. *The German Bundestag votes for German forces to participate in IFOR in Bosnia.*

14 DECEMBER. *The Bosnian, Serb, and Croat presidents formally sign the Dayton agreement.*

15–16 DECEMBER. *An EU summit in Madrid agrees that the single European currency should be called the "euro." Another intergovernmental conference, to review the implementation of Maastricht, will open at the end of March.*

17 DECEMBER. *Communists win Russian parliamentary elections, with right-wing nationalists in second place.*

20 DECEMBER. *In Bosnia, UNPROFOR hands over to IFOR, which divides the country into American, British, and French sectors.*

31 DECEMBER. *A customs union between the EU and Turkey comes into force.*

1996

8 JANUARY.   *Death of François Mitterrand.*

11–13 JANUARY.   Hanbury Manor, England. At a high-level Franco-British meeting, a senior French businessman gives me his view of the eastward enlargement of the European Union to include former communist countries. *"Il faut toujours en parler,"* he says, *"et jamais y penser."* "One should always talk about it and never think about it." I had always suspected that this was the attitude of much of the French elite to enlargement. But to have it expressed so clearly and elegantly is a kind of bitter delight. A wonderful thing, French *clarté.*

24 JANUARY.   *Józef Oleksy resigns as Polish prime minister following allegations about his collaboration with the KGB and its successors. He will be succeeded by Włodzimierz Cimoszewicz, former campaign manager for President Kwaśniewski.*

9 FEBRUARY.   *An IRA bomb explodes in London's docklands.*

3 MARCH.   *Spanish parliamentary elections end thirteen years of socialist rule and bring the center-right Popular Party to power. The prime minister will be José Maria Aznar.*

29 MARCH.   *An EU intergovernmental conference opens in Turin.*

5 APRIL.   Berkeley, California. We tell our Californian host that we are going to visit Czesław Miłosz, the great contemporary Polish poet, who lives near Berkeley. Later, our kind host collects us and asks, "Well, how is Milošević?" O happy California, where no one needs to know the difference between a Miłosz and a Milošević!

21 APRIL.   *Italian parliamentary elections result in victory for the center-left "Olive Tree" alliance.*

25 APRIL.   *The German government announces cuts in public expenditure, to meet "Maastricht criteria" for monetary union.*

MAY.   *Financial crisis in Bulgaria.*

1 JUNE.   *In Czech parliamentary elections, the Civic Democratic Party of Prime Minister Václav Klaus loses its overall majority.*

10 JUNE.   *All-party talks on the future of Northern Ireland open at Stormont Castle in Belfast.*

23 JUNE.   *Death of the veteran Greek socialist leader Andreas Papandreou.*

JUNE.   *Controversy in Poland over the postcommunist government's deci-*

sion not to save the Gdańsk shipyard, birthplace of Solidarity, from bank-ruptcy.

3 JULY. *Boris Yeltsin is reelected president of Russia, defeating the communist leader Gennady Zhuganov.*

14 SEPTEMBER. *Elections in Bosnia.*

15 SEPTEMBER. *In Italy, Umberto Bossi, leader of the Northern League, declares the independence of the state of "Padania."*

24 SEPTEMBER. *The United States, Russia, China, France, and Britain sign the Comprehensive Test Ban Treaty.*

SEPTEMBER. *Growing controversy about "Nazi gold" held by Swiss banks.*

15 OCTOBER. *The Council of Europe admits Croatia.*

17 OCTOBER. *President Yeltsin dismisses his national-security adviser, General Aleksandr Lebed.*

29 OCTOBER. London. I chair a meeting of more than 2,400 people with Mikhail Gorbachev in Westminster Central Hall, jointly arranged by *The Times* and Dillons bookshops to present his memoirs. Only in the central European revolutions of 1989 have I experienced such an explosion of spontaneous emotion as greets him the moment he steps onto the platform. At first, he is brief and sharp. What does he consider his three greatest achievements? I ask him. "Freedom, openness among nations, and an end to the arms race." He earns wave after wave of applause. But, as the evening progresses, his answers get longer and longer. After a twenty-minute tirade against Boris Yeltsin, he has almost lost the audience; but then he wins them back again.

At dinner afterward, Gorbachev proposes round after round of toasts, tapping his glass and crying, incongruously, *"Achtung! Achtung!"* (He has told a story about a Lufthansa pilot who kept saying that over the loudspeakers, so this is a kind of joke.) Close impressions: immense strength and warmth of personality. Above all, warmth—human, all-embracing warmth. A man settled in himself: happy to be Russian, happy to have been Soviet. A slightly surprising and very engaging simplicity, for all his experience of the world. His touching, obvious affection toward his wife, Raisa. And the sheer surreality of sitting here, in a London club, as this man who changed the course of the twentieth century proposes toasts with a jovial *"Achtung! Achtung!"*

Raisa seems to feel this surreality, too. At one point she feels it necessary to remind us, in her slightly schoolmarmish way, that no previous Soviet leader would have sat with us so informally. "No, Lenin would not have," she says. "Stalin would not have." Something between a giggle and a shiver goes around the table. "Not Khrushchev. Or Andropov. Or Chernenko." "Well, Andropov might have, you know," says Gorbachev, indulgently.

31 OCTOBER. *The European Commission accepts the legitimacy of a onetime payment by France Telecom to the French government to help France meet the Maastricht criteria for monetary union.*

FORTY YEARS ON

What happened in Hungary in 1956? Here is a fairly typical brief Western summary, from the *Columbia Encyclopedia*:

> On Oct. 23, 1956, a popular anti-Communist revolution, centered in Budapest, broke out in Hungary. A new coalition government under Imre Nagy declared Hungary neutral, withdrew it from the Warsaw Treaty, and appealed to the UN for aid. However, János Kádár, one of Nagy's ministers, formed a counter-government and asked the USSR for military support. In severe and brutal fighting, Soviet forces suppressed the revolution. Nagy and some of his ministers were abducted and were later executed. Some 190,000 refugees fled the country. Kádár became premier and sought to win popular support for Communist rule.

In Hungary itself, the history of the 1956 revolution was obliterated or traduced for more than thirty years, while János Kádár progressed from Soviet quisling to domestic father figure and the West's favorite "liberal" communist. Yet through all those years, Kádár himself seems to have been haunted and driven by the memory of the comrades he had betrayed and, finally, condemned to death. Imre Nagy was his Banquo—and he was always Macbeth.

A part of the true history was written abroad. Another part was gradually rediscovered by independent historians and oppositional writers inside Hungary in the 1980s, interviewing survivors, publishing suppressed writings, and drawing their own conclusions. Then, in June 1989, Imre Nagy and his closest associates were ceremonially reburied. Beside the coffins of the leaders lying in state on Heroes' Square, there lay a symbolic sixth coffin of the Unknown Insurgent. This was the great symbolic turning point in Hungary's transition from communism to democracy. Banquo's ghost was enthroned.

In a free Hungary, the true history of 1956 could surely at last be revealed. A whole institute was established for this single purpose: the Institute for the History of the 1956 Hungarian Revolution. Archives were opened. Survivors could now talk freely. Young historians set to work. The 1956 Institute produced a new short history of the revolution, which became the Hungarian school textbook.[1]

With the end of communism elsewhere, more evidence also emerged from the Soviet Union, from Yugoslavia, even from China. Not all the evidence, of course, but more. Meanwhile, American, British, French, and other Western official documents became available under the "thirty-year rule." Some, perhaps the most interesting, remained classified, but scholars pressed for further access and, in the United States, used the Freedom of Information Act to demand it.

1

Now, forty years on, scholars and survivors assemble in the handsome rooms of the Hungarian Academy of Sciences, its high windows looking across the Danube from naughty Pest to haughty Buda. Inside, it looks like just another academic conference.[2] We might be in London, at a conference about the Suez crisis that so fatefully coincided with the Hungarian revolution. This forty-year moment is an interesting one even in more normal countries: the first and generally the last occasion when reasonably digested findings from the archives can be confronted with the reasonably coherent memories of surviving participants. Thirty years after the event, most of the archives are still closed; fifty years on, most of the participants are no longer with us. Yet in Budapest, the witnesses have survived not just, say, too many good dinners at the Carlton Club in London but a death sentence commuted at the last minute to four-teen years in prison. So the occasion is not ordinary at all.

Being tested here is the central proposition of modern historical writing since Ranke: that with the passage of time we know more about the past. This is supposed to be the case because we have greater distance from the past; because we are (supposedly) more impartial; because we can see the longer-term consequences and therefore the larger historical "meaning" of the events in question; and, above all, because the documents are now available. The subti-tle of this conference is "The New Archival Evidence." Following Ranke, we should now learn "how it really was." But do we, can we?

In important ways, we certainly learn more. For example, here, from the Soviet archives, are the notes made by V. N. Malin, head of the General Department of the Central Committee of the Commu-nist Party of the Soviet Union, on the Soviet leaders' hectic debates in the Party Presidium.[3] We see them dithering and agonizing in the days after the outbreak of the revolution on 23 October: "C[omra]de Khrushchev [says] . . . the matter is becoming more complicated. . . . The workers are supporting the uprising." And, later, "The En-glish and French are in a real mess in Egypt. We shouldn't get caught in the same company." And their meetings with Chairman Mao's emissaries on 30 October. "Cde. Khrushchev . . . there are two paths. A military path . . . one of occupation. A peaceful path . . . the withdrawal of troops, negotiations."

So might it really have happened differently? What Gorbachev did in 1989, done by Khrushchev in 1956? These documents warn us against what the French philosopher Henri Bergson called "the il-lusions of retrospective determinism"—against the conviction, so hard to resist, that what actually happened had to happen. For years, most of us have lived with the assumption that the Soviet Union could never have tolerated what was happening in Hungary—other-wise, it would not have been the Soviet Union. But Soviet leaders plainly did not know that at the time. What would have happened if . . . ?

The openness did not last long. On 31 October, Malin records Khrushchev saying, "We should re-examine our assessment and should not withdraw our troops from Hungary and Budapest. We should take the initiative in restoring order in Hungary." What factors were decisive? How important, for example, were concerns about the unity of the international communist movement, with the Italian communist leader Palmiro Togliatti and, finally, also Chairman Mao urging the "restoration of order"? What difference was made by the assurance given by John Foster Dulles that "We do not look upon these nations as potential military allies"? What was the impact of Suez? "If we depart from Hungary," Khrushchev goes on, "it will give a great boost to the Americans, English, and French—the imperialists. They will perceive it as weakness on our part and will go on to the offensive . . . To Egypt they will then add Hungary."

"Agreed: Cdes. Zhukov, Bulganin, Molotov, Kaganovich, Voroshilov, Saburov"—and behind this sentence the Russian historian Vyacheslav Sereda hears a sigh of relief. The notes continue, "We should create a Provisional Revol. Gov't (headed by Kádár)." But then, incredibly, "If Nagy agrees, bring him in as dep. premier."

Another area of old controversy and new discoveries is the role of Radio Free Europe (RFE), the American-run radio station, which broadcast in all the languages of Eastern Europe. Here we have a hitherto unpublished memorandum from William Griffith, then political adviser to RFE.[4] Dated 5 December 1956, it reviews the Hungarian output of RFE and concludes that there were important "policy violations" by the Hungarian radio journalists involved. One program on 28 October gave detailed instructions to Hungarian soldiers on the conduct of partisan warfare. "In the Western capitals," a commentary on 4 November declared, "a practical manifestation of Western sympathy is expected at any hour." Griffith's own conclusion in December 1956 is that the Hungarian service did not *incite* the revolution and "(with one exception) made no *direct* promise or commitment of Western or UN military support or intervention. Its broadcasts may well, however, have encouraged Hungarians to have false hopes in this respect; they certainly did little or nothing to contradict them."

Now William Griffith, today a distinguished professor emeritus of political science at MIT, is on the platform, together with other surviving participants. He makes essentially the same argument that he did forty years ago. But a journalist who then worked for RFE's Hungarian service angrily suggests that the Hungarian journalists are being scapegoated. They were only following American policy guidance, which, in particular, urged criticism of the communist Imre Nagy and support for the militantly anticommunist Cardinal József Mindszenty. An American working in RFE at the time jumps up to support him. He remembers the discussions in the newsroom and quotes from the policy guidance given at the time by Griffith, who was, however, himself subject to policy guidance from New York. An old Hungarian, identifying himself as a listener to Radio Free Europe, emotionally declares that it was to blame for the deaths of thousands of Hungarian youngsters.

Pale-faced, her voice trembling, Mária Wittner, one of the street fighters who paid for her part in the revolution with more than four-teen years in prison, reads out extracts from RFE broadcasts in Hun-garian. The interpreter gives us some idea of the fiery language: "The tanks come in . . . invited by the bloody-handed Imre Nagy." (Basing their judgments too much on official Hungarian radio broadcasts, RFE initially thought Nagy was coresponsible for the first interven-tion by Soviet troops.) Or, again, "Where are the traitors . . . who are the murderers? Imre Nagy and his government. . . . Only Cardinal Mindszenty has spoken out fearlessly. . . . Imre Nagy is a base Mus-covite." But afterward there is some confusion. Are these quotations from RFE's own broadcasts or from Hungarian radio stations taken over by the insurgents—the "freedom stations"—some of whose pro-grams RFE rebroadcast? Jan Nowak, then head of RFE's Polish ser-vice, draws the important contrast with Poland, where both the freshly released Cardinal Stefan Wyszyński from inside and RFE from outside immediately and firmly backed Władysław Gomułka, the Polish Nagy.

After this dramatic confrontation of documents and memories, of written and oral history, we can see the historical picture more clearly. With the best of intentions on all sides, and quite under-standably, in a confused and drastic situation, which changed liter-ally minute by minute, both Hungarians and Americans at RFE got it wrong. Not all of them and not all the time, of course. But in the crucial days of late October, their broadcasts attacked Imre Nagy (while the Polish service was supporting Gomułka), and some encouraged armed resistance, with broad hints of imminent Western aid that, in fact, the United States (let alone the Suez-embroiled British and French) had no intention of giving. We can never know what difference this made to the course of events; it probably made little or none to the final result. That does not diminish the moral responsibility.

Here, then, are two cases which seem to justify the implicit, neo-Rankean assumption: that with the passing of time and careful study of the documents we know more about what really happened. Yet this is, on a moment's reflection, a very odd assumption. It was not shared by historians for more than two thousand years before Ranke. And it is not one we usually make in everyday life. Our rather reasonable everyday assumption is that the closer you are to an event, in both time and place, the more you are likely to know about it. "Well," we say, "of course you'd know better, because you were there."

The fact is that so much of history with a small *h*—most of it, in fact—is simply lost. To be sure, in some respects we do know more after forty years; but in others we know less. This is particularly true of times of crisis and rapid change, and above all of wars and revolutions. Tolstoy reminds us in *War and Peace* of the mystery at the heart of battles. So also with revolutions. Even now—especially now—do we really know how and why it came to the storming of the Bastille?

The Hungarian revolution of 1956 is an event of that kind—perhaps the last in Europe with the popular, violent, and genuinely spontaneous character that we still associate with the word *revolution*. All subsequent European revolutions—Czechoslovakia 1968, Portugal 1974, Poland 1980–1981, the many-in-one of 1989—have to be qualified with an additional adjective: "interrupted," "self-limiting," "peaceful," "velvet," "negotiated." For that reason, and because of the subsequent decades of political repression and historical falsification, there is a part of its history that is virtually impossible to recover. It may also be the most important part. It concerns, for example, the experience of the mainly young men and women who took up arms on 23 or 24 October 1956: the workers, students, street-fighting kids who, after all, actually made this a revolution. Without them, it might have remained a high-level political crisis, an attempt at radical reform, an affair largely of the party and the intelligentsia, with the people playing only a supporting role. Why did they act as they did? What was it like for them? What did they hope to achieve? What kept them fighting? What did they think of in the moments before they died?

I read the contemporary reports, watch the newsreels, look at the black-and-white photographs of those smiling boys and girls amid the broken glass, so like the photos of the Warsaw Rising in 1944. I think of Yeats: "a terrible beauty is born." Then I look at some of the meticulous reconstructions of the street fighting by Hungarian historians, using long interviews with survivors. I talk with Mária Wittner, described to me by another survivor as the revolution's Joan of Arc. It is a deeply moving conversation. But even she cannot really explain to me how, as a nineteen-year-old girl from a convent school, she came to pick up that ammunition belt and start reloading the guns for the boys on the roof, shooting back at the guards of the Budapest radio station on 23 October. She talks of "something in the air," of the "vibrations." But the filters of retrospection are too strong.

She wants to speak for those who can no longer speak: her dead comrades, the unknown insurgents. Much of her life since 1989 has been devoted to that purpose. Yet their experience is lost, irrevocably. We don't know, we will never know, what it was really like at the eye of the storm. Beside history regained, there is history lost. In history, too, there is always a sixth coffin.

2

The other thing that we are supposed to know more about is the consequences, and hence the larger "meaning," of the event. For this we plainly have to consider the alternatives. Purely hypothetical counterfactuals can be fun and illuminating too, but more important are the alternatives that were considered seriously at the time. As we have found from the documents, major alternatives were considered—for example, by Khrushchev. What if the advice from Togli-

atti, Tito, and Mao had been different? What i
been clearer, one way or the other? What if the b
had not launched the Suez adventure at exactly t
Might the Soviet leadership then at least have tried
path—withdrawal, negotiations—a little longer and more s

But what would have been the impact of that on Poland?
the Hungarian revolution started with a demonstration beneath
statue of the Polish General Bem, who himself had been a hero of
the Hungarian revolution of 1848–1849, the Polish October was
hugely influenced by what happened in Hungary. Khrushchev's
"peaceful path" in Hungary would surely have encouraged the Poles
to ask for the same or more. If the Soviet Union might just have been
prepared to countenance an Austrian status for Hungary—in which,
after all, even Stalin had proposed only a fifty-fifty split with the
West, in his famous "percentages agreement" with Churchill—it
was another thing to countenance that for Poland.[5] This, in turn,
would have meant countenancing it for Germany—the larger, Western part of which was already in NATO.

Or take another if: What if Hungary had stopped at radical reform, rather than revolution, as the reform communists around
Imre Nagy would have wished, and as Poland did? What might have
happened then? Well, look what happened in Poland, where the
hopes invested in Gomułka in 1956 were progressively and comprehensively disappointed. Is there any reason to believe that the same
would not have happened in Hungary?

Orwell once remarked that "All revolutions are failures, but they
are not all the same failure." The consequences appear different at
different times, and some emerge only decades later. To describe
1956 as "the victory of a defeat," as the exiled Hungarian historian
Miklós Molnár did in his book of 1968, was not merely romantic hyperbole and wishful thinking.[6] Perhaps the simplest and most direct
consequence is one that could be seen immediately but has en-
dured. This is quite simply the sympathy and positive feeling toward
Hungary on the part of people around the world who either had
hardly noticed its existence before or had had a rather negative
image of the country, seeing it as an oppressor of minorities before
1914 and Germany's ally in two world wars. This basic positive asso-

f American policy had
British and French
the same time?
the second
eriously?
For if
he

negative or nonexistent one, has
reasure—or asset, to use language
s the country strives to join the EU

nerged immediately but also en-
throughout the world. This was a
with Soviet communism, of grow-
and the parting of ways between
ialists. The Chinese historian Jian
he great split between communist
China and the Soviet Union.

Beyond this, however, someone reflecting on the tenth anniversary of the revolution, in 1966, would have been pushed to find
many more elements of positive legacy, of clear gain to set against
the obvious loss. On the twentieth anniversary, in 1976, one could
already add something more. By this time it was clear that the Kádár
regime was, if not more "liberal" than other communist regimes in
Eastern Europe—that label was always misplaced—then certainly
more cautious, circumspect, indirect, subtle, velvet-gloved in the
way it treated its own people.[7] This could be and was traced back to
the trauma of 1956, when the communist party and state had collapsed in a matter of a few days, and perhaps also, more even than
we guessed at the time, to Kádár's personal sense of guilt. On the
thirtieth anniversary, in 1986, one might have added the growing importance in Hungarian independent and oppositional thinking of
the rediscovery of intellectual and political tendencies of 1956—for
example, the work of the distinguished political thinker István Bibó,
author of a famous last declaration on behalf of the Nagy government.[8]

The great temptation, of course, is to draw a straight line from
1956 to 1989. There is a very narrow boundary between the historian's privilege of hindsight and Bergson's "illusions of retrospective
determinism." Nonetheless, there are connections to be made. For
example, I do not think that it is fanciful to make a connection between Soviet policy toward Eastern Europe in 1956 and that in
1989. Top Soviet policymakers, starting with Gorbachev, clearly remembered the political cost to the Soviet Union of the interventions

in 1956 as well as 1968. In 1956, the Soviet leaders did not know what to do and therefore used force. In 1989, the Soviet leaders also did not know what to do—but they did know what not to do: use force.

Nor is it fanciful to see Hungary 1956 as an important milepost in what may be described as the cumulative learning process of Central European oppositions and governments, from the sheer outburst of popular fury in East Berlin in 1953, through 1956 in Poland and Hungary, 1968 in Czechoslovakia, 1980–1981 in Poland, to the sophisticated peaceful change of system in 1989–1990, which I christened "refolution."[9] Moreover, it is undeniable that the largest symbolic event in the Hungarian refolution of 1989 was the ceremonial reburial of Imre Nagy on 16 June, the anniversary of his execution in 1958. The six coffins laid out on Heroes' Square, the revolutionary flags once again hanging from the lampposts: an occasion unforgettable to anyone who was there. And the past was a catalyst of the future.

However, the emergence of new evidence already slightly changes our view even of that very recent event. Documents found in the Interior Ministry archives by the longtime oppositionist János Kenedi now show how both the party leadership and the still active secret police used all possible means at their disposal—including, for example, "agents of influence" who had access to the American ambassador—to ensure that the reburial and attendant ceremonies passed off peacefully.[10] Kádár's successors, the new reform communists of 1989, appealed directly and indirectly to Nagy's surviving comrades, the reform communists of 1956.

The kaleidoscope does not stop turning. Now, in 1996, it is a free Hungary. The president of the republic, Árpád Göncz, was himself imprisoned for his attempts to mediate after the 1956 revolution, having been tried together with István Bibó. Wise, warm, avuncular, he is supremely fitted to mark the anniversary. The famous Plot 301 in a remote corner of the municipal cemetery, where Nagy and his comrades were given indecent burial after their execution in 1958, was a site of weeds and rubbish dumps when I first visited it in 1988 and still a place of freshly turned earth and recent clearing at the reburial in 1989. Now it has neat turf, marble tablets, paving stones, a monument—everything that belongs to an official place of public memory.

So far, so good. But the current government of the country is dominated by the Hungarian Socialist Party, the main successor to the ruling communist party. The socialists were elected, with a landslide majority, in 1994 and govern in coalition with the Alliance of Free Democrats, the main heirs to the liberal-democratic opposition of the 1980s, who now find themselves a junior and uncomfortable partner of the postcommunists. And the prime minister, Gyula Horn? Well, he was a reform communist in the 1980s, and as foreign minister he was partly responsible for opening the Iron Curtain to Austria in 1989 and letting the East Germans out later that year— thus beginning the end of the Berlin Wall. But in 1956? No, in 1956 young Gyula, aged twenty-four, was a member of the feared and hated volunteer militias, known on account of their distinctive heavy quilted jackets as the *pufajkások* (roughly, "quilted-jacket guys"), who fought, detained, and beat up those who continued to resist.

He has explained his actions. He was young, and he blamed the revolutionaries for the death of a much loved elder brother. He has, up to a point, apologized. He has, in a way, tried to make amends—for example, by increasing special pensions for the survivors. But his way of dealing with the problem is deeply ambiguous. For it also involves trying to draw a line under the past—and to claim Nagy's inheritance. Soon after becoming prime minister, he joined Imre Nagy's daughter in a ceremony at Plot 301 to mark the anniversary of the revolution. Then, earlier this year, it was Horn who proposed in parliament a special commemorative law to mark the hundredth anniversary of the birth of Imre Nagy. The Free Democrats did not know which way to turn. Of course Nagy should be honored, but at the initiative of a man like Horn? In the end, they abstained. This strange custom of the commemorative law, incidentally, has a history in Hungary reaching back into the nineteenth century. The hero of the 1848–1849 revolution, Lajos Kossuth, for example, was thus commemorated after his death. However, the last person to have been so honored by the Hungarian parliament was Joseph Stalin. And the man who proposed that tribute? The then president of the parliament, Imre Nagy. In Hungary, the ironies and ambiguities just never seem to stop.

How many more turns of the kaleidoscope will we see? As it looks now, Hungary has a very good chance of celebrating the fiftieth anniversary of the revolution as a full member of what we unreflectingly call "Europe" and "the West." Of the EU, that is. And of NATO. It will thus become, to recall John Foster Dulles's words in 1956, a military ally of the United States. But what will those two things mean in 2006? What will the internal condition of Hungary be then, and how will it affect Hungarians' views of 1956? How much more, and how much less, will we then know about the revolution? It is precisely the mark of great events that their meaning constantly changes, is forever disputed, with some questions never finally answered. Questions such as, What happened in France in 1789?

CHRONOLOGY

1996

1 NOVEMBER. *Slobodan Milošević's Socialist Party of Serbia wins Serbian parliamentary elections. In Bulgaria, opposition leader Petar Stoyanov is elected president.*

5 NOVEMBER. *Bill Clinton is elected for a second term as president of the United States.*

17 NOVEMBER. *In Serbia, the Zajedno ("Together") coalition win municipal elections in several major cities, including Belgrade, but the Milošević regime fraudulently denies them their victory.*

22 NOVEMBER. *Beginning of student demonstrations in Belgrade, protesting the fraudulent denial of opposition victories in municipal elections. In Romania, anticommunist Emil Constantinescu is elected president.*

24 NOVEMBER. *A referendum in Belarus gives President Lukashenka far-reaching powers, but these are contested by parliament.*

13–14 DECEMBER. *An EU summit in Dublin agrees on a "stability pact" that would penalize future EMU members who exceed budget-deficit targets.*

19 DECEMBER. *Denmark, Finland, and Sweden become full members of the Schengen group.*

20 DECEMBER. *A NATO "Stabilization Force" (SFOR) replaces IFOR in Bosnia.*

25 DECEMBER. *Italy rejoins the Exchange Rate Mechanism of the European Monetary System.*

1997

16–18 JANUARY.   Versailles. An Anglo-French meeting in the wonderful Petit Trianon hotel. A tablet in the dining room announces that in this very room M. Clemenceau dictated the terms of peace to the defeated Germans after the First World War. The French delegation to our meeting—a glittering collection of stars from the country's business, political, and intellectual elite, almost all of them graduates of the *grandes écoles*—argue with brilliance, lucidity, and near unanimity the French case for the Cartesian imperative of binding Germany into a European monetary union. I cannot help wondering if one day some Germans won't come to regard monetary union as the new "Versailles."

20 JANUARY.   *Bill Clinton starts his second term as president of the United States.*

JANUARY–FEBRUARY.   *In faxes apparently sent from a supermarket in Switzerland, a Kosovo Liberation Army claims responsibility for terrorist attacks on Serb police in Kosovo.*

5 FEBRUARY.   *The Swiss government agrees on a fund to compensate relatives of victims of the Holocaust whose assets were held in Swiss banks.*

11 FEBRUARY.   *The Serbian parliament recognizes opposition victories in municipal elections.*

19 FEBRUARY.   *The European Commission allows Italy to impose a one-time tax to help it try to meet the Maastricht criteria in preparation for monetary union.*

21 FEBRUARY.   *After student and opposition demonstrations force the Serbian regime to recognize the true results of municipal elections, opposition politician Zoran Djindjić starts work as mayor of Belgrade.*

MARCH.   *Albania collapses into anarchy. Arsenals are plundered.*

THE SERBIAN TRAGEDY

"PEOPLE COMPARE THIS TO THE 'VELVET REVOLUTION' IN PRAGUE," I say to Momčilo. "Yes," he retorts, "but the Czechs only lasted thirty-seven days!"

On the 104th day of the Belgrade student protest, Momčilo Radulović—thickset, with a two-day stubble, short dark hair, and black leather jacket—has just burst into the room exclaiming, "We've occupied the rector's office!" He is twenty-three and studies political science. As he leads me to the new center of action, he stops in the middle of the street to explain, "I just want to live in a normal country. I want to get up in the morning, go to a normal shop, read my books, have the rule of law and democracy. And to travel." "I'm not a child of the Internet," he adds, referring to a frequent characterization of the students, "but I'd like to be."

Around the heavy conference tables in the rectorate are packed some eighty students belonging to what they call the Main Board. "Silence!" people shout at the top of their voices. "Silence!" A tall, bespectacled history student named Čeda Antić tries to keep order: "Kolega Gavrilović to speak next." A girl with long brown hair and a little pink-and-white plastic handbag takes longhand notes in a ring-file binder, as if at a lecture. She is the official minute-taker. From the window I can see the student masses gathering below, with their flags, posters, and badges, while pop music blares out: "She loves you, yeah, yeah, yeah." How touching to hear the Beatles still.

The Main Board is discussing the route for today's Walk. Walking, with a capital *W,* is the students' characteristic form of protest. Today, they'll parade around the rectorate courtyard, then walk to the education ministry to support their deans. Instructions are given by mobile phone—a major technological advance on Prague in 1989. The mobile phones are a present from Bogoljub Karić, one of the country's best-known multimillionaires and until recently—or perhaps still—a close associate of the hated president Slobodan "Slobo" Milošević. "After ninety days, Karić decided that he supports us," Momčilo says, with nice irony. The student next to me has a multicolored badge saying "Propaganda." Their other departments included Information, Security, Culture, and Protocol. Information is for foreign visitors like me, Propaganda for their own rank and file. Protocol is now on the mobile phone to his colleague at the loud-speaker jeep outside.

The sound of singing comes from the square below. Everyone in the room rises to their feet, some standing to attention. This is the "Hymn of St. Sava," a patriotic hymn of nineteenth-century Serbia, celebrating the patron saint of education and only recently revived as the university anthem. Some sing along quietly, with expressions of mildly ironic affection on their faces; most are respectfully silent; one or two look embarrassed or resentful. At the end, a few—mostly the singers—cross themselves after the Orthodox fashion. Between St. Sava and the mobile phone this is no ordinary student protest.

Two days later—day 106—there is a vital decision. Early on, the students had formulated three demands. The victories by the Zajedno ("Together") opposition coalition in local-government elections on 17 November (by coincidence, also the starting date of the Prague events in 1989) should be properly recognized, the rector of the university should resign, and the student dean should also go. Milošević conceded the first, main demand several weeks ago, and Zajedno mayors have already moved into their offices. Today, the rector and student dean have offered their resignations. But are these resignations binding, or is it a trick? Professors from the law faculty are summoned to explain the legal niceties. Suddenly, we're in a law lecture.

Even if the resignations are binding, should the students stop here? Some faculties want to go back to lectures, others to raise new demands. Biljana Dakić, a fourth-year history student who is one of my guides, nods vigorously at a comment by the student chairman. What's he saying? "He says, 'Democracy is when the minority respects the will of the majority.' " But then a pale-faced man stands up and shouts, "This is a provocation! If you accept this, you'll all be fooled!" Čeda Antić intervenes. If the resignations are definite, he says, they should have a Victory Walk and then go back to lectures; if not, they should call for nationwide elections to a constituent assembly. Back to school or forward to the revolution! "You see, we have our Robespierres and our Dantons," Čeda wryly explains afterward, but he, the Girondin, was trying to outflank them.

Two CLICHÉS have been attached to this revolutionary theater of the Belgrade students and to the Serbian drama altogether: "velvet revolution" and "nationalism." Neither gets us very far. Certainly some students say things that sound nationalistic to a Western ear. Most seem rather confused in their political views. But is that true only of Serbian students? And who would not be confused if through the most impressionable years of childhood you had seen your country fall apart, in a war which had many Serb victims, too, and if, through those years, you were told constantly by state television, radio, your parents, teachers, and leading intellectuals that this terrible war was the fault of others: Slovenes, Croats, Muslims, Germans, Americans? "When I was seventeen," Momčilo tells me, "I wanted to go and fight for my fellow Serbs, like my older brother." Biljana was born in Knin, a city in the Krajina from which the Serbs, including many of her family, were driven out by the Croats' "Operation Storm" in 1995. Three of her uncles are now refugees in a Serbia that greets its fellow Serbs with far from open arms.

In the circumstances, it is remarkable that these students have produced a protest that has been so relatively peaceful, responsible, wittily inventive, and basically democratic. Despite all the propaganda and the poisoned mental environment in which they have grown up since the age of twelve or thirteen, and though many of them have never been to the West, they, like the "velvet revolutionaries" of Central Europe in 1989, embrace a model of "normality" that includes the fundamentals of Western democracy. What is more, they are trying to practice it in their own protest. Entirely gentle this was not. At the beginning, stones were thrown and windows broken. Then they reverted to eggs. But some put the eggs in a freezer first, so they came out as hard as stones. Perhaps deep-frozen eggs are the Serb version of velvet.

Against all the virulent denunciations of "Europe" by Slobo's hacks, the students still write on their placard, "EURO *polis,* EURO *demokratija,* EURO *standard,* EURO *pravo* [law], EURO *vlast* [authority]." We in the rich EURO-Europe hardly deserve such touching faith. Or, again, "AMERICAN PEOPLE HAVE: Bill Clinton, Stevie WONDER, Johnny CASH, and Bob HOPE! SERBIAN PEOPLE HAVE: Slobodan Milošević, no WONDER, no CASH, and no HOPE!" But a small wonder this was.

We must also distinguish between nationalism and patriotism. I walk over with Čeda Antić for a coffee at the Hotel Moskva. He, the talented history student, reminds me that the pre-1914 Serbian conspirators of the Black Hand used to meet in this café. Why, perhaps the future assassin of Franz Ferdinand sat in this very corner. But today's Young Serbia is not talking of assassination. Čeda is twenty-two. As a young child, with a Serb father and a Croat mother, he thought he was a Yugoslav. Then he found that he was really a Serb. In his search for identity, he discovered the glorious history of medieval Serbia—and the Orthodox church. He read the Bible, believed, and was baptized into the Church two years ago. His godfather is a fellow student, active in the protest. Čeda was one of those quietly singing the hymn of St. Sava.

Like many people I talk to in Belgrade, he now thinks that Yugoslavia was a mistake from the very beginning. "It was," he adds, "*our* mistake"—meaning that of the Serbs who thought their aspirations could best be realized in a larger state of all the southern Slavs. Now the Serbs' historic task is to start again, to build a modern, liberal, democratic Serbian nation-state.

It is a travesty to call someone like this thoughtful, idealistic young man a "nationalist" in the pejorative sense in which that term is now almost universally used. He is a patriot—someone who cares deeply for his country. If it were otherwise, he would not be demonstrating but trying to emigrate, as hundreds of thousands of younger, educated Serbs have already done.

He feels that the students have done what they can for Serbia, their new-old *patria*. Now it is up to the people and the opposition parties, three of which are supposedly united in the Zajedno coalition. The students have carefully kept their demonstrations separate from those organized by Zajedno, so as not to be "taken over" by any side, but we now walk out to observe the latest opposition demonstration, dedicated to the demand for free media.

1

More flags, more nineteenth-century patriotic hymns, more rousing speeches on Republic Square, before the National Museum. It looks like a scene from 1897 rather than 1997, except that one of the flags says "Ferrari." The crowd use their whistles—another hallmark of the Belgrade demonstrations—to blow like crazy at every mention of Milošević. Then off we stroll again, on what I'm told is "the Media Walk," past the egg-stained state television station, known as "TV Bastille," past white-haired "Grandmother Olga," an old lady who became a symbol of the protest, still cheerfully waving from her first-floor balcony, past Radio Belgrade, past the *Politika* newspaper, and so back to Republic Square. On the television in my hotel room, I find CNN reporting "a massive demonstration" with calls for Milošević's resignation. Well, it did not look massive to me, but what CNN says must of course be true.

Seen from outside, through the lens of such Western media coverage, and with the 1989 matrix still imprinted on our retinas, you might think that the Serb story is now "Zajedno versus Slobo" (like Civic Forum versus Husák, or Solidarity versus Jaruzelski) and the question is simply when Slobo will go. Seen from inside, it does not look like that at all. Even those parts of the opposition joined in the Zajedno—"Together"—coalition are still quite untogether in many vital ways. Despite the country's dreadful condition, Milošević and his allies still have many important sources of power, and he has nowhere else to go. Above all, the question of democracy is overshadowed by the still unresolved national question. And that is still, as it was a century ago, about the basic issue of the frontiers of states in relation to those of peoples, including the position of Serbs outside the present Serbian state—especially in Bosnia—and that of other nationalities inside the present Serbian state, especially the Albanians in Kosovo.

I talk to all three leaders of Zajedno—Vesna Pesić of the Serbian Civic Alliance, Vuk Drašković of the Serbian Renewal Movement, and Zoran Djindjić of the Democratic Party—as well as to Vojislav Koštunica, a "moderate nationalist" whose small but significant Democratic Party of Serbia was briefly in the Zajedno coalition but now stands separately again.

Koštunica—gray-suited, analytical, sober to the point of gloominess—harks back wistfully to the first Yugoslavia, a unitary state under a Serb king, before the dreadful bloodletting between Serbs and Croats during the Second World War confounded British-style nation building. (Serbs as English, Croats as Scots?) But he thinks Drašković's idea of restoring the monarchy is dotty. Why, the exiled Prince Alexander's Serbian is so poor they have to talk to him in English!

Vesna Pesić—a small, neatly dressed, energetic woman—is the only one with a consistent, impeccable record of commitment to civic, liberal causes, opposition to the war, and rejection of nationalism. But she also has the smallest following.

Vuk Drašković is the strangest character of them all; a tall, nut-brown, prophetic figure—although his long black locks are now more neatly trimmed and the prophet is cased in a very smart Italian suit. Politically, he is Dr. Jekyll and Mr. Hyde. When he talks about the past, about the atrocities committed by the Croat Ustasha during the Second World War, he is the old Mr. Hyde, the writer whose fiery language helped to inflame Serb nationalist feelings in the 1980s. When he talks about the present, he is a perfect Dr. Jekyll, swiftly hitting all the Western piano keys—"human rights," "regional cooperation," "peaceful change," "right for refugees to return to their home"—but also referring with justifiable pride to his own record of opposition to Milošević's war.

Behind this Jekyll and Hyde there is the unmistakable silhouette of an old '68er, one of that last defining generation of student activists, now to be found in high places all over Europe. To complete the picture there is his equally extraordinary wife, Danica, a tall, dark-skinned, orange-haired woman, bursting out of a gold-threaded designer jacket and skirt. In our short conversation, she lives up to her reputation for verbal extremism by suggesting that the Serbs should really set about getting rid of the communists "like the Albanians." (The Albanians are looting army arsenals as we speak.)

Finally, there is Zoran Djindjić, also an old '68er but now the very model of a modern politician. Neat in suit, white shirt, and tie, speaking excellent German (once a pupil of the sociologist Jürgen Habermas, he spent most of the 1980s in West Germany), he sits in his vast office as the new mayor of Belgrade and explains how he can do something from there. In the Balkans, he says, the difference between *pays légal* and *pays réel* is especially large. On paper, the city government may have few powers and less money, but in practice it has many properties and concessions (taxi stands, restaurants, bathing places) that can be privatized in an exemplary procedure, as well as other forms of informal power and influence. Also, the Serbs like a big man in power, and the mayor of Belgrade is that. I quote to him the Serb peasant who said, "I'll vote for the opposition when they are in power." Exactly so.

For Westerners, the skeleton in the mayor's cupboard is his past support for the Bosnian Serbs and his infamous meeting with Radovan Karadžić in Pale. He defends this vigorously. If he hadn't met Karadžić, he says, the national card would have been left entirely in the hands of Milošević. What is more, the West began to take him seriously only when, helped by this tactical nationalism, the Serb electorate started to take him seriously. Western criticism is so much humbug. (In fact—this is my comment, not Djindjić's—the West is not unlike that Serb peasant, supporting the opposition once it is in power.)

Diverse as they are, all the opposition leaders agree on one thing: They are still weak and divided, while Milošević has many cards to play. Despite recent donations by big businessmen such as Karić, now hedging their political bets, the opposition parties are still woefully underfunded and without proper organizations. The deep historical, political, and personal differences between the leaders are scarcely papered over by the facade of "Together"-ness. To give the opposition more time on the state-controlled media, as they demand at the rally, might actually be a clever move for Milošević. The more they talk, the more they will expose their differences, while Milošević can maintain his remote, statesmanlike silence. Though many claim the mantle of "the Serb Havel," there is no single figure to unite the opposition vote.

2

No one excludes the possibility of a sudden and violent overthrow of Milošević. The comparisons people make here are not with Poland or Hungary but with Romania (the end of the Ceauşescus), Bulgaria (the parliament besieged), and, of course, Albania. "Remember," everyone says, "this is the Balkans." The catalyst might be a further, precipitate worsening of the economy, leading to violent protests by the unemployed or underemployed workers and worker-peasants, rather than just students and city folk. (Vesna Pešić, a sociologist by profession, gives me a small lecture on how the usual social classifications no longer apply to Serbia, but the basic point stands.)

Barring this, however, people expect any peaceful political change to be long-drawn-out and messy. Serbian political scientists struggle to characterize the Milošević regime. It is not simply a dictatorship, says one. It is "half-legitimate," says another. A third adapts a Latin American term to say "*demokratura*": a new combination of democracy and dictatorship. Yes, Milošević still has an active secret police, though mainly for collecting information rather than for direct repression. Yes, the army is still vital, although during the demonstrations its commander signaled that it was not available for shooting students. But more important from day to day is the systematic manipulation of public opinion through the media and through the dubiously gained fortunes of business supporters both of Milošević's own Socialist Party of Serbia and of the neocommunist Yugoslav Unity League of his influential wife, Mira Marković, who in popular mythology takes the part of Lady Macbeth.

Yes, they tamper with the election results. But, even allowing for electoral fraud, Milošević has won a series of at least formally free elections since 1990. Although Zajedno came out ahead in the local-government elections in November 1996, the government coalition, of his and her parties, still won the more important federal elections held at the same time. According to the official figures, it got 45 percent of the vote, with a further, alarming, 19 percent going to the far-right nationalist party of Vojislav Šešelj, a notorious paramilitary commander in the Bosnian war.

The opposition leaders hope that Milošević's position has since been eroded by the demonstrations and their own arrival in local government, but everyone assumes that he still has significant popular support. For an outsider, this is the great mystery. Consider what Milošević has done for them. Ten years ago there was a country called Yugoslavia, "and I thought it was in Europe," says my friend Ognjen Pribičević, one of Belgrade's brightest political analysts. Economically, they were quite well off compared to the Czechs or Poles. Belgrade looked smarter than Warsaw. Schools and courts functioned more or less normally. They could travel freely. Yugoslavia had a good name in the world.

Now they live in a country known as Serbia, and it is—everyone agrees—not in Europe but in the Balkans. (Before I came out I looked in five popular tourist guidebooks to Europe. Serbia featured in none of them.) Serbia is an international pariah. To be a Serb abroad is like being a German after 1945. Provided, that is, you can even get abroad. You need a visa for almost everywhere. Distinguished professors stand in line for five hours in the cold and are then refused.

Physically, the whole place is battered and run-down. Belgrade reminds me of Warsaw in the late 1970s. If you look at the cars, the clothes, the shop windows, you feel that Poland and Yugoslavia have changed places. According to the (unreliable) statistics, average per-capita income has shrunk from around $3,000 to less than $1,000. The official unemployment figure is close to 50 percent. I visit Kragujevac, a town once made prosperous by the large Zastava car, truck, and arms factory. The war decimated the production of cars (since parts came from all over the former Yugoslavia) but was good for the arms factory. Now the peace has cut the production of arms. Most of the Zastava factory workers are paid some $20 to $25 a month for doing nothing. They line the streets selling black-market goods: trinkets, Nescafé, chocolate bars, cigarettes smuggled in via Montenegro.

Back in Belgrade, I am taken to a vast black-market bazaar, full of new Western consumer goods, all imported without paying taxes. There is a great double line of people hawking Western cigarettes, but watch out for the "Marlboros": They are made in Montenegro. Fake Calvin Klein, Versace, and Nike clothes adorn the stalls— mainly produced, I am told, in the Sandjak of Novi Pazar.

Crime, corruption, and lawlessness are endemic. A notice in the hotel foyer asks you to hand over your personal firearms to the hotel security department. A security man hovers watchfully with a metal detector: Does my tweed jacket suggest a local criminal or a Western businessman? I have never seen so many obvious gangsters, not even in Russia. I note that the phrase used about the election fraud is "when Milošević stole the elections." Elections are just one of so many things being stolen here.

People don't trust the banks, so they keep their money in cash. Here, as throughout former Yugoslavia, the deutsche mark is the real currency. "I don't take dollars," says one small businessman—"they are too easily forged." When your money is stolen, you have no redress. Insurance? You're joking. And the courts? A friend is meant, according to the law, to inherit a flat. But to get it he needs to pay DM 10,000—as a bribe to the judge.

Politics and corruption are deeply intertwined, as in all the post-communist *demokraturas*. The ruling parties run much of the state as a private business; private businesses protect themselves by supporting the ruling parties. But one would not like to inquire too closely into the finances of opposition parties, either. The moral environment is as degraded as the physical one.

And what of the Serbs for whom the nationalist standard was supposedly raised: the Serbs in Kosovo, the Serbs "across the Drina" in Bosnia, the Serbs in Croatia? The Serbs in the Krajina, in Croatia, have been completely expelled. The remaining Serbs in Bosnia, impoverished and brutalized, wander around the remnants of their tin-pot para-state. There are at least five hundred thousand Serb refugees in Serbia, most of them still without citizenship, let alone economic assistance from the state. In Belgrade, I talk to one woman whose plundered house I visited in the Krajina in 1995. She says, "I live here like a zombie."

WHAT A TRIUMPHANT RECORD of achievement! And yet people still support him. Why? Since I cannot talk individually to three million people, I have the usual frustrating experience of listening to intellectual, elite explanations of what "the people" think, supplemented by opinion polls, anecdotes, and a few personal encounters. ("Vox pop" in the foreign correspondent's knowingly ironic phrase.) First, this is, after all, a homegrown system, unlike the foreign-imposed regimes of the former Eastern Europe. Second, the intellectuals say, there is a Balkan, backward, authoritarian political culture, which always looks to a strongman in power. (Would they have said that fifteen years ago, in old Yugoslavia?) Third, there is a kind of residual socialist conservatism, fearing the plunge into economic freedom and clinging even to the pittance the Kragujevac worker has, for fear of losing that, too. (Milošević talks a lot about privatization but does relatively little—partly, it is said, because his wife is opposed to it on ideological grounds.) Finally, Milošević has created a national siege mentality, in which everything is blamed on the hostile outside world: the Croats, the Germans, Western sanctions. This has been a perfect self-fulfilling prophecy. He started by telling them that everyone was ganging up against the Serbs—then made it so.

As usual, the generalizations are impossible to prove; and if people soon speak otherwise, through the ballot box or on the streets, that may merely show how things have changed. But I do get a small personal sample of this mental state. A civil servant in one of the ministries, a nice family man and skilled technician, tells me he telephones the private television station BK to complain every time the pope appears on the screen, "because he's our greatest enemy." The pope, the Germans, the Americans: all against us. A retired major of the Yugoslav National Army—short, fat, bulging out of his grimy trousers—tells me he blames the current misery on what he calls "the American sanctions" and on the "immigrants" who come here taking all the jobs and scrounging. But these "immigrants" are actually the Serb refugees from Croatia and Bosnia.

Sanctions were imposed, he says, because Muslims bombed Muslims in the marketplace in Sarajevo. And Srebrenica? "That was also Muslims killing Muslims." He squats on his sofa like a wary toad. But why on earth would Muslims kill Muslims? Well, the Serbs tried to drive them out and they got frightened, "so they started killing each other."

The Zajedno opposition leaders are no good, the retired major continues, because they are not true Serbs: Djindjić was born in Bosnia, Drašković comes from Herzegovina and had a Muslim best man at his wedding. Oh yes, and his father was a communist. But wasn't Milošević once a communist? "No, he was a banker." The major doesn't approve of falsifying the local election results, but he's sure Milošević didn't know about that: "It was the people around him." Incidentally, he says, apropos of nothing in particular, he'd like me to know that his wife's best friend is Jewish. In fact, his own best friend is Jewish, too.

As I rise to leave, his wife—a schoolteacher—rather ceremoniously tells me that the Serbs still like the English, in spite of everything (i.e., everything we English have done to the poor Serbs). She hopes this conversation has given me a better picture of their country.

3

To make a modern liberal democracy out of this degraded, re-Balkanized society, suffused with national self-pity and psychological denial, would be difficult enough if the Serbs were alone with their problems in a single, clearly defined nation-state. But they are not. This is not just a matter of the remaining "Serbs outside Serbia." Inside the present rump Federal Republic of Yugoslavia, the Serbs comprise only some two thirds of the population (or perhaps slightly more if one were to count the Serb refugees). Another 6 percent are Montenegrins, with their own semi-independent republic within the federation. At least 15 percent are Albanians—perhaps as many as two million of them, concentrated in the southern province of Kosovo.

As so often before in Balkan and east European history, the unresolved national question cuts across, and frustrates, the attempt to democratize and modernize. As so often before, the Great Powers are called upon to sort out the mess—and end up making it worse. Diplomatic history is present in every conversation. I have never heard the Congress of Berlin mentioned so often. Talk of the frontiers, and people immediately say, "London Protocol!" The reference is to a secret treaty of 1915. "In the war . . ." they say, and you don't know if we are in the First World War, the Second World War, or the most recent war. In the political imagination, the last 120 years are wired in parallel rather than in series. Dayton (1995) exists simultaneously with the Congress of Berlin (1878). For all its claimed union, "Europe" still means Britain, France, and Germany. Russia, the Orthodox brother country, features only at the margin. For real solutions you look to America. That is the lesson they all draw from the agreement signed in Ohio, USA. But can Dayton seriously be described as a solution?

Bosnia features surprisingly little in discussions in Belgrade. The great outstanding national conundrum is now Kosovo. Kosovo is the question members of the opposition dread, because they have no answer to it. Kosovo reduces even the ebullient students to baffled silence. As all readers of Rebecca West's *Black Lamb and Grey Falcon* know, Kosovo, where the Serbs lost a great battle against the Turks in 1389, has traditionally been regarded by Serbs as the mystical heartland of their great medieval state and national identity. Vuk Drašković repeats to me the familiar description "our Jerusalem." The Serbian-Byzantine monasteries with their exquisite frescoes are still there. But 90 percent of the population is now Albanian. As you drive through the province, you see all around you, dotted across the fields, the unmistakable homesteads of Albanian extended families: several houses and sheds surrounded by a single high brick wall with a large wooden gate, like a makeshift castle. They have quite literally occupied the land.

In the 1980s, Kosovo was (under Tito's 1974 constitution) an autonomous province, with a largely Albanian administration. Although an Albanian rising in 1981 failed to achieve the status of a full republic, many of the Serbs were still leaving, often being forced out by discrimination and violence. In April 1987, Slobodan Milošević came to Kosovo and told the local Serbs, "No one should

dare to beat you!" With this battle cry, he mounted the Serb nationalist horse and rode it—assisted ably by politicians of other nationalities and especially by the Croat Franjo Tudjman—to the bloody
destruction of Yugoslavia. Kosovo itself was stripped of autonomy
and placed under direct Serb administration. The Kosovar Albanians responded with the declaration of an independent Republic of
Kosova (as they spell it) and extraordinary underground elections in
which a majority voted for a Democratic League of Kosova. Its
leader, Ibrahim Rugova, became "president of the republic."

Their headquarters is a large hut in the middle of a dusty bus
park, full of picture-book hawkers and spitters. At the door, I am met
incongruously by the "head of protocol," who ushers me in to see
"the president." In passable French, Mr. Rugova tells me about their
extraordinary underground state: the eighteen thousand school-
teachers they fund from unofficial taxes, which Kosovar Albanians
pay in addition to the official Serb ones; the independent university;
the attempt at health care, through an organization named after
Mother Teresa. Mr. Rugova's immediate demand is merely for an al-
leviation of the repression. While the Serb police dare not touch
him, they regularly harass lower-level activists. He insists on Gandhiesque peaceful means and has explicitly cautioned his followers
against following the example of armed insurrection across the border in Albania. But on the central goal he is quite unyielding: self-
determination for his people, statehood for the republic, which he
claims already exists.

His main rival, Adem Demaci—sometimes called "the Albanian
Mandela," on account of his twenty-eight years in prison—sits opposite me on a chair in his new party headquarters and, Gandhi-like,
pulls up his legs into the lotus position. He might settle for slightly
less than Rugova: a republic within a very loose confederation with
Serbia and Montenegro. But he wants more dramatic protest actions to achieve it. He has called on his followers to imitate the student and opposition demonstrations in Belgrade.

That is the Kosovar Albanian mainstream. But in the last year
there have also been a number of terrorist attacks, with responsibility claimed by a Kosovo Liberation Army. Are these the work of impatient young radicals, like the young Palestinians in Gaza? Or are

they secretly encouraged by the Serbian leader? Even sober political observers speculate that a cornered Milošević, faced with total economic collapse and massive popular calls for his resignation, might in desperation play the Kosovo card, provoking a terrorist assault or armed rising, which he could then heroically suppress.

For the time being, no one I speak to thinks the Kosovar Albanians are about to follow the example of their compatriots across the border. And this for one simple reason: Even if large quantities of small arms were to be smuggled in from the plundered arsenals of Albania, the heavily armed and professionally trained Serb army could immediately wreak terrible vengeance. "You see," both Serbs and Albanians tell me, with chilling matter-of-factness, "there are some seven hundred purely Albanian villages. So the people there could all be killed."

Yet everyone talks of the longer-term possibility of war—and the seeming impossibility of any peaceful solution. The positions are so far apart now, the Serb and Albanian communities so utterly alienated. When a local Albanian leader makes an appointment with my companion, a Serb journalist, he won't even say the name of the street in which he lives—because it's a Serb name. I visit a state school divided by an internal Berlin Wall, so that Serb and Albanian children never meet.

Each side speaks to you out of national martyrologies, underpinned with fantastic historical statistics. I ask the information secretary of the local Serb administration about the ethnic composition of the province. "In the twelfth century," he begins, "the Serbs were 98 percent of the population." "In the 1980s," says one of Mr. Rugova's key aides, "Kosovar Albanians served a total of twenty-seven thousand years in prison." The mutual stereotypes are equally fantastic. The Albanians portray the local Serbs as cock-a-hoop, triumphantly ruling the roost, whereas I find them, in fact, profoundly depressed and frightened. The Serbs see the Albanians as part of some diabolic conspiracy, *deliberately* having so many children and spreading across the land so as to realize the "Prizren program" for a Greater Albania. (The League of Prizren, as readers will doubtless recall, was the Albanian national grouping after 1878.)

What is to be done? Some nongovernmental talks between local

Serbs and Albanians have started, and are to be continued in New York. The Albanians look to the so-called international community. Like Drašković, they parrot the latest political buzzwords of the West: "full minority rights," "regional cooperation." But "parroting" is the wrong word. "Magpieing" would be more like it. For these Western terms are all adapted to their own local purposes, like a pen or pencil sharpener in the magpie's nest.

From Belgrade, from no less a figure than the novelist Dobrica Ćosić, has come the suggestion of peaceful partition. Serbia should take the main areas of Serb settlement, the mineral resources, and the holy places—the patriarchate at Peć, the beautiful monasteries of Gračanica and Dečani. The Albanians should have the rest. Albanian intellectuals have heard of this, of course. They even joke about it, when we talk in a cheerful basement restaurant hidden away beneath the dim, potholed streets of Priština. "Maximum fifteen percent for the Serbs!" "No, I'd go to twenty percent!" For a moment, I feel like the Edwardian British East Europeanist R. W. Seton-Watson, dividing up the Balkans on the back of an envelope. But seriously: The Serb holy places and main settlements are not contiguous to Serbia proper, there are large areas of Albanian settlement along the Serb frontier, and no one knows how it could be done without large movements of people and almost certain bloodshed.

David Owen has suggested an international conference on the Kosovo issue, under the auspices of the Organization for Security and Cooperation in Europe (OSCE). A Vance-Owen plan for Kosovo? But neither the Serb nor the Albanian side is ready for that. For the so-called international community, Kosovo is mainly an issue of "regional stability." The NATO generals' *cauchemar de Kosovo* is that violent conflict breaks out there and spreads to the large Albanian minority in Macedonia, thus also tearing the fragile former Yugoslav republic of Macedonia apart, involving Bulgaria and our NATO ally Greece. Then—hey nonny no!—we have the long-forecast "third Balkan war." Assuming, that is, we have not had it already.

For Serb democrats, by contrast, Kosovo is about the future of Serb democracy. One of them puts the case drastically: Serbia can have Kosovo, or it can have democracy. But which Serb politician would dare to suggest surrendering the mythical heartland of Serbianness? The leaders of Zajedno all feel it would be political suicide to open themselves to the charge of "losing Kosovo." Yet deep down everyone knows that somehow, some day, Serbia must address this issue if it is ever to become a normal, democratic nation-state.

Back in Belgrade, I have an extraordinary conversation with Dobrica Ćosić, perhaps the most important intellectual father figure of Serb nationalism in the 1980s and for a time president of the rump Federal Republic of Yugoslavia, until Milošević cast him aside, as he has so many others when they have served their turns. Ćosić receives me in his large villa in the famous suburb of Dedinje—where Tito used to live—amid ornate wooden furniture and towering bookshelves. A heavy, white-haired man, he speaks a heavy language of portentous national pathos. Yet his message is a surprising one.

It is this. He doesn't like the modern world, with its "technological civilization" and its dreadful, rootless Americanization. No, he abhors it. But that is the direction History is going. And if Serbia—now a small nation in the Balkans, on the outer edge of Europe—does not want to be left behind, to lose out completely in the great struggle of peoples for survival, then it must go with History. Specifically, then, Serbia should have a democratic and preferably a parliamentary rather than a presidential government (although keeping a federal presidency), a market economy, the rule of law, and a cooperative foreign policy. It must start to rebuild from the ruins. And then he—he of all people—speaks the memorable line "We cannot live from the myth of Kosovo."

4

For my last day, I go back to the students. I already have my "Walker's Passport," with, on the cover, the outline of Serbia filled with a photograph of protesters. (The outline shape includes Kosovo but not Montenegro.) Now they give me a badge: "Room 559: Epicenter of the Resistance." But Room 559 will soon be returning to its original use, as the departmental lending library for ancient history.

This has been a long moment of practicing democracy; of the new kind of peaceful, self-limiting popular protest that is one of the treasures of late-twentieth-century Europe; of excitement and hope. "Canada, don't give me a visa," said one of their placards, "the victory is near!" (It rhymes—in the language they now call simply "Serbian.") But privately, their assessments are sober. Biljana wants to go and study in America. Čeda fears a country populated largely by "old people and refugees" and sees the specter of fascism in its current politics.

True victory is still a long way off, and the past is such a heavy burden. "You know, there has been so much blood," says Aleksa Djilas, sitting in the apartment of his father, the great dissident Milovan Djilas. When I walked with the students a few days earlier, heading up toward Milošević's villa in Dedinje, we were stopped by a line of police just next to a large, new, monstrously vulgar, blue-and-white wedding cake of a building, thrusting out of the hillside. This is the house and headquarters of Arkan, one of the worst Serbian gangster-warlords in Bosnia, who still operates freely here, even appearing on television with his wife and baby child, all dressed up to the nines. Grotesque, utterly grotesque.

One day, in a new Serbian democracy, these young historians will have to address this heavy burden. But, looking at Kosovo, I feel the poisoned cup has still not been drained to the dregs. The tragedy that began on the field of Kosovo may yet end on the field of Kosovo.

Peering deeper into my crystal ball, I can dimly see the shape of a new Serbia. This shape is slightly smaller even than that on the cover of my Walker's Passport. It is the outline of a truncated imperial nation, which overreached itself and then lost, perhaps even more than it deserved to, in the cruel game of international politics. A suggestive comparison is with Russia: the other Orthodox postimperial nation, now also looking back before the First World War in search of a new-old identity. But a better comparison may be with a closer country of more equal size: modern Hungary, truncated since the 1920 Treaty of Trianon, which gave formerly Hungarian territory to neighboring states, including Yugoslavia. Like Hungary, this Serbia will be metaphysically depressed, much given to national self-pity, but eventually, slowly, painfully trundling back toward a place in Europe as a more or less liberal, democratic nation-state.

Then Momčilo may finally live his "normal life." Then Biljana may return from her university in America. Then Čeda may write the true history of a modern Serbia of which he can at last be proud. But how old will they be when that day comes?

For more of Biljana, Čeda, Kosovo, and Serbia, see below, pp. 318–39.

CHRONOLOGY

1997

2 APRIL. *Russia and Belarus sign a treaty providing for even closer ties.*

20 APRIL. *Fighting between Armenian and Azerbaijani troops in Nagorno-Karabakh.*

1 MAY. *The British Labour Party wins a landslide victory at a general election, ending eighteen years of Conservative rule. Tony Blair becomes prime minister.*

7 MAY. *The War Crimes Tribunal for the former Yugoslavia finds Dušan Tadić, a Bosnian Serb, guilty of crimes against humanity. He is subsequently sentenced to twenty years' imprisonment.*

25 MAY. *In a referendum, Poles vote for a new constitution.*

1 JUNE. *Socialists win parliamentary elections in France.*

16–18 JUNE. *An EU summit in Amsterdam agrees on the Amsterdam Treaty, which results from the intergovernmental conference to review Maastricht. It provides for complex but relatively modest steps of further integration.*

18–20 JUNE. Amsterdam. Just after the European summit, and the whole city is complaining about the disruption to traffic and everyday life. There is no single hint of pride in the "Amsterdam Treaty." In fact, I don't think it's ever mentioned.

20–22 JUNE. *A Denver summit of the group of seven leading industrial nations ("G7") is joined by Russia, making it a group of eight.*

25 JUNE. *Italy is admitted to the Schengen group.*

8 JULY. *At a summit in Madrid, NATO agrees to admit the Czech Republic, Hungary, and Poland by April 1999.*

9 JULY. *NATO signs a security pact with Ukraine.*

16 JULY. *The European Commission announces proposals for the EU to*

open membership negotiations with Poland, Hungary, the Czech Republic, Slovenia, Estonia, and Cyprus.

20 JULY. Warsaw. Lunch with my old friend Adam Michnik, ecstatic about the NATO and EU decisions to admit Poland. He takes me to an extravagant lunch at the Belweder restaurant—proud of being able to pay by credit card—and tells me, "I feel my life's work is done." The historic mission of his generation, he now thinks, was to guide Poland safely and peacefully from East to West, from communism to democracy. Poland could have blown it, like Slovakia under Mečiar. There were many dangers on the way. He still thinks that his dramatic Jeremiah-like warnings about the danger of a clerical nationalist authoritarianism (see above, pp. 76–77) were needed to prevent it becoming a reality. I still disagree. But no matter. The ship is nosing into harbor. Mission accomplished. And even a right-wing prime minister will not throw it off course now.

"Do you know the name of the prime minister of Switzerland?"

"No."

"Exactly! You see, it doesn't matter."

25 AUGUST. *Egon Krenz, the last communist leader of East Germany, is sentenced to six-and-a-half years' imprisonment for his responsibility for shootings of would-be escapers at the Berlin Wall.*

31 AUGUST. *Diana, Princess of Wales, dies in a car crash in Paris.*

21 SEPTEMBER. *The Solidarity Electoral Alliance wins Polish parliamentary elections.*

21 SEPTEMBER. Warsaw. The by now traditional election-evening party at the offices of the newspaper *Rzeczpospolita*. Canapés, exit polls, and media hullabaloo, just like any election in a Western country. It's as if Poland has been holding free elections for decades. While the Solidarity Electoral Alliance, a coalition of right-wing parties, is the winner, the more centrist, liberal Freedom Union does well, too. In spite of everything, there is pleasure at the prospect that two parties emerging from the post-Solidarity tradition can now form the government, albeit under a postcommunist president. This will be what the French call "*cohabitation*," but *à la polonaise*.

25–26 SEPTEMBER. Şibiu, Transylvania, Romania. Şibiu is now a Romanian town in Romania, but it used to be a German town in Hungary. The Germans had been settled here since the Middle Ages, and they called it Hermannstadt. Even today, it looks like a woodcut illustration to a book of Grimm's fairy tales: Gothic churches, houses with steep-pitched gables, cobbled streets. Yet virtually all the Germans have left. They started leaving under the communist regime. Nicolae Ceauşescu sold them to West Germany for about DM 8,000 a head. The rest left after the end of communism.

On the door of the large, handsome German church, I find a notice. It says something like this: "The member of our congregation Gertrud X died on 7 September. Our church bells will ring at the time of the funeral in Munich. The member of our congregation Hans Y died on 18 September. Our church bells will ring at the time of the funeral in Düsseldorf. The member of our congregation Hilde Z died on 24 September. Our church bells will ring at the time of the funeral in Frankfurt."

For whom the bell tolls? It tolls not just for the Germans of Transylvania. It tolls for that old Europe where people of different and of multiple nationalities lived mixed up together for generations, in a tense but creative coexistence. Now, having destroyed that world, we set about re-creating it. We call it "multiculturalism" and artificially nurture it with laws, subsidies, and government programs. The folly of it, Europe, the folly of it!

BAD MEMORIES

The sentence "We all have bad memories" can be read in two ways: "We all have memories of things that we found horrible, embarrassing, regrettable" or "Our faculty of memory is intrinsically weak, leading us to forget or misremember." The two may be connected, of course. We have a bad memory for bad memories.

In our post-Freudian English, this is usually called "repression," thus encouraging further wordplay: "After suffering under a repressive dictatorship, people repress the memory of repression." To say "repression," in the psychological sense, implies that the bad memory is the mind's way of handling bad memories. But that is just a theory. Before Freud, there was Nietzsche: " 'I did that,' says my memory. 'I can't have done that,' says my pride and remains adamant. In the end—memory gives way." And, before Nietzsche, there was Schopenhauer: "We do not like ruminating on what is unpleasant, at least when it wounds our vanity as indeed is often the case . . . therefore much that is unpleasant is also forgotten."

Comfort? Repression? Pride? Vanity? The explanations differ, but on the existence of this phenomenon, at least, the sages all agree. As Robert Louis Stevenson put it, we have "a grand memory for forgetting." But is "forgetting" an adequate word? In everyday life, we tend to operate with the binary distinction: remember/forget. And there is an awful lot that we do quite simply forget. Yet there are also many variations in between. There is, for example, the jumbling of memory. And there is the involuntary embroidering of memory. (When you recount an argument you had with somebody, it always sounds as if you won the argument.) Thomas Hobbes drew the most radical conclusion in his *Leviathan*. Discussing memory in a chapter entitled "Of Imagination," he concluded that "imagination and Memory are but one thing."

CLEARLY, this is a rich field. You may almost feel another little academic specialization coming on. There she goes, the bright young doctoral student heading straight for the Jonathan Aitken Chair of Memory Studies at the University of Westminster, after studying with the fearsome founder of the discipline, Professor Erich Teufelsdonck, Distinguished Professor of *Gedächtnisforschung* at the University of Braunau.

Let the joke die on your lips: The discipline is already here. French historians have been dwelling on this subject for more than a decade. The multivolume *Les Lieux de mémoire,* edited by Pierre Nora, is a centerpiece of recent French intellectual life. There is even—sure sign of the arrival of another academic subsubdiscipline—a learned journal, entitled *History and Memory.* Not accidentally, this is based at Tel Aviv University and centrally concerned with some very bad memories indeed: those of war, occupation, and the Holocaust.

By and large, the studies of the French school have been concerned with the history of collective memories. Often this involves a leap from a body of evidence about attitudes to the past—politicians' speeches, films, opinion polls—to a generalization about national memory. Thus, in his very interesting book *The Vichy Syndrome,* Henry Rousso uses the psychological notion of "repression" to describe the French collective memory of collaboration in Vichy. He even has a "temperature curve" charting the ups and downs of the syndrome, as if it were a fever. Stimulating though the argument is, these generalizations about some sort of national psyche are as hard to test as old-fashioned generalizations about "national character."

As A PLODDING Anglo-Saxon empiricist, I find it better to start with individual memory. My interest in this subject began—if I remember rightly—with the German memory (or forgetting) of Nazism, as I found it while living in Berlin at the end of the 1970s. The great change of 1989 was another stimulus. Trying to write the history of divided Europe in the cold war, I found that the end of communism had a remarkable transformative effect on individual memories. As after 1945, everyone suddenly discovered that they had been opposed to the fallen dictatorship. (In *Eichmann in Jerusalem*, Hannah Arendt notes that Dr. Otto Bradfisch, head of a Nazi *Einsatzkommando* that shot some fifteen thousand people, told a German court he was always "inwardly opposed" to what he was doing.) Meanwhile, politicians in the West suddenly remembered how they had "always" supported the dissidents and "said all along" that the division of Europe could not last.

Egon Bahr, the intellectual architect of Willy Brandt's Ostpolitik, now explained that he had always intended this policy to be subversive of communist regimes. Why was there no single record of his ever saying this over the previous quarter century? Ah, because he could never say this *in public*, for fear that the communists would wake up to what was going on. Not for nothing was he called "tricky Egon." Politicians' memories are, of course, made of especially flexible material. But we all do it.

The retrospective rationalization may be half conscious or even fully unconscious. A fine example is contained in the conversations between members of the German team who had been working on an atom bomb for Hitler, secretly recorded at Farm Hall, the British country house where they were being held. After they heard the news of Hiroshima, the German scientists were trying to work out why the Americans had succeeded where they had failed. "I believe the reason we didn't do it," ventured Carl-Friedrich von Weizsäcker, "was because the [German] physicists didn't want to do it on principle. If we had all wanted Germany to win the war we would have succeeded."

MORE RECENTLY, I have been plunged still deeper into the labyrinth of memory by working on a book about the strange experience of reading my own Stasi file. To read a secret-police file on yourself is a

Proustian experience. It brings back to you with incredible vividness many things that you had quite forgotten or remembered in a different way. There is a day in your life twenty years ago, described minute by minute with the cold, clinical eye of the secret policeman. There are conversations, recorded word for word. There are photographs taken with a concealed camera.

When I went on to talk to the friends, informers, and officers who figured in my life, I discovered further veils, wrinkles, and tricks of memory. One informer, whom the Stasi gave the code name "Michaela," firmly denied ever having been an "IM," the Stasi abbreviation for "unofficial collaborator." But her informer's file, which I subsequently saw, contained handwritten reports signed with the codename. She asked me, with a remnant of Marxist vocabulary, to "try to explain the subjective as well as objective conditions" when I wrote about her. "But," she added despairingly, "probably that's impossible. Even I can't really remember now." Another informer, an Englishman code-named "Smith," told me he had tried to talk to the Stasi only about general social and political conditions. In a tragicomic piece of retrospective rationalization, he "recalled" that by talking to the secret police—and, he fondly hoped, through them to the party leaders—he was trying to substitute for the missing "civil society." But his informer's file is full of detailed information on individual people.

As I traveled around with my bag of poisoned madeleines, I saw how people's memories—of events, of each other, of themselves—changed instantly, and then changed and changed again as the revelations sank in. There was no way back, now, to their previous memory of that person or that event. We say "X or Y jogged my memory" and usually mean simply "X or Y reminded me." But these "jogs" actually change the memory itself, like a digitized picture transformed in a computer: darkening that shadow, lightening this face. Except that, here, the process is involuntary. We are not the operators at the keyboard of memory.

So what we are dealing with, when we try to write history, is nothing less than an infinity of individual memories of any person or event. For these memories are changing all the time. There is, in all normal times, the slow fading that we call forgetting. But there are also the sudden changes that come with a dramatic change of external circumstances, like 1989, or with some new discovery, such as a file. L. P. Hartley famously wrote that "the past is a foreign country." But the past is much more than another country. It is another universe. The historian is a traveler through endless worlds of individual memory.

As a result, I have become even more skeptical than I was before about the value of *any* retrospective evidence. Yet that is what most historical evidence is. Most recorded history is the history of memories. What are described as contemporary, primary sources were usually recorded by an individual some time after the event, even if the interval between action and recording was only a few hours, minutes, or even seconds. We know from our own lives that people can have quite different recollections of a conversation or meeting the morning after. (Earlier this year, the leaders of the EU couldn't agree what they had agreed on in the last hours of the Amsterdam summit.) For a sobering experience, try comparing ten different newspaper reports of the same event.

The great exceptions to this rule are the tape recorder (overt or covert) and the camera. To be sure, these can lie too. Anyone who has watched a radio editor cutting and splicing a tape will never again believe what they hear. The new digital technology seems to create almost limitless possibilities of photographic manipulation. Still, properly used, they bring us an important step closer to Ranke's "how it really was." The television camera can lie, but at least it does not do what all human recorders do: both forget and involuntarily reremember. That is one reason why the best television documentaries are outstanding works of contemporary history. The television footage gives you not just the words but the body language that often belies the words, the facial expressions, the atmosphere, and telling detail that you can otherwise experience only as a participant or an eyewitness.

For the historian, the lesson is not just about the weakness of human memory but about its fecundity, its infinite creativeness, its ability—no, its elemental compulsion—endlessly to rearrange the past in constantly shifting patterns. Usually, the resulting patterns are more comforting to our self-esteem, pride, or vanity, as Nietzsche and Schopenhauer observed. But not always. Sometimes memory tortures people with remorse or guilt more than the circumstances really justify. The awful irony, explored harrowingly by Claude Lanzmann in *Shoah,* his film about the Holocaust, is that most often it is the victims who are cursed by memory, while the perpetrators are blessed by forgetting. Especially if the perpetrators were what the Germans call *Schreibtischtäter,* "desk murderers," bureaucratic coordinators of evil, like some of the chilling figures in Lanzmann's film. "That camp," said one—"what was its name? It was in the Oppeln district. . . . I've got it: Auschwitz!" Memory, this champion trickster, is thus the great adversary for anyone who tries to establish what really happened, whether as historian, journalist, or writer. Martha Gellhorn has written very movingly about this, in relation to her own memories of war, concluding, "What is the use in having lived so long, travelled so widely, listened and looked so hard, if at the end you don't know what you know?" But there is another set of questions about bad memories faced by all people and countries who have been through terrible experiences: hijacking, imprisonment, torture or—for the collective—occupation, war, dictatorship, genocide. These questions are not about how to reconstruct the past but about what is best for the individual, society, nation, or state now and in the future.

And that is the subject of the next essay, "Trials, Purges, and History Lessons"; see p. 256.

CHRONOLOGY

1997

1 OCTOBER. *SFOR troops in Bosnia take control of Bosnian Serb radio and television transmitters.*

15 OCTOBER. *Franjo Tudjman is elected president of Croatia for the third time.*

19 OCTOBER. *Milo Djukanović is elected president of Montenegro.*

27 OCTOBER. *British chancellor of the exchequer Gordon Brown says Britain will not join EMU in January 1999 and sets five economic tests for eventual membership.*

OCTOBER. *Major demonstrations by Albanian students in Kosovo.*

10 NOVEMBER. *Jerzy Buzek of the Solidarity Electoral Alliance becomes prime minister of Poland, with Bronisław Geremek, of the Freedom Union, as foreign minister.*

28 NOVEMBER. *The Kosovo Liberation Army publicly announces its existence at the funeral of a Kosovar Albanian schoolteacher killed by Serb police.*

26–29 NOVEMBER. Prague. Time for a brief visit to Václav Havel, convalescing from serious illness at Masaryk's presidential country house of Lány. He has a glass of beer on the table—"my medicine." But one thing seems to be acting as even better medicine: the news of the imminent downfall of the other Václav, prime minister Klaus.

30 NOVEMBER. *Czech prime minister Václav Klaus resigns, after more than five years in office.*

1 DECEMBER. *Britain is refused permission to attend meetings of the planned council for coordinating the economic policies of European states participating in monetary union—the "Euro-X."*

11 DECEMBER. Weimar. My favorite town in all of Germany. But now

it's a building site, with giant cranes towering over its houses and heavy lorries thundering through its quiet, cobbled streets. Why? Because it's to be "cultural capital of Europe" in 1999. I fear the delicate balance of its peculiar spirit, at once provincial and cosmopolitan, "small yet great," may be upset forever—in the name of culture.

12–13 DECEMBER. *An EU summit in Luxembourg agrees to open negotiations with six new applicants: Poland, Hungary, the Czech Republic, Slovenia, Estonia, and Cyprus—and to consider five others—Slovakia, Romania, Bulgaria, Lithuania, and Latvia—in a second wave.*

1998

20 JANUARY. *Václav Havel is reelected for a second and final five-year term as Czech president.*

21–24 JANUARY. Milan. I ask an acquaintance if there is a chance of hearing the Nobel Prize–winning anarchist playwright Dario Fo. Well, she says, as a matter of fact he's speaking at Milan University this evening. It's a ceremony to commemorate the death of a student killed by police twenty-five years ago. She says she has to be there anyway.

The large lecture room is packed. Dario Fo is amusing, loquacious, and insufferably pleased with himself. Much more interesting is the reason for my acquaintance being here. It turns out that her cousin was a left-wing student leader in the protests we are commemorating. Then he changed tack completely and went into business. He became the right-hand man of a senior industrialist who was deeply implicated in Italy's massive *tangentopoli* bribery and corruption scandal. In fact, her cousin was the man who actually gave the politicians the money. Now he is in prison. But he has been let out on bail for a couple of days, partly to attend this event. That's why she's here—to say hello to him and give him, as it were, moral support. The room is dotted with his cousins and friends.

Later, over dinner, my interpreter tells me that her father is a goldsmith. When the scandal broke, he suddenly found that most of his best clients were no longer coming. His business collapsed.

Ordinary lives, touched and changed by the *tangentopoli*. The human underside of great events.

TRIALS, PURGES, AND
HISTORY LESSONS

The QUESTION OF WHAT NATIONS SHOULD DO ABOUT A DIFFICULT PAST
is one of the great subjects of our time. Countries across the world
have faced this problem: Chile, Argentina, Uruguay, El Salvador,
Spain after Franco, Greece after the colonels, Ethiopia, Cambodia,
all the postcommunist states of Central and Eastern Europe today.
There is already a vast literature on it, mostly written by political scientists, lawyers, and human-rights activists rather than historians
and mainly looking at treating the past as an element in "transitions"
from dictatorship to—it is hoped—consolidated democracy. The
material for another library is even now being prepared in South
Africa, Rwanda, Bosnia, and The Hague.

Yet what exactly are we talking about? There is no single word for
it in the English language. German, however, has two long ones in
regular use: *Geschichtsaufarbeitung* and *Vergangenheitsbewältigung*.
These may be translated as "treating" the past, "working over" the
past, "confronting" it, "coping, dealing, or coming to terms with"
it—even "overcoming" the past. The variety of possible translations
indicates the complexity of the matter at hand. Of course, the absence of a word in a language does not necessarily indicate the absence of the thing it describes. But the presence of not just one but
two German terms does indicate that this is something of a German
speciality.

To be sure, many rivers flow into this ocean, and everyone comes
to the subject in his or her own particular way. The lawyer and

human-rights activist Aryeh Neier, for example, traces what he calls the "movement for accountability" back to Argentina in the early 1980s, and there is no doubt that a major impulse did come from Latin America, with its various models of a "truth commission." In the years since then there have already been close to twenty truth commissions, although not all were called that.[1] Yet Germany is the only country (so far) to have tried it not once but twice: after Nazism and after communism.

I have come to this subject through the curious experience of reading my own Stasi file and, more generally, through watching how the countries I know best, in Central Europe, have coped—or not coped—with the communist legacy. Here I shall concentrate on the Central European experience over the eight years since the end of communism. In particular, I want to compare the very special case of Germany with those of its east central European neighbors.

In doing so, I pose four basic questions: *whether* to remember and treat the past at all, in any of the diverse available ways, or simply to try to forget and look to the future; *when* to address it, if it is to be addressed; *who* should do it; and, last but not least, *how*?

1

The answer given to the first question—*Whether?*—in Germany since 1989 has been unequivocal: "Of course we must remember! Of course we must confront the history of the communist dictatorship in Germany in every possible way!" And Germany has set a new standard of comprehensiveness in the attempt.

The arguments made for tackling the past like this are moral, psychological, and political. Interestingly, the moral imperative, the commandment to remember, is often quoted in Germany in forms that come from the Jewish tradition: "To remember is the secret of redemption." Then there is the psychological notion, spelled out in an influential book by Alexander and Margarete Mitscherlich, that it is bad for nations, as it is for individual people, to suppress the memories of sad or evil things in their past and good for them to go through the hard work of mourning, *Trauerarbeit*. Above all, there is the political idea that this will help to prevent a recurrence of the evil. How many times has one heard repeated in Germany George Santayana's remark that those who forget the past are condemned to repeat it?

You can see at once why it is regarded in Germany as politically incorrect, to say the least, to question this received wisdom. After the Holocaust, how dare anyone talk of forgetting? Yet the basic premise has in fact been rejected in many other times and places. Historically, the advocates of forgetting are numerous and weighty. Just two days after the murder of Caesar, Cicero declared in the Roman senate that all memory of the murderous discord should be consigned to eternal oblivion: *"oblivione sempiterna delendam."* European peace treaties, from one between Lothar, Ludwig of Germany, and Charles of France in 851 to the Treaty of Lausanne in 1923, called specifically for an act of forgetting. So did the French constitutions of 1814 and 1830. The English Civil War ended with an Act of Indemnity and Oblivion.

Even since 1945, there have been many examples in Europe of a policy of forgetting. The postwar French republic was built, after the first frenzy of the *épuration,* upon a more or less conscious policy of supplanting the painful memory of collaboration in Vichy and occupied France with de Gaulle's unifying national myth of a single, eternally resistant, fighting France. In fact, much of postwar Western European democracy was constructed on a foundation of forgetting: Think of Italy, or of Kurt Waldheim's Austria—happily restyled, with the help of the Allies, as the innocent victim of Nazi aggression. Think, too, of West Germany in the 1950s, where determined efforts were made to forget the Nazi past.

The examples don't stop there. The transition to democracy in Spain after 1975 involved a conscious strategy of not looking back, not confronting or "treating" the past. The writer Jorgé Semprun speaks of "a collective and willed amnesia." To be sure, there was an initial explosion of interest in recent history, but there were no trials of Francoist leaders, no purges, no truth commissions. On the fiftieth anniversary of the beginning of the Spanish Civil War, the prime minister, Felipe González, issued a statement saying that the civil war was "finally history" and "no longer present and alive in the reality of the country."

What is more, we find something similar in Poland after the end of communism. Poland's first noncommunist prime minister in more than forty years, Tadeusz Mazowiecki, declared in his opening statement to parliament, "We draw a thick line [*gruba linia*] under the past." He has since repeatedly insisted that all he meant by this was what he went on to say in the next sentence: that his government should be held responsible only for what it would do itself. Yet the phrase "thick line," often quoted in the slightly different form "*gruba kreska*," rapidly became proverbial and was understood to stand for a whole "Spanish" approach to the difficult past. While this was unfair to the original context in which Mazowiecki first used the phrase, it was not unfair as a shorthand characterization of the general attitude of Mazowiecki and his colleagues.

As I well remember from conversations at that time, their general attitude was: let bygones be bygones; no trials, no recriminations; look to the future, to democracy and "Europe," as Spain had done. Partly this was because Poland in 1989 had a negotiated revolution, and representatives of the old regime were still in high places—including the government itself. Partly it was because by 1990 they simply could not imagine the postcommunist party being voted back into power in free elections. So there seemed to be no pressing political need to remind people of the horrors of the communist past, and many, many more urgent things to do—such as transforming the economy with the so-called Balcerowicz Plan. Yet it also reflected a deeper philosophy—one that Mazowiecki, a liberal Catholic and veteran Solidarity adviser, shared with many from the former opposition movements in Central Europe.

In Germany, it was the former East German dissidents who pressed for a radical and comprehensive reckoning. Elsewhere in East Central Europe it was the dissidents—those who had suffered most directly under the old regime—who were often most ready to draw that "thick line" under the past. Václav Havel in Czechoslovakia was a classic example, and his policy in his first year as president, like that of Mazowiecki, could be described as one of preemptive forgiveness. The Hungarian case was rather different. Here the conservative government of József Antall, composed of people who had not been in the front line of opposition to communism, indulged in a vivid rhetoric of reckoning—but their purgative words were not matched by purgative deeds. The sharpest contrast, as so often, was between Germany and Poland.

2

This brings me to my second basic question: *When?* For there is an intermediate position that says, "Yes, but not yet." An intellectual argument for this is the neo-Rankean one made against any attempt to write the history of the very recent past: We don't have sufficient distance from the events to understand their meaning; we are emotionally involved, and the sources are not fully available. Better wait thirty years for the relevant official papers to be available in the archives. In postcommunist Central Europe, however, the last part of the argument is circular, since those who say "The sources are not available" are often the same people who are keeping the archives shut.

Beyond this, the arguments are political. What is supposed to strengthen the new democracy might actually undermine it. To examine the difficult past too closely will reopen old wounds and tear the society apart. You need to integrate the functionaries, collaborators, and merely supporters of the dictatorship into the new democracy. Thus, Hermann Lübbe has suggested that it was precisely the fact that Adenauer's West Germany in the 1950s suppressed the memory of the Nazi past, with both amnesty and amnesia, that permitted the social consolidation of democracy in West Germany. It helped Nazis to become democrats.

Against this it can be argued, I think powerfully, as follows. First, the purely historiographical loss is as large as any gain in evidence or detachment. The witnesses die; others forget or, at least, rearrange their memories; and it is the worst horrors that are often the least well documented in the archives. Second, the victims and their relatives have a moral right to know at whose hands they or their loved ones suffered. Third, delay and suppression have their own psychological and political price. The fact that the torturers or the commanders go unpunished, even remain in high office, compromises the new regime in the eyes of those who should be its strongest sup-

porters. Dirty fragments of the past constantly resurface an
used, often dirtily, in current political disputes.

For France, Henri Rousso has described this vividly as the Vichy
Syndrome. He compares it to a chronic fever, an old malaria in the
bones of the French body politic. As we have seen in recent years
with the revelations about François Mitterrand's Vichy past, it still
has not gone away. So also with Germany. In her new book *Politics
and Guilt,* the Berlin political scientist Gesine Schwan sensitively
explores the political and psychological price paid by the Federal Republic for what she calls the *"Beschweigen"*—that is, the "deliberately keeping silent about" the crimes and horrors of Nazism—in
West German public life, schools, and, above all, families, in the
1950s. The systematic academic, journalistic, and pedagogic treatment of the Nazi past developed as part of an often angry reaction
against the suppression of the 1950s. In fact, the portmanteau terms
I mentioned at the outset, *Geschichtsaufarbeitung* and *Vergangenheitsbewältigung,* seem to date, in regular usage, only from the
1960s.

Many among the hugely influential West German "class of '68"
also thought the suppression of the Nazi past and the anticommunism of the older generation were two sides of the same coin. In reaction, they produced sympathetic, even rose-tinted, accounts of
communist East Germany, with, for example, no mention of the
Stasi. There is an interesting if perverse connection here. Their revolt against their fathers' failure to treat fully the past of the previous
German dictatorship contributed to their own failure to see clearly
the evils of the current one.

In any event, a sense of the high price of that delay in addressing
the Nazi past is one reason why the demand for an immediate, comprehensive "treatment" of the communist past was so swiftly accepted in Germany after 1989.

3

The German case also raises my third question: *Who?* Before the
long silence of the 1950s, there had, of course, been the attempt at
denazification, carried out by the occupying powers, and the

conducted by the victorious Allies. Both Nurem-
.cation have ever since been basic reference points
.ussions. To have the business done by outsiders,
eat, does have obvious advantages. There are no do-
l constraints to compare with putsch-happy militaries
in Lau. .ica or the still functioning security services in today's
Russia. Something gets done. But it also shows the disadvantages.
Indeed, one could argue that the suppression of the Adenauer years
was itself, in part, a reaction to what had been seen as "victors' justice"—and victors' history.

In most of postcommunist Europe we have the opposite position
to that of post-1945 Germany. Far from being newly occupied, most
postcommunist countries see themselves as newly emerged from occupation. Moreover, only in five countries—Poland, Hungary, Romania, Bulgaria, and Albania—is the communist past being faced
(or not faced) within the same state boundaries as those in which it
occurred. Everywhere else—in the former Soviet Union, the former
Yugoslavia, and the former Czechoslovakia—you have a number of
new, smaller successor states. Or rather, they might and do say, *not*
successors—not heirs to that past. In a country such as Lithuania,
genuinely emerging from an oppressive occupation and struggling to
build up a new national and state identity, the temptation to say,
"That was them, not us," is almost irresistible. Yet even for the Russians there is a large temptation to say, "That was the Soviet Union,
not Russia."

The German position is, once again, unique. Whereas Poles and
Hungarians are, so to speak, alone with their own past, East and
West Germans have to work it through together. Disgruntled East
Germans, mixing their historical metaphors, talk of an *Anschluss* followed by "victors' justice." But this was a voluntary *Anschluss,* voted
for by a majority of East Germans in a free election, and the boldest
steps of confronting the past were actually pressed for by East Germans. Still, the resentment is understandable. In many cases, West
Germans do sit in judgment, whether in courts of law or simply by
executive decision, over East Germans.

This extraordinary German self-occupation, or half occupation,
poses in a singular form the issues always raised by outside partici-

pation in the process. There is the practical issue of popular acceptance. But there is also the moral issue. What right have we, who never faced the dilemmas of living in a dictatorship, to sit in judgment on those who did? Do we know how we would have behaved? Perhaps we, too, would have become party functionaries or secret-police informers? So what right have we to condemn? But, equally, what right have we to forgive? "Do not forgive," writes Zbigniew Herbert, the great poet of Polish resistance:

> Do not forgive, for truly it is not in your power to forgive
> In the name of those who were betrayed at dawn.

Only the victims have the right to forgive.

4

This is a problem for those inside a country, too. Even inside, the question remains: Who has the right to judge? Parliament? Judges? Special commissions or tribunals? The media? Or perhaps historians? At this point, the question of *who* shades into the question of *how.* In my title, I have indicated three main paths: trials, purges, or history lessons. (I leave aside here the very important but also very complex issues of rehabilitation, compensation, and restitution for the victims or their relatives.)

The choice of path, and the extent to which each can be followed, depends on the character of the preceding dictatorship, the manner of the transition, and the particular situation of the succeeding democracy—if that is what it eventually becomes. Thus, for example, the political constraints in Central Europe are far less acute than in Latin America. But the preceding repression was also very different.

The American writer Tina Rosenberg has put it simply but well: In Latin America, repression was deep; in Central Europe, it was broad. In Latin America, there was a group of people who were clearly victims. They were tortured, murdered, or, in that awkward but strangely powerful locution, "disappeared" by a group of people—army and police officers, members of death squads—who were clearly perpetrators. In Central Europe, since the high-Stalinist period and with a few major exceptions, the regime was generally kept in power by a much larger number of people exerting less violent or explicit pressure on a much larger number. Many people were on both sides. Society was kept down by millions of tiny Lilliputian threads of everyday mendacity, conformity, and compromise. This is a point Václav Havel has stressed constantly. In these late or posttotalitarian regimes, he says, the line did not run clearly between "them" and "us" but through each individual. No one was simply a victim; everyone was in some measure coresponsible.

If that is true, it is much less clear who, if anyone, should be put on trial. Havel's implicit answer is: everyone, and therefore no one. Adam Michnik has made this answer explicit. Exceptions to prove the rule are individual cases of abnormal brutality, such as the Polish secret-police officers directly responsible for the murder of the Solidarity priest Father Jerzy Popiełuszko.

The record of trials in postcommunist Central Europe is, in fact, a very checkered one. In what was then still Czechoslovakia, two senior functionaries were convicted after 1990 for their part in the repression of antiregime demonstrations in 1988 and early 1989. In 1993, the Czech Republic's Law on the Illegal Character of the Communist Regime lifted the statute of limitations for crimes that "for political reasons" had not been prosecuted in the communist period. An Office for the Documentation and Investigation of the Crimes of Communism was established, and it brought charges against three former Communist Party leaders for their role in assisting the Warsaw Pact invasion of Czechoslovakia in 1968. In Poland, General Jaruzelski was investigated for ordering the destruction of politburo records and then, more substantially, indicted on charges relating to the shooting of protesting workers on the Baltic coast in 1970–1971. A number of senior figures were charged with causing the deaths of striking workers during martial law in 1981–1982. But, altogether, the judicial proceedings have been fitful, fragmentary, and usually inconclusive.

Germany has, unsurprisingly, been the most systematic. Border guards have been tried and convicted for shooting people who were trying to escape from East Germany. More recently, the country's last communist leader, Egon Krenz, was sentenced to six-and-a-half years' imprisonment for his coresponsibility for the "shoot to kill" policy at the frontier. Several other senior figures were found guilty with him. Yet even in Germany, the results are very mixed, to say the least.

The arguments generally made for trials are that they go at least some way to providing justice for the victims; that they help to deter future transgressions by the military or security forces; that they exemplify and strengthen the rule of law; and, finally, that they contribute to public knowledge and some sense of a wider catharsis. The first consideration—justice for the victims—certainly applies in some of these cases; the second applies to a much smaller degree, since, broadly speaking, where such deterrence might still be important (as in Russia) there have been no such trials, and where there have been trials (as in Germany) the deterrence is hardly needed.

Have these trials exemplified and strengthened the rule of law? It is very hard to say that they have. Equality before the law is a fundamental principle; but even in Germany, still more elsewhere, there has been a radical, arbitrary, and political selection of the accused. Then there is the familiar problem of trying people for crimes that were not crimes on the statute books of their countries at the time. How to avoid violating the time-honored principle of *nulla poena sine lege*?

Determined to avoid such a "Nuremberg" procedure, German prosecutors have therefore tried to identify crimes that were offenses in East German law at the time. However, this has involved a highly selective application of East German law, thus violating another basic principle. (Yet otherwise, the prosecutors should themselves be prosecuted for defaming the East German state, which was an offense under East German law!) And, when the case could still not quite be made to stick, they bridged the gap with an awkward invocation of "natural law." Meanwhile, the former minister for state security, Erich Mielke, was convicted not for his heavy responsibility in the regime but for his part in the murder of a policeman as a young street-fighting communist in 1931. The trial of Erich Honecker, the party leader from 1971 to 1989, was finally abandoned on the grounds of his ill health. He then flew off to spend his last months quietly in Chile.

None of this contributed much to any sense of popular catharsis. As for public knowledge: The thousands of pages of legal argument did little to illuminate the true history of the regime, certainly not for the general reader. Nor will future students of communism, I think, use the records of these trials as we do still use those of the Nuremberg trials to understand Nazism.

The Hungarian case is an interesting contrast. Here parliament initially passed a law that, like the Czech one, lifted the statute of limitations for acts of treason, murder, and manslaughter during the communist period, but the Constitutional Court struck that down on the grounds that it was retroactive justice. A new law was then passed specifically on Crimes Committed During the 1956 Revolution. This took a different tack and applied the Geneva and New York conventions on "war crimes" and "crimes against humanity" to what happened in 1956. Unlike the German prosecutors, and uniquely in Central Europe, they therefore claimed that some things done in the communist period did qualify for those Nuremberg trial categories—"crimes against humanity," "war crimes"—and that these provisions had at least notionally been in force in international law at the time.

THE SECOND PATH is that of purges. Or, to put it more neutrally, administrative disqualification. In this field alone it was not Germany that set the pace. Partly in reaction against Havel's policy of preemptive forgiveness, the Czechoslovak parliament passed a draconian law in the autumn of 1991. It laid down that whole categories of people—including high party functionaries, members of the People's Militia, agents, and what it termed "conscious collaborators" of the state security service—should be banned from whole, widely drawn categories of work in the public service. In Czech, the process was called not "purge" (a somewhat compromised term) but "*lustrace,*" a word derived from the Latin and implying both "illumination" and "ritual purification." Thanks to the Czechs, we can therefore revive an old English word: *lustration.* Among the meanings given by the *Oxford English Dictionary,* with supporting quotations from the seventeenth to the nineteenth centuries, are

"purification *esp.* spiritual or moral" and "the performance of an ex-
piatory sacrifice or a purificatory rite."

The Czechoslovak lustration was fully effective in its original
form for little more than a year, since Czechoslovakia then broke
into two. While the Czech Republic continued with a slightly modified version, Slovakia virtually dropped it. Yet there is no doubt that
the law did keep a number of highly compromised persons out of
public life in the Czech lands, while such persons remained to do
much damage in Slovakia. However, the original legislation was also
so crude and procedurally unjust that President Havel publicly expressed deep reluctance to sign the law, and the Council of Europe
protested against it. Disqualification by category meant that any particular individual circumstances could not be taken into account. A
commission determined, on the basis of a sometimes cursory examination of secret-police and other official records, whether someone
had belonged to one of the specified categories. The people thus
publicly branded often did not see all the evidence and had only limited rights of appeal. In effect, they were assumed guilty until found
innocent.

The German law on the Stasi files is more scrupulous. Employers
receive a summary of the evidence on the individual's file from the
so-called Gauck Authority—the extraordinary ministry set up to ad-
minister the 111 miles of Stasi files and colloquially named after its
head, Joachim Gauck, an East German priest. The employer then
makes an individual decision, case by case. Even in the public service, some two thirds of those negatively vetted have remained in
their jobs. The employee can also appeal to the labor courts. Yet
here, too, there clearly have been cases of injustice—even when de-
nunciatory media coverage has not ruined the person's life. And the
sheer numbers are extraordinary: As of the end of June 1996, more
than 1.7 million vetting inquiries had been answered by the Gauck
Authority. In other words, about one in every ten East Germans has
been, to use the colloquial term, "gaucked." Here, the strict, procedural equality may, in fact, conceal a deeper structural inequality.
East German employees are being subjected to tests that West German employees would never have to face.

Yet one also has to consider the cost of not purging. In Poland, that

was the original "Spanish" intent. Within a year, however, the contin-
uance of former communists in high places became a hotly disputed
subject in Polish politics. In the summer of 1992, the interior minister of a strongly anticommunist government supplied to parliament
summaries of files identifying prominent politicians as secret-police
collaborators. Of course the names leaked to the press. This so-called
noc teczek—or night of the long files—shook the new democracy and
actually resulted in the fall of the government. In December 1995,
the outgoing interior minister, with the consent of the outgoing president, accused his own postcommunist prime minister of being an
agent for Russian intelligence. The prime minister subsequently re-
signed, and the affair still rumbles on. In the latest parliamentary
election campaign, this autumn, it was suggested that the current
postcommunist president of Poland, Aleksander Kwaśniewski, himself had close contacts with the Russian agent who allegedly "ran"
the former prime minister.

So, in the absence of an agreed, public, legal procedure, Poland
has enjoyed not Spanish-style consensus but bitter, recurrent mudslinging and crude political exploitation of the files. As a long-
overdue antidote to all this, the Polish parliament has this year finally
passed a carefully drafted lustration law. It obliges people in senior
positions in public life, including in the state-owned media, to sign,
at the time they stand for elected office or are appointed to the job, a
declaration as to whether they did or did not "consciously collaborate" with the security services in the period June 1944 to May 1990.
At the recent parliamentary elections, I saw polling stations plastered
with long lists of the candidates and under each name the appropriate declaration. The admitted fact of collaboration does not in itself
disqualify you from standing for public office. Indeed, several candidates on the postcommunist list stood admitting their past collaboration. Only if you lie, saying you did not collaborate when in fact you
did, are you disqualified for ten years. The declarations of innocence
are to be checked, in secret, by a so-called Lustration Court.

Hungary passed a lustration law in 1997, and this is slowly being
implemented. There, a commission vets senior figures in public life,
but exposes them publicly only if they refuse to resign quietly.
Shortly thereafter, the prime minister, Gyula Horn, admitted that he

had been negatively assessed in the terms of the law, both on account of his service in the militia assembled to help crush the 1956 revolution and because, as foreign minister, he had been the recipient of secret-police information. However, he declined to resign and said he now regards the matter as closed. In both the Polish and the Hungarian cases, the circle of persons to be vetted is—wisely, in my view—drawn much more closely than in the German case.

Some analysts have taken the argument for purges a step further. Where there was no lustration, they say, as in Poland and Hungary—and elsewhere in eastern and southeastern Europe—the postcommunist parties returned to power. Only where there was lustration, in Czechoslovakia and Germany, did this not occur. Yet to deduce causality from correlation is an old historian's fallacy—*cum hoc, ergo propter hoc*. On closer examination, you find that in eastern Germany the postcommunist party has done very well in elections, and one reason for this is, precisely, resentment of what are seen as West German occupation purges and victors' justice. In fact, the number of votes the postcommunist PDS received in eastern Germany at the last Bundestag election, in October 1994, is remarkably similar to the number of people who have been "gaucked": about 1.7 million in each case. (Not that I would deduce causality from this correlation, but still.)

One should by no means simply assume that the return to power of postcommunist parties with impeccably social-democratic programs has been bad for the consolidation of democracy. Yet it is true that, in Poland and Hungary, the new democracy has been shaken by issues arising from the lack of lustration, including the current activities of the security services. And the return to power not just of the postcommunist parties but of historically compromised persons within them has furnished the populist, nationalist right with arguments against the working of the new parliamentary democracy altogether. "If such people are elected, there must be something wrong with elections."

FINALLY, there are what I call "history lessons." These can be of several kinds: state or independent, public or private. The classic model of a state, public history lesson is that of the "truth commission," first developed in Latin America and currently being used in South Africa. As José Zalaquett, one of the fathers of the Chilean truth commission, has noted, the point is not only to find out as much as possible of the truth about the past dictatorship but also to see that this truth be "officially proclaimed and publicly exposed." Not just knowledge but acknowledgment is the goal. In truth commissions, there is a strong element of political theater. They are a kind of public morality play. Archbishop Tutu has shown himself well aware of this. He leads others in weeping as the survivors tell their tales of suffering and the secret policemen confess their brutality. The object is not judicial punishment: In South Africa, full confession leads not to trial but to amnesty. It is formally to establish the truth, insofar as it can ever be established; if possible, to achieve a collective catharsis, very much as Aristotle envisaged catharsis in a Greek tragedy; and then to move on. In South Africa, as in Chile, the commission's aims are both "Truth" and "Reconciliation." The hope is to move through the one to the other.[2]

You might think that this model would be particularly well suited to the postcommunist world, where the regimes were kept in place less by direct coercion than by the everyday tissue of lies. But, again, only in Germany has it really been tried, and even there they somehow did not dare to use the word *truth*. Instead, the parliamentary commission, chaired by an East German former dissident priest, was cumbersomely called the "Enquete Commission in the German Bundestag [for the] 'Treatment of the Past and Consequences of the SED-Dictatorship in Germany' " (SED being the initials of the East German communist party). Hundreds of witnesses were heard, expert reports were commissioned, proceedings were covered in the media. We now have a report of 15,378 pages—and a successor Enquete Commission is working on another. There are problems with this report. The language is often ponderous. Some of the historical judgments represent compromises among the West German political parties, worried about their own pasts. Yet, as documentation, it is invaluable. For students of the East German dictatorship, this may yet be what the records of the Nuremberg trials are for the student of the Third Reich.

In Poland and Czechoslovakia, by contrast, the national commissions of inquiry concentrated on major crises in the history of the communist state: Solidarity and the Prague Spring. In each case, the focus was on the Soviet connection. Who "invited" the Red Army to invade Czechoslovakia in August 1968? Who was responsible for martial law in Poland in 1981? In Hungary, too, official inquiries have concentrated on the 1956 revolution and the Soviet invasion that crushed it. So, instead of exploring what Poles did to Poles, Czechs and Slovaks to Czechs and Slovaks, Hungarians to Hungarians, each nation dwells on the wrongs done to it by the Soviet Union. Instead of quietly reflecting, as Havel suggested, on the personal responsibility that each and everyone had for sustaining the communist regime, people unite in righteous indignation at the traitors who invited the Russians in.

Any explanation for the absence of wider truth commissions must be speculative. Part of the explanation, at least, seems to lie in this combination of two elements: the historically defensible but also comfortable conviction that the dictatorship was ultimately imposed from outside and the uneasy knowledge that almost everyone had done something to sustain the dictatorial system.

Another kind of history lesson is less formal and ritualistic but requires permissive state action. This is to open the archives of the preceding regime to scholars, journalists, writers, filmmakers—and then to let a hundred documentaries bloom. Yet again, Germany has gone farthest, much helped by the fact that the East German state ceased to exist on 3 October 1990. Virtually all the archives of the former GDR are open and provide a marvelous treasure trove for the study of a communist state. I say "virtually all" because a notable exception is the archive of the East German foreign ministry, in which are held most of the records of the often sycophantic conversations that West German politicians conducted with East German leaders. In opening the archives, West German politicians have thus fearlessly spared nobody—except themselves.

It has also helped that Germany has such a strong tradition of writing contemporary history. The research department of the Gauck Authority, for example, is staffed partly by younger historians from the Munich Institute for Contemporary History, famous for its studies of Nazism. Theirs are strange careers: progressing smoothly from the study of one German dictatorship to another, while all the time living in a peaceful, prosperous German democracy. The results are impressive. Whereas a West German schoolchild in the 1950s could learn precious little about Nazi Germany, every German schoolchild today can already learn a great deal about the history of communist Germany. Whether they are interested is another question.

Elsewhere in Central Europe, the opening of the archives has been more uneven, partly because of the political attitudes I have described, partly for simple lack of resources and trained personnel. Yet here, too, there have been some interesting publications based on the new archive material, and school textbooks have improved significantly. In Poland, there has been a lively intellectual and political debate about the nature, achievements, and (il)legitimacy of the Polish People's Republic. In Prague, a new Institute for Contemporary History concerns itself with the history of Czechoslovakia from 1939 to 1992. In Hungary, a whole institute has been established solely to study the history of the 1956 revolution. It has roughly one staff member per day of the revolution.

Beyond this, what Germany has uniquely pioneered is the systematic opening of the secret-police files, administered by the Gauck Authority, to everyone—whether spied upon or spying—who has a file and still wants to know its contents. The power is in the hands of the individual citizen. You can choose to read your file or not to read it. The informers on your file are identified only by code names, but you can request formal confirmation of their true identities. Then you have to decide whether to confront them or not to confront them; to say something publicly, just to tell close friends, or to close it in your heart. This is the most deep and personal kind of history lesson.

Maddeningly, the Gauck Authority's statistics do not enable us to say exactly how many people have gone through this experience. But a reasonable estimate is that more than 400,000 people have seen their Stasi files, over 300,000 are still waiting to do so, and more than 350,000 have learned with relief—or was it with disappointment?—that they had no file. I can think of no remotely scientific way to assess this unique experiment. People have made terrible personal discoveries: The East German peace activist Vera Wollenberger, for example, found that her husband had been informing on her throughout their married life. Only they can say if it is better that they know.

There has also been irresponsible, sensationalist media coverage—denouncing people as informers without any of the due caution about the sources or circumstances. In German, such exposure is revealingly called "outing." Here is a structural problem of treating the past in societies with free and sensation-hungry media. Against this, however, one has to put the many cases in which people have emerged from the experience with gnawing suspicions laid to rest, enhanced understanding, and a more solid footing for their present lives.

Elsewhere in Central Europe, the German experiment was at first strongly criticized and resisted, on the grounds that it would reopen old wounds and unjustly destroy reputations, and that the Polish or Hungarian secret-police records are much more unreliable than the German ones. (This last comment is made with a kind of inverted national pride.) Officers put innocent people down as informers or simply invented them—the so-called dead souls—in order to meet their assigned plan targets for the number of informers. Many files were later destroyed, others tampered with, and so on. So, instead, the secret-police files have remained in the hands of the current interior ministry or still active security service and have been used selectively by them and their political masters. Limited access has been given to just a few individual scholars.

Yet, interestingly, this is now changing. Hungary has provided for individuals to request copies of their own files. The precedent is clearly the German one, although the Hungarian rules demand even more extensive "anonymization"—that is, blacking out of the names on the copies. The Hungarian Gauck Authority has a simple but rather sinister name: the Historical Office. In sanctioning this access, the Hungarian Constitutional Court drew heavily on the judgments of the German Constitutional Court, notably in using the interesting concept of "informational self-determination." In plain English, I have a right to know what information the state has collected on me and, within limits, to determine what is done with it.

The Czech Republic has passed a law that provides for people who were Czechoslovak citizens at any time between 1948 and 1990 to read their own files, under similar conditions. The first applications were accepted in June 1997. Thus far there has been remarkably little debate about individual cases, and few prominent former dissidents have applied to see their files. Perhaps this will change when sensational material is found and published, but at the moment one is told in Prague that there seems to be little public interest. There is a strong sense that the Czechs have already "been through all this" with the great lustration debate of the early 1990s.

Poland is now following suit. The new post-Solidarity government has committed itself to making the secret-police files accessible to individual citizens. When I was there in mid-November 1997, a lively debate was going on about how best to do this. Frequent reference was made to the German experience. In the parliamentary debate on the government's program, the Catholic nationalist leader of the Solidarity Electoral Alliance, Marian Krzaklewski, called for a "lustration archive on the model of the Gauck Authority."

Altogether, it is remarkable to see how, in this of all areas, Germany has been not just a pioneer but also, in the end, something of a model for its eastern neighbors. Who would have imagined fifty years ago that, when it came to dealing with their own difficult past, the Poles would turn to the Germans for an example?

5

There are no easy generalizations and certainly no universal laws. So much depends on the character of the preceding regime and the nature of the transition. Even my first, basic question—*Whether?*—does not have a simple answer. The ancient case for forgetting is much stronger than it is comfortable for historians to recall. Successful democracies have been built on a conscious policy of forgetting—although at a cost, which often has not appeared until a generation later.

In Central Europe after communism, Germany's policy of a systematic, unprecedentedly comprehensive "treatment" of the past contrasted with Poland's initial policy of drawing a "thick line" between the past and the present. But the Polish attempt to follow the Spanish example did not work as it had in Spain. Within a year, the issue of the communist past had come back to bedevil Polish politics, and continues to be used in a messy, partisan way, with ill-documented accusations being made about past collaboration with the communist authorities. My conclusion is that if it is to be done it should be done quickly, in an orderly, explicit, and legal way. This also has the great advantage of allowing people then to move on— not necessarily to forget, perhaps not even to forgive, but simply to go forward with that knowledge behind them.

If the questions *"Whether?"* and *"When?"* are thus closely connected, so are the questions *"Who?"* and *"How?"* In Germany, the process has been made both easier and more difficult by West German participation: easier administratively; more difficult psychologically. Yet, doing it among themselves, Hungarians, Poles, Czechs, and Slovaks have all too humanly been inclined to focus on the responsibilities of others rather than their own.

There are places in the world where trials have been both necessary and effective. In Central Europe, trials have been—with a few important exceptions—of only questionable necessity and even more dubious efficacy. The attempt to use existing national laws has been contorted and selective and often ended in simple failure. It has hardly exemplified or strengthened the rule of law. This is one area in which the international component may be a real advantage.

Difficult though it is, the least bad way forward must be to try to establish a firm international framework of law on "crimes against humanity" or "war crimes." Building on the Hague tribunals for Bosnia and Rwanda, we need to move toward the permanent international criminal court for which Aryeh Neier, Richard Goldstone, and others have eloquently argued—a court to which all dictators, everywhere, should know that they may one day have to answer. Meanwhile, the Hungarian path of writing the existing international law into domestic law is an interesting precedent. It was, however, confined to just one event, the Hungarian revolution of 1956, now more than forty years past, and its implementation has been plagued by all the problems of evidence that we know so well from the trials of Nazi criminals in recent decades.

As for purges, there is probably no such thing as a good purge, even if it is politely called lustration. The Czechoslovak lustration was prompt and crudely effective but deeply flawed by procedural injustice. The German "gaucking" has been procedurally more just: careful, individual, appealable. But it has sometimes been perverted by media abuse, and it has suffered from elephantiasis. Did postmen and train drivers really need to be gaucked? Again we come back to the question of who is doing it, for would the West Germans ever have done this to themselves?

Yet Poland has shown the price of not purging. The Hungarians, with their nice habit of taking the German model and then improving on it, came up with a defensible refinement: It applied careful individual scrutiny only to those seeking senior positions in public life. But this was seven years late. Now Poland has finally followed suit, with a law that is probably the most scrupulous of them all.

I believe the third path—that of history lessons—has been the most promising in Central Europe. Much of the comparative literature comes to a similar conclusion for other countries: What is somewhat biblically called "truth-telling" is both the most desirable and the most feasible way to grapple with a difficult past. This is what West Germany did best in relation to Nazism, at least from the 1960s on. What united Germany has done in this regard since 1990 has been exemplary: the parliamentary commission, the open archives, the unique opportunity for a very personal history lesson given by access to the Stasi files.

To advocate the third path does, of course, assign a very special place to contemporary historians. In fact, I do think that if you ask "Who is best equipped to do justice to the past?" the answer is, or at least should be, historians. But this is also a heavy responsibility. *Truth* is a big word, so often abused in Central Europe during the short, rotten twentieth century that people there have grown wary of it. Studying the legacy of a dictatorship, one is vividly reminded how difficult it is to establish any historical truth. In particular, across such a change of regime, you discover how deeply unreliable is any retrospective testimony.

Yet studying this subject also strengthens one's allergy to some of the bottomless, ludic frivolities of postmodernist historiography. For this is too serious a business. Carelessly used, the records of a state that worked by organized lying—and especially the poisonous, intrusive files of a secret police—can ruin lives. To interpret them properly tests the critical skills that historians apply routinely to a medieval charter or an eighteenth-century pamphlet. But, having worked intensively with such records and read much else based on them, I know that it can be done. It is not true, as is often claimed, that this material is so corrupted that one cannot write reliable history on the basis of it. The evidence has to be weighed with very special care. The text must be put in the historical context. Interpretation needs both intellectual distance and the essential imaginative sympathy with all the men and women involved—even the oppressors. But, with these old familiar disciplines, there is a truth that can be found. Not a single, absolute Truth with a capital *T* but still a real and important one.

CHRONOLOGY

1998

JANUARY–FEBRUARY. *Parts of the Drenica area in Kosovo are claimed as "liberated" by the Kosovo Liberation Army.*

28 FEBRUARY–MARCH. *Violent repressive action by Serb forces against the extended families of Kosovo Liberation Army activists sparks large-scale armed insurrection in Kosovo.*

12 MARCH. *Leaders of the eleven states recognized as candidates to join the EU meet with EU leaders in London to launch enlargement. Turkey, not being so recognized, refuses to attend.*

25 MARCH. *The European Commission declares that eleven member states have met the Maastricht criteria for monetary union and wish to go ahead. Greece does not qualify; Britain, Denmark, and Sweden do not wish to join at this stage.*

THE CASE FOR
LIBERAL ORDER

THERE IS EUROPE AND THERE IS "EUROPE." THERE IS THE PLACE, THE continent, the political and economic reality, and there is Europe as an idea and an ideal, as a dream, as project, process, progress toward some visionary goal. No other continent is so obsessed with its own meaning and direction. These idealistic and teleological visions of Europe at once inform and legitimate, and are themselves informed and legitimated by, the political development of something now called the European Union. The very name "European Union" is itself a product of this approach. For a union is what it's meant to be, not what it is.

European history since 1945 is told as a story of unification—difficult, delayed, suffering reverses, but nonetheless progressing. Here is the grand narrative taught to millions of European schoolchildren and accepted by Central and Eastern European politicians when they speak of rejoining "a uniting Europe." Meanwhile, Western European leaders have repeatedly reaffirmed the goal of "ever closer union" since it was first solemnly embraced in the Treaty of Rome.

A classic example of this European self-interpretation is the French historian Jean-Baptiste Duroselle's *Europe: A History of Its Peoples*, published simultaneously in several European languages in 1990. Discussing different ways of viewing the post-1945 history of Europe, he writes, "One may, finally, see this phase of history in a European light"—by implication, the other lights must be un-European—"and observe how many objective factors have combined with creative acts of will to make possible the first step towards a united Europe."

The next chapter in this grand narrative is even now being written by a leading German historian, Dr. Helmut Kohl. Its millennial culmination is to be achieved on 1 January 1999, with a monetary union that will, it is argued, irreversibly bind together some of the leading states of Europe. This group of states should in turn become the "magnetic core" of a larger unification.

European unification is presented not just as the work of visionary leaders from Jean Monnet and Robert Schuman to François Mitterrand and Helmut Kohl, but also as a necessary, even an inevitable, response to the contemporary forces of globalization. Nation-states are no longer able to protect and realize their economic and political interests on their own. They are no match for transnational actors such as global currency speculators, multinational companies, or international criminal gangs. Both power and identity, it is argued, are migrating upward and downward from the nation-state: upward to the supranational level; downward to the regional one. In a globalized world of large trading blocs, Europe will be able to hold its own only as a larger political-economic unit. Thus Manfred Rommel, the popular former mayor of Stuttgart, declares, "We live under the dictatorship of the global economy. There is no alternative to a united Europe."

It would be absurd to suggest that there is no substance to these claims. Yet when combined into the single grand narrative, into the idealistic-teleological discourse of European unification, they result in a dangerously misleading picture of the real ground on which European leaders will have to build at the beginning of the twenty-first century. Here I shall make what many Europeans will regard as the heretical argument that unification is the wrong paradigm for European policy in our time. And I shall suggest a better one: that of liberal order.

1

In the index to Arnold Toynbee's A Study of History, we read, "Europe, as battlefield," "Europe, as not an intelligible field of historical study," and, finally, "Europe, unification of, failure of attempts at."

Toynbee is an unreliable source, but he raises important questions about the long sweep of European history. The most fundamental point is, of course, his second one. Is the thing to be united actually a cultural-historical unit? If so, where does it begin and end? It is, Toynbee claims, a "cultural misapplication of a nautical term" to suggest that the Mediterranean ancient history of Greece and Rome and modern Western history are successive acts in a single European drama. He prefers the Polish historian Oskar Halecki's account, in which a Mediterranean Age is followed by a European Age, running roughly from A.D. 950 to 1950, which in turn is succeeded by what Halecki called an Atlantic Age. Today we might refer to our period simply as a global age.

Yet, even in the European Age, the continent's eastern edge remained deeply ill-defined. Was it the Elbe? Or the dividing line between Western and Eastern Christianity? Or the Urals? Europe's political history was characterized by the astounding diversity of peoples, nations, states, and empires and by the ceaseless and often violent competition between them.

In short, no continent was externally more ill-defined, internally more diverse, or historically more disorderly. Yet no continent produced more schemes for its own orderly unification. So our idealistic-teleological or Whig interpreters can cite an impressive list of intellectual and political forebears, from the Bohemian king George of Podebrady through the duc de Sully and William Penn (writing already in America) to Aristide Briand and Richard Coudenhove-Kalergi, the prophet of Pan-Europa.

The trouble is that those designs for European unification that were peaceful were not implemented, while those that were implemented were not peaceful. The reality of unification was either a temporary solidarity in response to an external invader or an attempt by one European state to establish continental hegemony by force of arms, from Napoleon to Hitler. Yet the latter, too, failed, as Toynbee's index dryly notes.

2

The attempt at European unification since 1945 thus stands out from all earlier attempts by being both peaceful and implemented.

An idealistic interpretation of this historical abnormality is that we Europeans have at last learned from history. The "European civil war" of 1914 to 1945—that second and still bloodier Thirty Years War—finally brought us to our senses.

Yet this requires a little closer examination. For only after the end of the cold war are we discovering just how much European integration owed to it. First, there was the Soviet Union as negative external integrator. Western Europeans pulled together in face of the common enemy, as they had before the Mongols or the Turks. Second, there was the United States as positive external integrator. Particularly in the earlier years of the cold war, the United States pushed very strongly for Western European integration, making it almost a condition for further Marshall Aid. In later decades, the United States was at times more ambivalent about building up a rival trading bloc, but in broad, geopolitical terms it certainly supported Western European integration throughout the cold war.

Third, the cold war helped, quite brutally, by cutting off most of Central and Eastern Europe behind the Iron Curtain. This meant that European integration could begin between a relatively small number of nation-states—bourgeois democracies at a roughly comparable economic level and with important older elements of common history. As has often been observed, the frontiers of the original European Economic Community of six were roughly coterminous with those of Charlemagne's Holy Roman Empire. The EEC was also centered around what historical geographers have nicely called the "golden banana" of advanced European economic development, stretching from Manchester to Milan, via the Low Countries, eastern France, and western Germany. Moreover, within this corner of the continent there were important convergences or trade-offs between the political and economic interests of the nations involved. The crucial trade-offs were between France and Germany.

None of this is to deny a genuine element of European idealism among the elites of that time. But, the more we discover about this earlier period, the more hard-nosed and nationally self-interested the main actors appear. Contrary to the received view, the idealists are more to be found in the next generation: that of Helmut Kohl rather than Konrad Adenauer. There is no mistaking the genuine enthusiasm with which Helmut Kohl describes, as he will at the slightest prompting, the unforgettable experience of lifting the first frontier barriers between France and Germany, just a few years after the end of the war.

To be sure, the national interests were still powerfully present in the 1970s and 1980s. Britain, most obviously, joined the then still European Economic Community in the hope of reviving its own flagging economy and buttressing its declining influence in the world. In a book of 1988 entitled *La France par l'Europe,* none other than Jacques Delors wrote that "creating Europe is a way of regaining that room for manoeuvre necessary for 'a certain idea of France.'" The phrase "a certain idea of France" was, of course, de Gaulle's. In my book *In Europe's Name* I have shown how German enthusiasm for European integration continued to be nourished by the need to secure wider European and American support for the vital German national interest of improving relations with the communist East and, eventually, for the reunification of Germany. Besides this mixture of genuinely idealistic and national-instrumental motives, there was also a growing perception of real common interests.

As a result of the confluence of these three kinds of motive and those three favorable external conditions, the 1970s and 1980s saw an impressive set of steps toward closer political cooperation and economic and legal integration. Starting with the Hague summit of December 1969, they included direct elections to the European Parliament, the founding of the European Monetary System, the Single European Act, and the great project of completing the internal market in the magic year of "1992."

This dynamic process, against a background of renewed economic growth and the spread of democracy to southern Europe, contributed directly to the end of the cold war. One of the reasons behind Mikhail Gorbachev's "new thinking" in foreign policy was Soviet alarm at the prospect of being left still farther behind by a "Europe" that was seen as technologically advanced, economically dynamic, and integrating behind high protective walls.

How much more was this true of the peoples of east central Europe, who anyway felt themselves to belong culturally and historically to Europe—felt this with the passion of the excluded—and for whom the prosperous Western Europe they saw on their travels now clearly represented the better alternative to a discredited and stagnant "real socialism." Accordingly, one of the great slogans of the "velvet revolutions" of 1989 was "the return to Europe." In this sense one could argue, in apparent defiance of historical logic, that "1992" in Western Europe was one of the causes of 1989 in Eastern Europe.

The idealistic-teleological or Whig interpretation of recent European history, so widely taught and accepted in the 1980s, might not face the music of historical facts. But the very prevalence and wide appeal of this interpretation was itself a major historical fact. Nineteen eighty-nine seemed to be the ultimate confirmation of its rightness. Yet the end of the cold war also ended a historical constellation that was especially favorable to this particular model of Western European integration.

3

What have we witnessed since? It is possible to construe the 1990s as one more chapter, even a decisive one, in the pilgrim's progress to European unification. The Community has been renamed a Union. The major states of Western Europe have devoted extraordinary efforts to readying themselves for the unprecedented step of uniting their currencies. At the same time, preparations have been made to enlarge the union. Serious negotiations have started with five new postcommunist democracies and Cyprus, slightly less serious ones with five other postcommunist states. Certainly, there have been difficulties along the way; but never in its history has Europe been so close to the peaceful achievement of unity.

Against this optimistic, even Panglossian, view, we have to enter a number of objections. For a start, in this same period war has returned to the European continent: war and, in former Yugoslavia, atrocities such as we had not seen in Europe since 1945. Even in core states of the old European Community, we have seen a popular reaction against the technocratic, elitist model of "building Europe from above" epitomized by the impenetrable detail of the Maastricht

Treaty. The French referendum vote on the Maastricht Treaty, so narrowly won, was a telling symptom of this. And the Amsterdam Treaty of 1997 was no more accessible or popular. This popular resentment, and a sense that the institutions of the European Union are perilously short on democratic legitimacy, still persists.

While these years have seen further incremental diminution in the effective powers and sovereignty of established nation-states, they have also seen the explosive emergence of at least a dozen new nation-states. Indeed, there are now more states on the map of Europe than ever before in the twentieth century. In the former Yugoslavia, these new states emerged through ethnic cleansing and the violent redrawing of frontiers. In the former Czechoslovakia, the separation into two states was carried out peacefully, by negotiation. In the former Soviet Union, there were variations in between.

I do not suggest that these de-unifications reflected some deeper historical necessity. The specific etiology is different in each case, but very often rooted in the conduct of postcommunist politicians, making manipulative use of nationalist agendas to gain or maintain power for themselves. Yet the logic of de-unification is by no means always antidemocratic. It can be closely related to that of democracy. Democracy requires trust. It requires that the minority is prepared to accept the decision of the majority, because the minority still regards the state as fundamentally "theirs." The argument is hardly original—you find it already in John Stuart Mill's *Considerations on Representative Government*. "Among a people without fellow-feelings," writes Mill, "especially if they read and speak different languages, the united public opinion necessary to the working of representative government cannot exist."

Nor is this phenomenon of de-unification confined to the postcommunist half of Europe. The cliché of "integration in the west, disintegration in the east" does not bear closer examination. It is surprising, for example, to see the progressive disintegration of Belgium cited as evidence of the decline of the nation-state and the rise of regionalism. For the tensions that are pulling Belgium apart would be entirely familiar to a nineteenth-century liberal nationalist. Each ethnolinguistic group demands a growing measure of self-government. Britain has for decades been an unusual modern variation on the theme of the nation-state: a nation composed of four nations—or, to be precise, three and a part. But now the constituent nations, especially Scotland, are pulling away toward a larger measure of self-government.

And what of Europe's central power? It would be hard to dispute the simple statement that since 1989 Germany has reemerged as a fully sovereign nation-state. In Berlin, we are witnessing the extraordinary architectural reconstruction of the grandiose capital of a historic nation-state. Yet at the same time, Germany's political leaders, and above all Helmut Kohl, are pressing ahead with all their considerable might to surrender that vital component of national sovereignty—and, particularly in the contemporary German case, also identity—which is the national currency. There is a startling contradiction between, so to speak, the architecture in Berlin and the rhetoric in Bonn.

I do not think this contradiction can be resolved dialectically, even in the homeland of the dialectic. In fact, Germany today is in a political-psychological condition that can be described only as Faustian: "*Zwei Seelen wohnen, ach, in meiner Brust*" ("Oh, two souls live in my breast"). After monetary union has gone ahead and the German government moves to Berlin, then the country will wake up in its new bed on 1 January 2000, scratch its head, and ask itself, "Now, why did we just give up the deutsche mark?"

What is the answer? Of course there are economic arguments for monetary union. But monetary union was conceived as an economic means to a political end. In general terms, it is the continuation of the functionalist approach adopted by the French and German founding fathers of the European Economic Community: through economic integration to political integration. But there was a more specific political reason for the decision to make this the central goal of European integration in the 1990s. As so often before, the key lies in a compromise between French and German national interests. In 1990, there was at the very least an implicit linkage made between François Mitterrand's anxious and reluctant support for German unification and Kohl's decisive push toward European monetary union. "The whole of Deutschland for Kohl, half the deutsche mark for Mitterrand," as one wit put it at the time. Leading German politicians will acknowledge privately that monetary union is the price paid for German unification.

Yet, to some extent, this is a price that Kohl himself wants to pay. For he wants to see the newly united Germany bound firmly and, as he himself puts it, "irreversibly" into Europe. Even more than his mentor Konrad Adenauer, he believes that it is dangerous for Germany, with its erratic history and its critical size—"too big for Europe, too small for the world," as Henry Kissinger once pithily observed—to stand alone in the center of Europe, trying to juggle or balance the nine neighbors and many partners around it. So Dr. Kohl's ultimate, unspoken answer to the question "Why did we just give up the deutsche mark?" will be "Because we can't trust ourselves."

To which a younger generation will say, "Why not?" Many of them see no reason why Germany needs to be bound to the mast like Odysseus, to resist the siren calls of its awful past. They think Germany can be trusted to keep its own balance as a responsible, liberal nation-state inside an already close-knit community of other responsible, liberal nation-states. Certainly, Kohl's implicit argument will not convince the man in the Bavarian beer tent, especially when Kohl himself is no longer there to make it. In opinion polls, a majority of Germans still do not want to give up the deutsche mark for the euro. So Germany, this newly restored nation-state, will enter monetary union full of reservations, doubts, and fears.

4

Economists differ, and a noneconomist has to pick his way between their arguments. But few would dissent from the proposition that European monetary union is an unprecedented, high-risk gamble. As several leading economists have pointed out, Europe lacks vital components that make monetary union work in the United States. The USA has high labor mobility, price and wage flexibility, provision for automatic, large-scale budgetary transfers to states adversely affected by so-called asymmetric shocks, and, not least, the common language, culture, and shared history in a single state that make such transfers acceptable as a matter of course to citizens and taxpayers.

Europe has low labor mobility and high unemployment. It has relatively little wage flexibility. The EU redistributes a maximum of 1.27 percent of the GDP of its member states, and most of this is already committed to schemes such as the Common Agricultural Policy and the so-called structural funds for assisting poorer regions. It has no common language and certainly no common state. Since 1989, we have seen how reluctant West German taxpayers have been to pay even for their own compatriots in the east. Do we really expect that they would be willing to pay for the French unemployed as well? The Maastricht Treaty does not provide for that, and leading German politicians have repeatedly stressed that they will not stand for it. The minimal trust and solidarity between citizens that is the fragile treasure of the democratic nation-state does not, alas, yet exist between the citizens of Europe. For there is no "united public opinion," to recall Mill's phrase. There is no European *demos*—only a European *telos*.

Against this powerful critique, it is urged that "asymmetric shocks" will affect different regions within European countries, and the countries themselves do make provision for automatic budgetary transfers. In France, it is very optimistically suggested that reform of the Common Agricultural Policy and "structural funds" will free up EU resources for compensatory transfers. (But if we are serious about enlargement, some of these resources will also be needed for the much poorer new member states.) More economically liberal Europeans argue that monetary union will simply compel us to introduce more free-market flexibility, not least in wage levels. Yet none of this adds up to a very persuasive rebuttal, especially since different European countries favor different kinds of response.

The dangers, by contrast, are all too obvious. EMU requires a single monetary policy and a single interest rate for all. What if that rate is right for the German economy but wrong for Spain and Italy or vice versa? And what if French unemployment continues to rise? As elections approach, national politicians will find the temptation to "blame it on EMU" almost irresistible. If responsible politicians resist the temptation, then irresponsible ones will gain votes. And the European Central Bank will not start with any of the popular authority that the Bundesbank enjoys in Germany. It starts as the product of a political-bureaucratic procedure of "building Europe from above," which is even now perilously short of popular support and democratic legitimacy.

In fact, received wisdom in EU capitals is already that EMU will sooner or later face a crisis: perhaps after the end of a premillennium boom, in 2001 or 2002 (just as Britain is preparing to join). Euro-optimists hope this crisis will catalyze economic liberalization, European solidarity, and perhaps even those steps of political unification that historically have preceded, not followed, successful monetary unions. A shared fear of the catastrophic consequences of a failure of monetary union will draw Europeans together, as the shared fear of a common external enemy (Mongols, Turks, Soviets) did in the past. But it is a truly dialectical leap of faith to suggest that a crisis that exacerbates differences and tensions between European countries is the best path to uniting them.

The fact is that at Maastricht the leaders of the EU put the cart before the horse. Out of the familiar mixture of three different kinds of motive—idealistic, national-instrumental, and perceived common interest—they committed themselves to what was meant to be a decisive step to uniting Europe but now seems likely to divide even those who belong to the monetary union. At least in the short term, it will certainly divide those existing EU members who participate in the monetary union from those who do not: the so-called ins and outs.

Meanwhile, one consequence of monetary union has been seen even before it has happened. Such massive concentration on this single project has led to neglect of the great opportunity that arose in the eastern half of the continent when the Berlin Wall came down— an opportunity best summed up in George Bush's phrase about making Europe "whole and free." The Maastricht agenda of internal unification has taken the time and energy of Western European leaders away from the agenda of eastward enlargement. To be sure, there is no theoretical contradiction between the "deepening" and the "widening" of the European Union. Indeed, widening requires deepening. If the major institutions of the EU, designed originally to work for six member states, are still to function in a community of twenty-six, then major reforms, necessarily involving a further shar-

ing of sovereignty, are essential. But these changes are of a different
kind from those required for monetary union. While there is no theoretical contradiction, there has been a practical tension between
deepening and widening.

To put it plainly: Our leaders set the wrong priority after 1989.
We were like people who for forty years had lived in a large, ramshackle house divided down the middle by a concrete wall. In the
western half we had rebuilt, mended the roof, knocked several
rooms together, redecorated, and installed new plumbing and electric wiring, while the eastern half fell into a state of dangerous decay.
Then the wall came down. What did we do? We decided that what
the whole house needed most urgently was a superb, new, com-
puter-controlled system of air-conditioning in the western half.
While we prepared to install it, the eastern half of the house began
to fall apart and even to catch fire. We fiddled in Maastricht while
Sarajevo began to burn.

The best can so often be the enemy of the good. The rationalist,
functionalist, perfectionist attempt to "make Europe" or "complete
Europe" through a hard core built around a rapid monetary union
could well end up achieving the opposite of the desired effect. One
can all too plausibly argue that what we are likely to witness in the
next five to ten years is the writing of another entry for Toynbee's
index, under "Europe, unification of, failure of attempts at."

Some contemporary Cassandras go further still. They suggest
that we may even witness the writing of another entry under "Europe, as battlefield." One might answer that we already have, in
former Yugoslavia. Yet the suggestion that the forced march to
unification through money brings the danger of violent conflict between states in the European Union does seem drastically over-
drawn. For a start, there is the powerful neo-Kantian argument that
bourgeois democracies are unlikely to go to war against each other.
Unlike pre-1945 Europe, we also have a generally benign extra-
European hegemon in the United States. And to prophesy such conflict is to ignore the huge and real achievement of European
integration to date: the unique, unprecedented framework and
deeply ingrained habits of permanent institutionalized cooperation,
which ensure that the conflicts of interest that exist, and will con-

tinue to exist, between the member states and nations, are never resolved by force. All those endless hours and days of negotiation in
Brussels between ministers from fifteen European countries, who
end up knowing each other almost better than they know their own
families—that is the essence of this "Europe." It is an economic
community, of course, but it is also a security community—a group
of states that do find it unthinkable to resolve their own differences
by war.

5

Now one could certainly argue that Western Europe would never
have got this far without the utopian goal or *telos* of "unity." Only by
resolutely embracing the objective of "ever closer union" have we
reached this more modest degree of permanent institutional cooperation, with important elements of legal and economic integration.
Yet as a paradigm for European policy in our time the notion of "unification" is fundamentally flawed. The most recent period of European history provides no indication that the immensely diverse
peoples of Europe, speaking such different languages, having such
disparate histories, geographies, cultures, and economies, are ready
to merge peacefully and voluntarily into a single polity. It provides
substantial evidence of a directly countervailing trend: toward the
constitution—or reconstitution—of nation-states. If unity was not
attained among a small number of Western European states, with
strong elements of common history, under the paradoxically favorable conditions of the cold war, how can we possibly expect to attain
it in the infinitely larger and more diverse Europe—the whole continent—that we have to deal with after the end of the cold war?

"Yes," replied Pierre Hassner, the brilliant French analyst of international politics, when I made this case to him, "I'm afraid you're
right. Europe will not come to pass." "But, Pierre," I exclaimed,
"you're in it!" Europe is already here—and not just as a geographical
expression. There is already a great political achievement that has
taken us far beyond de Gaulle's *Europe des Patries* or Harold
Macmillan's vision of a glorified free-trade area. Yet, to a degree that
people outside Europe find hard to comprehend, European thinking

about Europe is still deeply conditioned by these notions of project, process, and progress toward unification. (After all, no one talks hopefully of Africa or Asia "becoming itself.") Many Europeans are convinced that, if we do not go forward toward unification, we must necessarily go backward. This view is expressed in the so-called bicycle theory of European integration: If you stop pedaling, the bicycle will fall over. Actually, as anyone who rides a bicycle knows, all you have to do is to put one foot back on the ground. And, anyway, Europe is not a bicycle.

If we Europeans convince ourselves that not advancing farther along the path to unity is tantamount to failure, we risk snatching failure from the jaws of success. For what has been achieved already in a large part of Europe is a very great success, without precedent on the European continent and without contemporary equivalent on any other continent. It is as if someone had built a fine if rather rambling palace and then convinced himself that he was an abject failure because it was not the Parthenon. Yet the case is more serious and urgent than this. For today it is precisely the forced march to unity—across the "bridge too far" of monetary union—that is threatening the very achievement it is supposed to complete.

But what is the alternative? How else should we "think Europe" if not in terms of this paradigm of unification that has dominated European thinking about Europe for half a century? How can we characterize positively what we have already built in a large part of Europe, and what it is both desirable and realistic to work toward in a wider Europe? I believe the best paradigm is that of *liberal order*. Historically, liberal order is an attempt to avoid both of the extremes between which Europe has oscillated unhappily through most of its modern history: violent disorder, on the one hand, and hegemonic order, on the other—hegemonic order that itself was always built on the use of force and the denial of national and democratic aspirations within the constitutive empires or spheres of influence. Philosophically, such an order draws on Isaiah Berlin's central liberal insight that people pursue different ends that cannot be reconciled but may peacefully coexist. It also draws on Judith Shklar's "liberalism of fear," with its deeply pessimistic view of the propensity of human beings to indulge in violence and cruelty, and the sense that what she modestly called "damage control" is the first necessity of political life. Institutionally, the European Union, NATO, the Council of Europe, and the Organization for Security and Cooperation in Europe are all building blocks of such a liberal order.

Liberal order differs from previous European orders in several vital ways. Its first commandment is the renunciation of force in the resolution of disputes between its members. Of course, this goal is an ancient one. We find it anticipated already in King George of Podebrady's great proposal of 1464 for "the inauguration of peace throughout Christendom." There we read that he and his fellow princes "shall not take up arms for the sake of any disagreements, complaints or disputes, nor shall we allow any to take up arms in our name." But today we have well-tried institutions of bourgeois internationalism in which to practice what Churchill called "making jaw-jaw rather than war-war."

Liberal order is, by design, nonhegemonic. To be sure, the system depends to some extent on the external hegemonic balancer, the United States—"Europe's pacifier," as more than one author has quipped. And, of course, Luxembourg does not carry the same weight as Germany. But the new model order that we have developed in the European Union does permit smaller states to have an influence often disproportionate to their size. A key element of this model order is the way in which it allows different alliances of European states on individual issues, rather than cementing any fixed alliances. Another is the framework of common European law. If the European Convention on Human Rights were incorporated into the treaties of the union, as Ralf Dahrendorf has suggested, the EU would gain a much-needed element of direct responsibility for the liberties of the individual citizen.

Liberal order also differs from previous European orders in explicitly legitimating the interest of participating states in each others' internal affairs. Building on the so-called Helsinki process, it considers human, civil, and, not least, minority rights to be a primary and legitimate subject of international concern. These rights are to be sustained by international norms, support, and, where necessary, also pressure. Such a liberal order recognizes that there is a logic that leads peoples who speak the same language and share the same culture and tradition to want to govern themselves in their own state. There is such a thing as liberal nationalism. But it also recognizes that in many places a peaceful, neat separation into nation-states will be impossible. In such cases it acknowledges a responsibility to help sustain what may variously be called multiethnic, multicultural, or multinational democracies, within an international framework. This is what we disastrously failed to do for Bosnia but can still try to do for Macedonia or Estonia.

Missing from this paradigm is one idea that is still very important in contemporary European visions, especially those of former Great Powers such as France, Britain, and Germany. This is the notion of "Europe" as a single actor on the world stage—a world power able to stand up to the United States, Russia, or China. In truth, a drive for world power is hardly more attractive because it is a joint enterprise than it was when attempted—somewhat more crudely—by individual European nations. Certainly, in a world of large trading blocs we must be able to protect our own interests. Certainly, a liberal order also means one that both gives and gets as much free trade as possible. Certainly, a degree of power projection, including the coordinated use of military power, will be needed to realize the objectives of liberal order even within the continent of Europe and in adjacent areas of vital interest to us, such as North Africa and the Middle East. But, beyond this, just to put our own all-European house in order would be a large enough contribution to the well-being of the world.

Some may object that I have paid too much attention to mere semantics. Why not let the community be called a "Union" and the process "unification," even if they are not that in reality? Václav Havel seems to come close to this position when he writes, "Today, Europe is attempting to give itself a historically new kind of order in a process that we refer to as unification." And of course I do not expect the European Union to be, so to speak, dis-named. After all, the much looser world organization of states is still called the United Nations. But the issue is far from merely semantic.

To consolidate Europe's liberal order and to spread it across the whole continent is both a more urgent and, in the light of history, a more realistic goal for Europe at the beginning of the twenty-first century than the vain pursuit of unification in a part of it. Nor, finally, is liberal order a less idealistic goal than unity. For unity is not a primary value in itself. It is but a means to higher ends. Liberal order, by contrast, directly implies not one but two primary values: peace and freedom.

CHRONOLOGY

1998

10 APRIL. *A multiparty agreement is signed on the future of Northern Ireland—the "Good Friday Agreement."*

24 APRIL. *Russian president Boris Yeltsin's youthful candidate for prime minister, Sergei Kiryenko, is accepted by the Duma at the third attempt.*

APRIL–MAY. *Armed conflict between Serb forces and the Kosovo Liberation Army escalates in Kosovo.*

1–3 MAY. *A special EU summit in Brussels announces that monetary union will be launched on 1 January 1999 with eleven countries participating.*

22 MAY. *In a referendum, voters in Northern Ireland approve the "Good Friday Agreement."*

31 MAY. *A coalition led by President Milo Djukanović, a critic of Serbian president Slobodan Milošević, wins parliamentary elections in Montenegro.*

1 JUNE. *An international aid package is announced in response to financial crisis in Russia.*

8 JUNE. *Threatening a strong Western response to Serb actions in Kosovo, British foreign secretary Robin Cook says, "I hope Milošević is listening. This is the last warning."*

20 JUNE. *All EU ambassadors are withdrawn from Belarus in protest at President Lukashenka's attempt to evict them from their embassies.*

25 JUNE. *Voting in Northern Ireland to elect a new assembly.*

7 JULY. *Former Italian prime minister Silvio Berlusconi is sentenced to two years and nine months' imprisonment for bribing tax officials.*

8 JULY. *Viktor Orbán of the "Young Democrats" (FIDESZ) becomes prime minister of Hungary.*

8–9 July. Gdańsk, Poland. I visit the former Lenin Shipyard, birthplace of Solidarity. It is now almost an industrial archaeology site, with head-high weeds, rusting hulls, and only a couple of ships being built this year. One of the shipyard halls has been converted into a techno-rock dis-cothèque. Lech Wałęsa tells me he feels a kind of "moral hangover" when he looks at the shipyard now. Certainly, all the radical, neoliberal changes to a free-market economy were essential. There was no other way. But he feels that somehow they should have done more for this place.

9 July. *A new Czech government is formed under Social Democrat prime minister Miloš Zeman, based on a pact with the center-right Civic Demo-cratic Party of former prime minister Václav Klaus.*

28 July. *Mališevo, unofficial capital of the Kosovo Liberation Army, is re-taken by Serb forces.*

August. *Financial "meltdown" in Russia.*

15 August. *A terrorist bomb kills twenty-eight people in Omagh, North-ern Ireland.*

23 August. *President Yeltsin sacks his cabinet for the second time in five months and replaces Prime Minister Sergei Kiryenko with Victor Cher-nomyrdin.*

26 August. *The Russian ruble loses 40 percent of its value against the deutsche mark after trading in dollars is suspended.*

9–11 September. Slovenia. A long conversation with President Milan Kučan, eloquent about his country's new-old location in Central Europe. Referring to the Serbs' view of Kosovo as the historic cradle of their nation, he says, "Our Kosovo is in Austria." He means Carinthia, the medieval duchy or Civitas Carantania, back to which the Slovenians trace their historic nationhood.

I assume that, as the man who led the first former Yugoslav republic to fight for its independence from Milošević's Serbia, he might support the Kosovar Albanians in their struggle for independence from Milošević's Serbia. But no. A lawyer by training, he insists that Kosovo was always part of the Republic of Serbia, not a constituent part of Yugoslavia, and therefore does not have the right to secede. Altogether, he shows remark-ably little sympathy for the Kosovar Albanians, whom he describes as a "rural patriarchal society" with an insatiable appetite for land. He speaks like a Central European contemplating some remote, slightly barbaric part of the Balkans. Yet ten years ago, they were part of the same country.

11 SEPTEMBER. *Postcommunist Yevgeny Primakov becomes the Russian prime minister.*

22 SEPTEMBER. *The Polish parliament votes to give people access to their own secret-police files from the communist period.*

23–26 SEPTEMBER. Poland, for publication of the Polish edition of my book about the Stasi files, *The File.* A young presenter on breakfast television interviews me about my experiences with the Stasi. Afterward he says, "But one thing I didn't understand. These people who informed on you. You write that they were afraid. But what did they have to be afraid of?" So swift is the forgetting, even in Poland.

25 SEPTEMBER. *Vladimír Mečiar is defeated in parliamentary elections in Slovakia.*

27 SEPTEMBER. *Bundestag elections in Germany.*

GOOD-BYE TO BONN

"THIS IS A HISTORIC MOMENT," A STALWART GERMAN CHRISTIAN Democrat whispered to me as the familiar giant figure of Helmut Kohl mounted the stage at party headquarters in Bonn, shortly before seven o'clock on the evening of Sunday, 27 September 1998. As if it needed saying! Given the scale of the Christian Democrats' electoral defeat, we all guessed that, after a staggering sixteen years in power, the chancellor of German and European unification would be stepping down. When the cries of "Helmut! Helmut!" had finally abated, he gave a dignified short speech. He congratulated the Social Democrat Gerhard Schröder on his victory and wished him "a happy hand for our land." As for himself, he would now also retire as party leader. It felt as if the Alps had suddenly announced their departure.

As the twentieth century draws to a close, we can safely say that Helmut Kohl is its last great European statesman. Watching him leave the stage, I thought of a memorable conversation we had a few years ago. At one moment, he took my breath away. "Do you realize," he said, "that you are sitting opposite the direct successor to Adolf Hitler?" The point of this startling, even shocking remark was that he—the first chancellor of a united Germany since Hitler—was going to do everything quite differently. Whereas Hitler had tried to put a German roof over Europe, he was determined to put a European roof over Germany. This amazing sally encapsulated several ingredients of Kohl's greatness: his acute instinct for power, his historical vision, and the bold simplicity of his strategic thinking. Add tactical adroitness, tireless attention to party-political details, and vast physical presence and stamina—the result is a provincial politician who changed the world.

The election of Sunday, 27 September, was not just the end of "the Kohl era." It marked several other ends—and new beginnings. This is the last federal election in which the parties' election expenses will be calculated in deutsche marks. Next time around, in 2002, the deutsche mark, that totem of postwar West German prosperity, stability, and identity, will be no more. Everything will be done in euros. It was also the last election for which we will go to Bonn. Next year, parliament and government move to Berlin. As Christopher Isherwood didn't write, "Good-bye to Bonn."

Walking up the modest highway that is the spine of that dank Rhineland city, with cheerful crowds thronging the pavements, their attention soon turning back from the election to a rock band, beer, and the Formula One championships just up the road, I felt a pang of regret. Bonn is a dull place, but what came to be known as "the Bonn republic" has been a good Germany—perhaps the best Germany we have ever had. In this election, it proved the maturity of its carefully constructed, quiet, civil democracy. Although the country has four million unemployed, German voters once again rejected the extremes of left and right. The old saying "Bonn is not Weimar"—that is, its democracy will not be torn apart by a flight to antidemocratic extremes, as in the Weimar republic—can now be adapted to a definitive, final form: "Bonn was not Weimar."

1

We knew we were saying good-bye to Bonn and the deutsche mark. We thought we would be saying good-bye to Kohl. What we didn't expect was a landslide that changes the whole political face of Germany. All the public-opinion polls except one showed Kohl closing the gap on Schröder. Electoral arithmetic based on these polls suggested the likelihood of a "grand coalition" in which Schröder's Social Democrats would govern together with the Christian Democrats, the latter under a new leader. This seemed about right for the

Bonn republic's style of gradual, consensual change. It is a remarkable fact that, in the whole previous history of the Federal Republic, the government has never completely changed as a direct result of the popular vote. Either the governing coalition has changed between elections or, in the rare event of it changing at an election, one previous coalition partner has remained in power.

This time, the voters decided otherwise. As if to show that, after half a century, German democracy has fully come of age, they produced a result that means that the Social Democrats replace the Christian Democrats as the senior partner, and the environmentalist Greens replace the Free Democrats as the junior partner. In this so-called red-green coalition, all the faces will be new.

Why was the vote so decisive? I saw three main reasons. First, and most important, after sixteen years people simply felt it was "time for a change." That was the answer that came again and again in my own conversations and those reported elsewhere. The old man and his team had run out of energy and ideas. Voters were plain bored of those same old faces. Boredom is an underrated factor in politics.

This was exactly what happened in Britain, after eighteen years of Conservative rule. A Conservative candidate in that 1997 election told me that when people asked him, "Isn't it time for a change?" he simply had no answer. In his heart of hearts, he thought it was too. So also here. Contrary to some predictions, the crises in Russia and Asia did not make voters feel that it was better to stick with the experienced statesman.

Second, the "Clintonblair" Schröder was a smooth, telegenic, attractive candidate, with an unusually well-disciplined Social Democratic Party behind him, led by his colleague and rival Oskar Lafontaine. Postelection research shows that the main component of the swing was straightforward: People who voted Christian Democrat last time voted Social Democrat this time. Among them were many pensioners, whose pensions Kohl had trimmed and Schröder promises to restore.

Third, there was the east. Back in the historic spring of 1990, Helmut Kohl won a crucial election in what was still East Germany by promising to create "blooming landscapes" out of the postcommunist wasteland. That vote meant East Germany became just eastern Germany: the eastern part of a larger Federal Republic. By the time of the last federal election, in 1994, with old communist factories rusting all around, and their workers on the dole, "blooming landscapes" had become a bitter joke. I saw people holding up placards at Kohl's election rallies saying "Where are the blooming landscapes?" or simply "Blooming landscapes!" But enough people still had enough confidence in Kohl to give the CDU the largest share of the vote.

This time, I spent much of the pre-election week in the east. In the city of Schwerin, I watched disillusioned youngsters, many of them unemployed, heckle the chancellor as he spoke glowingly of growth and jobs. They held up a satirical banner proclaiming, "Helmut: You Are the Way, the Truth and the Light." Then, on the hustings at a village on the outskirts of East Berlin, I was amazed to see a poster proclaiming, "Vote for Blooming Landscapes—CDU." The left-wing cartoonist Klaus Staeck was not amused. "That was my *joke,*" he protested. And a joke in the end it proved to be, since the CDU vote in the east plummeted from more than 38 percent in 1994 to just over 27 percent. In the west it fell less than half as much, from just over 33 percent to just under 28 percent. It was the east that turned a defeat into a rout.

There's a deep irony here. For Kohl has been voted away at a time when large parts of that eastern landscape actually are beginning to "bloom." Traveling around, I still found large patches of desolation, rust, unemployment, and the accompanying mixture of apathy among the old and often xenophobic anger among the young. But I also found impressive areas of large-scale construction, new jobs, energy, and hope.

Nowhere else in postcommunist Europe does one see such vistas of shining new steel, glass, and concrete. Hardly surprising, given that western Germany has pumped more than DM 1,000,000,000,000 into the east over the last eight years. And there is massive private investment too. The mayor of one community in the so-called bacon belt of prosperous commuter villages around Berlin showed me the newly made streets and fire station, the freshly renovated school, and a whole estate of detached, private houses, built by local people on savings and building loans. The old kingdom of Saxony in the south is booming, under its Christian

Democratic "king," Kurt Biedenkopf. Even in the poor northern province of Mecklenburg-Vorpommern, which has more than 17 percent unemployment, every village I drove through had some new building projects.

Still more important is the mental architecture. The picture you get from the British or American press is one of almost universal resignation and resentment. Yet I found people hungrily participating in a democracy that is still new to them. This was the liveliest campaign in the east since that vote for unification back in 1990. Walls were plastered with posters. Meetings were packed. More than 80 percent of those eligible turned out to vote, compared with 72 percent four years ago. And such civic activism is not confined to election time. The mayor of that "bacon belt" village tells me she is deluged with petitions and "citizens' initiatives." Many are dedicated to protecting the selfish interests of the new middle class. For example, the residents of that new private housing estate protest about being asked to contribute to the cost of a local "cycleway." This is "civil society" emerging, but civil society less as the Central European dissidents dreamed of it than as Karl Marx analyzed it—the self-defense of the bourgeoisie!

A comparison is sometimes made between the German east after unification and the American south after the Civil War. This is quite misleading. East Germany was always an artificial unit: the Soviet Zone of Occupation turned into a state. The flourishing southern *Länder* of Thuringia and Saxony now feel themselves closer to Bavaria than to Mecklenburg. East and West Berlin are slowly but surely getting mixed up together. The arrogance, condescension, and incomprehension that many western Germans display toward their eastern compatriots is still a big problem. It was rightly said after 1990 that Germany had been united, the Germans had not. But even that is beginning to happen. In the early 1990s, there continued to be a mass emigration of eastern Germans to the west. Last year, for the first time, almost as many western Germans came to live in the east.

All just as Kohl promised—though a lot more slowly, more painfully, and more expensively. Yet those ungrateful easterners have bitten the hand that fed them. So now Helmut Kohl will retire to his modest house in the small western town of Oggersheim, while Gerhard Schröder will move into the grand new chancellery in the big, raw, eastern city of Berlin. A half century of the Bonn republic has suddenly and decisively ended.

2

New government, new capital, new currency. As New Britain's Tony Blair likes to say, everything is new, new, new. But what can we say, or guess, about this New Germany?

It is already being called "the Berlin republic." Some German federalists object to the term. The Federal Republic, they argue, will still be a decentralized state. The business weekly *Wirtschaftswoche* ran a major article in election week arguing that Frankfurt, which narrowly failed to become the federal capital in 1949 and was again a candidate after unification, will remain the undisputed economic capital of Germany. Major newspapers are still in Hamburg, the Constitutional Court still in Karlsruhe. For all that, I think it will be "the Berlin republic," because I think the move to Berlin will have a profound psychological impact on the politicians and hence the politics of Germany.

Berlin is a city full of ghosts—Prussian militarist, Wilhelmine, Nazi, and communist, as well as the more attractive ghosts of Prussian intellectual life, Weimar culture, and anti-Nazi resistance. Amid these ghosts, vast, impressive new government buildings are thrusting up. These buildings do not speak of a nation that is proposing to surrender its only recently recovered sovereignty to a European superstate. Berlin is a metropolis, with many foreigners living there. Berlin is in the middle of eastern Germany, close to all the problems of the transition from communism. Berlin is just forty minutes' drive from the Polish frontier.

The Berlin republic, it is suggested, will be not only more eastern but perhaps also more Protestant than a Bonn republic shaped by the Catholic Rhineland tradition from which both Konrad Adenauer and Helmut Kohl came. Even in a highly secularized society, this matters. The Israeli political scientist Shlomo Avineri has observed that a Jewish atheist and a Christian atheist are not the same thing: They disbelieve in a different God. The same may be said of Catholic atheists and Protestant atheists.

Into this new setting moves a new generation of politicians, most in their fifties, some in their forties. Many of them, including Gerhard Schröder and the likely Green foreign minister, Joschka Fischer, are classic '68ers, shaped by that distinctive moment of student protest across the western world. Others were formed by the protest movements of the 1970s and 1980s: feminist, ecological, against nuclear weapons, and against nuclear power. As always in German politics, another formative influence is their diverse experience of policy-making in coalition governments in the federal states. Meanwhile, years of schooling themselves for power at the national level have made them adepts of the sound bite.

In theory, this red-green coalition will be able to stamp its mark on the new republic. Not only does it have a clear majority in the Bundestag, the lower house of parliament, it also has a majority in the Bundesrat, the upper house composed of representatives of the federal states. The coalition will be able to propose its candidate for federal president and to start nominating judges to the Constitutional Court. By 2000, all the key institutions of the republic might therefore be colored "red-green." They could even choose a president of the Bundesbank, although that is to be supplanted by the European Central Bank.

In opposition, the Christian Democrats, like the British Conservatives, will take some time to pull themselves together again, in alliance with the Bavarian Christian Social Union. Their new leader is Wolfgang Schäuble. When I spoke to the wheelchair-bound Schäuble, one of the most thoughtful and impressive figures in German politics, he was clearly looking forward to the task of regenerating a broadly based party—what in German is called a *Volkspartei*—that would, among other things, prevent disgruntled voters breaking away to the nationalist right. Yet German Christian Democracy will have to redefine itself in circumstances where its three traditional unifying forces have either disappeared or faded: anticommunism, Christianity, and a shared commitment to further steps of European integration. The last mentioned is most plainly challenged by the Bavarian premier, Edmund Stoiber, sometimes jokingly called Edmund Thatcher.

Meanwhile, in opposition from the left there is the ex-communist Party of Democratic Socialism, which just scraped over the 5 percent hurdle to get its full complement of members of parliament. While its electorate is still overwhelmingly in the east, it is now setting out to establish itself as a party of the "socialist left" in the whole Federal Republic.

For the time being, however, the coalition's main problems will be not with the opposition but within its own ranks. For this will be a coalition of coalitions. Schröder may be chancellor, but Oskar Lafontaine is the Social Democrats' party leader. They appeared together at virtually all the postelection meetings. Some even say, "Lafontaine makes policy and Schröder sells it." Lafontaine is an opportunist but an opportunist with close ties to the old left. And that old left is much more strongly represented among the Social Democrats than it is in Tony Blair's purged New Labour. Meanwhile, the Greens remain the most diverse and even chaotic of parties, with a strong pacifist wing.

What of Schröder himself? Though his rugged features are sharply cut, they are the sharpest thing about him. Except, perhaps, his suits. He looks very good on television. Indeed, he seems slightly more real on television than when you meet him in person. He is the epitome of the fifty-something, smooth, flexible, professional politician. But someone who knows him quite well told me that, unlike Clinton or Blair, he does not have any religious attachments (albeit, in the case of Clinton, honored in the breach) or perceptible value system. So he's a sort of Clinton without the principles.

He has never, this colleague pointed out, taken a courageous independent stand on any issue. In the past, he has embraced left-wing positions (opposing the deployment of NATO's cruise and Pershing missiles in the early 1980s, for example) and positions more associated with the right—for instance, last year he was suggesting the postponement of European monetary union. In each case, he has gone with the wind. In the public-opinion polls, more of those asked thought he would be a competent chancellor than thought Helmut Kohl would be. But my private opinion polls suggest that a lot of people, including some Social Democrats, share the doubts expressed on a recent *Economist* cover: "Would you buy a used car from Gerhard Schröder?" The polite word is *pragmatist*.

The elementary point of this catalog of observations is that the

Berlin republic begins with a whole series of unknowns. And a combination of unknowns is a larger unknown. In fact, the Germans have got more than they bargained for. They voted for a change, yes. But there was little of the popular enthusiasm for a new beginning that accompanied Willy Brandt's appointment as chancellor in 1969, with his famous slogan "Risk More Democracy." Instead, Schröder actually used the conservative Konrad Adenauer's motto "No Experiments." An experiment is what Germany has gotten, all the same.

3

This being so, all predictions are more than usually risky. But let me venture three guesses. My first guess is an optimistic one. It has to do with so-called foreigners living in Germany. The only disturbing element in this campaign was the popular hostility to these "foreigners" that was revealed. This was particularly true in eastern Germany, where one in five young men say they could imagine voting for a party of the far right. On the streets of Berlin, the posters of one of these parties proclaimed, "Criminal Foreigners Out!" The hostility extends not just to blacks and Turks but to the Poles they call "*Pollacken.*" And it reaches well into the Christian Democrat electorate. I saw Christian Democratic politicians receive tumultuous applause whenever they said that foreigners "should not abuse our hospitality" or "must respect our laws and ways."

This is a problem that Germany has made for itself, since it has been very liberal in taking people in but very restrictive in granting German citizenship. The result is that a staggering seven million people, out of a total population of eighty million, live as "foreigners" in Germany. Until quite recently, the main qualification for citizenship was to have German blood. Although the Christian Democrats changed the law to make it possible to gain citizenship after fifteen years' residence, they held out firmly against dual citizenship for, say, longtime Turkish residents in Germany. (Yet Germany itself is quite happy to grant dual citizenship to ethnic Germans living in Poland.) With a red-green government this should change, giving the country a normal, liberal citizenship law, more comparable with those in Britain and America. Altogether, it should encourage a more welcoming attitude to immigrants and to the whole idea of Germans being of different ethnic and cultural backgrounds.

My second guess is more pessimistic—for Germany, though perhaps not for its competitors. Helmut Kohl probably did larger things for his country than Margaret Thatcher did for hers. (To be fair, larger things needed doing. The United Kingdom did not need to be reunited.) But Kohl failed to do precisely those big things that Thatcher did: reducing the power of the trade unions, privatization, deregulation, lowering direct taxation, cutting public spending, and so on. In Britain, this is the foundation that Tony Blair can build on. Now Gerhard Schröder fought a campaign of Blair-like discipline and razzmatazz. But, to be a Blair in office, you need first to have had your Thatcher.

Virtually all German business leaders argue that if Germany is to remain competitive and to create new jobs, it needs some of that medicine. It needs Thatcherism with a human face. But can this new government deliver it? Schröder says economic and social reform is his top priority. He is famously close to business leaders and was on the board of Volkswagen. He understands some of what needs to be done. On the other hand, he was recently involved in a spectacular state bailout of a failing steelworks. The state of which he has been premier, Lower Saxony, has run up a large public debt. Moreover, he has promises to keep: that promise to restore pensions, for example. He also promised to defend the welfare state, promote "social justice," and finance job creation.

His own party, under Oskar Lafontaine, will surely try to keep him to that. Indeed, the Social Democrats actually favor a higher top rate of income tax than the Greens do: 49 percent, against the Greens' proposed 45 percent. But the Greens have their own pet scheme: a rapidly increasing tax on gasoline. German industry does not think that will help its competitiveness. If you add up the chancellor's track record and promises, his coalition of coalitions, the strength of the trade unions, and the whole postwar German tradition of change by consensus, you do not get a recipe for rapid implementation of the reforms that German business leaders think essential.

Finally, a guess about foreign policy, in which Schröder has promised "continuity." This promise is credible, but I suspect the character of this continuity will be "the same, only less so." The Greens and the Social Democratic left have a record of anti-NATO protest. A Green foreign minister may be bad for NATO military actions "out of area," since, whatever his personal convictions, he will have to pay some attention to his own party's pacifists. The outgoing defense minister, Volker Rühe, an outspoken advocate of both NATO enlargement and NATO intervention in Kosovo, told me he fears that the close partnerships for effective action that he has built up, especially with the United States, may be imperiled.

In the European Union, Schröder signaled continuity by paying his first foreign trip to Paris. Despite his past reservations about European monetary union, he'll try to make it work. But, like most of his generation, he will, I believe, be cooler and more hard-nosed about any further steps of European integration than were the postwar Euro-enthusiasts such as Helmut Kohl. Even if the inaugural speeches contain the usual visionary Euro-rhetoric, he won't in fact be pursuing any personal vision of ever closer union.

This will make him a more congenial partner for Britain. He has talked in the past of turning the Franco-German axis into a Franco-German–British triangle. On the other hand, there is at least one mighty argument ahead: about Germany's desire to reduce its outsize contribution to the EU budget. And cost will also be a problem when it comes to detailed negotiations about eastward enlargement of the union. Sitting in Berlin, the new government will see more clearly the necessity but also the difficulties of bringing in the neighbors just up the road. In this regard, too, we may expect more cool pragmatism, with close attention to both national interest and public mood.

THERE ARE my three guesses. But they are just guesses. What has been extraordinary about Germany in the 1990s has been the great continuity of its policies, despite the fact that the country's shape, size, internal composition, and geopolitical position have all changed with unification. This continuity was due to Helmut Kohl, the deutsche mark, and the Bonn republic. Now it's good-bye to all that. Like it or not, the Berlin republic may be more interesting.

CHRONOLOGY

1998

SEPTEMBER.   *Atrocities are committed by Serb forces in Kosovo. NATO responds with threats of air strikes against Serbia.*

12 OCTOBER.   *An agreement between U.S. envoy Richard Holbrooke and Serbian leader Slobodan Milošević provides for two thousand OSCE "verifiers" in Kosovo, NATO air surveillance, and negotiations for a political settlement.*

16 OCTOBER.   *Twentieth anniversary of the election of Pope John Paul II.*

OCTOBER.   *New German chancellor Gerhard Schröder indicates that eastward enlargement of the EU may depend on Germany getting a satisfactory reduction in its contribution to the EU budget.*

"BE NOT AFRAID!"

Brezhnev, Carter, Deng Xiaoping, Callaghan, Schmidt: Where are they now? These were the "world leaders" back in October 1978, when a little-known Polish cardinal stepped out onto St. Peter's Square as the new pope and proclaimed his electrifying message: "Be not afraid!" Twenty years on, those worldly leaders are long since retired or dead, but the "servant of the servants of God" is still with us, still traveling the world, still tirelessly proclaiming the same urgent, universal message to all humankind.

At seventy-eight, he is frail and bent now. That rugged, athletic figure has been worn down by Parkinson's disease, by the assassin's bullet that tore through his intestines in 1981, and by two decades of ceaseless toil. He used to ski for hours; now he leans on his old ski-sticks for support while taking undemanding walks. His voice used to be so powerful and clear, with a skilled actor's delivery that John Gielgud once described as "perfect." Now it is often slurred. His broad, smiling face used to radiate human warmth for a hundred yards around—a quality he shared with his "fellow Slav" Mikhail Gorbachev. Now the face is half frozen with Parkinson's. His left hand trembles uncontrollably.

Yet still you glimpse flashes of the old magic, as the distant figure, all in white, draws a whole crowd to him with a characteristic gesture: gently but repeatedly lifting two outstretched open hands. Then he speaks to half a million people as if he were talking to one person. It's the magic that I saw in communist Poland, where he dissolved the fear instilled by all Brezhnev's divisions with one wave of that now trembling hand. And still he goes on admonishing the rulers of this world, whatever their political color, whether Castro or Clinton. Still he offers succor to the poor, the weak, the sick, the oppressed in every land.

You might think from this opening hymn of praise that I'm a Catholic, even a papal groupie. Far from it. Indeed, if I were a Catholic, I might be much less enthusiastic. His fiercest critics are among his own flock. I leave it to them to argue about his restoration of a "monarchical" papacy and the stifling of debate inside the Church. As an agnostic liberal, albeit one rooted in a rich humus of Christianity, my concern is not with the Church but with the world. And I want to argue that Pope John Paul II is simply the greatest world leader of our times.

I say this not just because of what I saw him do in Poland, although of course that counts. Nor is it simply because I have experienced the force of his personality in a small gathering, although that was unforgettable. Over these twenty years, I have had the chance to talk with several credible candidates for the title of "great man" or "great woman"—Mikhail Gorbachev, Helmut Kohl, Václav Havel, Lech Wałęsa, Margaret Thatcher—but none matches Karol Wojtyła's unique combination of concentrated strength, intellectual consistency, human warmth, and simple goodness.

Yet my case rests on his public record. No one has conveyed a better message, more effectively, to more people. What is this message? When he arrived on St. Peter's throne, it was all there, fully formed, ready to go. He immediately wrote it down, in longhand, for his first encyclical, *Redemptor hominis* ("The savior of man"). But there's a problem here. A philosopher, poet, and playwright as well as a pastor, he writes in a dense, difficult linguistic blend of Thomism (the philosophy based on the teachings of Thomas Aquinas), phenomenology, and Polish Marian mysticism. After tackling his book *The Acting Person,* an American philosopher observed mildly, "I could not quite decide what the author was up to." Yet in conversation or on his travels, he can say what he means with stunning simplicity.

One common mistake is to suggest that he looks at the whole world through a Polish prism. Of course, he is profoundly Polish. If you ever doubt that—and he hardly conceals it—just listen to him speaking directly to the Virgin Mary before the great monastery of Częstochowa, emotionally addressing her as "Queen of Poland." (It's also deeply moving, for he really is like a man talking to a much-loved mother. His own mother died when he was eight.) But when I once had dinner with him, in a circle of Polish friends, speaking Polish, I was struck by the very opposite impression. Here was a man who, far from looking at the world through Polish lenses, looked even at Poland through the prism of his global experience, faith, and mission.

The other common mistake is to interpret him in conventional political categories, such as "left" and "right." Many in the West see him as just an old, dyed-in-the-wool reactionary. Gorbachev, by contrast, says the pope is a man of the left. In fact, he has always been fiercely critical of both capitalism and communism. But, as he insists in one of his encyclicals (*Solicitudo rei socialis*), the Church's doctrine is "not a 'third way' between liberal capitalism and Marxist collectivism." Tony Blair and Bill Clinton please note. Rather, it is "a category of its own." It is not ideology but theology. On the plane out to Poland for his first, great pilgrimage in 1979, he told journalists that the differences between communism and capitalism are superficial: "Underneath is where the people are."

His first concern is with what he believes to be the presence of God and Christ in the world. But, translated into the language of secular politics, his message becomes a set of demands to those who wield political, economic, or cultural power—demands on behalf of the people "underneath." And a matching set of appeals to those individual people. At the center is always what he calls "the human person" (comprising, in Catholic teaching, body, reason, and soul). He insists that each and every individual human being has an ineradicable dignity and inalienable rights—the poorest child in the worst barrio in Mexico City no less than the richest man in New York. John Paul II's passionate embrace of the language of human rights, previously associated with the heirs of the Enlightenment, was little short of revolutionary. And he preaches this gospel of human rights to one and all. He told Fidel Castro to respect his citizens' human rights, but also General Stroessner in Paraguay.

Everywhere, he takes the part of the poor. He may condemn "liberation theology," but his own Latin American homilies have been full of the liberation theologians' concerns for the structurally oppressed. His demands for "social justice" make pure neoliberal free-marketeers squirm. The right to work belongs to his core notion of human dignity. Again and again, he has denounced the evil of unemployment in capitalism, as well as that of "senseless work" in command economies.

Another great theme is tolerance and mutual respect between different peoples and faiths. He grew up with Jewish schoolfriends in prewar Poland, and reconciliation between Christians and Jews is very close to his heart. He has not gone as far as some Jewish leaders would like in acknowledging the Catholic Church's own historical responsibility for anti-Semitism, but he has gone farther than any of his predecessors. He also reaches out to Islam. Visiting Zagreb, he ordered Catholic Croats to respect the "outstanding presence" of muslims in the Balkans. If the Harvard political scientist Samuel Huntington is right that the next great world conflict will be "the clash of civilizations" (which, by the way, I don't think he is), it will certainly be no fault of this pope.

Everywhere, too, he preaches peace. On this he has been utterly consistent. Even in Nazi-occupied Poland, he refused to support armed resistance. "Prayer is the only weapon that works," he told a friend. In Japan, he cried, "Never again Hiroshima! Never again Auschwitz!" In Ireland, he told the IRA to abandon the violence that would "ruin the land you claim to love and the values you claim to cherish." In Britain, he criticized the Falklands War. And he opposed the Gulf War, too. All peoples have a right to justice and sovereignty, he says, but these may be achieved only by nonviolent means. As he told his fellow Poles in 1983, when General Jaruzelski had tried to dash their hopes with tanks, "You must defeat evil with good."

Not only has he kept saying these things on eighty-four foreign trips, from Argentina to Yamoussoukro. He has also dramatized them, with the skills of the professional actor he once nearly became. He has, as Princess Diana had, the ability to present compassion in a single photogenic image: the gentle embrace of a crippled child, the head bowed in sadness at a place of horror. Yet he can also make the mighty tremble. Literally so in the case of General Jaruzelski, whose knees we could see visibly shaking before he met John Paul II in 1983: "But only at the beginning," the pope commented kindly.

IT'S MAGNIFICENT, but has it been effective? This is much harder to judge than in the case of ordinary politicians. For how can you measure the effects of small changes in millions of human hearts? His old friend Father Józef Tischner said that the Solidarity movement in Poland was "a forest of awakened consciences." Such forests are usually invisible.

Politically, his most obvious contribution was to the end of communism. Gorbachev himself says, "Everything that happened in Eastern Europe would have been impossible without the presence of the pope." I would add "including Gorbachev." My argument is in two stages. First: without the pope, no Solidarity in Poland. His great pilgrimage in 1979 broke the barrier of fear and created the solidarity that paved the way for Solidarity. This was far more important than anything in his biographer Carl Bernstein's overexcited tale of a "secret alliance" between the Vatican and the CIA.

Second: without Solidarity, no Gorbachev. I don't mean, of course, that Gorbachev would not have emerged as Soviet leader. I mean that he would not have made his seminal revision of Soviet policy toward Eastern Europe unless the persistence of Solidarity—despite Jaruzelski's tanks—had shown him that the Soviet Union just could not carry on in the old way. When Gorbachev gave an inch, the Poles took a mile. Here is the specific chain of causation that goes from the election of the Polish pope in 1978 to the end of communism, and hence of the cold war, in 1989.

If this was his clearest positive contribution to world history, then his largest negative contribution has been his opposition to all forms of artificial contraception. Here, too, he has been nothing if not consistent. He came to this position after thinking deeply about love, marriage, and sexuality as a young priest. He personally encouraged Paul VI to take his stand against the pill in the fateful 1968 encyclical *Humanae vitae* ("On human life"). He once said to a friend who challenged him on the subject, "I can't change what I've been teaching all my life." But the result has been much needless, avoidable suffering, as poor women in the Third World, denied contraceptives or proper education on birth control, have brought unwanted children into lives of misery. Yes, that very poverty and misery against which his own heart cries out.

After seeing off communism in the 1980s, he has spent the 1990s attacking the evils of unbridled capitalism. He tells us, far more robustly than any of the supposedly left-wing parties that again rule in much of Europe, that the rich still exploit the poor and the North damages the South. He says we are caught up in the pursuit of "having" at the expense of "being." He says consumerism is "a web of false and superficial gratifications." Turning red in the face with anger, he rails against liberty decayed into license, sexual promiscuity, alcoholism, drugs, relativism, and postmodernism. Most people, even in his native Poland, ignore the old man's warnings. But are we really so sure there is no truth in what he says about our world—a world more free than it has ever been before?

As I WRITE, I have before me a little book, some five inches by three. A miniature anthology of the pope's teaching, it's called *Agenda for the Third Millennium*. Who else would dare such a title? I can't get anywhere with half of it, because I, like most of humankind, no longer believe. But there are things in the other half that I find magnificent, rich, and true. And important, too, for the next twenty years—never mind the next thousand. It may not be *the* agenda for our time. But do any of us have a better one?

CHRONOLOGY

1998

21 OCTOBER. *Former communist Massimo D'Alema becomes prime minister of Italy, forming the fifty-sixth Italian government since 1945.*

21 NOVEMBER. *New German foreign minister Joschka Fischer provokes controversy by suggesting that NATO should adopt a doctrine of "no first use" of nuclear weapons.*

CRY, THE
DISMEMBERED COUNTRY

ONCE UPON A TIME, THERE WAS A COUNTRY CALLED YUGOSLAVIA.
It was a medium-sized country in the southeast of Europe, and more
than twenty-three million people lived there. It was not democratic,
but it had a fair name in the world. Its king was called Tito. Being
both largely rural and socialist, this country was not rich. But it was
getting a little richer. Most of its children grew up thinking they were
Yugoslavs. They had other identities, too, and strong ones. Slovenes
already talked of the "narrower homeland," meaning Slovenia, and
the "wider homeland," meaning Yugoslavia. Its Albanians were always Albanians. Still, it was a country.

In the last decade of the twentieth century, this European country has been torn apart. At least 150,000 and perhaps as many as
250,000 men, women, and children have died in the process. And
how they have died: with their eyes gouged out or their throats cut
with rusty knives, women after deliberate ethnic rape, men with
their own severed genitalia stuffed into their mouths. More than two
million former Yugoslavs have been driven out of their homes by
other former Yugoslavs, and many deprived of everything but what
they could carry in precipitous flight.

In this former country, the grotesque spectacle of a whole village
burned, looted, and trashed has become an entirely normal sight.
"Yeah, the usual story," says the journalist, and drives on. A few have
grown rich: mainly war profiteers, gangsters, and politicians—the
three being sometimes hard to distinguish. The rest, save in Slove-

nia, have been impoverished, degraded, and corrupted too. Real wages in Serbia are estimated to be at the level of 1959—in the rare event of you actually being paid a wage. In Kosovo, the killing, burning, plundering, and expelling went on throughout the summer of 1998, even as West Europeans took their holidays just a few miles away. It went on though the leaders of the West had all repeatedly declared it would never, ever be allowed to happen again. Not after Bosnia.

If you look at a current political map of Europe, you may conclude that the former country is now five states: Slovenia, Croatia, Bosnia, Macedonia, and the Federal Republic of Yugoslavia (known to diplomats as the FRY, pronounced as in "French fries"). But the reality on the ground is at least nine parts. Bosnia is still divided between a "Serb Republic" (Republika Srpska) and a Croat-Bosniak Federation, which itself is effectively divided between Croat-controlled and Bosniak- (or "Muslim"-) controlled areas. The FRY is divided between what may loosely be called "Serbia proper," Kosovo, and the increasingly independent-minded republic of Montenegro. But even "Serbia proper" should be disaggregated to notice the northern province of the Vojvodina, with its large Hungarian minority, and—oh, delight to the diplomatic historian!—the still partly muslim-settled Sandjak of Novi Pazar. Perhaps one should also distinguish the Albanian-settled areas from the rest of Macedonia. That makes twelve ethnically defined parts to be going on with.

It's not just we in the West who are largely indifferent. Most inhabitants of most of these dismembered parts themselves live in growing indifference or active antipathy to each other. In Ljubljana, a cultured Slovene woman tells me sadly that her children cannot enjoy the wonderful work of Serbian writers because they no longer read the Cyrillic alphabet. Why, she exclaims, they don't even understand Croatian! In Sarajevo, a local veteran of the siege says, "You know, if I'm honest, we watched the television pictures from Kosovo this summer much as I suppose Westerners watched the pictures from Sarajevo." But the feeling is reciprocated. In Priština, the capital of Kosovo, a leading representative of the mainly muslim Albanians tells me, "We don't feel any fellowship with muslims in Bosnia, because they are Slavs." In fact, the two groups have diametrically opposed goals: Bosnian "muslims" want to keep together a multiethnic state, Kosovar Albanian "muslims" want ethnic separation.[1]

Across this landscape of extraordinary ethno-linguistic-religious-historical-political complexity crawl the white-and-orange vehicles of an international presence that, in its different, political-bureaucratic way, is just as complicated. SFOR, OHR, UNHCR, MSF, CARE, OSCE, USKDOM, EUKDOM, RUSKDOM: international alphabet soup poured over Balkan goulash. Americans may be the new Habsburg governors here, but French deputies tussle with British ones for priority at court, while earnest Scandinavians get on with laying the phone lines. At Sarajevo Airport, I sit next to a man whose shoulder badge proclaims "Icelandic Police." Perhaps that Icelandic policeman will now be sent to Kosovo, to keep peace among the dervishes of Orahovac.[2]

Faced with such complexity, it's no wonder newspaper and television reports have largely stuck to a few simple, well-tried stories: bang-bang-bang, mutilated corpse, old woman weeps into dirty handkerchief, ruined mosque/church/town, U.S. envoy Richard Holbrooke meets Serbian leader Slobodan Milošević, NATO bombers at Italian airbase, preparing not to bomb. Yawn. In truth, it needs a whole book to do justice to each single part. Here, I shall confine myself to reporting some of what I saw, in winter 1998, in just three closely related parts of the post-Yugoslav jigsaw: Kosovo, Macedonia, and Belgrade. But then I shall draw a few larger conclusions.

1
KOSOVO

The fresh red blood on the fresh white snow looks unreal, like a new avant-garde exhibit at the Tate Gallery in London. But it is entirely real. This is the blood of two dead Serb policemen, shot at dawn, almost certainly by the soldiers of a tough local commander of the Kosovo Liberation Army (KLA), violating the October cease-fire. The blood lies, symbolically, just beneath a ruined mosque, in the middle of an Albanian village that those Serb forces have systematically destroyed. Now the women of one of the few Albanian families daring to remain here are telling us how the Serb police beat them up after the assassination.

Earlier, we drive through the town of Mališevo, which has been called "the most dangerous place in Europe." This summer it was the bustling unofficial capital of the KLA's "liberated" heartland of Drenica. They even had their own KLA number plates. Now Mališevo is completely ruined and deserted, its shopping center reduced to rubble and pulverized glass. The only people visible are heavily armed Serb police, behind their sandbags in a makeshift, fortified police station. Instead of shoppers, there are large packs of dogs scavenging, as many as twenty together, presumably domestic animals gone feral. You see these dogs all over the province and their corpses lying on the roads.

Farther down the empty highway, we find a solitary Albanian farmer trying to rescue his car. As we stop to help him, we face a surreal sight. A large, orange-painted armored car, of the American type known colloquially as a Humvee, slowly and silently approaches. Right behind it trundles a long convoy of blue-painted armored vehicles, packed with heavily armed Serb police in their blue combat uniforms. In the middle of the convoy there are some very nasty-looking men in an unmarked white jeep. The farmer is terrified: "If the Americans weren't there, the police would beat us up."

Later, he shows us his farmstead. Behind the high rough walls with which the Albanians surround the property of an extended family, we find two substantial houses, both blown up and looted. The families huddle together in one small basement room. "We can't come back here while the Serbs are in the police station," they say. "We can't live under Serbia."

Farther on, we turn into the village of Dragobilje. Just a hundred yards off the main road patrolled by the Serb police, we meet the KLA in their brown-and-green camouflage gear. A thickset, bearded man, with hand grenades slung in a belt around his chest, speaks with us on behalf of the "122nd Brigade." When we ask his identity, he gives his code name: "Journalist." He explains that he actually was a journalist in Priština before the war. They are currently respecting the cease-fire, he says, but they are ready to fight again at any time for a free Kosovo. Meanwhile, several carloads of men in

KLA uniforms come bucking down the muddy back lane, dodging the horned cattle and the tractor trailers carrying old men wearing traditional white caps. It's their own local version of a Ho Chi Minh trail.

As we drive out of Dragobilje, we see the same orange-painted Humvee halted at the roadside. Beside it, a burly American monitor is talking to a local leader. "Don't let your guys in uniform be visible from the main road, because that will provoke them [i.e., the Serbs]," says the monitor. When the local leader starts talking about the bitter past, this quiet American says, "All you can do is look ahead—just look ahead." And he offers help to get their school and hospital open again. "What do you need? Plastic? Just tell us what you need."

Another day, another ruined village in the snow, another guerrilla stronghold: Lauša to the Serbs, Llaushe for the Albanians. This was where the KLA first showed its face in public, on 28 November 1997, when two uniformed soldiers unmasked themselves and delivered a liberation speech at the funeral of a local schoolteacher shot by the Serbs.[3] Now two of the Geci brothers contemplate their devastated homestead. It was once home to seven brothers and their families— some thirty-five people in all. Most are now refugees in Albania. Those who remain are living on aid. Their own crops have been burned, their cattle killed or lost. "The KLA is our self-defense," they say. "The soldiers are all local people." Can they imagine ever again living together with Serbs in Kosovo? The grandmother gestures to a bare wire dangling from the ceiling: "How can you live with those who hang people from light fittings?"

Our knowledge of the KLA is still fragmentary, partly because this guerrilla army is itself quite fragmentary. It has, as one Western military observer politely puts it, a "rather horizontal" command structure. Each region is different, and regional commanders behave like local bandit chiefs. Nonetheless, we can establish a few significant things about its history, leaders, and support.

First and foremost, its emergence is the result of Kosovar Albanians despairing of the nonviolent path that they adopted after the province was robbed of its autonomy by Milošević in 1989 and Yugoslavia began to fall apart in 1990–1991. Under their unofficially elected "President of the Republic of Kosova," Ibrahim Rugova, they organized an extraordinary alternative state, with its own taxes, parliamentary committees, private health service, and, most impressive, unofficial education system, from primary school to university. To the frustration of Western policy makers, Rugova was unbending in his commitment to the goal of independence. To their relief, he was equally unbending in his attachment to nonviolent means. How did he propose to square the circle? By the "internationalization" of the Kosovo problem.

Even in the early 1990s, there were those who thought change would come only with the help of more traditional methods. Many Albanians from this region go to Western Europe for training and to earn money to send home. So did they. Ramush Haradinaj, the local commander almost certainly responsible for that blood in the snow, went off to get his military training in the French Foreign Legion. In Priština, people recall first hearing of a KLA in 1993. But then it was something like one of the terrorist splinter groups from the Western European student movement of 1968. One of the KLA's more important current political leaders, Hashim Thaci, code name "Snake," was a student activist in Priština who then went to study in Albania and to raise funds in the West. But most of the political activists who came from three generations of formative student political protest—in 1968, 1981, and 1990–1991—were still for nonviolence.

What changed the balance? The startling answer I am given is: "Dayton." I'm told this by the veteran political prisoner Adem Demaci, who is now the KLA's political representative. He dates the true emergence of the KLA to spring 1996, just a few months after the November 1995 Dayton agreement on Bosnia. I'm also told this by Veton Surroi, a favorite source for visitors from the West, whose influential daily newspaper nonetheless supported (some even say inflamed) the armed struggle. And by several others.

They say they drew two lessons from Dayton. After more than five years of their Gandhiesque struggle for independence, the United States made a deal with Milošević over Bosnia without securing even a restoration of mere autonomy for Kosovo. So, lesson one: Nonviolence wasn't working. Meanwhile, in Bosnia itself, the Dayton agreement went a long way toward recognizing ethnic realities created by force. Lesson two: Force pays.

There's an element of retrospective rationalization in this account. This is not what these same people were telling me in Priština in March 1997.[4] But there is also an uncomfortable element of truth. So long as Rugova kept the lid on his own people, and so long as we felt we had to deal with Milošević over Bosnia, we weren't going to push him on Kosovo.[5]

The armed rising then grew from two further developments: the looting of arsenals during the violent implosion of Albania in spring 1997, which gave the KLA access to Kalashnikovs galore, and the brutality of Serbian "reprisals" against whole extended families and villages, starting in February 1998. As always, an oppressive army and police were the best recruiting sergeants for the guerrillas.

At each stage, more individuals from the peaceful resistance went for the gun. Thus, the KLA's spokesman, Jakup Krasniqi, had previously studied at the underground Pedagogical Higher School in Priština. *"Un bon étudiant,"* says his charming, francophone professor, Abdyl Ramaj, as he shows me around the tatty bungalow that is the school's temporary home. Most intriguing, most sobering, is the case of Shaban Shala. Until the spring of this year, Shaban Shala was the vice chairman of the Council for the Defence of Human Rights and Freedoms, a human-rights monitoring group supported by several Western foundations. Now he is a guerrilla commander in the hills of his native Drenica. "Well, in a way he's still fighting for human rights," says an embarrassed employee of the council. Well, in a way.

Though it's dangerous to generalize, those who joined or actively support the KLA often have three things in common. First, many of them were political prisoners in former Yugoslavia: Demaci for a record twenty-eight years, Shaban Shala for a pretty standard nine. Second, they often come from the worst-hit rural areas. In the countryside, extended family and clan loyalties are still very strong. And, in villages such as Llaushe, the KLA is now the local community in arms. Third, they are fiercely critical of what they see as the inflexible, authoritarian, but also weak leadership of Rugova.

These, then, are the fighters for national liberation—or "terror-

ists," according to the Serb authorities—who have comple
formed the situation here. Western military observers are pre
temptuous of their ragtag army, just as they used to be of the Bos
army in Bosnia. They say it was wildly irresponsible of the KLA,
the liberation euphoria of the summer, to take over larger towns
such as Orahovac, which they could not seriously defend. When the
Serbs came back, "they just ran." They must have known that the
Serbs would then wreak vengeance on innocent civilians such as
the family I visited. (In all, some quarter of a million people were
made homeless in this summer of war.)

This is true. But it's also true that the KLA are heroes to most
Kosovar Albanians. Their exploits are already the stuff of legend,
ready to enter the history books beside the doubtless equally mythol-
ogized deeds of the *kaçak* rebel fighters against the Serbs eighty
years ago. (Drenica was their stronghold, too.) Whatever its military
weakness, the KLA has growing political strength. Teasing out a
comparison with Ireland's 1916 Easter Rising that certainly occurs
to an Englishman, Veton Surroi says, "We now need a Michael
Collins." They need a political Sinn Fein to partner their IRA.

Moreover, the KLA in practice holds a large part of the land. The
division is roughly this. The Serb forces still patrol the main towns,
the main roads, and the borders with Albania and Macedonia; the
KLA has most of the countryside in between. In places, the two sides
are barely fifty yards apart. This is not peace. It is frozen war. The
war is frozen by the heavy snows that came down suddenly in mid-
November, although this has not prevented some serious fighting
from going on. It is also frozen, even less effectively, by the presence
of international monitors.

There have been diplomatic monitors officially accepted here
since July. Following the agreement reached by Richard Holbrooke
with Slobodan Milošević on 12 October, under the threat of NATO
bombing, they are becoming part of a much larger team of two thousand unarmed "verifiers" under the novel auspices of the Organization for Security and Cooperation in Europe (OSCE). At the
moment, they are trying to "verify" compliance with the cease-fire
and some rather unclear supplementary agreements on Serb police
and army numbers and locations. But the idea is that early in 1999

…ying" the implementation of a political agree-

… United States's impressive ambassador to
…er Hill, has been engaged in exhausting
…nacy to produce an outline for that new mas-
… has to reconcile the virtually unanimous in-
…Kosovar Albanians that they can no longer live "under
Serbia" and that after a transitional period a door must clearly be
open to independence, with the insistence of Milošević—but also of
most other Serb politicians—that Kosovo must remain in Serbia,
with the independence door firmly closed. Hill deals with a frustrat-
ingly disunited array of Kosovar Albanian leaders, including what he
calls "the KLA guys." On the Serb side, he deals with Milošević.

The local Kosovo Serbs fear Milošević will sell them down the
river. They are a nervous, sad bunch, hunched over their beers in
tatty, dim-lit pubs, while the Albanians take you to smart new cafés.
(The Serb-run Grand Hotel magnificently lives down to its reputation as the worst five-star hotel in the world.) How many Serbs are
left in this medieval cradle of Serbianness? The 1991 census showed
just over two hundred thousand. Some have since given up and left.
But Serb refugees from other parts of former Yugoslavia have been
resettled here, in prefabricated single-home settlements that stand
out amid the sprawling high-walled Albanian farmsteads.

Momčilo Trajković, leader of the so-called Serb Resistance Movement, says that a further twenty thousand Serbs have left the
province since March. Pathetically, he now talks of their desire for a
"multicultural, multiethnic" Kosovo. "Multicultural, multiethnic!"
he intones, almost like a Sarajevan. What would the local Serbs do if
Kosovo became independent? Some would fight, he says. Some
would flee. Pause. "I think most would flee."

2
Macedonia

"We all support the UCK," says the burly student, using the Albanian initials for the KLA. "All Albanians here are UCK." We are sitting
in the "Queen's Club" café, in the largely Albanian town of Tetovo,

in western Macedonia. Nearby, behind the closed metal doors of seemingly half-finished redbrick private houses, I have seen class-rooms packed with students of the unofficial Albanian University of Tetovo.

"Yes," agrees that student's professor, Zamir Dika, a lean, intense, black-bearded man, "there is total support for the KLA. We are one nation." But there's still a last chance to realize equal rights for Alba-nians peacefully, inside the present Macedonian state. And the po-litical party he represents, the Albanian Democratic Party, proposes to seize that chance as a member of the new Macedonian coalition government. His party demands the legal recognition of Tetovo Uni-versity, the release of political prisoners, ethnic Albanians' participa-tion in public service proportional to their numbers, and, finally, that the Albanians be recognized in Macedonia as what is called a *drza-votvorna nacija*—literally, a "state-creating nation." (This is a piece of Yugoslav ethno-constitutionalist jargon that presumably derives ultimately from Fichte's notion of a nation capable of creating a state.)

Later, I talk to his party leader, Arbën Xhaferi, a brooding, steely, black-bearded man, in a small, dark room in a headquarters fes-tooned with the black double-headed Albanian eagle on a red back-ground. He says people chant "UCK" at his rallies, not the name of his party. His own support for the Kosovar armed struggle is passion-ate—which is not surprising, since he spent most of his adult life as a journalist in Priština. (He was a colleague of "Journalist.") Kosovo is the cradle of Albanian nationhood, he lectures me, scene of 180 Albanian risings against Turkish rule. The Albanians are not peace-ful people by nature. They are warriors. Sooner or later, Kosovo will win its right to self-determination, even though Americans try to put it "in a straitjacket." Altogether, he informs me in a mesmerizing dis-quisition, the whole direction of European history is toward the sep-aration of ethnic groups into their own states. He personally wouldn't at all mind the Serbs annexing their "Serb Republic" part of Bosnia, if they give up Kosovo in exchange.

As for Macedonia, well, he accepts what he calls the "interna-tional framework." He knows the West jumps nervously at the mer-est whisper of secession for the Albanian part of Macedonia, fearing that its neighbors Bulgaria (which says that the Macedonian language is really a dialect of Bulgarian) and NATO member Greece (which obstinately insists that the state can't call itself "Macedonia" because Macedonia is in Greece) might then become involved, leading to a bad case of Balkan dominoes, even to another Balkan war. An interesting gloss is added by Bejtulla Ademi, a local politician from the other Albanian party, who himself served nine years as a political prisoner, together with several present leaders of the KLA. There was, he says, a coordinating body of Albanian political parties in the former Yugoslavia, which, after playing with much more radical variants, decided in 1992 that the Albanians in Kosovo should go for independence, the Albanians in Macedonia should aim for equal rights as a "state-creating nation" in the new state, while the Albanians in Montenegro and Serbia would have to settle for plain citizenship rights.[6] One step at a time.

Next day, I watch Xhaferi at a press conference to present the new Macedonian government in the capital, Skopje, together with the prime minister–elect, the fresh-faced Ljubco Georgievski, and the likely next candidate for president, a tubby old fox named Vasil Tupurkovski, formerly of the Yugoslav communist politburo. All three leaders privately assure me they didn't need the pressure exerted by the United States in order for the Albanians to be included in the new government. All agree that the Macedonian nationalists of Georgievski's party have become more moderate and pragmatic.

The Macedonian tragedy today, Prime Minister–elect Georgievski tells me in a subsequent conversation, is no longer foreign occupation, whether Turkish, Serbian, Bulgarian, or communist Yugoslav. It is poverty. The country has 30 percent unemployment. To revive the economy, they need to work constructively with Greece and Bulgaria. The challenge, says Tupurkovski, is simply to make a viable state. To do that, they must have the Albanians on board. And a lot of help from the West, too. Last year, the country got just six million dollars in foreign investment.

In the short term, things look moderately encouraging for this fragile new state of just two million people. Macedonia's Albanian leaders are not about to lead their people in an armed uprising. But in the long run? Young Macedonian Albanians tell you they are "all KLA." Talking to Arbën Xhaferi, I am reminded of Walter Scott's haunting romantic insurrectionary Redgauntlet. Indeed, the Albanians here may never need to reach for the gun. All they need to do is what they do anyway: have many, many children. Albanians are now at least one quarter of the Macedonian population. At current birth rates, they will be a majority in about 2025. And doesn't democracy mean rule by the majority?

3
Belgrade

"I will lead a movement of one million Serbs to liberate Kosovo," Vuk Drašković tells me. "My party is organized like an army. We will fight." Fight NATO? "There is no Serbia without Kosovo. I cannot betray it. I cannot betray Jesus Christ." And the leader of the Serbian Renewal Movement pulls from his inside pocket a map marking all the Serbian Orthodox churches across the province. This from the man who early last year was still part of the Zajedno ("Together") coalition that was supposed to bring democracy to Serbia.

But Kosovo upsets more than just the ranting Drašković. I tell the wife of an eminently liberal friend how in Kosovo I visited the medieval Serbian monastery of Dečani. It looked indescribably beautiful in the snow. But it is now occupied by soldiers. Suddenly her eyes are full of tears. She has such happy childhood memories of visiting her grandparents in the nearby town of Peć, of a Christmas with the nuns, of a magical cave where water runs uphill . . .

I explain to Biljana Dakić, one of my student guides through the great Belgrade demonstrations of 1996–1997, that I think Kosovo will become a kind of Western protectorate. "You know," she says, "my stomach really churns when you say that. It's such an emotional thing." Kosovo is somehow closer to her heart even than the fate of the Serbs beyond the river Drina, in Bosnia, and formerly in the Croatian Krajina, although her own family comes from there. Čeda Antić, a patriotic and religious young Serb whom I got to know as a leader of last year's student demonstrations, still uses the official Serb name for the province, "Kosovo and Metohija," Metohija being the historic lands of the Serb Orthodox Church. He is equally dismayed to contemplate its loss.

Never mind that their history of Kosovo, like the Albanians', is partly myth.[7] Never mind that they haven't been to Kosovo for years and would not dream of living there. Never mind that they know, in their heads, that the Albanians have already won, simply by multiplying and occupying the land. The prospect of losing Kosovo is so painful because it comes on top of many other bitter blows. The former Yugoslav metropolis of Belgrade is impoverished and depressed. Its population has been swollen by Serb refugees from the parts of former Yugoslavia that Milošević's adventurism has already lost but diminished by the emigration of much of the elite. Biljana tells me that 70 percent of her high-school classmates have left. Those that remain live in a cage, with only limited information from a few independent radio stations and newspapers and great difficulty in obtaining visas to travel to the West.

My Serb friends feel—and they are surely right—that even sophisticated men and women in the West no longer distinguish sufficiently between the Serbian people and their regime. To be a Serb in the world today is like being a German in 1945. They also fear—and in this they are probably also right—that, just as the Germans were the last victims of Adolf Hitler, so the Serbs will be the last victims of Slobodan Milošević.

I find that, if pressed, more and more people in Belgrade see partition as the least bad solution for Kosovo. But generally they prefer to talk about the prospects of political change in Serbia proper, rather than about Kosovo. "Democratization in Serbia" is, they insist, the key to progress in the whole of former Yugoslavia. But what chance of that? At the moment, things look worse than ever. Veran Matić, the forceful head of the independent Radio B92, sees a familiar pattern: When Milošević makes concessions externally (over Kosovo, as previously over Bosnia), he cracks down internally. This autumn saw the universities stripped of their autonomy and the passing of a draconian "information law" that threatens critical newspapers with confiscation of their assets. This has already happened, in a flagrant example of political justice, to the semi-tabloid *Dnevni Telegraf,* after its owner turned sharply against the regime.

How might change for the better come? Milošević's regime is an extreme postcommunist example of what has been called a *demokratura*: formally democratic, substantially authoritarian. These postcommunist *demokraturas* maintain their power through control of state television, the secret police, and the misappropriation of large parts of the formerly state-owned economy. Such regimes may be overthrown peacefully, but this requires a grand coalition of virtually all the forces opposed to them. I come to Belgrade from Slovakia, where the *demokratura* of Vladimír Mečiar has just been overthrown, at the ballot box, by just such a "coalition of coalitions": opposition parties, nongovernmental organizations, independent media, trade unions, parts of the Church.

In 1997, with the "walking revolution" and the "Together" coalition, it looked as if that might just be happening in Serbia. But the West gave little effective support, and "Together" soon fell apart disastrously. Drašković's partners reneged on their promise to support his candidacy for the Serbian presidency, and he then made a shocking tactical alliance with the regime, being rewarded with the ample spoils of running the Belgrade city government. Now he and his former ally Zoran Djindjić speak more bitterly of each other than they do of Milošević. Djindjić is trying to build a broad democratic alternative again, helped by Čeda Antić and other former student activists who have joined his Democratic Party. But their current public support is small, and the necessary "coalition of coalitions" seems more remote than ever.

Another recurrent idea is that the Milošević regime might crumble from within, perhaps being supplanted by a military coup. A recent bout of sackings, including the heads of the army and the secret police, and their replacement with confidants of Milošević's wife, Mira Marković (a.k.a. Lady Macbeth), has fueled such speculation. Romania is close, and people wistfully recall how Nicolae and Elena Ceauşescu met their end. But do these purges actually weaken Milošević or strengthen him? I, at least, don't know anyone who can really tell me what is going on behind the closed doors of this messy, embattled, yet horribly durable regime.

But I will venture one guess about the social psychology around it. There is a kind of chemical solution that is both deeply inert and highly unstable. It's not bubbling at all, but one tap on the test tube and—bang!—up it goes. Serbian society today may be like that. What could the tap be? Many serious observers agree that Western sanctions against Serbia produced a certain defiant popular solidarity with Milošević, while this autumn's NATO bombing threat occasioned a wave of xenophobia. Could concessions by Milošević over Kosovo, in the middle of an economically difficult winter, have an opposite effect? Might that be the final tap?

Yet even if that were so, it is possible—even likely—that power would at least initially be seized by radical nationalists such as Vojislav Šešelj rather than by conciliatory democrats. Things could get even worse before they finally get better. The tragedy of former Yugoslavia is in its sixth or seventh act. Many have observed that "it began in Kosovo and may end in Kosovo." Perhaps it is more accurate to say that it began in Belgrade, with Milošević's cynical exploitation of the Kosovo issue. And so the last act, too, may be in Belgrade, as Kosovo comes back to haunt him.

4

What have we learned from this terrible decade in former Yugoslavia? And what is to be done? We have learned that human nature has not changed. That Europe at the end of the twentieth century is quite as capable of barbarism as it was in the Holocaust of mid-century. That, during the last decades of the cold war, many in Europe succumbed to fairy-tale illusions about the obsolescence of the nation-state and war being banished forever from our continent. That Western Europe has gone on living quite happily while war returned almost every summer to the Balkans. And we have learned that, even after the end of the cold war, we can't manage the affairs of our own continent without calling in the United States. Wherever you go in former Yugoslavia, people say, "the international community—I mean, the Americans . . ."

Our Western political mantras at the end of the twentieth century have been "integration," "multiculturalism," or, if we are a little more old-fashioned, "the melting pot." Former Yugoslavia has been the opposite. It has been like a giant version of the machine called a separator: a sort of spinning tub that separates out cream and butter or liquids of different consistency. Here it is peoples who were separated out as the giant tub spun furiously around. Even half-formed nationalities (Macedonian, Bosnian) were solidified by the separator, while blood dripped steadily from a filter at the bottom. But, when separation was almost complete, the West finally stepped in to try to halt the bloody process: in 1995 in Bosnia, in 1998 in Kosovo. In Bosnia, we now have a Western quasi-protectorate. Soon we may have another in Kosovo.

At this point, I will make an argument that departs from the received wisdom of the West and political correctness. I believe that, if it were possible, probably the least bad framework in which the peoples of former Yugoslavia might now start their slow journey to join a civilized, liberal, democratic Europe would be as a group of small nation-states with clear ethnic majorities. (By that I mean, as a very crude rule of thumb, with at least 80 percent belonging to one nationality.) I am definitely not arguing that separating out into such nation-states was the inevitable result of "ancient tribal hatreds" in the Balkans. Buried hatreds there surely were, but to revive, exacerbate, and exploit them was the culpable responsibility of bad leaders: Milošević above all, but also Franjo Tudjman of Croatia. Nor am I arguing that earlier, more forceful Western intervention could not have created different possibilities. I am simply arguing that now, after all that has happened, peaceful separation, where it is possible, might be a lesser evil. To adapt Shakespeare to the Balkans, "Journeys end in haters parting."

If peoples really cannot live peacefully together, it is better that they should live apart. To be sure, there is always a loss—cultural, economic, and political—in descending from the larger to the smaller state. And there is a human cost. I think of Violeta, a plucky Priština journalist from a mixed Serb-Albanian marriage. What is she supposed to do? Cut herself in half?

But good fences might eventually make good neighbors. It is clear to every thinking person that this array of small and tiny states on the Balkan peninsula will sooner or later have to start cooperating again out of pure economic self-interest, if for no other reason. (One thing they already have, in practice though not in theory, is a common currency: the deutsche mark. I suppose when the DM disappears in 2002 they will have to start using the euro.) Some talk dreamily of getting together again inside the European Union. A faint hope, seeing the current pace of EU enlargement. Others, more realistically, would start with a Balkan customs union. Adem Demaci preaches a confederation that he calls "Balkania."

We are looking at an almost Hegelian dialectic here: separation as the path to integration. But is this dialectic so unfamiliar? After all, we in Western Europe have long since been molded into nation-states, in a process that lasted from the Middle Ages to the early twentieth century. There are a few exceptions, to be sure, but even those exceptions—such as Belgium, increasingly divided between its French- and Flemish-speaking parts, or Scotland in Britain—are now proving difficult to sustain. (Yes, I know, there's still trinational Switzerland, God bless her.) It's precisely on this basis of clear separation into nation-states that we have been getting together in the European Union, as well as becoming more ethnically mixed again, through immigration.

In Central Europe, the process happened later, in the mid-twentieth century, through war, genocide, ethnic cleansing, and the redrawing of frontiers. In the early 1990s, the process was completed by the peaceful "velvet divorce" of Czechs and Slovaks. In each case, it is a sad, hard truth that the resulting relative ethnic homogeneity has, in the medium term, helped the country return to the civilized, democratic community of states. And now the small, new nation-state of Slovakia is following suit. Again, I am not saying that history had to go this way. I am not peddling a philosophy of history. I am merely saying that this is the way European history seems to have gone. But, if that is true, then what we are proposing to do in our Balkan quasi-protectorates is not just to freeze war. It is also to freeze history.

The trouble is this. Intellectually, we may—although many Western policymakers still do not—see the case for separation, as a dialectical stepping-stone to integration. But the modern liberal conscience rightly recoils from the means used throughout most of European history to achieve it—namely war, partition, forced assimilation, and ethnic cleansing. Yet where in former Yugoslavia can it happen without them?

The former Yugoslav republic of Slovenia was fortunate not only in being the most northern and economically advanced but also in having a clear ethnic majority. As a result, it is today well on track to join the EU in the first wave of its eastward enlargement. In Croatia, we did in fact condone ethnic cleansing. We let Tudjman "cleanse" the Krajina of more than 150,000 Serbs in 1995, while his troops went on to do what we wanted them to do in Bosnia. (Yes, we protested, but very feebly.) The result is that Tudjman no longer has an ethnic "enemy within" to blame for the country's woes, and I believe the days of his nasty little *demokratura* are numbered. Here the West just has to work to hasten the advent of real democracy, as in Slovakia. Having got away with murder, Croatia, as a well-defined new nation-state, can then start its progress back to Europe. It may then also be more cooperative in respect of the Croat-controlled parts of Bosnia.

Some argue that Serbia without Kosovo would still be liable to further disintegration, with Montenegro, the Sandjak, and even the Vojvodina pulling away. This may yet happen, if Milošević carries on as he is, starting with the incremental secession of Montenegro. But a Serbia without Kosovo and without Milošević would have a reasonable chance of consolidating itself as a democratic federal republic. In this state, Serbs would constitute a clear majority.

In its policy toward Serbia, the West now has to work simultaneously with and against Milošević. This is a difficult trick that we nonetheless managed in relations with the leaders of Eastern Europe in the last half of the cold war. We have to work with Milošević to some extent, because of his direct power over Kosovo and his spoiling power in Bosnia. But we also have to work against him, to encourage much more energetically such fragmentary positive forces for change as there are in Belgrade. For, as Madeleine Albright rightly insists, Milošević is the single person most responsible for all the bloody dissolution of former Yugoslavia. When he finally goes, I'm sure the British government will be delighted to welcome him to the VIP lounge at Heathrow Airport, as it recently did General Pinochet. And then, over a glass of dry sherry, the Hague tribunal can present him with its sealed indictment.

In Kosovo, the intricate details of successive drafts of what has come to be known as "the Hill plan" are still disputed fiercely between Serbs and Albanians. But its basic elements are now clear. It would restore the far-reaching autonomy of which the province was robbed in 1989 but not explicitly remove Kosovo from Serbia. It would devolve much power to local communes, thus allowing purely Albanian areas to have Albanian authorities and police, while mixed areas would supposedly have mixed ones. It foresees direct international involvement, especially in the reconstruction of the police and the conduct of new elections within six to nine months. And the whole arrangement should be subject to "comprehensive review" in three years' time.

The hope is to move forward early in 1999 to direct negotiations between the Serbian and Kosovar Albanian sides, with American and EU negotiators present to help things along. But it is very far from certain that this will produce an agreement, even after deploying the political cruise missile called Richard Holbrooke. If the negotiations fail, fighting in Kosovo will surely escalate around our unarmed "verifiers," especially when the snows melt in the spring. It will only be a matter of time before we need to activate the French-led NATO "Extraction Force" (jokingly known as "the dentists") recently deployed in northern Macedonia, in order to extract an imperiled verifier. However fleetingly, NATO will then have invaded Serbia.

If negotiations succeed, we will have another Western quasi-protectorate. A conversation with Ambassador William Walker, the American head of the OSCE mission in Kosovo, makes it clear that he proposes to give a new dictionary meaning to the word *verifying*. The OSCE will mediate and supervise. In effect, the police will be OSCE-trained police, the elections will be OSCE-run elections, election-time television will be OSCE television. But what happens then?

I believe Kosovo is a case where we can and should think of working toward peaceful separation. The Albanians are more than 90 percent of the population in a well-defined territory. They have not achieved this preponderance by ethnic cleansing, as happened in Bosnia, so we would not be "condoning ethnic cleansing." By their conduct in the province over the last decade, the Serbs have seriously diminished their own moral right to rule. There is at least some legal basis for arguing that Kosovo was a constituent part of former Yugoslavia and therefore could be recognized on a similar basis to the other successor states.[8] Anyway, this is a special case, not an international precedent for ethnic self-determination.

Yet certainly this process would have to be managed very carefully over a number of years, with a major international presence. Those magnificent Serb monasteries do need a special status. More seriously, there is a real danger of another panic flight of innocent local Serbs. I ask an Albanian civil-society activist in Priština, a sophisticated woman speaking excellent English, what should be done about the Serbs in a free Kosovo. She slowly exhales the smoke from her cigarette and smiles at me. "Kill them all?" she says. A joke, you understand. Just a joke. But the hard men in the hills are not joking. Without firm preventive action, we will again be party to ethnic cleansing by terror.

Macedonia's Albanian leaders tell me that independence for Kosovo would stabilize the situation in Macedonia. In the short run, this may be right, since few things could be more immediately dangerous than those young Albanian Macedonians joining a renewed war in Kosovo. But in the long run I don't believe it. History suggests that a contemporary European state with a less than 80 percent ethnic majority is inherently unstable. If the large and growing minority happens to be Albanian and contiguous to the motherland, it is even more so. Albanians in former Yugoslavia have been victims, there is no doubt of that. But there is also complex, patient, and stubborn Albanian nationalism. Without continued American and Western European involvement in both Macedonia and the anarchic state of Albania itself and in coaxing along their relations with their neighbors, the last act in Belgrade may not be the last one after all.

Finally, there is insoluble Bosnia. My Sarajevan friends are delighted with the ten thousand foreigners living there, and the nine billion dollars being spent on the country every year. They tell me that Sarajevo has actually never in its history been so genuinely cosmopolitan. The new cafés are pulsating. Increasingly, the Office of the High Representative, headed by the Spanish diplomat Carlos Westendorp, rules like a colonial administration. It's tempting to say that Bosnia-Herzegovina has again become an Austro-Hungarian protectorate, as it was after the Congress of Berlin, with the Americans as the Austrian Habsburgs and we Western Europeans as the Hungarian junior partner (although picking up most of the bill). But it's not a real protectorate. Rather, it's a bizarre novelty in international relations. We have had protectorates before. We have had partitions before. This is half protectorate, half partition.[9]

The official ideology of all Western agencies in Bosnia is that the unitary state is being pulled together again. It's just taking rather a long time. Alas, I don't think this is true. I fear all the king's horses and all the king's men will not put Humpty-Dumpty together again. But final partition would be an even less acceptable option. For the Bosniaks to have a serious, viable state, you would need to give them at least part of the western half of the "Serb Republic." That would almost certainly mean more bloodshed and tens of thousands more people driven from their homes. If, on the other hand, you allowed the Serb- and Croat-run parts to secede as they are, you would be left with a landlocked rump Bosniak state. Bosniaks warn that this could turn their people into muslim-fundamentalist nationalists. The result would be a "Gaza strip in the middle of Europe."

In fact, the Bosniaks hold the conscience of the West in a powerful moral half nelson. In effect, they say, "We are the Jews of the Balkans *and* the Palestinians of the Balkans!" The Jews, because no people in Europe has suffered something as close to genocide since the Jews in the Holocaust. So how could we abandon them? The Palestinians, for the reasons already given. I very much doubt that a rump Bosnia would actually become a muslim-fundamentalist state. But in a sense this doesn't matter. Earlier this autumn, the former German defense minister Volker Rühe told me that the deepest issue in Bosnia and Kosovo was "whether the West sees a place for Islam in Europe." Powerful Islamic countries agree. Faced with these complementary perceptions of the powerful, the local truth is largely irrelevant.

So, in some parts of former Yugoslavia, violent separation has already happened. In Kosovo, there remains a difficult but still Humvee-navigable dirt road to peaceful separation. That road we should take. Elsewhere, in Bosnia, but in a different way also in

Macedonia, I see no morally acceptable alternative to a direct Western involvement lasting many years, probably decades. Even if, intellectually, we will the end of separation, we cannot will the means.

But why on earth should Americans be the new Habsburgs? Why
should American diplomats enter the twenty-first century trying to
solve problems left over from the dissolution of the Ottoman empire
at the end of the nineteenth? Why should sons of Kansas and daughters of Ohio risk their lives in these perilous, snow-covered mountains ("What do you need? Plastic?") to stop Europeans fighting over
obscure patches of territory? After all, the great-grandparents of
some of these Americans probably fled these very mountains to escape just these insoluble squabbles.

The vital national interest is indeed hard to see. The new catchall
bogey of "regional instability" hardly compares with the old fear of
the Soviet Union getting the upper hand in the cold war. But empires—especially informal, liberal empires—are like that. You muddle in; then somehow you can't quite muddle out. Somalia could
never apply the moral half nelson that Bosnia has. For the Balkans,
this has been a decade of Western bluster. First, we had the Western
bluster of intervention. Now we have the Western bluster of withdrawal. I don't believe this bluster either. I think the sons of Kansas
and the daughters of Ohio will be here for a good long time.

"Take up the White Man's burden," Rudyard Kipling wrote a hundred years ago, welcoming the United States's willingness, in the
Philippines, "To wait in heavy harness / On fluttered folk and wild."
There, and elsewhere, he prophesied, Americans would reap only
"The blame of those ye better, / The hate of those ye guard." Today,
some of the finest white men are, of course, black. And the local sav-
ages are Europeans.

LONG LIVE RUTHENIA!

WHENCE THEY CAME, NO ONE CAN TELL. NO ONE KNOWS EXACTLY who, how many, or where they are. They live in six states and in none. They are loyal to each of these states and to none of them. Their language is written in five different versions—in the Cyrillic alphabet but also in the Latin. Some regard themselves as Ukrainians, others as Slovaks, others again as Poles. Or Romanians. Or Hungarians. Or Yugoslavs. But many insist they are "Rusyns," or "Carpatho-Rusyns," or "*rusnatsi.*" Or they throw up their hands and give the ancient answer of the peasant from Europe's Slavic borderlands: "We're just from here."

Yet now they have a provisional government that wants to form a new nation-state. A state called Ruthenia.

And here I am, talking to the prime minister. We are sitting in the office he occupies as a pharmacologist at a large hospital in Užhorod, capital of what Ukrainians call Transcarpathian Ukraine but he insists is Sub-Carpathian Rus'. Professor Ivan Turyanitsa is a stout, cheerful, energetic man, with a shock of black hair, bright eyes, and the gift of the gab. He is dressed in what I find to be the current style among the Ruthenians: synthetic sports jacket above, pinstriped trousers below. He has just introduced me to the foreign minister, who has come specially from Slovakia, and the justice minister, who is a surgeon in the same hospital. "But," he hastens to add, "only two of the cabinet work here."

While the justice minister—still wearing his medical white

coat—makes me a cup of tea from a kettle in the corner, the prime minister expounds. In the December 1991 referendum on Ukrainian independence, he says, 78 percent of the people in this region voted for greater autonomy from the rest of Ukraine, on the far side of the high Carpathian mountains. But what he calls "the Ukrainian national fascist regime" ignored this popular wish. So in May 1993 he and his colleagues formed the provisional government of Sub-Carpathian Rus'—or, in English, Ruthenia.

How did the Ukrainian authorities react?

"*Normalnie!*" he replies. (As befits this transfrontier folk, we are speaking a mixture of Slovak and Polish.) "In the normal way. They arranged a car crash for me." Later, he takes me outside to show me the damaged car. At present, he says, he and his colleagues are tolerated but given no access to the media.

They want their own state, in the boundaries of the present Transcarpathian *oblast* of Ukraine but with close ties to fellow Ruthenians in Slovakia and Poland. As responsible politicians, they will leave defense and what they call "global" foreign policy to the Kiev government. Everything else—including "local and European" foreign policy, education, health, and so on—would be their domain. They would have their own currency, "though it could be called the same." Professor Turyanitsa hands me a lapel badge showing their national symbol: yellow and gold stripes, with a red bear, prancing. Rather handsome.

Do they have a national anthem? Yes, of course. Could I see the text? Well, er, um, they don't seem to have a copy to hand. "But," says the foreign minister helpfully, "we could sing it for you!" Yes, please! Unfortunately, they then get bashful, and instead of singing they dig around until they do find the words, written by Aleksander Dukhnovych, a nineteenth-century priest regarded as the father of the nation. "Sub-Carpathian Rusyns," the anthem begins, "Arise from your deep slumber."

IT'S TEMPTING to dismiss this all as a joke. Ruthenia even sounds like something out of a Tintin book; perhaps a neighbor to Ruritania. And the provisional government is certainly good for a laugh. Yet the

Ruthenian Question takes you to the heart of one of the most important problems of international politics in our time. For, in the decade since the end of the cold war, in the new freedom, these suppressed or sometimes only half-formed nationalities have reemerged and formulated political aspirations all over Europe.

To understand the Ruthenians' case, you need first to swallow a little potted history. The Ruthenians are a part of the family of east Slavic peoples, like the Russians, Belarussians, and Ukrainians, all of whom were at one time or another described as part of Rus'. One scholar wanted to call them "Rus'ians" as opposed to "Russians," but you can see why the fine distinction did not catch on. Everything about their origins, culture, language, and politics is disputed.

For most of their modern history, most of them lived in the Austro-Hungarian empire. They were mainly farmers or woodcutters in the heavily forested Carpathian foothills. (You still see peasant woodcutters at work in mountain villages that look like pictures by Chagall.) It was the Habsburgs who christened them *Ruthenen;* the English word derives from the German. When the empire was broken up after the First World War, they found themselves scattered between Poland, Hungary, Romania, Yugoslavia, and what would shortly become the Soviet Union, but the greatest concentration was in the new state of Czechoslovakia.

Czechoslovakia—the most democratic and liberal of those successor states—gave them considerable autonomy, in a province it called Sub-Carpathian Rus'. The book in which they found me the words of the national anthem was actually published in prewar Czechoslovakia. In those golden days of freedom, there was a great debate between Ukrainophiles, who argued that the Ruthenians were really Ukrainians; Russophiles, who thought they were closer to Russians; and Rusynophiles, who said they were altogether different. Today, the debate has revived as freedom has returned. In Slovakia, I visit two rival organizations: the Union of Rusyno-Ukrainians, who insist that they are just a kind of Ukrainian, and Ruthenian Renaissance, whose spokeswoman tells me it's impossible to be both Ruthenian and Ukrainian.

The autonomy of Sub-Carpathian Rus' reached a perilous height after Britain and France agreed to the dismemberment of Czechoslovakia at Munich in 1938. For six months, it was a separate unit in a rump federal Czechoslovakia. The official English name for this unit was Ruthenia. Then, as the Nazis marched into Prague, Ruthenia was gobbled up by Hungary. But that didn't last long either. At the end of the Second World War, Stalin seized it for the Soviet Union. When the Soviet Union collapsed, it became part of Ukraine.

Through all this, the Ruthenians went on chopping their wood. Professor Turyanitsa tells me the classic east European joke about the old man who says he was born in Austro-Hungary, went to school in Czechoslovakia, married in Hungary, worked most of his life in the Soviet Union, and now lives in Ukraine. "Traveled a lot, then?" asks his interviewer. "No, I never moved from Mukachevo."

One of the big questions that little Ruthenia prompts is whether the ethnically checkered successor states of the former Soviet Union might yet go the bloody way of former Yugoslavia. Are the Ruthenian rumblings an exception, inspired by the relatively recent experience of autonomy in prewar Czechoslovakia? Or are other suppressed nationalities even now forming provisional governments in remote hospital offices?

Perhaps as many as one million Ruthenians live in Ukraine. There are another one hundred thousand or so in Slovakia, some sixty-thousand in Poland (where they are called "Lemkos"), and smaller numbers in Romania, Hungary, and the Vojvodina province of rump Yugoslavia. (They also have one vital asset for any would-be nation: a large community in the United States.) So they live across half a dozen frontiers. One dramatic way in which they describe themselves is as "the Kurds of Central Europe."

Moreover, these are not just any old frontiers. Samuel Huntington argues in his influential book *The Clash of Civilizations* that the great dividing line in Europe, after the end of the Iron Curtain, is that between western (Catholic or Protestant) Christianity and eastern (Orthodox) Christianity or Islam. Here, according to Huntington, is the new eastern boundary of Europe and of "Western civilization," no less. The Ruthenians, true to form, cut right across it. They worship in both the Orthodox and the Uniate (or Greek Catholic) Church, which uses the eastern rite but acknowledges the authority of the western pope. If you drive through the Ruthenian mountain villages of eastern Slovakia, you often see two churches side by side: an old wooden one, which is Uniate, and a new Orthodox one. The original wooden churches were illegally given to the Orthodox by the communists after 1945, then returned to the Uniates after the end of communism, whereupon the Orthodox congregations stormed off and built their own churches next door.

More immediately, the Ruthenians will soon straddle the new eastern frontier of NATO. That will be true when Poland joins NATO in March 1999, and even more so if a now rapidly reforming Slovakia enters the Western alliance in a few years' time. Then you will have significant numbers of Ruthenians on both sides of the West's front line. The foreign minister tells me confidentially that his government is "delighted to see NATO coming closer to us."

The Ruthenian story is, in every respect, a quintessentially east European one, and those of us with the perverse taste for such things may love it for its own sake. But it's not just an east European question. In western Europe, too, we have nationalities, in varying degrees of formation, striving for anything from autonomy to statehood. Think of Scotland and Wales in Britain, or Catalonia and the Basque country in Spain.

And it's not just in Europe. When I ask the prime minister if his government has achieved international recognition, he proudly declares, "Yes, we've been accepted into UNPROFOR."

"UNPROFOR? But that was the military force in Bosnia!"

"Sorry, I mean UNPRO."

Finally, we establish that it's UNPO—the Unrepresented Nations and Peoples Organization. On my return, I visit UNPO's website and find a list of more than fifty members, starting with Abkhazia, Aboriginals in Australia, Alcheh/Sumatra, then on to East Timor, Kurdistan, Nagaland, and Tibet. And, in the middle, Kosova—the Albanian spelling of Kosovo.

All over the world there are these peoples who would be states. Or at least recognized political units. This is a problem in dictatorships, when established identities are brutally suppressed, as in Tibet or East Timor. It's also a problem in liberal democracies, when people wish to be governed by those who they feel speak the same language or are of the same kind. Perhaps most of all, it's a problem at the fragile halfway stage between dictatorship and democracy. So often the road that begins with an UNPO ends in the need for an UN-PROFOR.

THE RUTHENIANS are still far from being Kurds or Kosovars. For now, their "representatives" want some basic minority rights, such as education in their own language. Improvements in Slovakia will increase the calls for change in Ukraine. They demand that Ruthenian nationality should be an option in the Ukrainian census scheduled for 2001, and that Ukrainian state forestry companies should stop the mechanized stripping of the trees from their beloved hills. Those forests are their national heritage. They hope to prevent the Trans-carpathian *oblast* from being incorporated into a new, enlarged province ruled from Lviv, in a planned reform of public administration for which, they tell me, the International Monetary Fund has been pressing. And they look for more cooperation across the frontiers, in what is already the Carpathian Euro-region.

That's a long way short of statehood. But Professor Turyanitsa is a gifted demagogue. If the circumstances were right, and he was given access to the media, I could imagine him—or someone like him—persuading an audience of Ruthenian hill farmers, woodcutters, and impoverished town dwellers that they are heirs to a great tradition; that they were more prosperous and free as part of Czechoslovakia before the war; that the Ukrainian "national chauvinists"—a phrase he repeats often and with relish—are to blame for all their troubles; in short, that they'd be much better off governing themselves. As we speak, rainwater is pouring down from the Carpathians and flooding the lowlands on the borders with Slovakia, Hungary, and Romania. "You see," he exclaims, "the very waters are pushing us to the West."

Absurd as it may sound, I have a strange hunch that one day we will again see the name *Ruthenia* on the map, if not as a sovereign state, then at least as some sort of autonomous province. When that day comes, remember: You read it here first.

Chronology

1998

19 NOVEMBER. *President Bill Clinton is impeached for lying under oath.*

16–20 DECEMBER. *The United States and Britain bomb military installations in Iraq. The United States proclaims removal of Saddam Hussein to be a policy objective.*

DECEMBER. *Major cease-fire violations in Kosovo by both Serb forces and the Kosovo Liberation Army.*

1999

1 JANUARY. *Monetary union comes into force between eleven member states of the EU. Only Britain, Sweden, Denmark, and Greece do not participate.*

4 JANUARY. *The Euro makes a strong start on its first day of trading.*

14 JANUARY. *The European Parliament votes on a resolution to sack the whole European Commission, because of corruption in two commissioners' areas of responsibility.*

15 JANUARY. *Serb forces massacre forty-five Kosovar Albanian civilians in the village of Raçak.*

29 JANUARY. *The Contact Group on former Yugoslavia issues ultimatum to the Serbian regime and Kosovar Albanian rebels. If they have not agreed on an interim political framework in three weeks, NATO will take military action against both sides.*

6 FEBRUARY. *Negotiations chaired jointly by the French and British foreign ministers begin in Rambouillet between Kosovar Albanian and Serbian government delegations.*

17 FEBRUARY. *Kurds protest across Europe after the arrest of Addullah Ocalan by Turkish special forces.*

23 FEBRUARY. *The Rambouillet talks end inconclusively with provisional agreement by the Kosovar Albanian delegation to an autonomy deal. Tony Blair announces plans for the "changeover" from pound to euro.*

WHERE IS CENTRAL
EUROPE NOW?

"I'M DELIGHTED," SAID HENRY KISSINGER, "TO BE HERE IN EAST-
ern, I mean *Central* Europe." And for the rest of his talk he kept saying, "Eastern, I mean Central Europe." The place was Warsaw; the
time, summer 1990; and this was the moment I knew Central Europe had triumphed.

For nearly forty years after 1945, the term was almost entirely absent from the political parlance of Europe. Hitler had poisoned it;
the cold war division into East and West obliterated it. In the 1980s,
it was revived by Czech, Hungarian, and Polish writers such as
Milan Kundera, György Konrád, and Czesław Miłosz, as an intellectual and political alternative to the Soviet-dominated "Eastern Europe." At that time, I wrote a sympathetic but also skeptical essay
entitled "Does Central Europe Exist?"[1]

In the 1990s, Central Europe has become part of the regular political language. To mark the shift, both the U.S. State Department
and the British Foreign Office have Central European departments.
Although people still privately tend to say "Eastern Europe," every
greenhorn diplomat knows that one should refer to the whole postcommunist area as "Central and Eastern Europe"—a phrase so
cumbersome it is often reduced to an abbreviation: CEE in English,
MOE (*Mittel- und Osteuropa*) in German. Even Queen Elizabeth II
has spoken of "Central Europe," in the Queen's Speech to Parliament. So that's official. If the Queen and Henry Kissinger say it exists, it exists.

Just one problem remains: Where is it? "Central Europe," wrote the U.S. secretary of state Madeleine Albright in a newspaper article in 1998, "has more than 20 countries and 200 million people."[2] Yet we often find the term used to mean just the countries who are joining NATO this spring—Poland, Hungary, and the Czech Republic—or the "first wave" of postcommunist states negotiating to join the EU: the same three, plus Estonia and Slovenia.

Such disagreement is nothing new. In an article published in 1954, the geographer Karl Sinnhuber examined sixteen definitions of Central Europe. The only part of Europe that none of them included was the Iberian peninsula. The only areas they all had in common were Austria, Bohemia, and Moravia.[3] Tell me your Central Europe, and I will tell you who you are.

In the first half of the twentieth century, the debate about who did or did not belong to Central Europe had real political significance. So it has today. For to be "Central European" in contemporary political usage means to be civilized, democratic, cooperative—and therefore to have a better chance of joining NATO and the EU. In fact, the argument threatens to become circular: NATO and the EU welcome "Central Europeans," so "Central Europeans" are those whom NATO and the EU welcome.

The rival definitions are based on arguments from geography, history, culture, religion, economics, and politics. There are also major differences between how countries see themselves and how others see them. Since countries are not single people, and there are many "others," one has to generalize dangerously from a whole kaleidoscope of national and individual views. I am mainly concerned here with the way the concept is deployed in what we still often call "the West"—meaning primarily policymakers and opinion formers in the United States, Britain, France, Germany, Italy, and other members of NATO and the EU.

Since Central Europe is, by definition, somewhere in the center, every one of its boundaries is disputed: northern, western, southern, and eastern. By the same token, in delineating Central Europe we also delineate the other major geopolitical regions of Europe today.

1

Interestingly, and encouragingly, the boundary that was most hotly disputed at the beginning of the twentieth century is largely uncontroversial at its end: the western one. The idea of "Central Europe" exploded during the First World War as a furious argument between those, such as the German liberal imperialist Friedrich Naumann, who envisaged a German- and Austrian-ruled *Mitteleuropa,* and those, such as Tomáš Garrigue Masaryk, the future president of Czechoslovakia, who were fighting for a Central Europe of small states liberated from German, Austrian, and Russian imperial domination. This argument between visions of *Mitteleuropa,* on the one side, and of *Střední Evropa* or *Europa Środkowa,* on the other, continued throughout the "Second Thirty Years War" from 1914 to 1945. It culminated in the Austrian-German Adolf Hitler's attempt to impose his own grotesque version of *Mitteleuropa* on Germany's eastern neighbors.

So, when the term was revived in the 1980s, there was understandable nervousness both among Germany's neighbors and in Germany itself. Many German writers preferred to use the less historically loaded term *Zentraleuropa.* But recent years have been reassuring. After some discussion, the Masaryk of the 1990s, Václav Havel, invited President Weizsäcker of Germany to attend regular meetings of "Central European presidents," and the German president has done so ever since. Most German policymakers now accept that the reunited country is both firmly in Western Europe and in Central Europe again. As Havel once put it to me, Germany is in Central Europe "with one leg."

Of course, there have been tensions between Germany and its eastern neighbors—especially between Germany and the Czech Republic. And there will be more as the enlargement of the European Union slowly approaches, with Germans fearing that Poles and Czechs will take their jobs and Poles and Czechs fearing the Germans will buy up their land. (The latter fears are especially pronounced in the formerly German western parts of Poland and in what used to be the Sudetenland, in the Czech Republic.) Yet no one could now argue that there is any fundamental political difference between what a mainstream German politician means by *Mitteleuropa* and what a Czech leader means by *Střední Evropa* or a Pole by *Europa Środkowa*. Increasingly, they are just different words for the same thing. This is a tribute to wisdom on both sides, and one of the bright spots on the map of Europe at century's end.

Meanwhile, the Austrians quietly pursue their own dream of Central Europe, by which they mean nothing more nor less than the area of the former Austro-Hungarian empire. Symbolically, Austria celebrated its first presidency of the European Union with a "Festival of Central European Culture." More practically, flying Austrian Airlines is now the best way to get around the former Austro-Hungarian empire, and a new Central European Air Traffic Control center will be located in Vienna. At the same time, Austrians are even more hostile than Germans are to the idea of people from their former empire actually coming to live in their country and competing for their jobs.

For completeness, one should add the eastern parts of Italy that have very special ties with Slovenia, Croatia, and Austria—special ties consisting partly in the fact that Italy contains a small, still largely German-speaking piece of what used to be Austria (the South Tirol or Alto Adige), while Slovenia and Croatia have a little bit of what used to be Italy (eastern Friuli, the area around Trieste and the Istrian peninsula). Some would also include Liechtenstein and German-speaking Switzerland, although the Swiss generally hold themselves above this kind of thing. In all these cases, the historical legacy is still being played out in a hundred intricate ties and tensions. As I write I have before me a purely hedonistic *Guida alla Mitteleuropa,* published in Florence in 1992, which maps an Italian "*Mitteleuropa*" from Milan via St. Moritz, Vaduz, and Bayreuth to Prague, then back through Vienna, Budapest, and Zagreb to Trieste, Venice, and Verona.

I find it useful to distinguish between West Central Europe—meaning mainly Germany, but also Austria and that corner of Italy—and East Central Europe. But when people say "Central Europe" in English, they usually mean just the latter. As Poland, Hungary, and the Czech Republic become Western-style capitalist democracies, join NATO and (eventually) enter the EU, so the line between Central and Western Europe becomes increasingly blurred. Far from being dismayed, those who revived the terms in the 1980s should be delighted by this merging.

The frontier that need trouble us least is the northern one. In his anxiety to gather all the same nations under the flag, Masaryk included in his Central Europe everyone from Laplanders in the north to Greeks in the south. The region stretched, he implausibly suggested, from "the North Cape to Cape Matapan." But Scandinavia has a quite distinct identity. To be sure, the Baltic states are an important borderline case. Lithuanians, in particular, will tell you their country belongs both to the Nordic or Baltic area and to Central Europe. Lithuania, they argue, is a bridge between the two. Since, however, Scandinavia is part of the Western capitalist democratic world, and the Baltic states are small, their in-between position is not in itself a political problem, although Russia's objections to their membership in NATO and the status of the Russian exclave of Kaliningrad will be.

The major political argument now is about the eastern and southern edges. As revived by Kundera and others, the idea of Central Europe was directed against the East (with a large *E*), and specifically against Russia. Central Europe, Kundera suggested, was the "kidnapped West."[4] Until 1945, it had participated fully in all the great cultural movements of the West, from western Christianity, the Renaissance, and the Enlightenment to Expressionism and Cubism. But politically it was now imprisoned in the East. Out of a cultural canon he made a cannon—firing against the East. As Joseph Brodsky pointed out, this was quite unfair to Russian culture. But politically it was justified and effective as an antidote to the even more misleading notion of a single "Eastern Europe."

In the 1990s, the cultural ca(n)non has been directed against the south more than the east. The new democracies of Poland, Hungary, and Czechoslovakia set out early in the decade to pursue Central European cooperation, symbolized by the "Visegrád group" established in February 1991. They did this partly because they believed in the idea, which Havel and the new Hungarian president Árpád Göncz had preached in the 1980s, and wished to preclude any return to the petty nationalisms of the interwar years. But it was also because this right, tight little regional cooperation would win their countries favor in the West. Which it did.

They had little trouble distinguishing themselves from the new eastern (with a small *e*) Europe: Belarus, Ukraine, and European Russia. More difficult was the south. Romania tried to join the group at an early stage. The door was closed firmly in its face. A good reason for this was that Romania was at that time an undemocratic mess. A less good reason was that Polish, Hungarian, and (then still) Czechoslovak leaders thought they had a better chance of entering or (as the Central European ideology prescribes) "rejoining" the West in a smaller, more homogeneous group. Which they did.

Then came the bloody collapse of the former Yugoslavia. This revived another previously dormant geopolitical nation, "the Balkans," with connotations as negative as those of "Central Europe" were now positive. For politicians everywhere, and especially for Polish, Hungarian, and Czech politicians, the Manichaean contrast between "Central Europe," bathed in light, and "the Balkans," drenched in blood, was irresistible.[5]

To cap it all, the Harvard political scientist Samuel Huntington made his influential argument that the new cleavages of world politics would be based on "the clash of civilizations"—civilizations being defined mainly by their religious origins.[6] The Kunderaesque view of Central Europe, arguing as it does from culture to politics, fits perfectly into the Huntingtonian scheme, and it's no surprise to find Huntington enthusiastically adopting the term. But he goes further, suggesting that the eastern and southern boundary of Central Europe is simultaneously the frontier of Europe and "Western civilization."

What is this boundary, more fundamental even than the post-1945 Iron Curtain? According to Huntington, it is the dividing line between western (Catholic or Protestant) Christianity, on the one side, and eastern (Orthodox) Christianity or Islam on the other. This line has been in roughly its present position for about five hundred years, and its origins go back as far as the division of the Roman empire in the fourth century. Huntington even suggests that, because they are on the wrong side of the line, Turkey and Greece may not remain full members of NATO and, in the case of Greece, the EU.

Note, however, that the Baltic states, most of western Ukraine, half of Romania, all of Croatia, and even small parts of Bosnia and Serbia (i.e., the formerly Hungarian province of Vojvodina) fall on the "western" side.

At worst, the result has been an extreme cultural determinism. I call it Vulgar Huntingtonism, by analogy with Vulgar Marxism. It says: If your heritage is western Christianity, the Renaissance, the Enlightenment, the German or Austro-Hungarian empires, Baroque architecture, and coffee with *Schlagobers,* then you are destined for democracy. But eastern (Orthodox) Christianity or Islam, the Russian or Ottoman empires, minarets, *burek,* and Turkish coffee? Doomed to dictatorship! Of course, this is crude to the point of parody. But the way political ideas get used in real politics is very crude. And it has not been in the interest of the "Central Europeans" to restore any confusing nuances.

Yet this extreme cultural determinism curiously coexists with an equally extreme political voluntarism. For, in the political usage of the West, countries seem to jump in and out of "Central Europe" according to their current political behavior. The best example of this is Slovakia, and it's worth dwelling on for a moment.

2

In 1990, few people doubted that Slovakia belonged to Central Europe. It joined the Visegrád group as part of Czechoslovakia, and being in the same state as the Czech lands was certainly a help. Yet Slovakia had many of the historical qualifications in its own right, being geographically central, overwhelmingly Catholic, formerly part of the Austro-Hungarian empire, and with a capital that was once—though as Pressburg or Pozsony rather than as Bratislava—a cosmopolitan Central European city.

At the same time, its politicians were looking for more autonomy from Prague and a better deal in the Czecho-Slovak federation. These nationalist demands escalated under the demagogic populist Vladimír Mečiar, until the new Czech prime minister Václav Klaus suddenly gave more than most Slovaks (and probably Mečiar himself) wanted: full independence as a sovereign state, as of 1 January

1993. A headline in a Czech newspaper encapsulated the Klaus view. It said, "Alone to Europe or with Slovakia to the Balkans?"

For nearly six years thereafter, with one six-month intermission, Mečiar ran a corrupt, nationalist, semi-authoritarian regime of the kind that has been called, adapting a Latin American term, *demokratura*. It had more in common with the Tudjman regime in Croatia or even the Milošević regime in Serbia than it did with politics in the Czech Republic. The two parts of the former country—Masaryk's country—grew apart at extraordinary speed. ("Yes, we occasionally look at Czech television," a Slovak friend told me. "We watch it as we used to watch Austrian television in the communist times.")

The three pillars of Mečiar's *demokratura*, as of Tudjman's and Milošević's, were state television, the secret police, and the misappropriation of the formerly state-owned economy by regime members and supporters.[7] Television was grotesquely biased and manipulated. The secret police, called the Slovak Information Service (hence SIS, but not to be confused with the British Secret Intelligence Service), bugged, burgled, and intimidated Mečiar's opponents. SIS officers were almost certainly implicated in kidnapping the son of the country's president, Michal Kováč, Mečiar's most prominent critic, as well as in the subsequent murder of someone trying to spill the beans on their involvement in the crime. "Privatization" was a polite word for misappropriation. And then there was nationalist scapegoating of ethnic Hungarians, some 11 percent of the new state's population. They were denied basic minority rights, such as having street signs in their own language, and ranted against by Mečiar in what one Slovak democrat described to me as "hate hours." Relations with Hungary were abysmal.

In this fashion, Slovakia ejected itself from Central Europe. It fell off the "first wave" list of candidates for NATO and the EU. The Czechs, despairing of their former partner, took up instead with Slovenia, as that most northern, prosperous, and peaceful of the former Yugoslav republics successfully sold itself as a Central European state. (There were even quips about Czecho-Slovenia.) Early in 1998, Madeleine Albright—herself of Czech origin—warned that Slovakia could become "a hole on the map of Europe." As late as Au-

gust, Milan Šimečka, one of the country's leading independent journalists, wrote to me, "The situation here is worse and worse. Yesterday happened something bad [*sic*] in the private TV Markiza, Mečiar
is going to take it. He learns from Milošević and Tudjman."

Then, suddenly, everything changed. In September 1998, Mečiar
lost the election. He was peacefully and decisively defeated by a
grand coalition of opposition parties, supported by nongovernmental organizations, trade unions, independent media, and parts of the
Catholic Church. When I visited Bratislava in November, there was
a real sense of liberation. Slovakia did not have much of a popular
"velvet revolution" in 1989, and the sociologist Martin Bútora suggested to me that this peaceful overthrow of Mečiar was "our delayed velvet revolution." In previous years, people who joined in the
28 October manifestation to mark the founding of Czechoslovakia
had looked around nervously, fearing Mečiarite surveillance or
provocation. This year it was all smiles and celebration. The head of
the private Radio Twist told me he used to spend three quarters of
his time defending it against regime harassment: licenses revoked,
punitive taxes, power lines cut. Now he jokes that he has so much
free time he doesn't know what to do with it.

In parliament, I watched the dismantling of two pillars of the
demokratura, as deputies installed a new supervisory board for state
television and a new head of the security service. One deputy prime
minister told me how the new government was going to build a true
market economy. Another, himself a Hungarian, explained how the
rights of the Hungarian minority would be respected.

The governing coalition is a fragile one, but thus far it has made
all the right noises. And the West has responded in kind. Madeleine
Albright told the new foreign minister in January that "if Slovakia
continues these reforms and keeps improving its relations with its
neighbors" then it would be "a strong candidate" for the next round
of NATO enlargement. The French foreign minister encouraged
him to believe that the EU might start negotiations with Slovakia before the end of 1999. As if by magic, Slovakia is back in Central Europe again!

If you ask "Why did it fall out?" you can find several answers. One
is the presence of a substantial ethnic minority, who could be made

scapegoats—especially because the Hungarians are widely seen as a former oppressor. (Slovakia was part of Hungary until 1918 and subjected to "Magyarization.") It has been something close to a rule in the 1990s that the greater the ethnic mix in a postcommunist country, the more likely the country has been to take a nationalist authoritarian rather than a liberal democratic path. Those that have done best are also those that are ethnically most homogeneous: Poland, the Czech Republic, Hungary, and, yes, Slovenia. (Like all rules, this one has exceptions to prove it, such as Estonia, with its large ethnic Russian population.)

There's a great irony here so far as the Central European debate is concerned. The 1980s revival of the Central European idea involved a celebration of the region's prewar ethnic and cultural mélange: mixed cities, such as Prague or Czernowitz or Bratislava before it was called Bratislava, where people habitually spoke three or four languages; large minorities, especially Jewish and German ones; multiculturalism *avant la lettre*. Yet it seems that one of the preconditions for being seen as part of the political Central Europe in the 1990s was precisely *not* to be Central European in this earlier sense. Or, to put it another way, Slovakia's problem was that it was still a bit too Central European, in the older sense.

Other reasons offered for Slovakia's falling away include the weakness of its pre-1989 opposition. "There were really only two dissidents in Bratislava before 1989," the former dissident Miroslav Kusý reminded me. (The other was Milan Šimečka, father of the independent journalist.) This meant there was no liberal counterelite to take power after the communists fell, leaving the door open for a skillful populist thug like Mečiar. Then there was the fact that Slovakia's only previous experience of nation-statehood was the clerical-fascist state of Monsignor Jozef Tiso, established under license from Hitler during the Second World War. And this was an agrarian society, with a relatively small bourgeoisie. In other words, Slovakia was missing some vital elements on the 1980s Central European checklist.

But then you have to ask why it succeeded in bouncing back again. Well, there was the proximity to better examples: Slovakia is sandwiched between Poland, Hungary, and the Czech Republic, while Bratislava is an hour's bus ride from Vienna. And there was significant pressure from the West—both active criticism and what has been called the "passive leverage" of NATO and the EU (i.e., if you don't do X and Y, we simply won't let you in).[8] But perhaps most important was another key item on the 1980s checklist: civil society.

Even in the worst moments of Mečiarism, Slovakia had a vibrant civil society—or what Slovaks call "the third sector." There was the powerful Catholic Church. (Although its leaders were rarely outspoken in criticizing Mečiar, prominent lay Catholics were.) There were independent radio stations, magazines, and the private television channel Markíza. And there were numerous nongovernmental organizations. Some sixty of these got together before the elections in a countrywide campaign to persuade people to turn out and vote, starting in the remotest mountain villages and working down toward Bratislava. There were mass meetings, posters, pamphlets, T-shirts, buttons, baseball caps, and "Rock the Vote" concerts. Arguably, this swung the election. The number of votes cast for Mečiar's party actually increased marginally from the previous election in 1994, but, at least partly thanks to this campaign, the electoral turnout went up much more—from 75 percent to 84 percent. It was these new voters who vanquished Vladimír the Terrible. When I described this civic campaign to opposition friends in Serbia a week later, they threw up their hands in envious despair. So perhaps this was a triumph for Central Europe, in yet another sense.

In sum, the phenomenon of Mečiar shows that a positive political outcome (in shorthand, "democracy") is not culturally predetermined by a Central European heritage. But the circumstances of his ousting do suggest that it helps.

3

Geopolitical boundaries are not just lines drawn on maps by officials in gilded conference chambers. If they are real, then things change when you cross them on the ground. The Iron Curtain was like that: Walk ten yards from Checkpoint Charlie and you were in a different world. If you want to experience such a dividing line in today's Europe, then I suggest you go by foot, as I did on a cold November evening, through the border crossing between Vyšné Nemecké in Slovakia and Užhorod in Ukraine.

The shock is instantaneous. Well-made asphalt roads give way to potholes and cobblestones. The Ukrainian border post seems to have been overrun by shaven-headed, thickset men, dressed in black boots, black jeans, black sweaters, and bulging black leather jackets—the uniform of the postcommunist mafiosi. I watch them taking customs officials by the elbow for a quiet word in a dark corner. I can almost hear the word *corruption* hiss through the freezing fog. Murmuring into their mobile phones, they jump into dirty black Volvos—of the latest, most powerful model—and screech off down the road.

Pausing only to set our watches forward one hour from Central to East European time, my companion and I proceed, more sedately, past large, extravagant villas, with giant satellite dishes, security cameras, high walls, and metal gates. "New Ukraine!" exclaims our guide, a professor at Užhorod University, whose own salary is barely fifty dollars a month—and he hasn't been paid for three months. He accepts the hard currency that I give him for a day's guiding services (the equivalent of a month's salary) with a mixture of gratitude and wounded pride, while we both desperately try to keep up the pretense that this is just normal academic collaboration between two of the world's great universities, Oxford and Užhorod.

The hotel demands payment in advance—cash only—and remember to lock your door from the inside. A friend tells how his father-in-law had a small collision with one of those black Volvos. Four men in black jumped out: "This will cost you $4,500. Cash. We come to your office tomorrow morning." He rang the police, gave them the Volvo's license number, and they promised to check it out. An hour later, the police rang back. They said, "When those men call tomorrow, you pay." This is a different world. Its essential qualities, as in Serbia, are habitual corruption, arbitrariness supported by violence, and a state that either cannot protect you or is itself criminal.

Today, the boundary between Central and Eastern Europe—Ukraine, Belarus, and European Russia—is clear and deep and real. I've made the case anecdotally, almost flippantly, but one could do so systematically and at length, with supporting statistics and graphs.

This is emphatically not to argue cultural predestination. The Huntington line, our new successor to the Curzon line, runs many miles east of here. The line you cross at Užhorod is the western frontier of the former Soviet Union, not the eastern frontier of western Christendom. Nor am I suggesting that these countries are eternally doomed to corruption, chaos, and poverty. Indeed, there is a real possibility that western Ukraine and western Belarus, which, like the Baltic states, were part of the Soviet Union for only two generations rather than three, might recover more quickly than the rest. But both the quality and the sheer scale of the problems of postcommunism in the states of the eastern Slavs make for a political dividing line that will probably last for at least another decade. Today, the eastern frontier of the West runs no longer along the river Elbe, nor along the Oder and Neisse, but along two rivers most people have never heard of: the Bug and the Už.

The crossings to the south, by contrast, between Central Europe and what we again call the Balkans, are much less sharp. To walk from Hungary into northern Romania is not to enter a different world. Partly that is because Hungarians live on both sides of the frontier. Both Transylvania and the Banat, which between them make up more than a third of Romania, are positively marked by the Austro-Hungarian heritage. But even if you take the southern parts of Romania that belonged to the Ottoman empire, the differences in society, politics, and economics between Hungary and Romania are nothing like as marked as those between Slovakia and Ukraine.

If you go from the Slovenian part of Istria to the Croatian part, you hardly notice the difference at all. As my *Guida alla Mitteleuropa* rightly suggests, Catholic, formerly Habsburg Croatia clearly qualifies historically as part of Central Europe. Politically, in the 1990s, Croatia has been part of the Balkans. But there is a good chance that it will come back, with Tudjman's *demokratura* crumbling either before or after his death. A new ethnic homogeneity—achieved by ethnic cleansing while the West looked the other way—provides favorable conditions for a return to Central Europe.

There is work for at least another ten years ahead before all those states that have credible claims to belong to Central Europe by virtue of geography, history, and culture will also be part of Central

Europe, in the 1990s sense, on account of their current politics and the way they are viewed in the West. It will be longer still before this Central Europe becomes just central Europe, another region of Western Europe, as northern Europe and southern Europe are today. Meanwhile, countries such as Ukraine may lift themselves up, especially if the West does more to help them.

Yet Central Europe does have to stop somewhere. To have a purely political, voluntarist definition of it is as absurd as it is to have a purely cultural-determinist one. It has been reasonable enough for the West to make political behavior the prime criterion of acceptance, saying, in effect, "Central European is as Central European does." But you can't go on forever suggesting that whichever among the postcommunist states exhibits the rule of law, democracy, tolerance, respect for minority rights, and interest in peaceful international cooperation will ipso facto become part of Central Europe. For example, even if Serbia one day meets all these political criteria, it will not be part of Central Europe. It will still be in the Balkans.

The trouble is that, at the moment, these are not neutral statements. They are heavily charged: positively in the first case, negatively in the second. This is the danger in making any association of a geographical expression with a set of values or aspirations. It's a problem not just with "Central Europe," but with "Europe" (as in "European values") and "the West" (as in "Western civilization" or "Western values" contrasted with "Asian values").

Yet the difficulty lies precisely in the fact that this association with Central Europe (as with Europe and the West) is *not* completely arbitrary. There is some truth in it. There was a core and a periphery in European historical development. The difference between western Christianity—with its seminal separation of Church and state—and eastern Christianity—with its legacy of "Caesaro-Papism"—has deeply marked the political history of, say, France as opposed to Russia. And this truth is not just historical. It is also hard contemporary experience. As I was preparing to fly to Slovakia from Heathrow Airport, I met a banker of my acquaintance who travels extensively in CEE. He bluntly summed up his personal findings thus: "The further east and south you go, the more corruption and chaos."

The cardinal fault, it seems to me, is to turn probabilities into certainties, gray zones into lines between black and white, and, above all, working descriptions into self-fulfilling prophecies. We know, for example, that the following pairings will be difficult to achieve: Balkan tolerance, Ukrainian prosperity, Russian democracy, Turkish respect for human rights. But to suggest that these are contradictions in terms is not just to relativize our own values. It is also to betray the many, many people who are fighting for these things in these places, against the odds, and sometimes at the risk of their lives.

I have made the case for Central Europe over two decades. I believe it has been a good cause, which has helped to transform the central region of Europe for the better. But I am appalled at the way the idea has now been recruited into the service of these politics of relativism and exclusion. Whatever and wherever Central Europe is, it should never be part of that.

HELENA'S KITCHEN

ONE GLOOMY AUTUMN AFTERNOON IN 1980, A PALE, SHORT, slightly built woman, with untidy brown hair and intense gray-green eyes, greeted me at the door of her small apartment in one of the ugly new housing estates that the communist regime had thrown up around Warsaw. I was in Poland to witness the workers' revolution led by the Solidarity movement, the greatest challenge to the Soviet empire in Eastern Europe since its creation at the end of the Second World War, and I had been told that Helena Łuczywo would be a good source.

Her tiny kitchen, cloudy with cigarette smoke, was packed with people arguing, gesticulating, and laughing, pausing only for rapid sips of tea, drunk from glass mugs. In the living room, someone was laying out the next edition of a samizdat magazine called *Robotnik* ("The worker"), while a real, live worker from Gdańsk, birthplace of Solidarity, held forth in one corner. In another corner sat a pretty seven-year-old, Łucja, Helena's daughter. The phone was ringing—it seemed always to be ringing—and Helena picked it up, shouted into it, talked to me, took a drag on her cigarette, and giggled, all at the same time. Life in this crowded apartment was being lived at a mad tempo. Partly this was because there was a revolution on and at any minute Russian tanks might roll across Poland's eastern frontier. But mainly it was because this place was, well, Helena's.

I visited Helena's kitchen many times during the revolution, until, in December 1981, General Jaruzelski declared martial law to crush Solidarity. Then the authorities made it difficult for me to reenter the country. But whenever I could get a visa, I headed straight for Helena's—not telephoning beforehand, for fear of alerting the secret police, just turning up at the door. Poland was a police state again, and Helena was now running an underground paper covertly distributed among Solidarity members and supporters. Our conversations in the kitchen were interrupted by her colleagues—wan, intense women, dashing in with news of some crisis. But now, rather than shouting, they scribbled their messages on scraps of paper. Then they burned the paper in a candle while chattering loudly about something else, for the benefit of hidden police microphones.

Helena and I became firm friends, but I would never have imagined the development that has led me to write about her now. Today, she is the key figure behind the most successful newspaper in the whole of postcommunist Europe. *Gazeta Wyborcza* (The Electoral Paper), of which she is deputy editor and an executive-board member, sells more than half a million copies on weekdays and an additional two hundred thousand on the weekend. On its own custom-built web offset presses, it prints a full-color weekly magazine, a television guide, eighteen different local sections, and book, property, car, job, and computer supplements, plus acres of highly lucrative advertising. It employs more than 2,400 people. Its parent company, Agora, has invested in radio stations and satellite television.

This is a multimedia giant in the making—a Polish multimedia giant. And a hugely profitable one: so profitable that it is about to go public. Advised by Credit Suisse First Boston, Agora will soon be making an initial public offering on the Warsaw and London stock exchanges. Its senior managers will be wooing institutional investors in a road show through Europe and the United States. Estimates put its value as high as $600 million. Suddenly, my old friend Helena is a very powerful woman. She is about to be a rich one, too.

"The Electoral," as most people call it, has a distinctive style—sometimes abrasive, often sarcastic, always irreverent. The political line laid down by its editor in chief, Adam Michnik, is a source of constant and even venomous controversy. The nationalist right attacks the paper for being part of a conspiracy—a Jewish–ex-Bolshevik–capitalist conspiracy, you understand—that is sapping the moral fiber of a nation in which to be Polish should mean to be Catholic. Others, such as *Trybuna*, the paper of the former communists, denounce "Adam Michnik's media cartel," screaming, "Agora builds an empire!" *Trybuna* has called for the company's radio and television interests to be referred to Poland's Anti-Monopoly Office—an ironic demand from what was once the central organ of the communist party.

I don't like everything about the new paper. But I do like the way it perfectly upends so many Western clichés about Poland as a nation of tall, drunken, bragging, mustachioed, male-chauvinist, anti-Semitic noblemen, making doomed cavalry charges against tanks. Or the old German jibe about *polnische Wirtschaft*, implying that "Polish economy" is a contradiction in terms. Or another cliché—meant to characterize the whole of postcommunist Europe—which has former communist apparatchiks raking in the millions while embittered former dissidents sit in freezing attics, wrapped in nothing but a blanket of woolly memories.

The truth is that Poland is rapidly and quietly building a normal consumer democracy. It has a burgeoning middle class and one of the highest growth rates in Europe. It has started negotiations to enter the European Union and will join NATO in the spring of 1999. And near the heart of the Polish miracle is this hugely successful paper run by ebullient former dissidents, several of them Jewish and many of them women.

How do you write about someone who has become a close friend? Helena and I had our first formal "interview" seated in a quiet, modern conference room in the paper's Warsaw offices, talking over the Polish version of a light executive lunch—thick soup, then meat and potatoes. We both laughed at our predicament. There were so many basic things I didn't know. For example, when and where was she born?

During the first winter after the war, in Warsaw. Her father, Ferdynand Chaber, the son of wealthy Jewish wine merchants, had become a communist during the 1920s, spent the war in Russia, and returned after the Polish communists came to power on the back of

Russian tanks. He worked in the propaganda department of the new ruling party. The detail suggests an obvious conceit: "from the father's communist propaganda to the daughter's battle against communist propaganda." But Helena resists this fiercely. Her mother, she says, had been the more influential figure in her life.

Dorota Guter, who came from a family of Jewish small traders, was a model of industry, discipline, commitment—and deep Polish patriotism. She earned a university degree in law; when the Germans invaded, she fled to Russia, where she took a second degree, in engineering, and was reunited with her husband. On their return, she raised two children and held a position as a senior engineer at a car factory near Warsaw. At the same time—and this is so important—this determined Jewish mother was deeply immersed in the Polish Romantic tradition represented by poets such as Adam Mickiewicz, the Polish Byron.

Helena was brought up to think of herself as simply Polish. That proved to be difficult. In 1968, while she was studying economics at Warsaw University, she experienced a revolting anti-Semitic campaign orchestrated by communist leaders. Week after week, the communist press was full of tirades against rootless cosmopolitans, parasites on the Polish nation. Polish Jews were denounced as "a gallery of traitors." When Warsaw students protested, some were beaten up and others imprisoned, including Adam Michnik, one of their leaders. Most of Poland's surviving Jews—few enough already, after the Holocaust—left the country as a result, and those who stayed were marked for life. Yet the experience also shaped an extraordinarily dynamic generation of Polish '68ers, both Jewish and non-Jewish activists, so similar in some ways to Western '68ers (informal dress and lifestyle; much drink, sex), so different in other, more important ways. Many came to revere an older generation of fighters against communism, whom their Western counterparts tended to abhor, and, while permanently immunized against utopian politics, they found ideals worth suffering and even dying for.

The year 1968 formed Helena's generation, but her own personal moment of truth came later. She went on to complete her degree in economics, worked in a bank for three years, got married to a bearded engineer named Witold, and gave birth to Łucja. Then she went back to Warsaw University to study English, intending to be a translator and interpreter: set fair, it seemed, for an ordinary, unpolitical, life. But in the summer of 1976, a message reached her from an opposition leader, Jacek Kuroń. She had good English, so would she accompany a Swedish television team to interview persecuted workers in the industrial town of Ursus? She agonized for three days. She did not want to be a political activist. She was afraid of another anti-Semitic campaign. And what about her three-year-old daughter?

Finally, she decided to go. Why? She lights a cigarette, glances away for a second's thought, then says in her quick way, "Oh, I don't know. Just a sense of decency." Decency, Orwell's cardinal virtue. She doesn't stop to reconstruct the way she was then. Yet this was what in Poland is sometimes called "the Conradian moment"—that single personal decision that makes or mars a whole life. Conrad's Lord Jim jumped the wrong way when he abandoned what he thought was the sinking ship. Helena jumped the right way.

A year later, in 1977, she joined a group of friends—'68ers all—to start the samizdat paper that I found her producing when I visited her three years later. The first issue of Robotnik—the title was taken from a famous paper edited by the Polish independence hero Józef Piłsudski before the First World War—appeared that September: four letter-size sheets of paper, with smudged print on one side only. Helena was among those who insisted that its opening editorial should express a clear commitment to the ultimate goal of Polish independence. With Leonid Brezhnev still in power in the Kremlin, that seemed like aiming your bicycle at Mars. But the romantic tradition taught that politics is the art of the impossible. As Byron put it, in lines memorably translated into Polish by Adam Mickiewicz:

> For Freedom's battle once begun,
> Bequeath'd by bleeding Sire to Son,
> Though baffled oft is ever won.

Or, in this case, bequeathed by reading mother to daughter.

More immediately, she discovered the first requirement of being an editor: saying no. She remembers one article that her colleagues thought they should print because it was by a friend. She read it. It was no good. She told the author so and spiked it. *Basta*—an editor is born. The style they developed in this and other publications connected with KOR, the Workers' Defense Committee, was short, sharp, factual, colloquial. Friends jokingly referred to it as the "popgun" style. (In Polish, a popgun is a "corky"—*korkowiec*—thus making a pun on KOR.) Partly this was a conscious reaction against the bloated Newspeak of the communist media. Partly it was because the magazine had so little space. Partly, I think, it was because they just wrote the way they spoke: bang, bang, bang.

The "printing" of that first issue was done on an ancient duplicator, three hundred copies rolled from a revolving drum covered in blue ink. Later editions were produced by a homemade process involving a wooden frame and an inked silk-screen across which a squeegee was run by hand. Despite frequent harassment by the secret police, the paper's print run grew; by early 1980, they were distributing twenty thousand copies. In August of that year came the Solidarity revolution, and for sixteen months the paper was produced without fear of immediate police action. Since she also ran a news agency for the movement, Helena scarcely slept.

Then, on 13 December 1981, everything changed with General Jaruzelski's declaration of a "state of war." That night, as army and police patrols arrested Solidarity members on Warsaw's snow-covered streets, Helena went into hiding. Within two months, she and her colleagues had organized twenty hidden printing places—a small offset press in a cellar, a duplicator in an attic, an old silk-screen machine pressed back into service—and were publishing a new underground paper for the Warsaw region of Solidarity: *Tygodnik Mazowsze* (The Mazovia Weekly). Many of the staff were women. They puttered around the city in their tiny Fiat 126 cars, with samizdat in the trunks, benefiting from the male chauvinism of the police. For how could a pale young woman, with a small child, in a little Fiat, be any threat to the manly police state? The publication, with the jumbly red Solidarity logo on its masthead (and a quotation from the union's leader, Lech Wałęsa, "Solidarity will not allow itself to be divided or destroyed"), continued to appear regularly for seven years, until 1989, with print runs eventually as high as sixty thousand copies.

Helena remembers this time as awful and exhausting. Although she no longer had to spend her whole life in hiding, everything to do with the paper had to be conspiratorial. The experience, she says, was "insufferable"—especially with a young daughter to look after. Her marriage disintegrated. Most of her energy was spent on dodging the police. And there was "no perspective": She did not know—none of us knew—that it would all end in 1989. As far as she could see, it would go on and on and on.

One spring day, she found herself walking past someone's allotment garden and looking at it almost longingly. What the hell was she doing with her life? Would she end up an isolated, fanatical activist, as her father had been as a communist before the war? After five years, she needed a break, and the communist authorities let her out to spend a year in the United States, as a "peace fellow" at Radcliffe College in Harvard. It took an effort to return to Warsaw and go back to the endless grind of underground work. But she carried on producing *Tygodnik Mazowsze* out of cussed loyalty. Loyalty to the great idea of Solidarity. Loyalty to the readers who went on buying the weekly. Loyalty, above all, to her own underground team.

Then, in 1988, after a new wave of Solidarity strikes, the political ground began to move. The Jaruzelski regime, encouraged by Mikhail Gorbachev, sought dialogue with Solidarity, and, early the next year, all parties sat down to negotiate at a "Round Table"—a model that was later imitated in Hungary, East Germany, and Czechoslovakia. By April 1989, they had agreed that elections should take place, that the opposition would participate, and that it should have a newspaper for the election campaign. Lech Wałęsa asked Adam Michnik to be its editor, and Michnik, in turn, asked Helena and her team from *Tygodnik Mazowsze* to run it. Michnik, that is, would be the public, political head of the paper; Helena would actually get the thing out.

There was very little time. The elections were set for 4 June 1989. With scarcely eight weeks to go, a limited company, Agora, was formed to publish the new paper (its founding shareholders—there were twenty-four—included the film director Andrzej Wajda and the Solidarity leader Zbigniew Bujak). A month later, the first issue appeared, with an editorial declaring that its editors wanted to produce a "normal" newspaper. It seems now such a modest ambition, but the country had not known a normal newspaper for more than forty years. The newspaper, its editors promised, would be "multifaced, quick, objective"—and, most important, it would clearly separate commentary from news.

Yet this first issue was openly partisan. In tabloid format, it carried a front-page appeal to its readers to vote for Lech Wałęsa, beneath a large photograph of him. On the masthead was the slogan that I had so often heard protesters chant in the streets: "*Nie ma wolności bez Solidarności.*" "There's no liberty without Solidarity." And six of the paper's eight pages were filled with potted biographies of what it called "our candidates" for parliament. In fact, for the first couple of years, *Gazeta Wyborcza* was still a long way from its proclaimed ideal of a "normal" newspaper: fact sacred, comment free. Its news stories could be selective and sarcastically partisan. Critics punned that the paper was not "The Electoral" but "The Selectoral" (*Wybiorcza* rather than *Wyborcza*).

In those early days, its poor-quality paper and print made it look very much like the old communist papers—not surprising, since it was actually printed on the same press as the communist party daily *Trybuna Ludu*. Adam Michnik had to wrangle with communist leaders to get the paper that was needed. The type was set up in lead, by hand; the typesetters drinking vodka by the liter and suffering from lead poisoning. Upstairs at the print shop sat the censor. Once, during the election campaign, I asked Helena if I could take a cartoon up for approval. I found a frumpy woman in a cheap floral dress, with a glass of tea and a cigarette hanging from her lip, who examined the cartoon carefully and then signed it on the back.

Its first editorial office, at 19 Iwicka Street, was a former nursery school. It still had low tables and child-sized chairs. On warm days, editorial meetings were held around a sandpit in the garden. When I visited the office shortly before the elections, I found an atmosphere of creative chaos, with people dashing about amid plumes of cigarette smoke, shouts, laughter, crying, and telephones ringing all over the place—Helena's apartment writ large. The underground veterans of *Tygodnik Mazowsze,* who came to be known internally as "the Mazovians," were joined by a few distinguished journalists from other camps and by a rapidly growing band of the very young. Helena would sit with them at the nursery-school desks, like a schoolteacher, and show them how to write a news story.

"The Electoral Paper" was the organ of the Solidarity opposition in the first free election in Poland for more than fifty years. How much did it contribute to Solidarity's victory? It's an open question. The Poles had more than enough reasons to vote out the communists after so many years of unelected misrule. But the paper contributed decisively to the next step: the appointment of a noncommunist prime minister—the first in Eastern Europe since 1948 —and the installation of General Jaruzelski as president, to reassure Moscow. It was the paper that first suggested this. In a characteristic division of labor, Michnik wrote the editorial advancing the radical proposal; Helena thought up the historic banner headline YOUR PRESIDENT, OUR PREMIER. His article, her headline. With interventions like this, *Gazeta Wyborcza* wrote itself into the history of Poland's negotiated revolution, rather as the Spanish newspaper *El País* had done during Spain's transition from dictatorship to democracy.

Like so many revolutionaries before them, Solidarity's leaders began fighting among themselves soon after their triumph. In the aftermath of this "war at the top," as Wałęsa described it, the official Solidarity leadership told the paper to remove from its masthead the familiar red logo and the slogan "There's no liberty without Solidarity." There was not much solidarity left now that liberty had arrived. In an election in late 1990, Lech Wałęsa stood for president against his own former adviser, Tadeusz Mazowiecki. The paper backed Mazowiecki, but Wałęsa won.

It was high time to do what they said in the first issue they would do: make a "normal" newspaper. The editors moved out of the nursery school and took over two floors of a nearby office building. Today, those offices do look, at first glance, much like those of a normal Western paper: modern, open plan, highly computerized, with a cool aesthetic of pale blues and grays, so unlike the strident red, white, and black of the years of struggle. And yet they aren't. Helena shares a cramped office at the end of the newsroom with another senior editor. Both have small modern desks rather like something you might buy for a teenage daughter. Casually dressed journalists crowd into this small room for the afternoon conference, standing in the doorway or sitting on the floor. No instructions are barked from the head of a long editorial conference table. Instead, people argue to and fro through the cigarette smoke, with Helena joining in from her little desk. If I half close my eyes I can almost imagine myself back in Helena's old kitchen.

But insiders warn me that appearances can deceive. When I use the word *egalitarian* to describe the ethos of the paper, one of them exclaims, "Egalitarian shmegalitarian! You should see the way Helena talks to an intern." She can lose her cool and bawl out older colleagues. There's a toughness there that I, as a friend, may not have seen. I ask Helena if she feels that her new power has changed the way people relate to her. She reflects for a moment and says, "Well, perhaps a little, yes." I'm afraid it may be a little more than she thinks. Another insider, who preferred not to be named (and that in itself was revealing), told me that younger members of the editorial staff go in fear of her. Several talented journalists have left after arguments. Most painfully, she has ceased to be friends with two of her closest associates from the underground resistance team—those pale, intense women I remember dashing into the old kitchen and burning messages in a candle flame. It's an old story: together under oppression, divided in freedom.

Everyone but everyone says that the whole editorial side of the paper revolves around Helena. The only person to dispute this is Helena herself. She is there from morning to night and is renowned for going over pieces line by line. Even close friends sometimes don't have her private number, because you can always reach her at the office. And she likes other people to be there, too. I was told that one afternoon word got about that Helena had gone out for a few hours to the beautician. Within twenty minutes, the office had emptied. Even if not literally true, the story expresses a deeper truth.

WHAT IS the paper like now? The offhand, mildly sarcastic tone persists. It's a tone that is impatient, even contemptuous, of an older, stuffier, conservative, Catholic, nationalist Poland, for which Warsaw slang has the delightful term *bogoojcžyniany*—roughly "god-fatherlandized." ("Mrs. Z is very nice, but a little god-father-landized.") The tabloid-format paper's front page still carries its short, lively, "popgun-style" stories. Picking up a copy at random, I find the headline FED TNIE STOPY—that is, FED CUTS RATES. (Ten years ago, most Poles would not have known what the Fed was, let alone cared about its rates.) There are high-quality color photographs—in this copy, the lead picture is of a new Renault car. And there are short items flagging the longer stories inside. But these inside news stories are still written in a sharp, readable style. When I've been interviewed by journalists from the paper, I have found that my sentences get chopped up into short, snappy ones, so I started sounding like one of them: bang, bang, bang. There is strong foreign coverage and—reflecting the country's rapid advance to capitalism—a growing amount of business news. And it has excellent reportage, often written by young journalists on the regional supplements, who track down stories of local corruption, mafias, the drug scene, and so on.

In the weekend edition, there are long essays—about history, the Polish Catholic Church, Polish-Jewish relations, developments in other postcommunist countries—of the kind more usually found in intellectual monthlies and quarterlies. It's like having *The New York Review of Books* in the center pages of a tabloid newspaper. Finally, there is the personal contribution of the editor in chief, Adam Michnik, who sets the political line. His sharply written, signed commentaries have provoked fierce protest even from his own staff—as when, in the middle of the 1995 presidential campaign, he seemed implicitly to give his support to the postcommunist (and ultimately successful) candidate Aleksander Kwaśniewski, against none other than Lech Wałęsa. He was also one of very few people in Poland to criticize, albeit from a position of profound respect, some of the statements made by the pope on his last visit to his native land.

WANDA RAPACZYNSKI explained to me the commercial strategy of what the rest of the Polish press enviously calls "Agoraland." Wanda is the paper's business supremo. She and Helena were childhood friends and attended the same secondary school. Wanda left Poland after the anti-Semitic campaign in 1968 and, at the age of twenty-one, moved to the United States, where she studied to be an academic psychologist, married, had a daughter, then went to the Yale School of Management and worked for Citibank in New York before Helena persuaded her to return.

The company had to grow and diversify, Wanda said—accounting for the business's expansion into radio and television. It needed to protect itself against a possible future recession, in which advertising revenues might slump. Advertising—which until 1989 rarely featured in any Polish periodical—now accounts for more than 70 percent of the paper's revenue: the kind of healthy ratio that you'd expect to find in any British or American publication. Anyway, to diversify was simply "the law of the market." But where to find the capital? "My borrowing capacity far exceeds the lending capacity of any Polish bank." Hence the decision to go public. But, before doing so, they had to restructure the company.

The paper is no stranger to foreign investors. In the heroic early days, it had help from Western friends. The French newspaper *Libération* sold a special issue on the paper's behalf. *Le Monde* donated an old printing press, and a group of American supporters, including Robert Silvers and Rea Hederman of *The New York Review of Books,* lent money to transport the press from France. Although that press was never actually used, it served as useful collateral for loans from Polish banks. (So much have things changed that a couple of years ago the paper got a letter from *Le Monde* asking if *Gazeta* would now like to invest in it.) The editors found a substantial American private investor, Cox Enterprises, and they obtained an $8.5 million loan from the European Bank for Reconstruction and Development.

Until recently, the company was a business anachronism, a financial world's wonder: worth millions of dollars, but without any clear owner. It had twenty-four founding shareholders but, true to the idealistic collective spirit in which it had begun, their shares had no financial value. What was to be done? Finally, they came up with a solution that creates two kinds of stock: special voters' shares, called

A shares, which protect the company from hostile takeovers but cannot be traded, and B shares, which can be traded and will soon have substantial financial value. The three members of the executive board, Helena, Wanda, and the thirty-nine-year-old publisher, Piotr Niemczycki, together with one other editor and a senior manager, control the A shares. The five of them also own B shares, along with ninety-five others. In addition, there is a stock-purchase scheme for 1,700 employees, and an annual incentive plan will reward managers and journalists with further stock. "Hardly a case of heartless, cold capitalism," comments Wanda.

Yet however liberal, meritocratic, and broad-based they have tried to make the dividing of the cake, the fact is that in a few years some of those involved in the paper will be very much richer than the others. Seriously rich, by Polish standards. I'm told people already have plans to buy new apartments. "I worry about the day when department heads start arriving in their new BMWs," one younger journalist told me. What will happen then to the casual, informal, still outwardly egalitarian atmosphere of the paper? And, in this capitalist multimedia giant, what place is there for the trade-union movement whose organ "The Electoral Paper" originally was? Not much, it would appear.

I ask Helena if there is a Solidarity branch in the paper. No, there isn't. And she is unapologetic: "I'm not going to pretend to you that it's in my interest, as an employer, to have a Solidarity branch here." But she says the paper is an exemplary employer, giving generous work conditions and benefits. The story is complicated by the fact that Solidarity has now become a movement of the political right. It led a coalition of right-wing parties called Solidarity Electoral Action that won the 1997 election, promising, among other things, more state help for workers. Helena, by contrast, is a vehement supporter of the free-market liberalism of the Freedom Union, itself born of the Solidarity movement of the 1980s.

When I first sent her a note about this essay, I recalled how years ago I had described her as "the Rosa Luxemburg of Solidarity"—an allusion to the early-twentieth-century left-wing Polish-Jewish-German revolutionary. She wrote back, "I am Thatcher now, not RL any more." Later, as we talked in Helena's apartment, Adam Michnik teasingly remarked that what she likes about Margaret Thatcher is the "strong woman." She retorted that what she really admires is the way the "Iron Lady" revived Britain's moribund economy by tough, neoliberal economic policies. Just as she admires the way the Polish economy was transformed after 1989 by the neoliberal "shock therapy" of Leszek Balcerowicz, now leader of the Freedom Union. Nonetheless, she insists the paper is still true to the broader ethos of the original Solidarity, with its goals of democracy, civil liberties, and human rights.

Meanwhile, one person who won't have the awful problem of deciding what to do with all the money is Adam Michnik. He has flatly declined to take any shares at all. In effect, he has just turned down a million dollars. He told me that his intellectual independence and editorial judgment might be jeopardized if he was always thinking, "What might this do to the value of the shares?"

So no one can now credibly accuse Adam of heading the paper for personal gain—which doesn't mean they won't still try to. As people realize just how rich and powerful Agora has become, the Jewish theme may reemerge in the right-wing press—since Adam, Helena, and Wanda are all of Jewish origin—with implicit, if not explicit, use of some classic stereotypes. Helena thinks this subject of Polish-Jewish tensions is often greatly overplayed in the West. But she is the first to accept that the relationship is still far from normal.

The continuing tensions are illustrated by one small regular feature in the paper. In a supplement called "Supermarket," they publish a long list of helplines: AIDS, drugs, suicide, and so on. At the end of the alphabetical list appears "Żydowski" ("Jewish")—"telephone of the Jewish Forum for people who have problems with Jewish origins." Ring 652-2144 on a Thursday evening.

Normal this isn't. But the new Poland for which the paper stands is precisely one in which people can be Jewish Poles or Catholic Poles or agnostic Poles or Protestant Poles or Ukrainian Poles; white, black, or brown Poles. Here is the great battle that runs through the Polish—and the European—twentieth century: the battle between a narrowly ethnic nationalism and a broader civic patriotism. Even if *Gazeta Wyborcza* has not always managed to practice the tolerance that it preaches toward those who live or think differently, at least it has always preached it.

I FIND MYSELF wondering where the paper, and Poland, will be in another ten years. Both have traveled such a vast distance toward a Western-style "normality" over the last decade and traveled it so exuberantly and so well. Yet still, at every turn, you find some Polish peculiarity. Will these peculiarities, too, gradually disappear? Will the editorial mix become more like that of any other Western paper, with more entertainment and fewer ideas? Perhaps in the new editorial building they are currently planning, to cost an estimated twenty-five million dollars, there will be large offices and desks, and men in suits and ties barking orders from the end of long conference tables. But perhaps this new Poland will also be a place where, at long last, people can be Jewish Poles as they can be Jewish Americans.

Must the gains and losses always balance out, like entries in an accountant's ledger? More prosperity, less equality. More freedom, less intensity. More tolerance, less solidarity.

I would like to think that some positive singularities will remain. But if I had to lay a wager, I would bet that they will go. The pressures of a Western consumerist, entertainment model of "normality" may prove more difficult to resist than those of the Soviet-type communist "normalization" that Solidarity so roundly and unexpectedly defeated. Perhaps this is the last irony of freedom's battle: The compulsory could be defied, but the voluntary may be irresistible.

CHRONOLOGY

1999

11 MARCH. *Oskar Lafontaine resigns as German finance minister and leader of the SPD.*

12 MARCH. *Poland, Hungary, and the Czech Republic formally join NATO at a ceremony in Independence, Missouri.*

15 MARCH. *Kosovo peace talks resume in Paris rather than Rambouillet.*

16 MARCH. *The whole European Commission under Jacques Santer resigns after a damning independent report on its corruption and mismanagement.*

19 MARCH. *Kosovo peace talks in Paris end with Kosovar Albanian delegation signing but Serb side refusing to sign the agreement.*

23 MARCH. *NATO gives order to bomb Serbian military targets after special envoy Richard Holbrooke fails to persuade Slobodan Milošević to accept the Rambouillet agreement.*

23–25 MARCH. *At an informal summit in Berlin, EU leaders agree to nominate former Italian prime minister Romano Prodi as president of the European Commission and discuss the outlines of a budget for 2000 to 2006.*

24 MARCH. *NATO bombing campaign ("Operation Allied Force") begins against targets in Kosovo, Serbia, and Montenegro, the first time in its fifty-year history that NATO has attacked a sovereign state. Serbian forces conduct a campaign of terror and "ethnic cleansing" in Kosovo that results in the flight of some one million Kosovar Albanians.*

14 APRIL. *Misdirected NATO bombing attack kills more than fifty refugees in a convoy.*

19 APRIL. *The German Bundestag meets for the first time in the restored Reichstag building in Berlin.*

23–25 April. *NATO's fiftieth-anniversary summit in Washington is dominated by the Kosovo war.*

6 May. *Elections to new parliamentary assemblies in Scotland and Wales. The G8 (the G7 countries plus Russia) agree on general principles for ending the Kosovo war.*

7 May. *NATO bombs the Chinese embassy in Belgrade, by mistake.*

21 May. *The Clinton administration suggests increasing the size of the proposed Kosovo peacekeeping force to fifty thousand.*

War over Kosovo

"I'll tell you the truth," says the Kosovar newspaper editor. "They really don't know." We are sitting in Tetovo, Macedonia, in the Café Arbi, where the exiled intellectuals of Priština meet the world. *They* in this comment are not the intellectuals but the KLA commanders still in Kosovo, to whom Baton Haxhiu talks daily by satellite phone. Besieged on their hilltops, they can see a burning village here, a Serb patrol there, a tank at a crossroads, but they have no overall picture. Yet a large proportion of NATO's bombing targets in Kosovo come from this same source: from the KLA commanders, via satellite phone. So *they* is also NATO.

We ordinary mortals imagine that NATO, with its almost godlike technology, its satellite cameras that can see an ant at ten thousand miles, its secret special forces reportedly deployed inside Kosovo, must really know. Then they bomb the Chinese embassy. Of course, we can piece together, from thousands of individual stories, a picture of the terror that has probably driven more than a million Kosovars from their homes since the bombing started. But we don't know what is happening on the ground right now. We don't know the combat readiness, fuel and ammunition supplies, communications, and morale of the Serb forces.

Similarly, we have numerous excellent reports from Belgrade. I talk by phone and e-mail to friends and acquaintances there. We know what they are saying. But we don't know what is really happening inside the Milošević regime: between the military, the police, the business kleptocracy, and, not least, him and his wife. And even they don't know what is going to happen next.

War, like love, changes everything. The beginning of wisdom is to realize that, behind those confident pronouncements of our generals, prime ministers, and presidents, nobody knows. Still, there are a few things that can be said after two months of this war about its causes, its course, and even its consequences.

1

The long-term origins lie in a struggle that dates back at least 120 years, to the time of the Congress of Berlin and the League of Prizren—a struggle between Serbs and Albanians for control of this European Palestine. This is probably its last, decisive battle. Now, as then, outside powers will decide who wins.

The medium-term origins lie in a decade of appeasement by the West of an evil postcommunist politician who has exploited Serbian nationalism to bring power and riches to himself and his family. As they end, the 1990s remind us of Auden's "low, dishonest decade"— the 1930s. Milošević is not Hitler, but the basic pattern of appeasement is comparable: The longer you wait, the higher the price. Hitler should have been stopped when he remilitarized the Rhineland in 1936; Milošević, at the siege of Vukovar in 1991.

There are many Neville Chamberlains in this story. One is certainly William Jefferson Clinton. Washington's fierce rhetoric has been accompanied by feeble deeds. In the Balkans, Clinton has inverted Theodore Roosevelt: He speaks loudly and carries a small stick.

As a European, I prefer to dwell on the beam in our own eye rather than the mote in our transatlantic brother's. After all, this is a conflict in Europe. The Kosovo war supports an argument I have made throughout the decade: The leaders of Western Europe set the wrong priorities at the end of the cold war. Instead of seizing the chances and recognizing the dangers that arose from the end of communism in half of Europe, they concentrated on perfecting the integration of the western half. They put Maastricht before Sarajevo. Now we are paying the price.

The immediate origins of the war lie in a major miscalculation by the leaders of the West. They took too literally Clausewitz's famous saying that war is the continuation of politics by other means. Misled by the Bosnian precedent, they thought they could bomb Milošević into accepting a version of the Rambouillet deal for Kosovo. Some of those leaders expected a tough military and police action by Milošević against the KLA and supporting civilians, in response to bombing. None expected the scale, speed, and brutality of what he did.

Of course, it's easy to be wise after the event. The only people I know who actually forecast this horror are politicians from former Yugoslavia. Last September, I remarked to President Milan Kučan of Slovenia, "but surely Milošević can't 'ethnically cleanse' 1.8 million people?" He looked at me quizzically and replied, "You don't know Milošević." Early last year, President Kiro Gligorov of Macedonia called for a "corridor" to bring large numbers of Kosovar Albanian refugees through his country to Albania. Now, in Skopje, I asked him why he had seen this coming. The shrewd old man looked at me and shrugged, as if to say, "Wasn't it obvious?"

Well, it was not obvious to us who live in a more normal world. I, too, did not anticipate it. But what we can fairly hold against NATO is that it did not plan for this contingency. After all, that's what a political-military alliance is meant to do: plan for contingencies, even remote ones. Since then, the action has patently gone wrong. Let me be clear. I more than accept the end. I believe it had become imperative to threaten force so as to get a new dispensation for Kosovo. When the threat failed, NATO was fully justified to use force in and over Kosovo. But the means chosen have compromised the end. To conduct the campaign entirely from the air, and that mainly at fifteen thousand feet; to conduct it increasingly by bombing civilian infrastructure in Serbia proper—bridges, roads, railways, factories, the TV station—rather than destroying Serb forces in Kosovo; this has been disastrous.

Why have we chosen the means of an aerial war against Serbia proper? First, we were not prepared for any other sort of war, and hardly even for this one. Second, it turns out that with all our godlike technology, we can't find Serb tanks hiding in garages, let alone paramilitaries who stop over in a different Albanian house every night; so Milošević has been winning in Kosovo itself. Third, the president of the United States is not prepared to risk a single casualty in this conflict and will not even send a significant number of ground troops to neighboring countries to increase the pressure on Milošević, let alone actually use them. Clinton's emotional comment on the three captured U.S. soldiers—"We look after our own people"—unintentionally says it all. So the bombers fly at fifteen thousand feet, and, inevitably, their bombs sometimes hit the very civilians they are meant to be saving.

2

The list of disastrous consequences is long. First and foremost, most of the Albanians who live in Kosovo have been kicked out of their homes; many have lost everything; young women have been raped, men killed. It is wrong to call this a holocaust, but it is, together with the events in Bosnia, the most terrible single thing to have happened in Europe in fifty years. It is wholly comparable with Hitler's and Stalin's forced deportations of whole ethnic groups—Poles, Estonians, Crimean Tartars—and with the postwar expulsions of the Germans from Eastern Europe.

On a plane to Skopje, Blerim Shala, a member of the Kosovar delegation at Rambouillet, tells me about his own perilous trek to Macedonia: Ordinary Serb soldiers shared their hunks of bread with the Albanians and even promised to protect them from the marauding paramilitaries. Then he starts explaining the topography of deportation, as whole cities were transported to different frontiers. "Priština went to Macedonia," he says. "Prizren went to Albania." Incredible sentences. As if one said, "Washington went to Mexico" or "Paris went to Spain."

Moreover, this was precipitated by NATO's bombing. Certainly, Milošević had driven something like three hundred thousand Kosovars out of their homes the year before. Clearly, what is apparently called "Operation Horseshoe" had been planned in advance. But elementary logic indicates that we cannot know what would have happened if we had not started bombing. What we do know is that the

Serb action escalated dramatically as soon as the air campaign began.

Standing in front of his tent (sixteen people sleeping in a space the size of an average living room) at the Stenkovec 2 refugee camp in Macedonia, Jusuf Mustafa, a once prosperous building contractor, told me how he and his family had gone out onto the balcony of their home to applaud the first NATO bombs. Within fifteen minutes, the Serbs started throwing grenades into their neighborhood. A few days later, the whole family was driven out at gunpoint. His story stands for many. This is not to say that NATO was wrong to bomb. It is to say that the West now has a direct responsibility for getting these people back to their homes.

With the mass expulsion, Milošević almost certainly intended—I say "almost certainly," for who knows what really goes through that poisoned mind?—to spread havoc by destabilizing the neighboring countries. NATO fights with bombs; he uses civilians. He has very nearly succeeded. Albania, already in a state of near anarchy, has been swamped by close to half a million dispossessed compatriots. Montenegro, a country of some 600,000 people hosting more than 60,000 Kosovar expellees, struggles bravely to keep its half independence from Serbia. And I saw firsthand what the war has done to Macedonia.

This small, poor country of just two million people has been shaken to its foundations. Its economy is in shock, since 20 percent of its exports went to Serbia and more depended on trade routes through Serbia. Meanwhile, it has—slowly, reluctantly, often with low-level police brutality—taken in more than 230,000 expellees. It's as if the United States had to take in thirty million Mexicans.

Albanians already made up roughly a quarter of Macedonia's population. Suddenly, they are more than a third. Throughout the 1990s, the country has been plagued by ethnic tensions between the Albanians and the Slav Macedonian majority. In the mainly Albanian city of Tetovo, where many of the expellees are living with local families, I found an explosive situation. An acquaintance told me that Slav Macedonians have even received anonymous threatening telephone calls: "Get out of here, it's our city now, and NATO is behind us." Then, back in Skopje, a Kosovar refugee said that she was leaving because she had received threatening phone calls from Macedonians.

The political leaders of the Macedonian Albanians have so far displayed great restraint. "Milošević's aim is to destabilize Macedonia," Arbën Xhaferi of the Albanian Democratic Party explained, "so my priority is not to allow him to succeed." And President Gligorov insisted that his country is struggling to remain what is effectively the only functioning multiethnic state in former Yugoslavia. He emphasized that there is no significant history of ethnic conflict between Macedonians and Albanians, unlike between Serbs and Albanians. "If our forefathers were able to live together," he said, "why shouldn't we be able to?" But already there have been several nasty confrontations between Macedonian police and Albanian expellees. One big incident—perhaps an attempted breakout from a camp met by police shooting—and the tensions between Albanians and Macedonians could explode. So the reality behind that anodyne phrase "regional stability" is another Balkan country on the verge of collapse.

Meanwhile, in Serbia itself the NATO campaign has shot the legs out from under the small democratic opposition. These are the people I mostly talk or e-mail to, and they are in despair. It may not be true that the whole country has united behind Milošević, nor are they proud of what Serbia has done in Kosovo. Yet even the most pro-Western among them are furious at the bombing and the nations behind it—that is, us. These attitudes can change again after the war is over, especially if Milošević is defeated and seen to be defeated in Kosovo and only in Kosovo. But for now, this has been another calamitous effect.

Oh yes, and then NATO managed to infuriate one fifth of the world's population, who had nothing at all to do with the conflict, by bombing their embassy.

This is the balance sheet two months into the war. This is how NATO has celebrated its fiftieth anniversary.

3

How do we get out of this bloody mess? What is the minimum political objective upon which we must insist? The minimum is an international protectorate for the whole of Kosovo, to which the majority of those who have been expelled will both wish and feel safe to return. With each week that passes, the difficulty of achieving this increases.

The auspices for this protectorate should be those of the United Nations. To achieve that, you need the assent of two seriously offended permanent members of the security council, Russia and China. The conditions to which they would agree might not be those under which the majority of Kosovars would actually return. On the ground, a large international force would be needed to protect those returning. If Serbia proper were not defeated militarily and Milošević not replaced by someone more reasonable, then our troops would have to secure Kosovo's external security against a revanchist Serbia as well as its internal security against any remaining Serb soldiers, police, paramilitaries, and simply armed civilians. The Rambouillet agreement envisaged an implementation force of 28,000 troops. On 21 May, President Clinton proposed a NATO ground-force presence in neighboring countries of 50,000. Partly, of course, this is a (long overdue) threat of invasion, to put pressure on Milošević. But it is probably also a realistic estimate of the numbers that would now be needed, initially at least, to implement any new agreement.

Again and again, I asked the expellees in the camps what they would need in order to return. Their answers could be summed up in a single phrase: "no Serbs with guns." But if the Serbs are disarmed, what about the KLA, to whose colors young Kosovars in exile are now flocking? The KLA would surely flood back as the Serbs retreated, firing their Kalashnikovs in the air, as they did after the cease-fire agreement last October. And they would terrorize any remaining Serbs. If the place is to be halfway peaceful, the international force would need to make a stab at disarming them. But decommissioning a guerrilla army is a very difficult task, as we have seen in Northern Ireland.

Then, who would maintain law and order? A whole new police force would have to be created from scratch. Someone would have to train it. NATO soldiers say that is not a job they are either equipped or ready to do. Meanwhile, many people have no homes to go back to and no crops or cattle to see them through the winter. So a massive effort would be needed, first by the UNHCR, to put roofs over their heads and to feed them, then by governments and charities, probably coordinated by the EU, to reconstruct the infrastructure destroyed by Serb forces and by NATO bombs. "Kosovo is lost for me," one articulate exile exclaimed, "the place is just destroyed; it will take twenty years to rebuild it." Even if Milošević is defeated, we will still face the enemy called Despair.

To vanquish despair, the Kosovars will need their own political leadership. We talk all the time about the international framework. In the acronymic jungle of planning for peace, the OSCE is assigned the role now curiously called "nation building": supervising elections, building up democratic institutions, and so on. But what about the people whose homeland this is supposed to be? One voice that has been singularly missing over the last two months is that of Kosovo itself. We have heard the refugees and, as Hillary Clinton mawkishly put it, feel their pain. But the Kosovars have featured only as victims—as objects rather than subjects of history.

The trouble is that their political leadership is hopelessly divided. There is the pacifist president, Ibrahim Rugova, widely discredited by appearing on Serb television with Milošević while his people were being rounded up and killed. There's the "prime minister in exile," Bujar Bukoshi, who controls the money collected from Kosovo Albanians living in the West. There are the KLA commanders besieged in mountain pockets across Kosovo, and KLA leaders squabbling in Albania. Finally, there are the liberal intellectuals of Priština, now to be found at the Café Arbi in Tetovo, desperately looking for their new Havel or Mandela.

In one respect, and one only, Kosovo should be easier than Bosnia. In Bosnia, the international community is trying to maintain the semblance of a multiethnic state, but the reality on the ground remains one of ethnic partition. In Kosovo, the West must certainly strive to see that there is a place for innocent Serb civilians in a territory that holds so much Serb history. We must not ourselves become party to a revenge ethnic cleansing, as we were in the Croatian Krajina. But I fear that, in practice, all the Serbs will flee. As innocent Germans paid the price for Hitler's crimes after 1945, so innocent Serbs will pay the price for Milošević's crimes. Even if some of them stay and are given all possible minority rights, the combination of demography and democracy would mean that this would still be essentially an Albanian political entity. As a result, a viable home-grown polity could eventually develop under international tute-lage—in a way that is, alas, most unlikely ever to happen in Bosnia.

Eventually, it probably would become an independent state. The legal basis for its independence would be the very plausible claim that Kosovo was a constituent part of former Yugoslavia: the same basis on which Croatia, Slovenia, Macedonia, and the other re-publics of former Yugoslavia were recognized. So it would not set a dangerous precedent, let alone enunciate some universal right of ethnic self-determination: Catalonia for the Catalans, Ruthenia for the Ruthenians, Cornwall for the Cornish! But at the moment, the question of its formal status in international law is far less important than the reality on the ground. (Milošević knows this, too. After all, he rejected the Rambouillet agreement, although it gave him full, formal sovereignty.) Wise Kosovars acknowledge that a new Kosova (the Albanian spelling) will need international foster parents for a long time before it can walk on its own feet.

The Russians will have to be part of this international framework. They are an essential part of the solution. They are also part of the problem. The Kosovars don't trust them at all. "They are worse than the Serbs," one Albanian patriarch told me. "They are all Slavs," his son explained. If Russian soldiers stand at the frontier, refugees will be reluctant to go back. But there is a worse variant, which Milošević will almost certainly try for. This is a Russian zone of occupation in the north and east of Kosovo, where the mineral wealth and some of the main Serb monasteries are. What this would mean in reality is partition. Serbs would go to the Russian part; Albanians to the rest.

One has to be very clear about this: Such a "face-saving compro-mise" would be a defeat for NATO. As noted in earlier essays, even Serb nationalists have for several years been talking about partition as the only solution for Kosovo. It would also encourage Albanians to say: All right, if you, the West, are ready to accept the partition of Bosnia and Kosovo on ethnic lines, we will divide Macedonia on ethnic lines. It would be a disaster—and Milošević could plausibly claim victory, strengthening his hold on power.

The trouble with this war is that it is being fought in the wrong place. A war in Kosovo for Kosovo seems to me wholly defensible. A war fought—because of NATO's lack of contingency planning and the American paranoia about taking casualties—from the air over Serbia proper, against increasingly civilian targets, is much more difficult to defend.

What we should aim for is exactly the opposite: a situation in which, in Serbia proper, Milošević loses rather than gains popular support, while we at last do something effectual in Kosovo itself. The distinction between fighting for Kosovo and fighting against Serbia may seem a fine one—too fine for wartime—but it remains vitally important. Rather than bombing Serbian towns, we should be liberating Kosovan ones.

The key to doing this has all along been the presence of ground troops. With hindsight, we can see that we should have had substantial ground troops ready nearby before we started bombing. I referred earlier to NATO leaders being "misled by the Bosnian precedent." Many people still believe we bombed Milošević to the Dayton peace agreement. But that was possible only because we already had French and British troops on the ground—who could direct the bombs accurately to their targets, in a way that besieged KLA commanders with satellite phones obviously cannot—and because the Croatian army, trained by Americans, had changed the military balance against the Serb forces on the ground.

Some have suggested that we should have used the KLA in an analogous way. If you're not prepared to change the balance on the ground yourself, use the local barbarians to do it for you. But the Croatian army was at least the more or less regular army of a recognized, sovereign state. Even then, the horrible side effect was that we became party to the largest single act of ethnic cleansing until Kosovo: the expulsion of at least 150,000 Serbs from the Krajina in 1995. The KLA has, of course, never been the regular army of a sovereign state. Last year, it was still a ragtag, irregular, guerrilla army with some very wild local commanders. They made few distinctions between guilty and innocent Serbs. In the capitals of the West, people loosely say, "They are a bunch of drug dealers." Although some of the funding may have come from Kosovar drug dealing, a knowledgeable senior Western official comments wryly that "drug dealers is about the only thing they aren't." I think it would have been neither right nor militarily effective to arm and train them last year. And now? Well, we don't have the time. And then, thinking ahead to the protectorate, it would seem a very curious strategy to arm people today in order to disarm them tomorrow.

No, there is no alternative to doing it ourselves. We should have had the ground troops there at the beginning. We have wasted two months not building up a credible force. The deadline drew near for bringing in the necessary troops and equipment so we could go in opposed, if the worst came to the worst, and start getting the refugees back before the winter snows descend. Now, at last, President Clinton has been persuaded by the Pentagon and Tony Blair to go up to fifty thousand.

But Milošević has to believe that we are actually prepared to use them. No one ever won a fight by saying at the outset, "All right, I'll fight, as long as I never get hurt." Having seen British troops training to take casualties—with a realism that almost matched that in Steven Spielberg's *Saving Private Ryan*—I do not write these words lightly. To look after your own people is the first duty of a leader. Yet it is a perverted moral code that will allow a million innocent civilians of another race to be made destitute because you are not prepared to risk the life of a single professional soldier of your own. What are soldiers trained for? What kind of superpower is this? What kind of morality?

The irony is that if we had had the ground troops there in sufficiently impressive array at the beginning, we might never have needed to use them. Milošević has this, too, in common with Hitler and Stalin: His programmatic evil and strategic madness is mixed with supreme tactical realism. As the Romans knew, if you want peace, you must prepare for war.

4

In two months, we have learned or been reminded of some deeply sobering lessons. About the human capacity for evil. About the

Balkans. About the Clinton administration. About the United States, a superpower that believes in no-loss war. About NATO, the emperor who turns out to be naked in his high-tech birthday suit. Yet this is also a story of a European failure to deal with a European problem.

Talking to the European soldiers in Macedonia, I asked them whether European forces could, if it came to the worst, liberate Kosovo on their own? Well, they said, there was a problem with the transport of heavy armored divisions and with air support. But otherwise: Yes, in military terms we could do it. We have the men. We have the equipment. We have the money.

Isn't this just the kind of operation that has been discussed ever since the end of the cold war: European troops with NATO support? I doubt it will happen this time. German opinion has moved a very long way, but Chancellor Gerhard Schröder says it is "unthinkable" that German ground troops would participate in an invasion of a country that was last occupied by Hitler's Wehrmacht. His red-green coalition would fall apart if they did. The Italians are also unwilling. Britain and France alone would not be enough. But this should surely be a catalyst for the closer European defense cooperation that has been talked about for so long.

The countries of the European Union are bound to take a leading role in the economic and political effort to reconstruct not just Kosovo but the whole region after the war. Macedonia, Montenegro, Albania, and Bulgaria all need urgent help, especially if a fudged diplomatic solution means that a significant number of refugees decide not to return to Kosovo. Already, there is talk of speeding up EU enlargement (I'll believe that when I see it), and a conference has been summoned in Germany to discuss a "stability pact" for the Balkans—politely called "Southeastern Europe." At last, European policy makers are beginning to use some imagination about what the world's economic superpower—the EU—can do to prevent still more of its neighbors from descending into war and to rebuild those that have already gone through war. Writing, somewhat incongruously, in a British tabloid, *The Mirror*, Mikhail Gorbachev jeers that the war has shown Europeans their true place: "Yes, you are strong economically, but politically you are pygmies."

Will it help us to grow up? Heraclitus famously said that war is the father of all things. The experience of the Second World War was the father of the European Union as we know it today. Perhaps this war will lead us to start doing at the end of the decade what we should have done at the beginning: build a liberal order for the whole of Europe. Knowing Europe, I wouldn't count on it.

When Milošević caved in, just ten days after this essay was completed, some former critics of the bombing campaign threw up their hands and declared that they had been wrong. This heralded, they suggested, a new era of high-tech wars won from the air. Indeed, the victory was sudden, unexpected, and complete. It remains a challenge for historians to work out exactly why Milošević gave in when he did. But, while I patently did not expect this outcome so soon, I will not join that chorus of "we were wrong." For it remains true that a million Kosovars paid the price for NATO's failure to anticipate Milošević's reaction to the bombing and for the United States's insistence on waging the war without a single American casualty.

CHRONOLOGY

1999

27 MAY. *International War Crimes Tribunal in The Hague announces that it has indicted Slobodan Milošević and other Serbian leaders.*

3 JUNE. *Slobodan Milošević accepts the peace plan presented jointly by EU envoy Martti Ahtisaari and Russian envoy Victor Chernomyrdin.*

3–4 JUNE. *Cologne summit of EU. Javier Solana is appointed as the EU's first high representative for foreign and security policy. Agreement is reached on the outlines of a common defense and security policy and a "stability pact" for southeastern Europe.*

9 JUNE. *Yugoslav and NATO representatives sign a military-technical agreement on the withdrawal of Yugoslav forces from Kosovo. Romano Prodi presents his proposed new European Commission.*

10 JUNE. *UN Security Council Resolution 1244 approves international administration for Kosovo while reaffirming full Yugoslav sovereignty over it.*

10–13 JUNE. *Elections to the European Parliament. Low turnouts across Europe.*

11–12 JUNE. *Kosovo peacekeeping force (KFOR) enters Kosovo. Two hundred Russian troops arrive unexpectedly at Priština airport, having come from Bosnia via Serbia.*

18 JUNE. *Meeting of G8 in Cologne.*

20 JUNE. *Serbian forces complete their withdrawal from Kosovo.*

21 JUNE. *KFOR signs agreement with the KLA for its progressive demilitarization over a ninety-day period: "K-Day."*

2 JULY. *Bernard Kouchner, a French human-rights activist and founder of Médecins sans Frontières, is appointed head of the United Nations Interim Administration in Kosovo (UNMIK).*

RETURN TO KOSOVO

At half past six on a fresh summer morning, the voices of invisible nuns ring out from the Serbian monastery of Gračanica. This was the first place I ever visited in Kosovo, more than twenty years ago, and here, behind the high monastery walls, you can, for a moment, imagine that nothing has changed. Still the black-bearded priests in their white, red, and gold robes celebrate a never-changing God in the ancient, undulating chants. I recognize one of the nuns, who has a round, nut-brown face, and she gives me a serene smile.

But the visitors' book tells a different story. From 11 June, the day before NATO troops marched into the devastated province, a defiant inscription in Serbian declares, "Kosovo is the heart of Serbia and the monasteries are its soul." But now Kosovo is part of Serbia only in name. Day by day it becomes ever more Albanian and more international. "May peace return to Kosovo," reads an entry in English dated 20 June, "and the people live together in harmony and prosperity." Signed: Richard Cieglinski, KFOR—the acronym for the international military force whose tanks, armored cars, and soldiers you now see churning up every dusty, potholed road across the devastated land.

I came to Kosovo for the second time in the early 1980s. Albanian student protests had just been brutally suppressed, and the atmosphere was heavy with menace. I wrote an article entitled "Belfast in

Yugoslavia." Today, the troops who were then on the streets of Belfast have actually come to Kosovo. Everywhere, I hear the accents of London, Leeds, and Glasgow. Twenty years on, the once remote, exotic world of the other Europe and the familiar world of Britain have suddenly and surreally met.

There's a British KFOR post in the former Serbian police station close to the Gračanica monastery. "It's OK, they're English," shouts the guard to his mate as I approach with a colleague from *The Independent*. Stuart Watson, a young second lieutenant from 52 Battery, Royal Artillery, tells us how last night the senior churchmen from the monastery came to say that the people in this mainly Serb village were frightened by the sound of gunfire from the nearby capital, Priština. Lieutenant Watson tried to reassure them, and they went back to calm their flock. Since there are no ordinary police, the locals come to the KFOR soldiers to complain: "He stole my pig," "No, he nicked my radio!" There's still no civil administration in sight here, so British soldiers and Serbian priests try to run the place between them.

Everyone says the experience of Northern Ireland equips the British best of all the foreign troops for the job in Kosovo. A corporal of the Parachute Regiment who stands guard at the door to the Grand Hotel in Priština tells me it's like serving in Belfast—only better. There, in their own country, the Paras were spat at in the streets. Here, the Serbs look anxiously to them for protection, and the Kosovar Albanians greet them like heroes. Large graffiti on the facade of a nearby theater offer thanks to one "Tony Bler" and proclaim "God Save the Quin."

My next trip was in the spring of 1997. For eight long years, the Kosovars had organized entirely peaceful resistance against the Milošević regime, which in 1989 had stripped the province of its autonomy. But patience was running out. There were reports of a shadowy organization called the Kosovo Liberation Army, killing Serb police in the hills of the central region of Drenica. Yet friends in Priština warned me, "There are some seven hundred purely Albanian villages, so the people there could all be killed." When I was last here, in November, the KLA rising had met with brutal, utterly disproportionate repression; already there were miles of ruins, hundreds of thousands of the refugees, much blood in the snow.

Now I return to visit the places and the people I knew. In the meantime, they have been to hell and back. Or at least to Macedonia or Albania and back. You see the returnees on every road, trailers piled high with mattresses and children, the red-and-black Albanian flag flying from the tractor in front. Everyone I meet has some extraordinary tale of suffering and endurance. There are ten thousand novels here. Misery is a writer's gold mine.

Yet beyond the tragedy, I find a phlegmatic determination to rebuild, as well as a real sense of liberation: liberation not just from a few months of horror but from ten years of oppression by the Milošević regime. And, for those who see the longer perspective, from more than eighty years of living under Serbian rule. The Kosovar Albanians have suffered terribly, but most of them also feel that they have finally won.

Priština itself I find relatively undamaged. Every day, there are more people on the streets, and another café reopens. A surprising number of people stayed here throughout the bombing, though under extreme duress. Veton Surroi, the leading independent newspaper publisher, was in hiding the whole time—obsessively listening to radio news and watching satellite television: "BBC World was the best." I meet him on his way back from Holland, where he's just bought a new printing press for his paper. Professor Abdyl Ramaj, a small, charming, cultured man, survived in his own home, harassed constantly by Serb police and officials, who tried to persuade him to collaborate. He is exhausted, even traumatized, the words coming only slowly in half-forgotten French. But as I leave he stands on the verge, eyes sparkling again, and gives the V-for-victory sign.

To see the real destruction, you have to go into the countryside. So I steer my Russian-built jeep past the endless columns of KFOR military vehicles, along dirt tracks, and across makeshift bridges that replace the ones we bombed. The small town of Mališevo, in the heart of Drenica, was described by Richard Holbrooke as "the most dangerous place in Europe." When I went there last autumn, it was a ghost town, utterly destroyed, with heavily armed Serb police controlling the road into town. Graffiti on the walls boasted "Serbia to Tokyo" and "burning houses, beautiful houses." Now I find Albanians cheerfully cleaning out the police station. There's a market in the main street with vendors selling bottled water, some vegetables, fruit, and great piles of the real essential of Balkan life: cigarettes.

I visit a family that I had then found cowering in one cellar room of their ruined farmstead, terrified of the police. One brother was originally a schoolteacher, the other a bus conductor. The men survived the war in the woods, creeping down for food at night; their wives and children fled to Albania. When it was over, the schoolteacher walked for seven days and nights, crossing illegally into Macedonia, then into Albania, to fetch his family. How did it feel when they met? His hands go up: "It was the happiest moment of my life." They have just a few blankets between them. No food, no flour, no oil, no work. Only aid and a little money from relatives abroad. But they say they feel free—"so long as NATO is here."

In the town that Serbs call Peć and Albanians call Pejë, Selim Moriqi, a gnarled fifty-one-year-old woodcutter, sits in a wheelbarrow amid the ruins. He escaped to Montenegro, walking with his children through the snows. Another epic. The Serbs killed his uncle. His house is ruined, his woodcutting equipment stolen. His family of ten has received a little aid but not enough. So here he is, with his five-year-old grandchild, trying to make a few deutsche marks by selling, yes, cigarettes. So it goes on, tale after tale.

I track down the local KLA commander, Ramush Haradinaj, a man with a ferocious reputation. Still in uniform, he talks English with what I think must originally have been the Birmingham accent of an earlier English girlfriend, now modified by that of his present Finnish wife. He says "foighting" for *fighting*: "The nation is going to respect the time of this foightings."

Last autumn, I saw the fresh blood of two Serb policemen shot by Commander Ramush's men in the nearby village of Prilep, a flagrant violation of the cease-fire. Now I charge him with responsibility for it. His reply: "I hope it was more than only two." He was so happy to see dead police. After all, they had killed two of his own brothers. "Me," he remarks memorably, "I couldn't be no Mother Teresa."

Yet even Commander Ramush insists that he is committed to demilitarizing the KLA, although he would still like his best soldiers to form the nucleus of a Kosovo professional army. He is, in fact, brighter and less thuggish than I expected, and he even claims they can live together with innocent Serbs: "The Albanian people can forgive . . . in the time of Tito it was no trouble."

I drive on to Prilep. It is a collection of ruins, yet still the people are coming back. Last autumn, I visited a family in a still-intact house near the mosque. Now the mother, Gale Latifaj, stands before a pile of rubble that was once that house and weeps. Her husband is dead. Her eldest son, a KLA soldier, was killed fighting for Commander Ramush. Her youngest son has gone to try to find a tent from one of the aid organizations. Meanwhile, she has put a little water in a rusting can to heat in the midday sun, so she can wash, and carries bricks from the rubble, slowly, one by one, to build a shelter for the night. She is fifty-eight and looks about seventy.

Back in Priština, I talk to the political leader of the KLA, Hashim Thaci, formerly known as Commander Snake. In his slightly wooden Swiss German he says, "Freedom always has a price, but we have won." Of course, it's not people like him—now a budding young politician in jacket and tie, programmed for sound bites—but people like Mrs. Latifaj who pay the price.

YET THE WISE among the Kosovar Albanians recognize that the ultimate losers are the Kosovo Serbs. Most of them have fled already. Those who remain feel imperiled or live in ghettos. A Dutch tank stands guard at the entrance to the purely Serb village of Velika Hoča, in the KLA heartland. Local Serbs pathetically ask me if I could get them some tomatoes and water from the local town. They don't even dare to go shopping there. A large, blowsy woman named Snjezana complains, "We were told it would be UN control but now look at your badge"—and she seizes my KFOR identity badge—"it says NATO. I don't like people like you who come and look at us for fifteen minutes, as if we are animals in a zoo, then go away."

The town of Kosovska Mitrovica is effectively divided at the river Ibar, with Serbs dominating the northern part of the city, Albanians the south, and French troops on the bridge over the Ibar. I watch a bunch of Serbian men, wearing sunglasses and wooden crosses around their necks, line up to chant abuse at a few Albanian kids who venture halfway across the bridge. "We're waiting for the Russians to come here," one says. How does he know they are coming? "I heard it on the Voice of America."

However hard KFOR tries to persuade the Serbs and Albanians to live together, the Serbs are already reduced to tiny pockets in an essentially Albanian place. Suddenly, thanks to NATO, the tables are turned. The only authority the Serbs have left is the church. And church leaders are now saying out loud who is really to blame.

I seek out, as I always do, the exquisite monastery of Dečani, a medieval wonder nestled in the wooded foothills of the Accursed Mountains, on the border with Albania. When I have negotiated my way past the Italian armored car blocking the entrance, I am received by the black-robed and black-bearded abbot, Father Theodosius. Talking through young Brother Leonard, who speaks fluent English with a strong taste of the King James Bible, he says that during the war they "felt great injustice and great evil." Everything was wrong: While NATO bombed Serb civilians, Serbs wreaked vengeance on Albanian civilians. Many ordinary Serb soldiers came to unburden their heavy consciences to the monks.

So has Milošević lost Kosovo for Serbia? "He has not only lost Kosovo but completely destroyed his own people, physically and spiritually." This monastery will survive international rule, or Albanian rule, as it survived five hundred years of Ottoman rule. But the time of Slobodan Milošević will be remembered as the worst in the whole history of the Serbian nation. Brother Leonard translates: "It is not meet, in this sanctuary, even to mention that name."

THE PROTECTORATE

IN THE VILLAGE OF VELIKA HOČA—NOW A SERBIAN GHETTO GUARDED
by Dutch tanks—a woman called Snjezana jabbed an angry finger at
me. "I don't know where I live anymore," she said. "Is it Serbia? Is it
Yugoslavia? Is it . . . whatever?"

The correct answer is: whatever. In Kosovo, the so-called international community has embarked on an extraordinary adventure. We
are setting out to build a whole new state while pretending not to.
Even in Somalia or Cambodia, the UN never had a job as ambitious
and complex as this. Every aspect of the state has to be built literally
from ruins. Yet at the same time, because of the ambiguity of the
peace deal with Milošević and the subsequent UN Security Council
resolution, attention has to be paid to the continued formal sovereignty of the Federal Republic of Yugoslavia over the devastated
province.

It's a test case for post–cold war liberal internationalism. A war
justified as a humanitarian intervention leads to an international
protectorate, which in turn is supposed to end with a viable, self-
governing—um, er—something. How can it possibly work?

The job starts with the most elementary necessities of life: water,
shelter, food, electricity for heat and light. Crops have been destroyed. You see the severed heads of dead cattle along the roads.
Rubbish lies all over the place, stinking. It is not cleared, unless the
local NATO troops do the job. The troops are also getting the hospi-
tals working again. But soldiers can't go on doing these jobs. Civil-

ians have to take over. Here, in the essentials of life, we have one major ally: the hardiness and resourcefulness of the Kosovar Albanians. It's incredible, and moving, to see people who have lost their houses, their life savings, their equipment, cattle, everything, just starting over with a wry shrug of the shoulders. They're used to adversity.

But some of them are stealing what they need to rebuild their homes, and a few are killing Serbs in revenge. In early July, there were still virtually no civilian police—although in the northern town of Kosovska Mitrovica I did meet a spruce colonel of the French gendarmerie, fresh from Versailles. If you occasionally wonder why we need a state at all, you should visit a place like Kosovo that has none. This has advantages, of course. For example, you don't need to worry about speeding fines. But you can also get robbed or killed at night, and no one will take any notice.

Everyone agrees that the top priority at the moment is law and order, which means bringing in international civilian police and appointing judges to support them. Then local police are to be trained: The gendarme from Versailles or the bobby from Liverpool is to patrol the streets side by side with a local cadet. But what laws will they enforce? At the moment, the proposal is: the criminal code of the Federal Republic of Yugoslavia, modified by international human-rights conventions when Yugoslav law violates them.

Then there is the matter of schools for the children who currently line the roadside, selling cigarettes and giving the V-for-victory sign to any passing Westerner. And what about work for their parents? I was shocked to learn that, after three weeks, the UN administration still had no senior economic expert in place, for the economy is central to the prospects of recovery. Here, the problems deriving from the ambiguity of status are acute.

Cafés, restaurants, and shops may reopen easily enough, but most of the larger companies still have Yugoslav owners. Then, who will set and collect the taxes? And what about border controls and customs duties? (At the moment, the only control at the infamous Blace frontier crossing is by gum-chewing American soldiers.) And a currency? The deutsche mark is the universal unofficial tender. A restaurant owner turns up his nose when my companion offers Yugoslav dinars. A formal currency reform, such as in Bosnia, where the official currency is now the *konvertibilna marka* (exchange rate fixed at one KM to one D-Mark), would be the best thing for the economy. But wouldn't that tear away even the pretense of Yugoslav sovereignty?

Meanwhile, the newly reopened cafés of Priština are filled with handsome, idealistic, suntanned foreigners—earnest Danes, charming Chileans, quiet Americans. They hardly knew where Kosovo was six months ago; now they are running it. "Hello, we met in Rwanda," they greet each other, or "Weren't you with the OSCE in Kazakhstan?" Their byzantine, polyacronymic structures of international administration are to be superimposed on a "transitional council" of Kosovar Albanians and Serbs, with local consultative commissions for various practical aspects of reconstruction.

Beyond this formal, polit-bureaucratic pattern there is the informal, sometimes inspiring, often corrupting reality of interaction. The names of the military occupation force, KFOR, and the skeleton civilian administration, UNMIK, have already become Albanian and Serbian words. *UNMIK* is pronounced with a short *u*, as in *unpick,* and *KFOR* is pronounced *kufaw,* as in *guffaw.* Prices of any decent apartments soar. A whole local industry grows up servicing the internationals: restaurants, drivers, interpreters. Blerim Shala, editor of the leading Kosovar Albanian weekly *Zeri,* tells me he is having difficulty getting his journalists to come back to work for him, since they can all earn three times as much working as interpreters for international organizations. Some of the pretty girls among them will get married and start new lives in Stockholm, Paris, or a small town in Texas.

In the longer term, Kosovo simply can't work as a colony. The international architecture alone is far too complicated. There are endless disagreements and turf wars between the international organizations involved, starting with intense rivalries between the UN's own different agencies. There are even greater differences between the participating nation-states, including all those absurd matters of prestige. Thus, Britain has the military commander so France has to get the civilian governor—and poor old Kosovo is lumbered with a Bernard Kouchner. Meanwhile, the Americans are taking a whole street of houses for a fifty-strong embassy (sorry, nonembassy) to run the show from behind the scenes. Then, having all stuck their fingers in the pie, the major powers will all lose interest before the job is done, as domestic political priorities turn elsewhere.

The key to making this unprecedented experiment work therefore lies in enabling the Kosovars to govern themselves, as much as possible, as soon as possible. Full, formal independence is not the most urgent thing—that must and can wait until Serbia itself becomes more democratic and cooperative, and perhaps even longer. What matters is giving substance to those "democratic self-rule institutions" to which even Milošević has already agreed. One great advantage here, as against Bosnia, is that the vast majority of the population is of one nationality. Even special minority privileges for the few remaining Serbs—and there is, ironically enough, a case for such privileges—will not change that.

The great problem is the fissiparous nature of Albanian politics. Already, this small territory with fewer than two million people has one unofficial president, two unofficial prime ministers, and at least five political parties or protoparties. (Another one was founded, or relaunched, while I was there.) For the Kosovars themselves, this is a historic test. There is a real danger that they will prove incapable of governing themselves in a halfway organized, civilized fashion. And, as we all know, long-term dependency breeds irresponsibility.

So I find myself, over an evening drink with a sophisticated British official, discussing whether old Rugova can still pull the votes; whether something can be made of young Thaci; or if Kosumi might be a "player" after all. Almost as my grandfather, who was an imperial civil servant in India, must have sat on a veranda in Delhi in 1929, wondering what old Gandhi was up to, and if young Nehru could be brought on.

It's a rum way to end the twentieth century.

CHRONOLOGY

1999

1 JULY. Doubice, Czech Republic. A day in a beautiful rural part of northern Bohemia, accompanying Václav Havel on one of his presidential meet-the-people tours. In the evening, over a drink in the local pub, I ask him if he personally feels more free than ten years ago. "Of course I don't feel more free," he says. "Even in jail I felt more free in some ways." He is imprisoned in his role, hounded from one appointment to the next by aides, security men, and the ever-prying media. But, he suggests, his own loss of freedom is the price he pays for others to be free.

8 JULY. Bruntal, Czech Republic. A very different Czech encounter. Ludvik Zifčák was the secret policeman who, during the student demonstration that started the velvet revolution on 17 November 1989, pretended to be a student beaten to death. The news of his "death" was immediately passed to the media by other secret police agents. The purpose of this secret police plot was to provoke a little local unrest, which would give a pretext for more dynamic communist leaders to take power. They hoped, as he says frankly, to save communism; in fact, they precipitated its demise. Conspiracy theories are generally a branch of fiction. Occasionally, there really are conspiracies in history; but even then, they usually go wrong, as this one did.

I ask him how he died. He laughs and says, "Well, really I just fell over. That was the whole death." After a short spell in prison, he now works in this gray, godforsaken north Moravian town, as a pawnbroker.

23 JULY. *Fourteen Serbs are murdered, presumably by Kosovar Albanians, while harvesting at a village near Lipljan in Kosovo.*

30 JULY. *President Clinton and Tony Blair attend summit in Sarajevo to launch the Stability Pact for southeastern Europe.*

5 AUGUST.   *Former British defense secretary George Robertson is confirmed as new NATO secretary-general.*

9 AUGUST.   *President Yeltsin nominates longtime KGB officer Vladimir Putin as Russian prime minister, the fourth in twelve months.*

19 AUGUST.   *Large demonstration against Slobodan Milošević in Belgrade.*

23 AUGUST.   *German government moves to Berlin.*

AUGUST.   *Chechen rebels invade Dagestan, clashing with Russian forces there.*

SEPTEMBER.   *Bomb explosions in Moscow are blamed on Chechen terrorists.*

9 SEPTEMBER.   *Former Hong Kong governor Chris Patten publishes his report on the reform of policing in Northern Ireland.*

5, 12, AND 19 SEPTEMBER.   *In Germany, the Schröder government suffers a series of defeats in provincial and local elections.*

21 SEPTEMBER.   *KLA leaders agree to become a Kosovo Protection Force with a maximum of three thousand members and just two hundred guns.*

  In a deliberate gesture by the German government, the prime minister of Israel, Ehud Barak, is the first foreign leader to visit the German government in its new-old capital, Berlin.

23 SEPTEMBER.   *Russian forces begin a major air offensive against Chechnya.*

27 SEPTEMBER.   *Pro-Yeltsin politicians form "Unity" block to fight Duma elections in Russia.*

27 SEPTEMBER.   London. I talk to a senior NATO official about the Kosovo bombing. He says nobody at NATO headquarters in Brussels anticipated the length of the campaign. Before it started, all efforts were devoted to the herculean task of getting the nineteen member states to agree on what to do. Seen from inside the organization, to achieve internal consensus was already the great victory. No one there, so far as he could see, was thinking seriously about the possible consequences in former Yugoslavia of the action agreed upon. He hopes that, in future, the organization will be better at what he memorably calls "consequence management."

30 SEPTEMBER.   *Russian prime minister Vladimir Putin says Russian ground forces are moving in and out of Chechnya, which he claims as part of Russia.*

3 OCTOBER. *In parliamentary elections in Austria, Jörg Haider's Free-dom Party becomes the second strongest party in parliament, campaigning on an anti-immigrant and Euroskeptic platform. In Serbia, the brother-in-law and security guards of opposition leader Vuk Drašković are killed in a road accident, in suspicious circumstances.*

10 OCTOBER. *Social Democrats sink to a record low in Berlin elections, won by Christian Democrats. The postcommunist PDS wins nearly 40 per-cent of the vote in East Berlin.*

13 OCTOBER. *In the Czech town of Ustí nad Labem, a two-meter-high wall is erected to separate local Czechs from their Roma neighbors.*

15–16 OCTOBER. *In a special summit in Tampere, devoted mainly to cooperation on justice and home affairs, EU leaders agree in principle to open membership negotiations with a further six candidate states and with Turkey.*

18 OCTOBER. *A report from "three wise men"—Richard von Weizsäcker, Jean-Luc Dehaene, and Lord (David) Simon—recommends further insti-tutional reforms to prepare for an EU of twenty-eight member states.*

21 OCTOBER. *Russian troops advance to within ten kilometers of the capital of Chechnya, Grozny. An estimated 180,000 refugees, one tenth of the Chechen population, have fled.*

27 OCTOBER. *Former Italian prime minister Giulio Andreotti is cleared by a court in Palermo of charges of collusion with the Mafia.*

31 OCTOBER. *The first round of presidential elections in Ukraine leads to a runoff between incumbent Leonid Kuchma and Communist leader Petro Symonenko.*

2 NOVEMBER. *French finance minister Dominique Strauss-Kahn resigns following allegations of financial irregularities.*

8 NOVEMBER. Berlin. I chair a remarkable discussion between former chancellor Helmut Kohl and former presidents Mikhail Gorbachev and George Bush, on the tenth anniversary of the fall of the Berlin Wall. On the top floor of the tower block that the conservative publisher Axel Springer deliberately built right next to the Berlin Wall, its windows offering stun-ning views over the vast building site that is Berlin, the three grand old men celebrate the end of the cold war as a triumph for personal diplomacy.

Helmut Kohl recalls how Mikhail Gorbachev resisted siren calls from Soviet hard-liners in the hours immediately after the opening of the Wall. "I'll never forget it, Mikhail," he says, turning to him as to an old friend, and using the familiar *Du*, ". . . that you trusted us, after you and I had got to know each other in our long nighttime conversation during your visit to Bonn." The personal warmth between the two is unmistakable. Afterward, seated near them at dinner, it seems to me that "Helmut" treats "Mikhail" like a nice but slightly boring younger brother. George Bush, the old gentleman from Texas, is cooler and more detached, but he, too, stresses the paramount importance of personal diplomacy. Gorbachev remembers with gratitude Bush's promise that he would not "dance on the Wall."

When I ask them if they think there are any important secrets about those events still in the archives, Bush and Kohl suggest that there are not many left; Gorbachev hints that there may still be a few in the Russian files. The show is crowned by the Russian cellist Mstislav Rostropovitch, who ten years ago spontaneously flew to Berlin to play at the Wall and now performs a joyful piece of Bach.

Afterward, someone tells me a joke about the evening: "Which of the great men revealed most secrets?" Answer: Rostropovitch.

9 NOVEMBER. Berlin. Exactly ten years since "the night the Wall came down." Then, in 1989, this was a true manifestation of people power. Large crowds of East Berliners gathered at the main checkpoints in response to a misleading West German television news report that the Wall was "open," following a bungled announcement of a new regulation on free travel by East German Politburo member Günter Schabowski. It was only the pressure of these crowds that led to the unplanned opening of the frontier. This spontaneous, popular breakthrough produced the unforgettable night when Berliners, East and West, danced on the Wall and fell into each other's arms.

Now, ten years on, the celebration is a purely political and media event. The scenes from 1989 have been replayed so many times on television that they have lost their impact. Every politician wants to be here, to grab his or her share of the limelight. But most ordinary Berliners say, "I'm staying at home, or just having a drink with a few friends." Special television studios have been set up around the Brandenburg Gate, in expectation of vast crowds. In fact, the crowds are quite small and subdued. They spend much of their time watching the main German television program about the anniversary, which is rebroadcast on large outdoor screens.

So, instead of sitting at home watching television, they stand outdoors, in the rain, watching television. Occasionally, the big screens show shots of them, the people at the Brandenburg Gate. So then what they see on television is themselves on television. They watch themselves watching themselves watching themselves watching themselves, in a kind of eternal iteration.

Of course, television itself does not tell you that this is what is happening. When I go to be interviewed by CNN, which is broadcasting from an outdoor platform just the other side of the Brandenburg Gate, their monitors seem to be showing a large, celebrating crowd behind us. And when, in the course of the interview, I tell Christiane Amanpour that I think the Germans have a lot to celebrate, she gestures at the people behind us and says words to the effect of "and so they are." Thus does television create its own story.

The anniversary of the ultimate modern event is marked by the ultimate postmodern event.

11 NOVEMBER. *British House of Lords Bill receives the royal assent. Hereditary peers no longer sit of right in the House of Lords.*

14 NOVEMBER. *Leonid Kuchma is reelected president of Ukraine in the second round of presidential elections. In Macedonia, Boris Trajkovski is elected president, with a significant vote from the Albanian minority, but faces accusations of electoral fraud.*

17 NOVEMBER. Prague. Another capital, another tenth anniversary: this time, that of the velvet revolution. Here I chair a discussion in Prague Castle, with the Berlin Three—Kohl, Gorbachev, and Bush—augmented by Václav Havel, Lech Wałęsa, Danielle Mitterrand (representing her deceased husband), and Margaret Thatcher. Unexpectedly, it produces real controversy, as Lady Thatcher's forceful neoliberal, Anglo-American triumphalism is challenged by her old sparring partner, Mikhail Gorbachev. Hearing her pep talk on the one true way, Gorbachev says, reminds him of listening to an old communist. The West cannot go on dictating terms like this. Pluralism means that there are many possible ways and combinations of ways. Unfortunately, this very pertinent response is only the beginning of a twenty-minute tirade, in which he himself goes on to lecture his largely Czech audience in the hectoring oratorical style of an old Russian communist. They had more than enough of that in the years before 1989. His style defeats his content.

18–19 NOVEMBER. *Istanbul summit of the now fifty-four members of the Organization for Security and Cooperation in Europe (OSCE). The summit is dominated by criticism of the continuing Russian military campaign in Chechnya.*

28 NOVEMBER. *The Basque separatist organization, ETA, announces an end to its cease-fire.*

29 NOVEMBER. *In Belfast, the Northern Ireland Assembly confirms in office a new Northern Ireland cabinet, under the Unionist leader David Trimble, with the participation of both unionists and Sinn Fein, the political wing of the IRA. In Priština, Kosovo, an Albanian mob kills an elderly Serb professor and beats up two elderly women, thus marking the Albanian "flag day."*

ANARCHY AND MADNESS

Balushe is back! With a quiet smile on her pleasant face, she stands under a blue UN tarpaulin in a makeshift wooden hut. They found her wandering nearby, bemused, hungry, but otherwise unharmed. Balushe is the Latifaj family cow, and her return is a small sign of what has gone right in the place we should now, realistically, call Kosova.

The Latifajs used to live in a large house next to the mosque in the village of Prilep, at the foot of the Accursed Mountains that separate Kosova from Albania. Now they live amid the rubble that was their house, next to the ruined mosque, in a village that Milošević's artillery and special forces have almost entirely destroyed. A year ago, I found the whole family cowering in their yard. Serb forces had just beaten them up after a KLA ambush of Serb police outside the mosque. Five months ago, I found Granny Latifaj standing alone, weeping, in the rubble. She was trying to heat some water in a bucket by placing it in the sun.

Today, half the family has returned. They've built a large wooden hut in the snow-covered ruins, with materials supplied by international agencies and charities. They have a wood-burning stove and enough wood to see them through Kosova's freezing winter. (One daughter tells me they received an extra allowance of firewood because her brother died in the war, fighting alongside the KLA's legendary Commander Ramush.) Like so many Kosovars, they are helped out financially by family members working in Germany. They hope their fields will be cleared of land mines in time for the spring sowing. Meanwhile, with international aid and family help, they have just enough to eat. The children go to a rudimentary school, with the same teacher who used to instruct them illegally before the war. Most people in the village have come back, and, yes, they finally feel free. "We'd like to thank you," says the *hoxha,* the local clergyman from the ruined mosque, whom I find repainting his own house, "you Americans and Europeans, for doing so much for our freedom."

This is the good news, and it's repeated all over the battered province. The main street of every town looks like a do-it-yourself exhibition. Small shops contain everything you need to rebuild a house, from bricks and timber, through electrical cables and drainpipes, to the all-important rugs and coffee cups. A family I have visited several times in Mališevo, once the capital of the KLA and "the most dangerous place in Europe," have such a shop, newly built with money sent from Germany by their *Gastarbeiter* son. The father cautiously estimates his profit at thirty-five to forty deutsche marks a day. He hopes to reconstruct his own house on the earnings from selling reconstruction materials to others.

In the trashed bazaar of what used to be the Serbian city of Pec and is now the Albanian city of Pejë, local children have painted the ruins with brightly colored frescoes. There's a thriving market, and even a couple of jeweler's shops. Young girls stand in the mud, distributing calendars for Ramadan.

In sum, most of the Kosovars who were expelled have come home; they are surviving and will eventually rebuild. Here, however, the good news ends. For Kosova today is an almighty mess. The province for which NATO fought the first war in its history is now the most ambitious project of truly international administration in the whole history of the United Nations. The experiment is not going well.

1

Thanks to us, Kosovo ends with an *a*—the Albanian as opposed to the Serbian spelling. *A* stands for Albanian. It also, at the moment, stands for anarchy. Take A for Albanian first. It's now entirely clear that our intervention has decisively resolved, in favor of the Albanians, a Serb-Albanian struggle for control of this territory that goes back at least 120 years. This was neither the stated nor the real intention of Western policy makers.

Although most Serbs don't believe it, the representatives of the so-called international community are genuine and even passionate in their desire to see a future for the Serbs in Kosova. Dr. Klaus Reinhardt, the impressive German general who now commands the multilateral, NATO-led military force (KFOR), thumps his right fist into his left palm as he tells me that he *will* bring Serbs back to live again in their homes, even though those homes have been torched and plundered by Albanians since KFOR marched in. Bernard Kouchner, the very French head of the United Nations mission (UNMIK), tells me, "history will judge us on our ability to protect a minority [i.e., the Serbs] inside another minority [i.e., the Albanians in Yugoslavia]."

These are bold terms on which to invite history's judgment. For the reality on the ground is one of almost total ethnic separation. Many Serbs fled to Serbia proper when KFOR marched in. Most of the rest have been driven subsequently into Serbian enclaves by intimidation and outright terror from returning Albanians. Particularly among the younger generation of Albanians, who have known Serbs only as remote oppressors, there is a growing intolerance of all ethnic others (including Roma and muslim Slavs). People under thirty make up more than half the population, and young Kosovars manifest a thirst for revenge that sickens not just foreigners but also many among the older generation of Kosovars, who still have personal memories of peaceful coexistence with the Serbs.

Just before I arrived, an elderly Serb professor was lynched by a mob celebrating the Albanian "flag day" in Priština. There used to be some forty thousand Serbs living in Priština; now there are just a few hundred. The isolated Serbian monastery of Dečani has lost all the lay Serbs who used to sustain it. When the monks need to go shopping, they travel under Italian KFOR escort to Montenegro. In Podujevo, British troops mount a twenty-four-hour guard over two remaining Serb grannies—"and the Albanians would slot them if we didn't," a British officer remarks, using a slang term for *kill*. It is entirely fitting to speak, in this context, of reverse ethnic cleansing. Yet this ethnic cleansing has been carried out under the very noses and tank barrels of more than forty thousand international troops.

Momčilo Trajković, the leading Serb politician still in Kosova, fled Priština after being shot through his front door by an Albanian. He now lives in what he calls the Serb "ghetto" around the monastery of Gračanica, an area a few miles across. When he wants to travel anywhere outside the ghetto, he needs a KFOR escort. "This means," he explains, "that I can go to Priština to meet President Clinton but I can't go there to buy a loaf of bread." He's still indomitable. When I ask him how long people can live in such a ghetto, he replies, "A thousand years!" They outlived more than five hundred years of Ottoman rule, he says, and they'll survive this! But he is alone in his heroic optimism.

Beside these enclaves, which contain perhaps some twenty thousand to thirty thousand Serbs, there is an area north of a line running roughly east–west through the city of Kosovska Mitrovica. This area compromises less than 10 percent of the whole territory. It contains some (though not all) of the valuable Trepča mines, and is contiguous with Serbia proper. Here, an estimated 70,000 Serbs still rule the roost. The situation in the divided city of Kosovska Mitrovica is amazing. When I pass the barbed-wire barriers on the bridge over the river Ibar, my papers are checked by French soldiers as I enter the Serb-controlled northern sector. French, British, and Scandinavian troops patrol this part, too, but within a few yards of a British armored car I am accosted by burly Serbs in plain clothes, armed with walkie-talkies. They sharply ask my business, and my resourceful Albanian interpreter rapidly becomes "Dragan Trajković from Belgrade." We walk up through a peaceful-looking Serb town—schoolgirls giggling on their way home, couples quietly going shopping—to the regional hospital, which is run by Serbs, though with a French director and French soldiers at the gate.

Here we meet a doctor who is also a member of a Belgrade-based, moderate nationalist opposition party. He explains that all their salaries are paid from Belgrade, and their electricity, water, and other supplies come from the north. "The multiethnic concept of

Kosovo is finished," he says. Partition is the only answer. Back in the southern part of town, the KLA-appointed unofficial Albanian mayor, Dr. Bajram Rexhepi, a surgeon who tended the KLA wounded, earning the affectionate nickname "Doctor Terrorist," retorts that this is intolerable. If nothing changes by the spring, he says, the Albanians will again resort to pressure, even force, to storm the bridge over the river Ibar. Some of the local French soldiers have been seen carousing with Serb paramilitaries, he claims, and are pro-Serb, but he thinks their commanders are not.

In truth, the refusal to force open the bridge over the Ibar is not French policy but that of the whole international administration, both civil and military. For if we let the massed Albanians surge across, the Serbs would either fight or flee—probably first one, then the other. We would again be party to ethnic cleansing. So instead, KFOR and UNMIK struggle ineffectually to implement a few schemes for Albanian-Serb cooperation—in the hospital, in a factory—that do nothing to change the overall reality of partition. Indeed, Kouchner has now tacitly acknowledged this, proclaiming his medium-term goal to be no longer a "multiethnic" society but "peaceful coexistence" between largely separate communities.

Yet this hate-filled Albanian-Serb separation is only half the story—and for the future of Kosova not even the most important half. More important is that the *a* in Kosova stands increasingly for anarchy. It's hard to convey what a chaotic, threatening place the Albanian 90 percent of Kosova is this winter. In the dark, through freezing fog, along potholed, icy roads, race endless columns of cars, many of them probably stolen in Western Europe. Half the cars display no registration plates and have black-clad, unshaven young men at the wheels, driving like madmen. Once, our column stops because a kid has thrown a brick through the windscreen of what he thinks is a Serb car. More often, it's because a car has spun off the road. I have never in my life seen so many serious traffic accidents. At one particularly nasty one, a KFOR armored car trundles past while a car lies upside down in the snow, its warning lights flashing in the dark and its driver presumably crushed. There are still virtually no police, and there is no effective law. I keep thinking of Graham Greene's title: *The Lawless Roads*.

Meanwhile, the Albanian mafia has entered with a vengeance. Young women are afraid to go out at night in Priština, for fear of being kidnapped into forced prostitution. Drug consumption among the students has soared, as the pushers get to work. In the last week of November, there were twenty-two recorded murders; several of them cold-blooded executions. The independent newspaper publisher Veton Surroi, who in the summer courageously denounced Albanian revenge killings against Serbs, sees his prophecy coming true: What began with Albanians murdering Serbs ends with Albanians murdering each other. Before and during the war, Kosovars kept assuring me that Kosova would not be like Albania: corrupt, anarchic, ruled by the gun and the gang. Increasingly, it is. Here is the Albanization of Kosova in a way no ordinary Kosovar Albanian wanted. The gangsters have stepped into a vacuum left by the slowness of the West.

KFOR tries to do what it can. Sometimes its efforts are simply comical. As cars speed down the main street of one small town, a Swedish soldier steps out waving a little sign reading "30 kph" (kilometers per hour). The cars ignore him, of course. On the other side of the road I see a local man—unshaven, toothless, probably a little drunk—holding his sides and shaking with uncontrollable laughter at this ludicrous yet emblematic scene. The West meets the Balkans.

More seriously, the KFOR forces have detention camps, with hundreds of suspected murderers and violent criminals. "But then," an exasperated officer tells me, "the Albanian judge comes and releases all the Albanians, the Serb judge does the same for the Serbs." Mere looting and plundering earns just "a cuff round the ear and don't do it again." The soldiers always knew they could never be a substitute for a proper police. The then KFOR commander, General Sir Michael Jackson, told me in May last year, when they were still waiting in Macedonia, that the key to success would be international police. Disastrously, UNMIK has gotten only some 1,800 of the 6,000 international police Kouchner requested when he arrived in July. And 6,000 would still be too few.

Some of these police are from third-world countries, such as Bangladesh and Malaysia, and critics say they are mainly here for the money. They sit in the cafés while crime goes on all around. The more professional ones mix grim determination with despair. They include sixty officers of the Royal Ulster Constabulary, fresh from the streets of Belfast. "It's just like home," one of them remarks, after discussing last night's particularly nasty summary executions. Just a couple of hundred local police have graduated from the new police academy. Behind them, there is still no proper structure of law, judges, courts, and prisons. UNMIK has taken half a year to secure agreement even on which body of law should be applied, let alone to start applying it.

This is the greatest failure of international administration but not the only one. Six months after the world moved in, the province still has nothing that could be called a proper government.

2

There are, it seems to me, five main reasons for the way this unprecedented experiment in the local application of world government has thus far gone wrong. First, you could hardly think of a more difficult place to try. It's not just the physical devastation, with more than a third of the houses destroyed or damaged. It's also the social and psychological devastation wrought by ten years of oppression, followed by war, forced exile, and return. Further dislocation is caused by the tens of thousands of country people flooding into Priština because they have nowhere to live for the winter.

Second, there is the disunity, corruption, and irresponsibility of the local Kosovar Albanian politicians, among whom Kouchner looks for partners in a joint administration. Five years ago, we would still have had one relatively well-defined local structure to deal with, the underground administration of the Democratic League of Kosova (LDK), headed by the unofficial president, Ibrahim Rugova— no shining light, but at least committed to peaceful change. Now there is another major movement, the KLA, which—together with its new Sinn Fein, the PPDK—believes that it has matchless legitimacy flowing from the armed struggle for independence. Several lesser competitors swirl in the background.

The leader of the unofficial KLA government, Hashim Thaci, known here as Albright's Darling, greets me in a smart blue suit and smoothly makes all the right noises about human rights, tolerance, and stability. "We didn't make war to have this anarchy," he says. But all the time a curious, slightly sinister smile plays on his lips, as if he's really thinking, "What a huge joke that the United States and the whole Western world and this man from Oxford are all treating me, the kid from Drenica and the Zurich Bahnhof, with such respect." Well-informed, very senior Western sources think it is a bad joke, since they claim to have firm evidence that Thaci has been directly involved in KLA racketeering and strong-arm tactics.

In small towns and villages, the self-appointed KLA bosses behave as if they are the masters now. Local people complain bitterly about the unjust way the bosses distribute international aid. (The mother of my Mališevo family shows me all they have received: one cardboard box, marked, in some Sussex spinster's hand, "Teenage Girls' Underwear.") In many places, they intimidate the local LDK leaders, still loyal to Rugova—so much so that in one village in the KLA heartland of Drenica, the LDK representatives did not even dare to turn out to meet Dr. Kouchner. "Thaci thinks he's Castro," the independent newspaper editor Baton Haxhiu says. And even Dr. Kouchner wearily comments, "Thaci wants to run the whole thing."

Yet this insolent arrogance of power alienates many Kosovars. Wherever I go, I find evidence of strong support for the LDK and especially for Ibrahim Rugova. Rugova himself is back and receives me in stately style in his large suburban house, full of heavy furniture and rich carpets. He wears a suit and tie but not, for once, his trademark paisley scarf. In his passable French, he tells me how he was detained by the Serbs in this very room with fourteen people and forced to go to Belgrade and be shown on Serbian television shaking hands with Milošević. Don't people blame him for that? I ask. "No, because every Kosovar was in the same situation." Like Thaci, he offers me smooth clichés about tolerance, stability, and democracy, but his problem is the weakness of his party, especially since the Serbs killed Professor Fehmi Agani, the éminence grise who held it together. At parting, Rugova shows me his mineral collection and presents me with a semiprecious lump of Kosova.

Rugova wants three sorts of election as soon as possible: local elections, what he calls national (i.e., all-Kosova) elections, and direct presidential ones. The KLA wants local and national ones, then for parliament to elect the president, because they fear that Rugova would win a direct election. Kouchner hopes to start with local elections; but first the citizens and voters have to be registered, and that process has barely begun. Autumn 2000 seems the earliest likely time, and anyway such a contest is likely to sharpen the local rivalries.

In the background, there is a second unofficial government headed by Bujar Bukoshi, who allegedly has hundreds of millions of deutsche marks collected from Kosovars living abroad during the 1990s. Thaci charmingly calls it "the mafia of Bukoshi." There's also another party, headed by a leading Kosovar intellectual, Rexhep Qosja, which, like the KLA and Rugova's LDK, was represented at the Rambouillet peace talks in early 1999. In case you were wondering, the Islamic clergy seem quite incapable of acting as an integrating and pacifying force. "We try," says the nice *hoxha* of Prilep, "but the anger is stronger, the anger is stronger." When I ask the newspaper publisher Veton Surroi why he does not take a lead, he replies, "Me, I'm a moral authority." But he says it with a weary, almost cynical shrug, as if he would add, "Whatever that means, in a place like this."

The third reason that things are going wrong is the complexity and chaos of the international presence itself, which matches and compounds the local Kosovar confusion. Locals comment proudly, "We're Balkanizing the international community!" But the international community does that all by itself. On paper, there's a structure which is drawn in KFOR documents—this is not a joke—as a Greek temple. The base is KFOR, providing security. Then there are four columns: UNMIK, for civil administration; the United Nations High Commission for Refugees (UNHCR), for restoring people's homes; the Organization for Security and Cooperation in Europe (OSCE), for elections and media; and the European Union (EU), for economic reconstruction. The pediment is marked "a stable and peaceful Kosovo." Very neat. But the practice, ah, there's a different matter.

All these international organizations have their own marked bureaucratic styles and political constraints. All compete with the others. All are subject to innumerable national pressures. Their separate propaganda sheets make revealing reading. The European Commission has a *Reconstruction Weekly.* Lead item in the 21–27 November 1999 issue is a report of a one-day workshop on management training that apparently concluded that "top-level managers in socially-owned companies . . . would require training on change and organisational behaviour, quality management, public relations, international markets, as well as general management development." The bureaucratic language takes one straight back to Brussels. One wonders what polished consultant was paid what enormous fee (a year's living for ten large Kosovar families?) to compose this ringing statement of the blindingly obvious. The report goes on to discuss the small and medium-size enterprise (SME) sector: "To acquire a fully comprehensive assessment of training needs, it was recommended that a survey of all existing SMEs be undertaken to define more clearly training and related requirements (such as technology, markets, clients, and partnerships)." To anyone who knows the chaotic reality on the ground, this idea of a "survey of all [!] existing SMEs" in Kosova is utterly ludicrous. It's stuff like this that can make even the staunchest friend of the EU despair of the Europe our fathers have built.

Turning to the *KFOR Chronicle,* I particularly enjoy one headline: GREEKS ORGANISE THE CHAOS. Well, exactly. General Reinhardt tells me he has thirty-four different national contingents under his command, "and don't think they do something just because I order them to." No, they all go off and ask their national governments first. I find that people from KFOR, UNMIK, and OSCE privately spend much time blaming each other—just like the Kosovar politicians. In fairness, one should say that the UN has never before been charged with such a complex piece of international government and at such short notice. Many dedicated, idealistic, professional people work long hours doing real things. There is something truly touching about this Babel of Azerbaijani soldiers, French intellectuals, Swedish diplomats, and Zambian policemen, trying to make a reality of a liberal internationalist dream. I wish it could work. I really do.

Behind the conflicts of the local mortals, there are the demigods squabbling in New York, Washington, London, Paris, Berlin, Moscow, and Beijing. It is no secret that Kouchner has spent much of his time trying to secure agreement from the UN Secretary-General and Security Council to this or that minute step of local self-government. When I ask him about this, he replies startlingly, "New York does not exist!" (I think it might sound better in French.) In a conversation that I would characterize as unfocused, Dr. Kouchner gives me the impression of passion and Gallic eloquence but not of masterly administrative skills. Yet to make this thing work needs a politician-administrator of genius.

The problems run from the very top to the very bottom. For example: UNMIK is trying to recruit judges, customs officials, and teachers at salaries of some DM100 to 500 a month. But the same people can earn DM1,000 to 2,000 a month working as interpreters or simply as drivers for those same international organizations. Thus, the international community unwittingly defeats its own objectives. ("And," a Kosovar friend adds, "do you think customs officials on DM500 a month are going to collect many customs dues? Of course, they'll take bribes instead.") My own driver-interpreter is a judge, dismissed by the Serbs in 1991. He won't go back to being a judge, for three reasons: because of the money; because he fears his own dear fellow Albanians will make trouble for him if he convicts some of their choicer brethren; and because he wants to emigrate to Canada anyway, to give his children a better life.

In mid-December, shortly after I left, Kouchner finally persuaded his multiple international masters and the three Kosovar Albanian parties represented at the Rambouillet peace conference to agree on a structure of interim administration. This is supposed to last until elections produce something more democratic and permanent. It places him at the top as civilian governor of the province, with a mixed UNMIK and local administrative council beneath him and nineteen executive ministries under that. Competent persons are to be proposed by the Kosovar parties to head these ministries, but Kouchner will decide who gets the jobs. Well, we shall see.

The fourth reason for the mess is the deep ambiguity of UN Security Council Resolution 1244, which, as a paper bridge between the Western and the Russian/Chinese positions, declares that the province is at once subject to the sovereignty of the Federal Republic of Yugoslavia and will enjoy substantial autonomy and self-government. Virginity and motherhood combined. This is, as one senior UNMIK official puts it candidly, "a nightmare." The Russians and Chinese cry blue murder at every step to self-government, such as having a budget in deutsche marks rather than Yugoslav dinars or instituting customs controls or issuing separate identity papers. Yet such steps are the only way out of anarchy.

Last but by no means least, it's a mess because the world really does not want to be here. We stumbled into this experiment as we stumbled into the war itself. Each individual member state counts the cost. The reason why the international police officers, to take the single most important failure, have been so slow in coming is that national governments have not found them and won't pay for them—including, as Kouchner bitterly remarks, his own, French government. (There are gendarmes in Kosovska Mitrovica, but the gendarmes are a military not a civilian force.) All Africa cries: What about us? International attention has already moved on to other crises. Chechnya, not Kosova, now produces the CNN effect. UNMIK had to go around with a begging bowl to raise the $250 million needed for this year's core administration budget. It's often been said but still bears repeating: For the price of a few days' bombing, we are throwing Kosova away.

This place supposedly took its name from "the field of the blackbirds" (*Kosovo Polje*), and in the bleak midwinter blackbirds still gather in vast numbers to squawk and caw in the trees of Priština. As I write up my notes in the early morning of my last day here, they flock and swirl outside my window, blackening the dawn sky above the offices of the International Criminal Tribunal, as if to shriek, "We know where the rest of the bodies are buried!" Then they swarm above the main headquarters of the UN administration, as if to crow, "You'll never bring peaceful order to this place!" It's a scene from Hitchcock's *Birds,* and it eerily heightens my sense of grim foreboding as I leave for Serbia. The West won the war. I fear we are losing the peace.

3

To return to Serbia proper from occupied Kosova is a surreal experience. In the freezing fog, I say farewell to my Albanian judge/driver/interpreter. Cheerful Canadian soldiers at the sandbagged checkpoint take my passport details—"Just in case something happens to you." My Serbian driver waits on the other side, to take me past the Serbian police checkpoint. Then we drive through what still looks, by comparison with Kosova, to be a civilized and orderly landscape to Belgrade. There, I tell friends and acquaintances about life in the chunk of their country we've just occupied and what the German general proposes to do with it.

These are not easy conversations. Surprisingly, Kosovo/a is not itself a major subject of contention, although the state media do make propaganda out of the suffering of Serbs at the hands of vengeful Kosovars and out of the general chaos in the province. In a public-opinion poll conducted in October for the National Democratic Institute—amazing that a U.S. public institution can commission a poll in what is still virtually enemy territory—only 5 percent of respondents said that the loss of Kosovo was the most important problem facing Serbia, compared with 26 percent who singled out poverty and social problems, and 14 percent who mentioned the regime of Slobodan Milošević. A year ago, Vuk Drašković, leader of the half-oppositional Serbian Renewal Movement, spent most of our conversation ranting about Kosovo. This time, in a long talk at his large, comfortable family home, he mentions it only once, almost in passing: "Of course Kosovo is lost." Among other opposition politicians, who for years have been struck dumb by the Kosovo issue, I sense something like relief: "At least it's not our problem anymore."

The war, however, especially the bombing of their own cities and towns, is a major subject for conversation with an Englishman. Aleksa Djilas, son of the famous dissident Milovan Djilas and, I like to think, a friend, greets me warmly in his apartment and then says, "Do you realize, if Britain had conscription and the war had gone on, we might have been fighting each other?" Quite a thought. Everyone has a story of the bombing. A woman who works for one of the most genuinely liberal (and therefore small) opposition parties recalls that when her six-year-old daughter asked, "Why are they bombing us?" she tried to explain along the lines of "there are bad people in Serbia doing bad things, and they are bombing those bad people, but unfortunately that means they're also hitting us." The little girl didn't understand. (I'm not quite sure I do either.) Instead, she now goes around singing a popular rude song against "Clinton Bill." The double-edged bitterness felt during the bombing was perfectly summed up in a graffito that read simply "*Slobo Klintone!*" "Slobo, you Clinton!"

Generally, the bombing has reinforced the Serbs' already highly developed sense of national victimhood. I talk to the angry former mayor of a village in Serbia's wooded rural heartland, the Šumadija. As I take my leave, he says, generously, "We Serbs can forgive, but we cannot forget." No notion that Serbs might themselves need to ask anyone else for forgiveness! At the same time, there's an overwhelming awareness that Serbia has to start rejoining the civilized, developed world. Even this man, who belongs to Milošević's Socialist Party, thinks there is no alternative.

Yes, the Milošević regime accuses the opposition of being NATO lackeys. But, an opposition leader observes wryly, ordinary Serbs also respect power, and the bombing was nothing if not a crude lesson in power. Psychologically, even more than economically, the country is in a horrible condition, stewing in a witches' broth of resentment, cynicism, conspiracy theories, and humiliated pride. The same Belgrade intellectuals who one minute berate me for the sins of Western policy are, next minute, privately asking me for a letter of recommendation or other assistance in getting to the West. So many of the brightest and best have left already. Those who remain are often reduced to semilegal small business or plain black-marketing to make ends meet.

"To understand this country now," says a political scientist whose judgment I respect, "you don't need a political scientist. You need a clinical psychologist. We're all crazy somehow." And he mentions a black-humor diagnosis: Political Serbicide Syndrome. They feel they belong to a society being led into collective political suicide by Slobodan Milošević, himself the son of parents who both committed suicide.

In such a society, in such a moment, serious political analysis is very difficult, and prognosis near impossible. Nonetheless, almost everyone I talk to agrees on three things. First, and self-evidently, Milošević has survived the immediate consequences of defeat. There has not yet been the "Galtieri effect" hoped for by the opposition and by the West—and perhaps especially by the Clinton administration. (The Argentine dictator was, of course, deposed for losing the Falklands War.) There are shortages. People get up at five in the morning to line up for milk. They are very hard up. But there are far more power outages in NATO-occupied Priština than in Belgrade. Somehow, Milošević is getting through the winter. He has a favorable barter arrangement for Russian gas supplied via Hungary. He has received what is said to be $300 million of aid from China. He has probably cut some backdoor deals for fuel through Bulgaria. His policy of systematically selling off state property (including those Trepča mines in Kosovo/a) to cronies and foreign investors has apparently still left some minimal hard-currency reserves. And he does a cash-flow juggling act that consists in not paying each group of public-service workers for a month or two in turn.

A slick advertising campaign on state television shows his regime heroically rebuilding the bridges and buildings that NATO destroyed. Serbia defies the world! These public works are paid for partly by not paying the workers at all, partly by printing money, and partly by using the country's ample reserves of very cheap labor—including the approximately eight hundred thousand impoverished Serbian refugees from other parts of former Yugoslavia. (Thus, Milošević's own destructive policies have created a pool of cheap labor for him to exploit.) Politically, the street demonstrations called by the Alliance for Change, a loose coalition of opposition parties, started with a bang in the summer; they have ended with a whimper. They have failed in their stated objective of securing early elections. The 1980s ended with the fall of Honecker, Husák, and Ceauşescu; it would have been wonderful to end the 1990s with the fall of Milošević. But no.

This does not mean, however, that Milošević will be Europe's Saddam Hussein. For there is also widespread agreement that we have entered the last act of the Serbian tragedy, with Slobo and his

powerful wife, Mira Marković, still playing Lord and Lady Macbeth.
Two major opinion polls, the NDI one and another commissioned by
the local Center for Policy Studies, show a vast majority of respondents blaming Milošević for the country's woes and wanting him to
go before the end of his term. There is much anecdotal evidence of
the regime crumbling: border guards congratulating opposition figures on their television appearances and so on. Quite big rats seem
to be preparing to leave the sinking ship so as to save their own skins
and the wealth Milošević has enabled them to accumulate in return
for their support. I talk to a banker formerly close to the leading couple and—pulling at a large cigar as he weighs how far he dares go in
conversation with a Westerner—he describes Serbia as being in a
"pretransition period."

Unfortunately, the third thing on which all local observers agree is
that this transition is most unlikely to be peaceful. One must distinguish between the rational and the real. Rational projections suggest,
for example, that the Alliance for Change, a fragile coalition of some
of the more liberal opposition parties, might win popular support by
joining in a "Trilateral Commission" with the United States and the
European Union to distribute Western aid. "See, we can deliver!"
they would say. "Oil to opposition-run cities [the so-called Energy for
Democracy plan], supplies for a hospital here, a school there." Rational projections suggest elections—local and federal ones have to be
held in 2000, the crucial republican ones in 2001 at the latest. The
opposition parties have long been hopelessly disunited, and their
most prominent leaders, Vuk Drašković and Zoran Djindjić, are
in different ways widely discredited. Even so, Milošević's Socialists,
his wife's United Yugoslav Left (JUL) party, and their extreme-
nationalist coalition partner, the Radicals, would almost certainly
not win enough votes to form another government. But there the rational ends and the real begins. For how would Milošević peacefully
concede power, even assuming he was prepared to? And where would
he then go? The Hague?

Milošević is now more dangerous than ever. Drašković suggests to
me that until this year, Milošević was still restrained by fear of the
West's reaction. Now the West has done its worst—it has bombed
him—and he has little more to fear. On the other hand, because of

the public indictment by the International Criminal Tribunal for the former Yugoslavia ("The Hague Tribunal"), he has no safe exit. He has his back to the wall. Wounded, cornered tigers are liable to strike out—as he has. The universities, wellsprings of the great student protests of 1996–1997, have been brought firmly back under regime control. He used the pretext of the war to seize the assets of some of the most important independent media, such as Radio B92—though the indomitable Veran Matić now runs a Radio B292. The remaining independent media are being punished with huge fines under a draconian public-information law. Opposition activists are regularly arrested and roughed up.

What is more, Serbian politics are becoming a matter of life and death. During the war, the newspaper editor Slavko Čuruvija, once close to Milošević's wife, Mira Marković, but subsequently an outspoken critic, was gunned down outside his home. In early October, the brother-in-law of Vuk Drašković was killed, together with three of Drašković's bodyguards, in a highly suspicious traffic accident. Some speculate that this was a factional security service or even a gangland killing, since that brother-in-law was in charge of the lucrative and corrupt Belgrade city construction office. Drašković, however, has denounced the Radicals and Mira Marković's JUL party (but not Milošević's Socialist Party) as being responsible for "state terrorism." His Serbian Renewal Movement has formed armed self-defense units from among its own members.

He clearly fears for his own life, as does Ognjen Pribičević, a friend and former member of my Oxford college who threw in his lot with Drašković during the war. I sit with Pribičević in a restaurant in central Belgrade and he says, "I don't think they'll shoot me here, in this restaurant, but perhaps something will happen on the road, another 'traffic accident.' " He is meant to chair a talk I propose to give in the hope of engaging Belgrade intellectuals in dialogue. He arrives five minutes late and says breathlessly to Aleksa Djilas, "I can't do this now, the armed struggle has begun!" This is one of the more interesting excuses I have heard for being unable to chair a talk. It turns out there's a tense standoff with police who have come to interrogate three party leaders about their statement denouncing "state terrorism."

Well, the armed struggle does not actually begin—and old Belgrade hands say they have heard it all before, a hundred times—prerevolutionary hysteria as a way of life. But that does not mean that violent change will not one day, finally, happen. There are widely differing speculations about what the spark for revolution might be. Drašković suggests it might be an attempt by Milošević to reassert control over the last remaining constituent part of the Federal Republic of Yugoslavia, Montenegro, which is carefully carving out its own de facto autonomy. The next day, there is a confrontation between Serbian soldiers and Montenegrin police at Montenegro's main airport. Yet the shrewd and cautious Montenegrin president, Milo Djukanović, has again and again managed to avoid a showdown in which many of his people, identifying themselves as Serbs, might actually side with Serbia.

Dragoslav Avramović, the wily old economist who once worked for Milošević and now leads the Alliance for Change, speculates that the spark might be another bout of hyperinflation. He says the current rate of 40 to 50 percent a month, though desperately difficult for anyone without a hard-currency income, is just about sustainable. But if it passes 100 percent a month, then the balloon goes up. Zoran Djindjić of the Democratic Party thinks no one can predict what the spark would be. After all, one of the Serbian risings against Ottoman rule in the nineteenth century began when an Ottoman soldier shot a Serbian boy lining up for water at a well.

What one can identify are the many groups waiting to act, when the moment comes. Students are organized outside the universities, in a movement called Resistance. One of their leaders tells me they are conserving their energies for the right occasion and deliberately focusing on a single demand: "Slobo must go." There are the opposition parties, of course. Then there are several opposition-controlled cities. I visit one, Čačak, and talk to its popular mayor, Velimir Ilić, a private entrepreneur built like an ox, who survived the war hiding in the woods to escape Milošević's security men. He tells me, "We're waiting for Belgrade." There are the independent media, including an impressive network of regional television stations. Then there are the opportunists—politely called pragmatists—who are held to be especially numerous in Milošević's own Socialist Party. There is the mass discontent evidenced in the opinion polls, as well as the miserable refugees—although their revolutionary potential may be doubted. Western observers always speculate about a possible army coup, but there is scant external evidence of that possibility. On the other hand, the incidents involving Ćuruvuja and Drašković do suggest a real fragmentation of the security apparatus. Who knows if one day their guns could not be turned against Milošević himself?

Asked what the West can do to increase the rather small chances of a change that is both swift and peaceful, people from all points of the political spectrum join in making two firm statements. First, Milošević must be given a way out. They hate him. They wish him dead or in prison. Morally, they think the Hague indictment is right (though some of them say the recently deceased Croatian president, Franjo Tudjman, and the Bosnian president, Alija Izetbegović, should have been indicted, too). But politically it is proving disastrous. Milošević has nowhere to go, so they fear he will fight "to the last Serb." Even the radical young student leader says Milošević must, instead, be offered some safe exit. With the fantasies of limitless American Machiavellianism that are rife here, those I talk to conjure images of some new Ollie North covertly spiriting Slobo off to a Caribbean hideaway in an unmarked Stealth fighter.

Second, everyone says that sanctions are counterproductive. Sanctions against the regime, yes. Barring some six hundred people associated with the regime from getting visas to Western countries has been an excellent move. And they strongly approve of the steps taken to block the foreign bank accounts of Milošević and his associates. But sanctions against the people only increase the possibilities for illegal earnings by Milošević's cronies. They impoverish ordinary Serbs. Above all, they reinforce the very image that his propaganda has so successfully exploited for so long: innocent, heroic, suffering Serbia, a Christ among nations, persecuted by the whole world.

So let fresh air in. Let people travel again. Then they can see for themselves how Milošević has ruined their country while all their neighbors have moved on. ("The most painful thing for me," says one Serb who does travel, "is visiting the other former Yugoslav republics. Why, even Skopje looks better than Belgrade.") Wouldn't lifting sanctions enable Milošević to say, "Look, you can have me *and* the West"? No, they unanimously insist, quite the reverse. After all, the biggest challenge to his regime so far—the demonstrations of 1996–1997—came after the easing of UN sanctions in 1996.

I don't see how we can even contemplate doing the first of these things—giving Milošević a way out—however strong the political logic. This would undermine one of the pillars of the international liberal order we are trying to build for the twenty-first century. But I think we can and should do the second—lift the sanctions against the people—as many West European governments are inclined to. This is not a replay of old cold-war arguments, with West Europeans being soft on the Soviet Union out of cravenness and material self-interest. I have always felt that we should be guided by domestic oppositions in the application of sanctions. That's why sanctions were right against Poland in the 1980s, where Solidarity wanted them, and against South Africa, where the ANC wanted them, and are right against Burma today, where Aung San Suu Kyi emphatically supports them. By the same token, they should be lifted here. But that would mean the Clinton administration admitting, in an election year, that it had got something wrong.

4

I make the long drive back north to Budapest, through the rich, dark fields of the Vojvodina plain. After waiting hours at the frontier for that little exit stamp, I face another shock: neat, modern highways; tollbooths with the prices already shown in Euros; American-style out-of-town shopping centers; a gleaming modern airport. The West!

This is no Huntingtonian frontier between clashing "civilizations." Eighty years ago, the Vojvodina was part of pre-Trianon Hungary. It belongs to exactly the same historical civilization. Nor is this a cold-war divide. For much of the cold war the people living on the Yugoslav side of this frontier were in many ways better placed than those on the Hungarian side. No, this shocking contrast is a product of the politics of one decade: the broadly positive politics of Central Europe and the terrible politics of former Yugoslavia.

The consequences of those terrible politics are nearly played out. Slovenia is already sailing west. Croatia, after the death of Tudjman, has a chance to follow it. The domestic tragedy of Serbia has still to reach its bitter end. We also have yet to see whether tiny Montenegro is pushed to independence or if it can make a future in a loose federation with a reformed Serbia. Equally, we shall see whether the greater autonomy promised to the Albanians in western Macedonia by Boris Trajkovski, the successful candidate in Macedonia's recent presidential elections, spells stabilization or further disintegration for that still imperiled country. Bosnia remains an ethnically divided international protectorate.

I have argued for several years now that this separating into small states or substate units with clear ethnic majorities, driven though it has been by manipulative and often cynical postcommunist nationalism, nonetheless has powerful precedents and counterparts in the rest of Europe. Elsewhere in Europe, too, people generally prefer to be ruled by those they consider somehow "of their own kind." Only once thus constituted, in some version of a nation-state, are they prepared (up to a point) to come together in larger regional and all-European units. A realistic liberal internationalism for the twenty-first century needs to take on board the insights of liberal nationalists from the nineteenth.

So there is, alas, a logic in the madness. Yet I come away from this journey feeling, more than ever, the futile folly of it. It's not as if these nations want to live in quite different ways in their different houses. What you find in each individual, small, battered, impoverished part of the Balkans are people—especially young people—looking at exactly the same Western advertisements, worshiping the same Western pop stars and fashion models, watching the same Western films and television shows, yearning for the same Western way of life. This is true in Serbia, despite the anti-Western sentiments, just as much as in Kosova, where the West is liberator-king.

My judge/driver/interpreter in Kosova happens also to be the president of the leading Priština basketball club, and on my first evening there he invited me to a match. Players wore smart Adidas gear. Young fans had baseball caps, T-shirts, scarves, and flags. They jumped up and down, clapped rhythmically, chanted "olé, olé, olé,

olé," and did all the other things they had obviously seen Western fans do on television (although I think they had gotten slightly confused between basketball and football rites).

I sat in the freezing stadium and mused on the madness of these small and tiny nations, who have spent years fighting and murdering each other so that, in the end, they can all go off to their separate little patches of land, and there—each and all of them—try to live just like Americans.

CHRONOLOGY

1999

DECEMBER. *Russian forces continue their action in Chechnya, working toward the capital, Grozny.*

5 DECEMBER. *Boris Trajkovski is confirmed as the new president of Macedonia, after a partial reballot to remedy electoral fraud.*

10 DECEMBER. *Croatian president Franjo Tudjman dies.*

10–12 DECEMBER. *EU summit in Helsinki agrees to open membership negotiations with Turkey, Slovakia, Bulgaria, Romania, Lithuania, Latvia, and Malta and to create a European rapid-reaction force. British prime minister Tony Blair clashes with his European colleagues over the ban on British beef and a proposed Europe-wide tax.*

19 DECEMBER. *Russian parliamentary elections give victory to the pro-Kremlin forces, although the communists remain the largest single party.*

31 DECEMBER. *Russian president Boris Yeltsin announces his early retirement, due to age and ill health, and names Prime Minister Vladimir Putin as acting president and his chosen successor.*

ENVOI

T his book is a kaleidoscope. I hope a few truths about Europe emerge from these mirrored images of colored fragments, constantly rearranged into different patterns as time's hand twists the tube. Perhaps one truth is that Europe is itself a kaleidoscope. The real Europe, I mean: a jagged, diverse continent of more than six hundred million individual men and women, speaking more than fifty languages, living in more than thirty-five states, making food, love, and politics in countless subtly different ways.

Such a book can no more end in a summary than a kaleidoscope can be turned into an organization chart. History of the present must acknowledge its own limitations. Systematic conclusions need a greater distance of time. Since the privilege of historians of the present is to record what we ourselves see and hear, our favored tools are fine brushes and smaller canvases.

Nonetheless, it is occasionally worth taking up the broad brush to paint what journalists call "the big picture." I have tried this at a couple of junctures, especially in the essays entitled "Catching the Wrong Bus?" and "The Case for Liberal Order." Let us revisit this big picture briefly at the end of both decade and book.

Throughout modern European history, periods of a given order have alternated with generally shorter ones of violent disorder, during which the political map is redrawn. The last decade of the twentieth century was one of these formative times. A glance at the maps of Europe in 1989 and 1999 will remind you that the political face of Europe changed more between those dates than in any other decade since the hellish one of 1939 to 1949. The disorder of the 1990s was not as violent as its predecessors. Still, in former Yugoslavia it was violent enough to puncture West European leaders' comforting platitude that "war has been banished from our continent."

There is no reason at all why order should descend neatly at the end of an arbitrary division of time. As it happens, the main elements of a new order did seem to be in place by the end of the decade and the millennium. Most of the states of Western Europe, joined together in a slightly larger European Union, had taken the great leap to monetary union. For good or ill, this would determine the shape of West European development for years to come. Germany had absorbed the former East Germany without seriously upsetting its own political system. Its capital moved to Berlin shortly after the Federal Republic's first-ever complete change of government through the ballot box. The core states of Central Europe had crossed the bottom of the valley on their journey from communist dictatorship to capitalist democracy and from East to West. Poland, Hungary, and the Czech Republic had become members of NATO. Even if joining the EU takes much longer, we know which slope they are climbing. In the Balkans, the former Yugoslavia has been dismembered into a patchwork of small nation-states, together with one or two international protectorates. That process was almost complete.

There are still long ragged edges and large unanswered questions. Won't the effects of one interest rate for all create intolerable political strains among the countries participating in monetary union? How will the Berlin republic reconcile the two souls in its Faustian breast: sovereignty regained and sovereignty surrendered, restored Berlin and sacrificed deutsche mark? What about those states on the borderlines between central Europe and the Balkans or Eastern Europe? And all that unfinished business of Kosovo/a, Macedonia, Albania, Bosnia, Montenegro, and Serbia itself? But only in the former Soviet Union is the shape of the new order still quite unclear. In these four major parts, Western Europe, Germany, Central Europe, and the Balkans, the basic direction is apparent.

None of us knew that things would go this way. (Look at the fears expressed early in this book.) The changes for the better experienced by friends in Warsaw, Prague, and Budapest have outstripped all our dreams. What happened to those in Belgrade, Sarajevo, and Priština has been worse than our worst nightmares.

None of this was inevitable. At every stage, there were other possibilities, paths not taken. In extraordinary times, political leadership is more important than it is in ordinary ones. A large part of the responsibility for two of these four great castings of the die—European monetary union and the shape of German unification—lies with one man: Helmut Kohl. The personal leadership of a Havel or a Göncz was at moments decisive. In the opposite direction, so was that of Mečiar, Tudjman, and Milošević. The received wisdom of the early 1990s had suggested that the economy was the key in both Western Europe and the former Eastern Europe. Instead, we experienced the primacy of politics.

The new European order has no name as yet. Previous ones have often been known in shorthand by the name of a great international conference. Following the Thirty Years War and the Peace of Westphalia, there was "Westphalia Europe." After the Napoleonic Wars came the Congress of Vienna and "Vienna Europe"; after the First World War, "Versailles Europe." Most recently, we had "Yalta Europe," which was a result of the Second World War but frozen in place for forty years by the cold war. There was no single grand international conference to redraw the map of Europe at the end of the cold war. German politicians, in negotiating their unification, deliberately set out to avoid that. The last thing they wanted was a new Versailles.

We might think of calling the new order "Paris Europe," after the November 1990 Paris Charter for a New Europe, signed by all the states of the Conference for Security and Cooperation in Europe. But the Paris Charter bears as much resemblance to what happened afterward as our personal New Year resolutions do to our subsequent behavior. Contemplating the EU and monetary union, some might say "Brussels Europe." Those who overdramatize Germany's return as the great power in the center of Europe might counter with "Berlin Europe." Then again, if I look at Central Europe or the

Balkans, I am tempted to suggest "Washington Europe." With the enlargement of NATO and the United States' leading role in the Balkans, the United States is as heavily involved in Europe now as it was in 1989.

WHATEVER ITS NAME, this is not the order I hoped for. In this respect, I feel a painful contrast with the 1980s. In the 1980s, I argued that the Soviet empire in what was then called Eastern Europe was both illegitimate and fragile. Peaceful change could come only from pressure from below. The West had not just a moral but also a political interest in supporting the so-called dissidents. During the velvet revolutions of 1989, I enjoyed a sense of triumph and vindication. I felt that I had contributed, in a very small way, to a great change for the better.

Throughout the 1990s, I argued (mainly in newspaper commentaries, lectures, and conference talks not reprinted here) that the West's top priority should be to seize the opportunity offered by the peaceful ending of the Yalta division of Europe and build a liberal order for the whole of Europe. A "Europe whole and free," as George Bush put it, in one of his few memorable phrases. So NATO should want to take in the new democracies. The European Union should concentrate on preparing for eastward enlargement and on the close coordination of our national foreign and security policies to meet the challenges that were sure to arise from the upheavals of postcommunism. I wanted Britain to take a lead in this direction.

The NATO argument was won by the end of the decade, mainly thanks to the advocacy of others, especially in the United States and Germany. The argument about priorities for the European Union was largely lost. We did not prevent war from returning to our continent. We fiddled while former Yugoslavia burned. The United States had once again to step in to sort out Europe's mess. Preparations for eastward enlargement of the EU were sluggish and niggardly, as if the community's secret motto was what that French businessmen said to me in January 1996: *Il faut toujours en parler, et jamais y penser.* If Central Europe is now joining the West, 90 percent of the credit belongs to the Central Europeans themselves, scarcely 10 percent to us. As I feared in my essay of July 1990, we have been Dr. Johnson's Patron: "One who looks with unconcern on a man struggling for life in the water, and, when he has reached ground, encumbers him with help." Britain was too hobbled by its own "European debate" to take much of a lead in the direction I had urged.

This failure of advocacy is hardly surprising. If you think you have influenced policy as a commentator it is usually an illusion anyway. All commentary is a kind of blowing in the wind. When the wind is blowing in the same direction, as it was for me at the end of the 1980s, you may imagine it's your breath that is bending those trees. When the wind is against you, the spit comes back in your face. Nonetheless, I still have a personal sense of failure.

The leaders of Western Europe concentrated their energies on the amazing adventure of monetary union. I admire the titanic efforts of statesmanship and political will that made this happen. Only a fool or a bigot could not see potential benefits. But I think it was simply the wrong priority for the 1990s. After the miraculously peaceful end of the cold war, we should have concentrated our efforts on building that liberal order for the whole of Europe. And I'm afraid that EMU is a bridge too far for Western Europe itself. Some of the countries now in the monetary union are not ready for it. I fear the resulting strains will make Western Europe a very bad-tempered place—perhaps even worse—at some point in the next ten years. The only consolation in making such a guess is that I would be glad to be proved wrong.

However, the last months of 1999 did bring a rash of developments that I had hoped to see since 1990. European governments, strongly encouraged by a new European Commission under Romano Prodi, resolved to open EU enlargement negotiations with a further six postcommunist states, as well as with Turkey. Together with the already agreed "first wave" of enlargement, this is to lead eventually to a community of twenty-eight rather than fifteen states. The timescale was very unclear, and the devil would be in the details of negotiations, but at least the course had been set. Simultaneously, the new commission identified, for decision at a new intergovernmental conference, the areas in which the EU would have to become more integrated (with a further sharing of sovereignty) if such an enlarged community was to work properly.

In the same period, the EU appointed its first foreign-policy representative, choosing former NATO secretary-general Javier Solana. Henry Kissinger's famous question—"I want to talk to Europe, but what telephone number should I call?"—was not yet answered, since on any important issue a U.S. secretary of state would still have to speak to at least three or four major national governments. This was nonetheless a step in the right direction. And European leaders agreed to build up a European rapid-reaction force, as part of more coordinated European defense and security policy.

So at the end of the decade we started in earnest the work upon which we should have embarked at its beginning. Perhaps advocacy had some effect after all. Yet far more important was the impact of another bloody war in the Balkans—one that directly involved all the major West European powers.

These developments coincided with celebrations to mark the tenth anniversaries of the velvet revolutions of 1989. As I turned from one to the other, I could not help wondering whether the problem with what happened in 1989 was that it had been *too* peaceful, velvet, and magical. The great drive for the "construction of Europe" after 1945 came out of the traumatic experience of the Second World War, together with its preceding and succeeding horrors. Have we learned nothing? Are we so complacent and shortsighted that it has taken another war for us to start doing what we should already have done?

Most of the fragments in this kaleidoscope come from faraway countries of which most American readers know little. The political argument I made in the 1990s, like that of the 1980s, was of course influenced by my personal involvement in Germany, Central Europe, and the Balkans. To be thus deeply engaged in the affairs of other countries brings the danger of being partisan or quixotic—and certainly of being seen as such. Yet to be judged on your arguments rather than your motives is a basic intellectual right, and I maintain that the argument is valid for the whole of Europe. Where, however, does it leave the country in which I live and about which I care still more deeply?

Although Britain stands a little apart from Europe, the singularity of its apartness and ambivalence is often overstated. For example, it is said that Britain is one of only two European countries in which people talk about Europe as being somewhere else. ("Jim's just back from Europe.") The other, we are told, is Russia. Yet I have encountered this way of speaking about Europe in many other European countries, from Portugal to Poland and Sweden to Greece. Swedes, Poles, and Greeks insist their countries are parts of Europe but also worry that there's a political, economic, or cultural reality to which they might not fully belong.

In fact, about the only European countries that never question their own belonging to Europe are France, Germany, Belgium, the Netherlands, and Luxembourg. Yet even in those core countries of Western Europe there is ambivalence about the shape that the political project known as "Europe" has assumed in the 1990s. Remember that only a bare majority of French voters approved of the Maastricht treaty in the referendum of September 1992. Until well into 1998, more than half the Germans asked in opinion polls said they were opposed to giving up the deutsche mark for the euro. One of the chronic British fallacies about "Europe" is the notion that over there, on the Continent, three hundred million people are lined up behind a single grand design, like a Napoleonic army.

Britain also vibrates to some deeper European rhythms, often without knowing it. Take "sleaze," for example, one of the big themes of British politics in the 1990s. If you look through the chronologies in this book, you will find that the exposure of political corruption was a feature of European politics altogether. In Italy, France, Spain, and Greece, serving or former prime ministers were accused, indicted, imprisoned, or committed suicide as a result. Why did political corruption become a major issue across Europe? Was it because the end of the cold war meant people felt free to expose corruption where previously this would have been seen as playing into the hands of the other side? Because more than forty years of the same system had encouraged the slow erosion of standards? Because, since elections are now won by television and advertising, politicians need ever more money to fund it? Whatever the reasons, Britain had a rather mild bout of an all-European disease.

Or take devolution. Is it pure accident that Scotland and Wales voted for their own new national assemblies at a time when smaller peoples all over Europe were pressing for greater autonomy or seizing independence? Catalonia and the Basque country, Wallonia and Flanders, Slovakia, Croatia, Slovenia, Moldova, Ruthenia. . . . Again, the local causes are diverse, but there is a deeper pattern, a dance to the music of Europe.

That said, in some respects Britain really is different. The most obvious of these include common law, the unwritten constitution, and the sovereignty of Parliament; our deep affinities with what Churchill called "the English-speaking peoples"—Americans, Canadians, Australians, New Zealanders; and the Anglo-American version of capitalism, as opposed to the Franco-German or "Rhenish" model that predominates in what is now popularly called "Euroland." While many European peoples doubt whether they belong fully to Europe, we are one of the few who also doubt whether we want fully to belong. (Who are the others? Russia certainly. Perhaps Ukraine and Serbia. Denmark? Sweden?) So we once again stand aside from a major continental development as we agonize over whether or not to join Euroland.

Our choice will matter to Europe, since Britain is the fifth-largest economy in the world, politically and militarily one of the EU's big three states, and home to its most important financial center. If Russia is the great unknown in Europe's east, Britain is the major unknown in its west. This choice coincides with the incremental disuniting of the United Kingdom, in Scotland, Wales, and Northern Ireland. Together, these two developments pose fundamental questions about where and what we wish Britain to be—and, for us English, about England. As the historian Geoffrey Hosking has suggested, the English have this in common with the Russians: Our national identity has for centuries been bound up with an imperial one. So the Matter of England is set fair to be one of Europe's more interesting subjects over the next ten years.

The trouble with the choice about entering monetary union—shall we call it The Choice?—is that it hinges on economics and on speculative assertions about the political consequences of economic actions. In this it differs from other great foreign-policy choices such as the Suez crisis or Vietnam, where interested citizens could readily grasp the main facts. This is much more complex, impenetrable, and imponderable. (Am I alone in feeling that it is also more boring?)

As a noneconomist, I can say only three things about The Choice with any confidence. First, if one cares at all about the rest of Europe, one must now hope for the existing monetary union of eleven states to succeed, even if one wishes (as I do) that it had not been tried in this decade. Second, it is possible to be in favor of the European Union and opposed to Britain joining monetary union. Some British opponents of monetary union really are "anti-European," but it is quite wrong to disqualify all opponents with that tag. Third and most important: Don't believe those who maintain that the course they advocate—to go in, to stay out—is without large dangers.

Both courses are heavy with risk. If Britain goes in, we risk sacrificing some of our hard-won flexibility and competitive advantages, joining an enterprise that is flawed, having an interest rate that may not fit our economic circumstances and diminishing democratic, parliamentary control over vital areas of national policy. If we stay out, we risk loss of influence over European decisions that will directly affect us, long-term decline in the foreign direct investment that has created many jobs in Britain, discrimination against British exports to our largest market, and being downgraded as a political partner of the United States. For us in Britain, the chief legacy of Europe's nineties is this unenviable choice.

THE CONTRAST WITH GERMANY could hardly be sharper. Germany's great decisions were already made in the 1990s. Moreover, it was remarkable to observe how the doubts and fears that surrounded Germany at the beginning of the decade had disappeared almost entirely by its end. If, today, you asked a politician in Rome, Paris, London, or Warsaw, "What are the main problems in Europe?" the chances are that Germany would not even be mentioned in the answer. Here is evidence of an extraordinary achievement.

The summer of 1999 saw another milestone: the participation of German troops in the liberation and occupation of Kosovo. As an Englishman, I found it moving to watch how, sixty years after the outbreak of the Second World War, British and German soldiers risked their lives together so that the Kosovar Albanians could go home.

The history of Europe in the twentieth century might be told as a short sequence of unforgettable photographs. The Second World War is that little Polish Jewish boy, hands in the air, bewilderment on his charming, innocent face, as German soldiers drive him out of the Warsaw ghetto. The Soviet invasion of Czechoslovakia in 1968 is the man standing defiantly in front of a Russian tank on Wenceslaus Square, in the center of Prague. Now I would add a photograph from Prizren, Kosovo, in June 1999. A German officer, unarmed except for the pistol in his holster, resolutely approaches a heavily armed Serbian soldier in order to wrench the gun from his hands. The Serb's fellow soldiers stand around, angrily, and under their steel helmets they look just like the Germans in the photograph from the Warsaw ghetto. An old story is over, a new one begins.

I don't speak lightly of "normalization" or "a new normality," since for Germany, as for Poland, normality is historically abnormal. Certainly, there are still large questions in and for Germany. The question, for example, of the depth of its commitment to the eastward enlargement of the European Union, not just in words but in deeds that require paying a short-term cost in order to secure a long-term benefit. Or the question of its ability to reform a once exemplary "social market economy" so that it remains globally competitive. And, closely linked to that, awkward questions about the lasting acceptance of the Euro.

Yet for now one must record, with wonder, the most startling outcome of this formative decade: There is no longer a German Question. Instead, we have an English Question.

WHAT, finally, of the United States and Europe? As I have noted already, the United States was no less involved in European affairs at the end of the decade than it was at the beginning. On a moment's reflection, this is quite surprising. Most alliances in history have collapsed after the common enemy was vanquished. Having abruptly departed Europe after the end of the First World War, the United States was brought back into Europe during the Second World War by one common enemy, the "Axis" of Nazi Germany, fascist Italy, and imperial Japan, and then kept there for the duration of the cold war by another: Soviet communism and its allies. When the cold war ended, some foresaw the demise not just of NATO but of "the West" altogether: "The political 'West' was not a natural construct but a highly artificial one," wrote Owen Harries in 1993. "It took the presence of a life-threatening, overtly hostile 'East' to bring it into existence. It is extremely doubtful whether it can survive the disappearance of that enemy." [1]

But it has—thus far, anyway. Why? Partly, no doubt, because of the deep substrata of shared history, culture, and values. In a world at once more globalized and more consciously multicultural, such commonalities are accentuated. The formerly dominant Western culture is more widespread but also more contested. The strange survival of the West also has to do with the habits of cooperation, built up over at least fifty years—sixty in the case of the United States and Britain—and institutionalized as never before, whether in secret intelligence sharing, the formal organizations of political, military, and economic coordination, or the countless nongovernmental, transatlantic talking shops.

Another small contributing cause was the enthusiasm of the new arrivals from Central Europe. Poland, in particular, is one of the most pro-American countries in Europe. Polish, Czech, and Hungarian politicians irk the French by constantly describing what they want to join as "the Euratlantic structures." The enlargement of NATO also reinvigorated the alliance. As I write, a brigade of Poland's King Jan Sobieski Armored Cavalry has just taken over from Italy's San Marco Battalion in the unruly divided city of Kosovska

Mitrovica. Last but not least, there were still common enemies in the wider world: rogue states, terrorists, the international drug traders. And there were common challenges, such as the new Asian great powers in the making—and China above all.

None of this means that the transatlantic alliance, which has defined the modern "West," is eternally secured. Nor will any of this prevent the U.S.-European relationship from being racked by discord. In 2000, a major row seems to be brewing over Washington's plans for a national missile-defense system and European fears of a consequent "decoupling." But this row feels so familiar. In every decade of NATO's history there has been at least one major transatlantic disagreement. Can there be a family without family arguments?

What is qualitatively new is the extent of European integration and the possibility of gradually extending it to embrace the whole continent. The United States is now called upon to define its attitude to processes about which it has sometimes seemed ambivalent. As an English European, my view is that the United States should unequivocally welcome the general direction of these two historical developments—for Europe's sake but also out of enlightened American self-interest. Without "interfering in internal affairs," it can also legitimately support certain priorities. Thus, for example, it should surely encourage the development of a European rapid-reaction force, particularly if—as we saw in the Kosovo war—the United States itself is not prepared to risk the life of a single U.S. soldier in order to make peace or remedy gross violations of human rights in Europe. Similarly, the United States is obviously crucial to the balancing act between the essential enlargement of NATO and the European Union and the equally vital relationship with Russia. The latter, in particular, is too large for Europe to handle on its own.

As for the further integration that may be catalyzed by monetary union; there is, to be sure, a Gallic vision of "Euroland" that envisages it as a rival to the United States. But there is also an alternative conception that sees the European Union as a "partner in leadership" with the United States—to recall another helpful phrase of George H. W. Bush. Altogether, there is a struggle going on for Europe's soul. Crudely stated, this is a new version of the old argument between the Atlanticist, liberal, global free-trading and the Gaullist, etatist, protectionist orientations. Obviously, a victory for the former is in the American interest (and, I believe, in Europe's own). More difficult is the question of how the United States might help to bring it about. It is not for me to design such a strategy. The starting point, however, must be to see Europe plain and to see it whole.

Europe in 2000

INTRODUCTION

1. See Reinhart Koselleck, "Sprachwandel und Ereignisgeschichte," *Merkur* 8/43, August 1989.

2. E. J. Hobsbawm, "The Historian between the Quest for the Universal and the Quest for Identity," *Diogenes* 42/4, no. 168.

3. Neal Ascherson, "Fellow-Travelling," *London Review of Books*, 8 February 1996.

4. On this, see my "Orwell in 1998," in *The New York Review of Books*, 22 October 1998.

5. The don was Harry Willetts—an otherwise lovable, wry, and learned historian of Russia and Poland and translator of both the pope and Solzhenitsyn.

THE SOLUTION

1. Armin Mitter and Stefan Wolle, eds., *Ich liebe Euch doch alle! Befehle und Lageberichte des MfS, January–November 1989* [But I love you all! Orders and situation reports of the Ministry for State Security, January–November 1989] (Berlin: BasisDruck Verlagsgesellschaft, 1990). But see note 3 below.

2. See the chapter on Germany in my *The Magic Lantern: The Revolution of '89 Witnessed in Warsaw, Budapest, Berlin, and Prague*, new ed. (New York: Vintage, 1999).

3. Like many of the most famous quotations in history, this is generally misquoted. It is usually given as *"Ich liebe Euch doch alle,"* as in the book title cited in note 1. But in the televised record of the People's Chamber session he says just, *"Ich liebe doch alle . . . alle Menschen."*

INTELLECTUALS AND POLITICIANS

1. See my account in *The Magic Lantern*.

2. Václav Klaus, *Proč jsem konzervativcem?* (Why am I a conservative?) (Prague: TOP Agency, 1992).

3. A very useful exploration of this subject, partly inspired by Havel's earlier writings, is Ian MacLean, Alan Montefiore, and Peter Winch, eds., *The Political Responsibility of Intellectuals* (Cambridge: Cambridge University Press, 1990).

4. I first used this phrase in my essay *"Après le Déluge, Nous,"* see above, p. 24.

5. Published in English as George Konrád and Ivan Szelényi, *The Intellectuals on the Road to Class Power* (New York: Harcourt Brace, 1979). Szelényi notes in his introduction that the manuscript was completed in 1974.

6. The full title of the English-language volume is *Toward a Civil Society: Selected Speeches and Writings, 1990–1994* (Prague: Lidové Noviny, 1994). A note on the copyright page indicates that this volume is edited by Paul Wilson, with the translations by Paul Wilson and others. A slightly different edition has now been published as *The Art of the Impossible: Politics as Morality in Practice: Speeches and Writings, 1990–1996* (New York: Knopf, 1997). The Czech collections are Václav Havel, *Projevy leden–červen 1990* (Speeches: January–June 1990) (Prague: Vyšehrad, 1990); Václav Havel, *Vážení občané, Projevy červenec 1990–červenec 1992* (Dear citizens: Speeches, July 1990–July 1992) (Prague: Lidové Noviny, 1992); and *Václav Havel 1992 & 1993* (Prague: Paseka, 1994).

7. The Czech original is even more emphatic, saying literally, "All lie who tell us that politics is a dirty business."

8. Václav Havel, *Vážení občané,* pp. 198–99.

9. The sequel is amusing. After being instrumental in reactivating the PEN club, Klíma was summoned for interrogation by the security police. Their main concern was that Václav Havel should not become president of Czech PEN. Three months later, he was president of Czechoslovakia.

BOSNIA IN OUR FUTURE

1. This and many other details come from the superb documentary series *The Death of Yugoslavia* (made for BBC Television by Brian Lapping Associates, series producer Norma Percy) and the book that accompanies the series, Laura Silber and Alan Little, *The Death of Yugoslavia* (London: Penguin/BBC, 1995). See also Misha Glenny, *The Fall of Yugoslavia,* rev. ed. (London: Penguin, 1993).

2. The decision to adopt the term *Bosniak* as the name of the nation previously described as the Bosnian Muslims was taken by the Second Bosnian Assembly in 1993 and reaffirmed in the Dayton agreement and constitu-

tion. (I am most grateful to Robert Donia for this information.) I use the term not only because it is the correct one, but also because, in my experience, many Bosnian "Muslims" are not at all muslim in the sense that, say, an Iranian or a Saudi would recognize.

3. In fact, it was the linguist Max Weinreich who observed in 1945, "A language is a dialect with an army and a navy." I am most grateful to Tim Snyder for this information. Perhaps one could also say that a state is a language with an army.

Forty Years On

1. The excellent English-language edition is György Litván, ed., *The Hungarian Revolution of 1956: Reform, Revolt, and Repression, 1953–1963*, ed. and trans. János M. Bak and Lyman H. Legters (London: Longman, 1996).

2. Entitled "Hungary and the World 1956: The New Archival Evidence," the conference was organized by the Institute for the History of the 1956 Hungarian Revolution and the Hungarian Academy of Sciences, in Budapest, and the National Security Archive and the Cold War International History Project, both of Washington, D.C.

3. The Malin notes are translated and expertly annotated by Mark Kramer, a Harvard specialist on Soviet–Eastern European relations, in a compendium of declassified documents prepared for the conference by the 1956 Institute and the National Security Archive. A larger collection of documents is due to be published by Central European University Press.

4. The memorandum is included in ibid.

5. See my review essay "From World War to Cold War," *The New York Review of Books,* 11 June 1987.

6. *Victoire d'une défaite* is the title of the original French edition (Fayard, 1968). The English edition is entitled *Budapest 1956: A History of the Hungarian Revolution* (London: Allen and Unwin, 1971).

7. Suitably enough, Miklós Haraszti's book on the position of artists under Kádárism was entitled *The Velvet Prison* (New York: Basic Books, 1987). See also my "The Hungarian Lesson" in *The Uses of Adversity: Essays on the Fate of Central Europe,* new ed. (London: Penguin, 1999).

8. See István Bibó, *Democracy, Revolution, Self-Determination: Selected Writings,* ed. Károly Nagy (Boulder, Colo.: Social Science Monographs, 1991).

9. "Refolution in Hungary and Poland," *The New York Review of Books,* 17 August 1989.

10. János Kenedi, *Kis Állambiztonsági Olvasókönyv a Kádár-korszakban* (A small reader on the state security services in the Kádár period) (Budapest: Magvetö, 1996).

TRIALS, PURGES, AND HISTORY LESSONS

1. I am grateful to Priscilla Hayner for confirming this tally. Her book about truth commissions is due to be published as *Unspeakable Truths: Confronting State Terror and Atrocity* (New York: Routledge, forthcoming).

2. I look at the work of the South African truth commission in "True Confessions," *The New York Review of Books,* 17 July 1997.

CRY, THE DISMEMBERED COUNTRY

1. I put "muslims" in quotes in both cases, because Islamic observance seems to be even more lax in the Kosovar case—certainly in the towns—than in the Bosnian one. There is also a small but significant community of Kosovar Albanian Catholics.

2. "Dervishes" is no mere figure of speech. Although the dervish orders were officially closed down in 1952, I was shown a mosque in Orahovac where the dervish rites are now again observed.

3. This and much other invaluable information is to be found in two excellent reports by the International Crisis Group, *Kosovo Spring* and *Kosovo's Long Hot Summer,* both available from www.crisisweb.org.

4. See "The Serbian Tragedy," above, p. 195.

5. It is striking that the few references to Kosovo in Richard Holbrooke's *To End a War* (New York: Random House, 1998) concern the time before or after he was active in the Bosnia negotiations. The only mention of Kosovo that I can find in his account of the actual Dayton negotiations is this: "Once, as Milošević and I were taking a walk, about one hundred local Albanian Americans came to the outer fence of Wright-Patterson with megaphones to plead the case for Kosovo. I suggested we walk over to chat with them, but he refused, saying testily that they were obviously being paid by a foreign power."

6. Mr. Ademi told me he has not seen a copy of this document, although "Mr. Rugova must have one in his drawer." In her *Between Serb and Albanian: A History of Kosovo* (London: Hurst, 1998), p. 253, Miranda Vickers quotes an October 1991 statement by the "Coordinating Committee of Albanian Political Parties in Yugoslavia"—presumably the same body—which canvases more radical options, including an Albanian Republic embracing all the Albanian-settled parts of Kosovo, Macedonia, Montenegro, and Serbia proper, or, in the event of a change to the external frontiers of former Yugoslavia, territorial unification with Albania "within the boundaries proclaimed by the First Prizren League in 1878." However, the only source she gives is a study by a Serb scholar in good standing with the Milošević regime, and one would wish to be sure that the text and context of the Albanian original are fairly given.

7. For a scholarly and acerbic dissection of these myths, see Noel Malcolm, *Kosovo: A Short History* (London: Macmillan, 1998).

8. The claim would be that, contrary to what President Kučan of Slovenia told me (see above, p. 255), Kosovo, as an "autonomous province," was a constituent part of former Yugoslavia and therefore has the same right to secede as all other constituent parts. Malcolm, *Kosovo,* pp. 264–65, argues with fiendish ingenuity that, when Kosovo was taken from the Ottoman empire by the Serbs in 1912–1913, it was never properly, legally incorporated into Serbia at all.

9. I owe this insight, as I owe many others, to Pierre Hassner.

Where Is Central Europe Now?

1. "Does Central Europe Exist?" *The New York Review of Books,* 9 October 1986. The essay is reprinted in my *The Uses of Adversity.*

2. "Nato Enlargement: Build a Europe Whole and Free," *International Herald Tribune,* 30 April 1988.

3. Karl A. Sinnhuber, "Central Europe—Mitteleuropa—Europe Centrale: An Analysis of a Geographical Term," *Institute of British Geographers Transactions and Papers* (1954).

4. Milan Kundera, "The Tragedy of Central Europe," *The New York Review of Books,* 26 April 1984. The version of this essay published in *Granta* 11 (1984) bore Kundera's own title: "A Kidnapped West or Culture Bows Out."

5. Vesna Goldsworthy explores the literary-political past and present of these negative images of the Balkans in her *Inventing Ruritania: The Imperialism of the Imagination* (New Haven: Yale University Press, 1998), as does Maria Todorova in her provocative *Imagining the Balkans* (New York: Oxford University Press, 1997).

6. See his *The Clash of Civilizations and the Remaking of World Order* (London: Touchstone Books, 1997). His original article on "the clash of civilizations" was published in *Foreign Affairs* in summer 1993.

7. On Milošević's and Tudjman's *demokraturas,* see "Cry, the Dismembered Country," above, p. 318.

8. See the forthcoming book by Milada Vachudova, *Revolution, Democracy, and Integration: The Domestic and International Politics of East Central Europe since 1989* (Oxford: Oxford University Press). The argument in this essay is also indebted to the article by Tim Snyder and Milada Vachudova, "Are Transitions Transitory? Two Types of Political Change in Eastern Europe since 1989," *East European Politics and Societies* 11 (1), and to comments by Tim Snyder, Vladimir Tismaneanu, and Charles King.

Envoi

1. Owen Harries, "The Collapse of 'The West,'" *Foreign Affairs* (September/October 1993), quoted in Christopher Coker's stimulating *Twilight of the West* (Boulder, Colo.: Westview Press, 1998).

ACKNOWLEDGMENTS

I am most grateful to my outstanding editors: Robert Silvers of *The New York Review of Books,* Bill Buford, first at *Granta* and now at *The New Yorker,* Ian Birrell at the restored *Independent,* Ferdinand Mount at *The Times Literary Supplement,* Fareed Zakaria at *Foreign Affairs,* and, last but not least, Stuart Proffitt at Penguin Books and Jason Epstein at Random House. They have improved these texts by asking the quintessential editor's question, "What do you really mean?"

My Oxford college, St. Antony's, is a model of reaching out across the frontiers that I describe in the introduction. I thank particularly its two wardens of the 1990s, Lord Dahrendorf and Sir Marrack Goulding, and the many colleagues and students who have commented on, or garnered information for, the essays in this book.

For financial support, I am grateful to the Körber Foundation, the European Cultural Foundation, and the Thyssen Foundation.

Finally, there are the friends and acquaintances across Europe who contributed in so many different ways: sometimes unknowingly but more often with deliberate generosity. This book would not merely have been impossible without them. It is, in a deeper sense, all about them.

PERMISSIONS

Grateful acknowledgment is made to the following for permission to reprint previously published material: Routledge, Inc., a Taylor & Francis Company for "Solution" from *Bertolt Brecht: Poems 1913–1956* by Bertolt Brecht, translated by Derek Bowman. Copyright © 1976, 1979 by Methuen London. Reproduced by permission of Routledge, Inc., http://www.routledge-ny.com; HarperCollins Publishers, Inc., for an excerpt from "The Envoy of Mr. Cogito" from *Mr. Cogito* by Zbigniew Herbert, translated by John Carpenter and Bogdana Carpenter. © 1974 by Zbigniew Herbert. Translation ©

INDEX

This index lists only personal names and place-names